THE PHILIPPINE ISLANDS

LONDON : HUMPHREY MILFORD
OXFORD UNIVERSITY PRESS

PRESIDENT SERGIO OSMEÑA

THE PHILIPPINE ISLANDS

Revised Edition

BY

W. CAMERON FORBES

Cambridge, Massachusetts

HARVARD UNIVERSITY PRESS

1945

PRINTED AT THE HARVARD UNIVERSITY PRINTING OFFICE
CAMBRIDGE, MASSACHUSETTS, U.S.A.

PREFACE

THIS volume is an abridged copy of the two-volume edition of *The Philippine Islands* brought out in 1928. For those who desire the fuller text, with notes, appendices, references, and a fairly full documentation the original edition should be sought.

The book was originally brought out with the approval of the then Secretary of War who desired that the subject matter should be made of record. Access was given to the archives of the War Department, and General Leonard Wood who at that time was Governor-General of the Philippines caused his bureau chiefs and secretaries to make the archives of the Philippine Government available. The author was fortunate in securing the full-time assistance of the Honorable Frank W. Carpenter who had held important positions in the Islands for a protracted period of time, including that of Executive Secretary of the Insular Government and that of Governor of the Moro Province, and who assisted in supplying information and seeking original material.

Recently the Honorable Sergio Osmeña, shortly after assuming the position of President of the Philippines in the summer of 1944, suggested the appropriateness of a smaller volume at a reduced price so that those seeking information regarding the Philippines would have the meat of the former volumes within reach.

The book gives a brief description of the Islands and a summary of the earlier history, tells of the American Occupation, and has a number of chapters that deal with the operation of the different departments of the government, emphasis necessarily being laid on the period of ten years during which the author was active in the administration.

It seems to be unnecessary to repeat here the acknowledgments carried in the foreword of the original book to the many kind people who gave assistance or permission to use their material in the formation of the book, as that has been fully set forth in the earlier edition.

Most of the new material in this book is to be found in the next to last chapter, The Independence Movement, which contains a summary of events leading up to the dark 7th of December, 1941, when the war broke out between the United States and Japan.

W. C. F.

January 3, 1945

CONTENTS

CONTENTS

ILLUSTRATIONS

FOREWORD

THE NAME of W. Cameron Forbes has long been associated with the development of Filipino-American friendship. Going to Manila in 1904, he served as Secretary of Commerce and Police on the Philippine Commission. Because of his extremely devoted labors in this and other capacities, he was promoted to Vice-Governor and then to Governor-General, a post which he held with distinction from 1909 to 1913. During that period my responsibilities as Speaker of the National Assembly brought me in frequent contact with him. Our personal relations were always mutually pleasant, even though the problems of government were complex and difficult.

Many of the projects for which Governor Forbes was personally responsible in the Philippines continued to be of great value after he finished his official duties there. An incident connected with the current war bears out this point. During the years which followed the end of the armed conflict between Japan and Russia in 1904–1905, it was rumored that the Japanese intended to seize the Philippines. Although such a development was not considered likely at the time, Governor Forbes felt that the Islands should be prepared to cope with any external emergency. With this thought in mind, he quietly proceeded to construct underground vaults on Corregidor; this project was completed unknown to the general public before he departed from the Philippines. His farsightedness enabled the Commonwealth Government to transfer valuable records and large amounts of money to those bomb-proof vaults shortly after the Japanese treacherously attacked my country in December, 1941.

Governor Forbes has never ceased to display an interest in the welfare of the Filipino people. More than a decade ago he devoted a great deal of time and effort to the writing of a two-volume study on the Philippines which has been universally accepted as a standard work in its field. Now that he has condensed this book and brought it up to date, I feel certain that his new volume will be read eagerly by many Americans whose interest in the Philippines has been increased by the events of the war.

SERGIO OSMEÑA
President of the Philippines

April 9, 1945

CHRONOLOGY

1521. March 16. Discovery of the Philippine Islands by Magellan.

1543. The name Filipinas (Philippines) given the Islands by the Spanish explorer, Villalobus.

1565. First Spanish settlement founded at Cebu by Legaspi, who established Spanish sovereignty in the Islands.

1571. Establishment of the city of Manila by Legaspi as the Spanish capital of the archipelago.

1762–1764. British occupation of Manila.

1837. Port of Manila opened to foreign trade.

1872. Cavite Revolt.

1892. Revolutionary secret society, the Katipunan, organized.

1896. August. Beginning of Philippine revolution against Spain.
December 30. Execution of Philippine patriot, José Rizal.

1897. July. Proclamation of independence issued by General Aguinaldo.
December 14. Agreement known as the Pact of Biac-na-bato made between the Philippine insurgent leaders and the Spanish Governor-General.

1898. April 21. Beginning of war between the United States and Spain.
May 1. Battle of Manila Bay, resulting in the destruction of the Spanish Philippine squadron by Commodore Dewey.
June 18. Dictatorial government proclaimed by Aguinaldo.
August 6. Appeal to foreign governments by Aguinaldo to recognize Philippine independence.
August 13. Capitulation of Manila to the American forces and establishment of military government.
December 10. Signing of Treaty of Paris between the United States and Spain.

1899. February 4. Beginning of Philippine insurrection against the United States.
February 6. Treaty of Paris ratified by United States Congress.
March 4. Arrival in Manila of the Schurman Commission.
March 31. Malolos, insurgent capital, occupied by American troops and Aguinaldo's government moved to Tarlac.
May 6. At Baliuag, Bulacan, first organization, under American administration, of municipal government with popular election of officials.
November 21. Insurgent government broken up by reason of occupation of Tarlac by American troops, Aguinaldo retiring to the mountains.

1900. June 3. Arrival in Manila of the Taft Commission.
June 21. Amnesty proclamation issued by the American Military Governor.
September 1. Legislative power transferred from the Military Governor to the Philippine Commission.
November. Organization of the Federal Party by representative Filipinos.

1901. March 2. President authorized, by the 'Spooner amendment' to an act of Congress, to establish civil government in the Islands.

March. Capture of Aguinaldo by General Funston.

July 4. Inauguration of William H. Taft as first Civil Governor.

September 1. Appointment of three Filipinos as members of the Philippine Commission.

1902. February. First elections of provincial governors.

July 1. Enactment by Congress of organic act for civil government in the Islands.

July 4. Official recognition of the end of the Philippine insurrection.

Amnesty proclamation issued by President Roosevelt.

Military government terminated.

1903. March 2. First Philippine census taken.

Provision by Congress for a new Philippine currency on a gold basis.

1904. February 1. Inauguration of Civil Governor Luke E. Wright succeeding Governor Taft, who had been appointed Secretary of War. (Title of chief executive of the Islands later changed from Civil Governor to Governor-General.)

1906. April 2. Inauguration of Governor-General Henry C. Ide.

May 24. Creation of Philippine Postal Savings Bank.

September 20. Inauguration of Governor-General James F. Smith.

November 15. Majority of members of provincial boards made elective.

1907. October 16. Philippine Assembly inaugurated as the lower house of the Legislature.

Representation of the Islands by two resident commissioners at Washington.

1909. August 5. Enactment by Congress of the Payne Tariff Law authorizing limited free trade between the United States and the Philippine Islands.

November 24. Inauguration of Governor-General W. Cameron Forbes.

1913. October 3. Enactment by Congress of the Underwood Tariff Law authorizing unlimited free trade between the United States and the Philippine Islands and abolishing Philippine export duties.

October 6. Inauguration of Governor-General Francis B. Harrison.

October 30. Filipinos given majority on the Philippine Commission.

1916. August 29. Enactment by Congress of the Jones Law, the new organic act for the government of the Islands.

October 16. Elective Philippine Senate inaugurated as the upper house of the Legislature in place of the appointive Commission.

1918. December 31. Second Philippine census taken.

1921. May 4. Arrival in Manila of Wood-Forbes Mission.

October 15. Inauguration of Governor-General Leonard Wood.

1927. August 7. Death of Governor-General Wood.

1928. March 1. Inauguration of Governor-General Henry L. Stimson.

1929. June 4. Dwight Davis appointed Governor-General.

1932. February 29. Theodore Roosevelt appointed Governor-General.

1933. January 17. Hawes-Cutting bill passed over the President's veto.

1933. October 17. Hawes-Cutting bill rejected by the Philippine Government.

1933. May 10. Frank Murphy appointed Governor-General.

1934. March. Tydings-McDuffie bill passed by House March 19; by the Senate March 22; signed by the President March 24.

1934. May 1. Tydings-McDuffie bill accepted by the Philippine Legislature.

1934. July 10. Elections to the Constitutional Convention held.

1935. May 14. Plebiscite election on the Constitution held.

1935. September 17. Election of the officers of the Commonwealth of the Philippine Islands: Manuel Quezon, President; Sergio Osmeña, Vice President; and others.

1935. November 15. Frank Murphy appointed High Commissioner.

1937. February 27. Paul V. McNutt appointed High Commissioner.

1939. August 8. Francis B. Sayre appointed High Commissioner.

1941. December 8. United States declared war on Japan.

THE PHILIPPINE ISLANDS

CHAPTER I

THE PHILIPPINE ISLANDS

ON THE FIRST of May, 1898, the American people were startled with the news of the battle of Manila Bay, and thrilled with excitement on reading of the heroism shown by American sailors and the overwhelming victory won by Admiral Dewey and his ships. Little did they dream that a new era had been opened in the foreign relations of their country and in the extension of its influence toward the west, for up to that time most of the trade of their country had been conducted along its eastern shores. Startled American citizens, even those who prided themselves on a fair degree of education, pulled down their atlases to learn where and what were these Philippine Islands about which they had known practically nothing but the name. But no map could give any appreciation of the size and latent possibilities of this archipelago, those thousands of islands, with their fertile plains, great rivers, ranges of high, forest-covered mountains; their forty-six million acres of virgin forests, and vast resources of luxuriant tropical vegetation and marine growth; their history of romance and adventure; and the long, laborious, and admirable work carried on through the centuries by their mother country, Spain, which had resulted in their supporting the only Christian people in the Orient. Nor is it probable that many of those who took down their atlases realized the strategic position held by these islands as a gateway from the United States to the Orient.

A glance at the map of the Eastern Hemisphere will show the continent of Asia separated from the Pacific Ocean by a chain of islands extending all the way from Kamchatka on the north to Borneo on the south. Between these islands and Asia lie various seas — the Sea of Okhotsk, the Sea of Japan, the Yellow Sea, the Eastern Sea, and, on the south, the China Sea. The southern end of the islands overlaps the southern end of the continent of Asia, and thus shipping bound from either of the Americas to Asia, in order to reach any of the great ports of that continent, must pass through this chain of islands, which control the approach to Asia from the Pacific Ocean.

Most of these islands are now in the possession of Japan, from the Kurile Islands on the north to Formosa on the south. The lower third of the chain comprises what are known as the Philippine Islands, extending southward from near Formosa for a distance of about twelve hundred miles to Borneo, the southern end being just north of the Equator. Their east and west extent is nearly six hundred miles. There are numerous natural harbors, and the principal ports have been made accessible to large transoceanic vessels.

The Philippine official census of 1918 shows 7083 islands, and even then the enumeration of some smaller islands had not yet been completed by the Coast Survey. Of these 1095 are inhabited; 463 have an area of more than one square mile each, and 11 of more than one thousand square miles.

The total land area of the Philippine Islands is 114,400 square miles, or three-quarters that of insular Japan. About 95 per cent of the land area lies in the eleven largest islands, and approximately two-thirds in the two great islands of Luzon with 41,000 square miles and Mindanao with 37,000 square miles of area. These large islands bear heavily wooded mountains, cultivable hills, fertile lowlands, and rolling upland prairies, some of which attain an elevation exceeding two thousand feet.

The principal islands are traversed by large rivers, many of which are navigable. There is abundant water-power in numerous streams. The sources of practically all the rivers and smaller streams are in the heavily forested uplands, with the result that there is a dependable, and in many cases abundant, flow of water, not only for power, but also for irrigation, without the necessity of building reservoirs for impounding the excess precipitation in the rainy season.

In the interior of some of the larger islands there are extensive lakes, some of which are navigable and in most of which there is abundance of fish. Near the sea are large areas of swamps, important by reason of their growth of mangrove, nipa palm, and wood for fuel. Some of these have been ingeniously developed for use as controlled fisheries, and others for salt works.

The seas, within and adjacent to the archipelago, teem with natural resources. Besides the food fishes, there are profitable pearl fisheries and an abundance of commercially valuable shells and sponges.

In the lowlands the climate throughout the year is warm, moist, and rather enervating to white people, who, during the hotter months, seek refuge from it in the mountains, where there are pleasant resorts. The average temperature in Manila, 79.5° F., is typical of the lowlands throughout the archipelago. The temperature at night, even in the lowlands and at all seasons of the year, is agreeably cool, and in January and February, the coolest period, is sometimes as low as 59° at Manila.

The seasons are divided into the northeast monsoon, which brings frequent rains on the east coast of the islands, and the southwest monsoon, which brings the rainy season in Manila and on the west coast. In the southern and narrow part of the island of Luzon and from there down through the southern part of the archipelago, the rainfall is well distributed throughout the year. The rainfall is very heavy, in certain sections as much as two hundred and fifty inches annually, and occasionally more. The hottest months are April and May.

Typhoons are of occasional occurrence, usually during the southwest monsoon. Although the wind reaches terrific velocity as it circles around the center of a typhoon, often reaching one hundred miles an hour, the forward movement of the typhoon is very slow, perhaps eight to twelve miles an hour, and is nowadays accurately forecast. The path of a severe typhoon is marked by destruction, houses blown down, trees uprooted, ships wrecked, and crops ruined. Fortunately its path is narrow, seldom exceeding ten or twelve miles, and serious damage is always of limited extent. Destructive typhoons generally pass to the northward of Luzon, and of those striking the Philippine Islands about twice as many pass to the north as to the south of Manila. The southern portion of the archipelago, including the central and western regions of the great island of Mindanao, southern Palawan, and the Sulu Archipelago on the south, is remarkably free from typhoons.

There is a notable chain of volcanoes from the Batan Islands on the north down to the noble Mount Apo, over 9600 feet in height, in southern Mindanao. Some of these are still active. Although the seismograph in Manila frequently registers earthquakes, they are seldom strong.

One of the most beautiful sights of the Philippine Islands is Mayon Volcano, an almost perfect cone, which rises from sea level to a height of 7943 feet in the southernmost part of Luzon.

The Islands are generally of volcanic origin, the higher portions of a partly submerged mountain mass. The slopes of some of the mountains are so steep and rock strata so shattered as to be in a state of unstable equilibrium. The serious geological disturbances which brought these mountains into being have resulted in frequent faults in the mineral deposits. The Islands are connected with Borneo by two narrow, interrupted land bridges, Palawan and the Sulu Archipelago.

Some islands, like Bohol and Cebu, are in great part overlaid with coral, which, disintegrating, has given soil characteristics of marked difference from those of most of the larger islands, where lava overflow and volcanic tufa and ash deposit have affected extensive districts and resulted in some curious phenomena — areas of extremely fertile soil adjacent to land almost incapable of successful cultivation. Some of the small islands in the southern seas are wholly of coral formation, fertile, but without dependable springs or other sources of potable water. The soil in many districts is rich. There is no wholly arid region.

The archipelago comprises three natural divisions: on the north, Luzon, Mindoro, and adjacent islands; in the center, the Visayas, of which the island of Samar is the largest, while Cebu, Panay, and Negros are preponderant in population and commerce; and on the south the great island of Mindanao and the Sulu Archipelago extending to the very shores of Borneo. Of all the islands in the group Mindanao has the largest area of undeveloped agricultural land. There are also great areas of undeveloped fertile land naturally adapted to agriculture in the Visayan Islands, especially in Leyte and Samar, as well as on the large islands of Mindoro and Palawan; and, although it supports by far the largest population, there are still extensive uncultivated fertile regions in Luzon.

Before the American Occupation gold, copper, and iron had long been produced in a small way on various islands. Since the later days of the Spanish régime there has been a limited production of gold by European and American mining enterprises in Luzon, Masbate, and Mindanao, as well as from the more primitive operations carried on by Filipinos.[1] Americans, as will be shown later, had developed large gold producing mines,[2] and it is probable that the industry extended back into prehistoric times. Copper and iron are also mined in a very small

[1] The word "Filipino" has the Spanish spelling derived from Felipe, while the adjective "Philippine" has the English spelling of Philip. In writing this book, the word "Philippine" has been used wherever reference is made to the Islands in a geographical sense, and "Filipino," both noun and adjective, where reference is made to the people. When the people are described geographically, however, the term "Philippine people" is used. These distinctions are not always observed in quoted matter, where, of course, passages are copied without change.

[2] A gold mine developed by American enterprise in Benguet, island of Luzon, has proved extremely profitable.

way in Luzon. The largest known deposit of iron is in the island of Mindanao. Efforts on the part of individuals, corporations, and the government have been made to exploit other minerals, such as asbestos, petroleum, and asphaltum, but without notable success. Coal of various grades is found in many places. There have been efforts, both by private enterprise and by the government, to develop commercial production, but up to 1927 these efforts had met with no important measure of success.

Mineral and thermal springs are found in many places in the Islands, and some are notable for their beneficial effects in the treatment of diseases.

The Philippine forests are of great economic value.[3] There are many varieties of the choicest cabinet woods, and of timber well adapted for all kinds of structural and other economic uses; and they produce large quantities of tan barks (cutch), dyewoods, gutta-percha, gum copal, and other valuable gums, resins, oils, rattans, and fibers, and nipa palm, the sap of which is used for the manufacture of alcohol.

Philippine hard woods are classified by the Bureau of Forestry according to degree of hardness and there are a number of the first class of a specific gravity greater than water, capable of taking the finest finish, and useful for a variety of structural purposes. About three thousand varieties of wood ("arboreous species") are distinguishable in the Islands.

Narra, which is of two shades, light or "white narra" and blood-red, was the favorite wood of the Spanish artisans for making furniture. This is much harder than the average wood sold as mahogany, and much of the fine old furniture in the Islands is made of it, including table tops as large as eight feet in diameter cut from the buttress roots of the trees. Ebony of fine quality is found. Molave, known in the Philippine Islands as the king of woods, is most resistant to the elements.

The Philippine forests, estimated at 72,224 square miles, comprise about two-thirds of the total land area of the Islands. Of this forest area, nearly ninety per cent, or 64,127 square miles, are commercial forests, the balance being classed as second growth capable of furnishing timber of small dimensions and abundant supplies of firewood. Practically all these forests are public domain and are administered by

[3] It has been asserted by competent authority that the stand of hard wood timber in the Philippine Islands is now probably the finest in the world.

the Philippine Bureau of Forestry, only one per cent being privately owned.

The forests in many places begin at the sea and extend across the lowlands to the very crests of the mountain ranges. Entirely unlike the temperate zone, there is here a wealth of varied vegetation in addition to the stately towering trees. In the shade of these dense forests there is an exuberant growth of plant life — great climbing rattans, some of which are hundreds of feet in length and of such strength that they make excellent ferry cables; innumerable varieties of orchids and other parasitical plants, as well as an abundance of plants and shrubs. As night falls hordes of great fruit bats come and flap slowly and thickly about among the tree-tops.

Many medicinal plants, including quinine, camphor, chaulmoogra,[4] and others not indigenous, find favorable climatic and soil conditions in many parts of the Philippine Islands.

Still more important are the agricultural resources of this fertile and well-watered country. It might provide for an additional population of about eighty million souls.

The Filipinos have the true Oriental skill in terracing lands for irrigation. Their finest work is the ancient terraces built on the steep mountain-sides by the tribal peoples in the interior of northern Luzon.

During the Spanish administration of the Islands, the Filipino farmer still used rather primitive methods. The typical farm was generally less than five acres.

The most important agricultural food product is rice, which is the staple article of diet. To a lesser degree, and more recently, corn has come more into general favor. As late as 1926 neither rice nor corn was produced in quantities sufficient to meet the needs of the people, and much rice was imported, partly because there was an apparent economic advantage to the Filipino in raising the more profitable crops of hemp, copra, sugar, and tobacco.

The Philippine Islands are the only region in the world extensively to produce abaca, known as "Manila" hemp, which is superior to all other fibers for marine cordage and other purposes requiring an especially long, strong, durable fiber. Maguey, sisal, and other fibers are also produced for local use, and to an appreciable extent for export.

---

[4] A specific for the cure of leprosy is obtained from the seed of the chaulmoogra tree.

The fibers of various other plants, including cotton and pineapple, are used for the manufacture of fabrics for local use. Piña cloth, made from the pineapple fiber, is used for those exquisite embroideries for which the Islands are famous, but which are not produced for export in quantities comparable with the commercial embroideries on imported cotton and linen fabrics.

Most tropical and subtropical fruits and nuts of economic value, including coffee and cacao, have been demonstrated to be capable of commercial growth in the Islands.

Production of plantation rubber has been carried on to a degree which indicates that it can be commercially profitable. So far this has been the result of small private ventures by Americans and Europeans without adequate capital. After several years of commercial production, these small plantations have demonstrated that conditions of the Philippine climate, soil, and labor are eminently favorable to rubber production.

Racially the Filipino is a Malay and throughout the Islands the bulk of the population is sufficiently similar in type to indicate no great differences of origin. There has been continued infusion of Mongolian blood, and limited infusion of that of other Asiatic and of Polynesian peoples. There is little appearance of Caucasian blood in Filipinos except in the city of Manila and a very few other localities. In the composition of the race the Negroid elements are negligible. There are in various localities a few aboriginal dwarf people with black skin, some with very dark, frizzled, and some with straight hair.

The typical Filipino has straight black hair, dark brown eyes, and light to dark brown skin. He has a graceful, lithe physique, at maturity not usually exceeding five feet and four inches in stature. There is also a numerous sub-type of more stocky build and frequently with oblique eyes in which the Mongoloid element is manifest. Noteworthy, though less numerous, is a type distinctive chiefly in greater height, approaching that of some of the peoples of northern India or of Polynesia. All these physical types are found as individuals and groups among both civilized and tribal peoples, Christians, Mohammedans, and pagans.

The earliest estimate of the population is given as 500,000 people at the time of the conquest of the Islands by Legaspi about 1570. In 1899, during the first year of American occupation, the population, not including tribal peoples, was estimated to be 6,700,000, an increase that bears eloquent testimony to the advance made under the Spanish rule.

The official census in 1903 gave a total population of 7,635,426, of which 6,987,686 were civilized and 647,740 were tribal.[5] The resident foreigners in the Philippine Islands according to the census of 1918 were 64,037.[6]

In 1940, according to the census of that year, the population was 16,356,000.

The Christian Filipino woman holds a very different position in the family from that given to her sisters in India or in some other Oriental countries. She is usually the business manager of the household, keeps the keys, does the providing, receives all cash earned by any member of the family, including the proceeds from the farm produce, and supervises the expenditure. It is she who makes the budget. A man who fails to turn in his receipts for his wife's direction somewhat injures his standing in the community.

The more wealthy Filipinos assimilated something of the Spanish practice of surrounding the women with all sorts of physical means of protection. The windows of their houses, built during the Spanish régime, were heavily barred, and wife or daughter was not supposed to go out in the street unaccompanied by a duenna. Coeducation was not to be thought of, and the free and trusted association of boys with girls was not allowed. The introduction of American ideas and practices rapidly modified these customs.

The educated Filipino women throughout the lowlands are quiet, modest, unassuming, and carefully dressed. They have excellent man-

---

[5] "The civilized people, with the exception of those of foreign birth, were practically all adherents of the Roman Catholic Church, while of the peoples here classified as wild, a large proportion, probably more than two-fifths, were Mohammedans in religion and were well known in the Islands as Moros. The remaining three-fifths belonged to various tribes differing from one another in degrees of barbarism." (*Census*, 1903, II, 15.)

[6] The following table shows the distribution of the foreign residents in Manila and the provinces:

Citizenship	Total	Manila	Provinces
American	5,774	2,916	2,858
Chinese	43,802	17,760	26,042
Japanese	7,806	1,612	6,194
Spanish	3,945	2,050	1,895
English	1,140	664	476
German	286	201	85
French	182	121	61
Swiss	125	71	54
All other	977	474	503

(*Census*, 1918, II, 32.)

In 1926 the Chinese residents in the Philippine Islands were estimated at 60,000, and the Japanese at 10,000.

ners, pleasant, quiet voices, and under most circumstances comport themselves with great self-possession.

The family life of the Filipino is generally happy. There are usually several children and frequently aged and other dependent relatives, all of whom are welcomed members of the household. The development and education of the children soon come to be the absorbing interest of the older members of the family, who as a rule make whatever sacrifices may seem necessary. The parents are very indulgent, but are usually recompensed in later years by filial affection and care. It is rare to see a homeless aged or crippled person. Those without near relatives are taken into the homes of acquaintances among the more affluent members of the community or receive aid otherwise from private persons. The Roman Catholic missionaries appear to have encouraged these admirable traits of the people. An interesting sight is the aged poor leaving the monasteries on certain days of the week with food and other alms. It is noteworthy that there is no almshouse outside the city of Manila.

In commerce, Filipino women are notably more numerous than men in retail trade, and they are often local jobbers in agricultural produce and Philippine textiles as well as imported merchandise. In many instances women successfully manage substantial investments in agriculture, fisheries, and other industries. They compete with the men in the professions of medicine, dentistry, and pharmacy, and are entering the practice of law.

In public affairs, women are taking an increasingly important part through individual leadership and club organizations. These are engaged in welfare work rather than political activities. There seems to be little popular demand for woman's suffrage, but many Filipino women hold important positions in government service, including such posts as assistant attorney in the Bureau of Justice, medical officer with the rank of senior surgeon in the Bureau of Health, and municipal treasurer.

It is especially notable that a Moro woman was appointed president of a municipality in Mindanao upon the request of a majority of the men of the district expressed at a *viva voce* election. In Sulu more than once a woman has been the acknowledged ruling influence in the public affairs of the Sultanate, and one assisted in conducting most important negotiations with the Spanish and American governments.

The social structure found in the Islands by Americans was essentially feudal. In the rural districts genuine loyalty as well as feudal land-tenure existed between the *cacique* [7] and his retainers.

Villages rather than scattered homesteads are characteristic of Filipino rural life, and fondness for their social life causes them to be unwilling to live on the lands they cultivate except for the brief periods of seedtime and harvest. The annual festival of the patron saint of the village attracts crowds from other villages. Religious services and processions from the church through the principal streets are conducted with pomp and solemnity. These are followed by open air theatricals, feasting, music, dancing, and other entertainments all of an Occidental character due to the influence of the Spanish missionaries. Except for a few attractive folk dances which survive in the Christian communities, it is only among the Mohammedan and tribal peoples that the pre-Spanish music and dancing are still to be found. The arrival of persons of distinction is generally celebrated by banquets and a grand ball. Presentable strangers of all classes find in these villages a hospitality so invariable that hotels rarely exist except in the cities and a few of the largest towns.

Manila is not only the political capital, but also the great commercial center of the Philippine Archipelago. It is situated on the shores of Manila Bay at the mouth of the Pasig River and is the terminus of the main railway lines on the island of Luzon. At the time of American occupation the city had a population of about 300,000, which comprised Filipinos from all parts of the Islands, about 3000 Americans, and foreigners of almost every nationality. The most numerous foreigners are the Chinese. Of these there are nearly 18,000, most of whom are engaged in commerce.

The total area of the city is about fifteen square miles, and includes in addition to the walled town many suburban villages. There are spacious parks and many wide avenues, so that the greater part of the city is pleasantly free from crowding.

In the delta of the river Pasig there are, besides the main channel of the river, many canals, or *esteros*, of which some were formerly branches of the river and others were opened for thoroughfares.

[7] *Cacique* is the term customarily used to indicate a Filipino of dominating local influence, and so used is usually suggestive of such a person who uses his power arbitrarily. This word was taken by the Spaniards from the Caribbean Indian dialects, in which it appears to have been used to indicate the chief of a group or tribe, and subsequently applied by the Spaniards to local chiefs among the natives of the Philippine Islands and other islands of the Pacific.

The city is peculiarly free from slums due to the efficiency of the public health and police authorities. It has electric light, street railways, telephone, gas, and other services. Also there are good hotels, whole-sale and retail merchandise establishments, banks, express companies, ice and cold storage plants, abundant supplies of meats, fish, fresh fruits and vegetables, and other modern facilities for business convenience and comfortable living.

Manila possesses many historic monuments of Spanish construction, of which the most impressive is the walled city built by Legaspi at the mouth of the Pasig River. The portion next to the river is the citadel known as Fort Santiago, the construction of which in its present form was begun in the year 1590. From this citadel defensive walls were extended parallel with the sea beach and along the south bank of the river Pasig for considerable distances and then brought together on the south, enclosing the area within which were constructed the principal government offices and residences of the Spanish officers and their families. The total extension of the wall, about two and three-quarters miles, was completed during the eighteenth century. After the evacuation of the city by the English in 1764, extensive changes were made in the fortifications, including the excavation of a wide moat outside the wall, since filled.

Of the many churches, monasteries, and other buildings within the walled city the oldest is that of the Augustinian friars, the construction of the present building having been begun in the year 1599. Its walls were built strongly enough to have withstood the earthquakes and storms of three centuries. The churches of the Dominicans, Franciscans, Recollects, and Jesuits, are also located in the walled city. The most imposing of the church edifices is the cathedral. The University of Santo Tomas and the Jesuits' college for young men have museums which contain much of historic and scientific interest.

Throughout the Islands there are more than fifteen thousand villages, or *barrios* as they are termed, and these are grouped for governmental purposes in nearly twelve hundred municipalities. The typical village is small in population; the houses in orderly location on one or two streets, a schoolhouse and a chapel being the only public buildings. The seat of municipal government is generally larger, with a public plaza, fronting on which are the government office building or "town hall," the church, and perhaps the public school building, the market, and residence of one or more of the wealthy families. Cebu, the site of the first European settlement in the Islands, with a population of 66,000, is, next to Manila, the largest city. Among other cities of importance are the seaports of Iloilo, Legaspi, and Zamboanga. Jolo, said to be the smallest walled city in the world, is attractive with its background of hills and mountains, and its pier where traders deal in pearls and many unusual marine products.

The Filipinos use a variety of dialects, chiefly of Malay origin, which are usually spoken in the homes and in local social relations and trade among themselves. The Spaniards found them using a system of writing which had come to them through Hindu-Javanese channels. One of the early missionary friars stated that these islanders were given to reading and writing and that there was "hardly a man, and much less a woman," that did not "read and write in the letters used in the island of Manila." The leaves of a palm were used in the absence of paper, which appears to have been introduced by the Spaniards.

It appears that the Filipino manuscripts were chronologies, poems, and songs, the latter especially recounting the exploits of ancestors. The use of these old alphabets or syllabaries continued to a diminishing extent until the eighteenth century, when one of the missionary fathers remarked that in 1745 it was rare to find a person who could use them. A few Tagbanuas, a tribal people on the island of Palawan, and Mangyans on the island of Mindoro, still use similar alphabets to a very limited extent. There is no authentic specimen of pre-Spanish manuscript now known to exist, a very few alleged to have been found in caves in the Visayas being said to be of doubtful antiquity and of little or no value.

Although Spain gave its religion to the people, it never made any effort to impose its language, but rather discouraged the Filipino from learning anything but his local dialect, for which they substituted the Roman for the native alphabets. Neither was there any effective effort to give general primary education to the common people.

The dialects used by the largest groups are Visayan, Tagálog, and Ilocano. Besides these, the more important are Pampangan, Pangasinese, and Bicol. There are several localized dialects peculiar to the various groups constituting the tribal peoples and Mohammedans. The Negritos appear now to have no distinctive language of their own and use the dialects, more or less modified, of the other tribal or Christian peoples with whom they come most in contact.

Many Americans in writing of the Philippine Islands have construed the great diversity of languages, which some ethnologists believe they can divide into as many as eighty-seven different dialects, as evidence of lack of unity and cohesion of the Philippine people. While the difference in language makes common understanding more difficult, the fact is that the people are all reasonably similar in type, generally so in religion, have the same ideals and characteristics, and are imbued throughout with a great pride in their race and desire for its advancement which should make them capable, under a common language, of being welded into a united and thoroughly cohesive body politic. Those who question Filipino capacity should look for arguments against it in other directions than that of language or of tribal division.

The domestic animals in the Philippine Islands include carabao, or domesticated water buffalo, cows, horses, swine, sheep, goats, poultry, dogs and cats. The carabao is the commonest draught animal and is generally useful. It plows the land, hauls the cart to and from the market, supplies milk for the family, and finally is killed for beef. Domestic oxen are also used and found to be more efficient for field work and transportation during the season of minimum rainfall, as they are not so much affected by the heat and the sun.

The vast areas of unplowed grassland and abundant water supply from numerous mountain streams offer natural advantages for the cattle industry. Cattle were probably originally introduced from the mainland of Asia, and subsequently from Spain. Both cattle and water buffalo became very abundant and remained so until the importation of some dangerous communicable diseases, especially foot-and-mouth disease and rinderpest, brought in from Asia during the latter part of the Spanish régime. These caused devastating losses. During the serious disturbances of public order in the years 1896 to 1902, these diseases spread from island to island and to most of the interior regions of the largest islands. Before protective measures were well understood and applied, infection was reintroduced through the continued importation of cattle and water buffalo from Asia. With the present knowledge of methods of prevention of these diseases, the livestock industry, both for draft and food purposes, may become one of the great economic resources of the Philippine Islands.

Some authorities claim that the horse is indigenous to Sulu but it is probable that horses were imported from western Asia into the Sulu Archipelago at an earlier date than elsewhere in the Philippine Islands. Mongolian ponies probably found their way into the northern islands from China. Later, importations of Arab and Barb types came from Spain. Almost all the local northern dialects make use of the Spanish word for horse, which indicates that he is a relatively recent addition to the domestic animals of the Islands. Moreover, the Filipino displays less understanding in the care of his horse, which is used exclusively for saddle and the lightest draft purposes, than in the care of his carabao or draft bull.

The introduction of the Arab type and the crossing with the Mongolian pony have greatly improved the beauty and spirit of their progeny, which is distinctly of the diminutive pony type, but of admirable endurance and often quite handsome in appearance. Donkeys do not thrive in the Philippine Islands, and the only mules are those imported, generally by the government.

Of distinctive indigenous animals the most noteworthy is the tamarau, a species of small buffalo found only on the island of Mindoro. This animal is fierce and has never been domesticated.

The only other large animal that is dangerous to hunt in the Islands is the wild water buffalo, or *cimarrón* as this animal is locally known. He is practically identical with his tame brother, the carabao. One of the warlike tribal peoples in Luzon, the Kalingas, hunt the wild carabao on horseback with spears — a sport that not infrequently ends fatally for man and horse.

There are wild boar and deer on many of the islands and their meat is an important element in the food supply in many localities. The scarcity of other varieties of large wild animals is noteworthy because in the adjacent island of Borneo there are orangutans, panthers, tigers, bear, elephants, and rhinoceroses.

There are periodic swarms of locusts which bring ruin and devastation to the crops of those who are so unfortunate as to have plantations lying in their path. Organized defense against this periodically recurring pest would save many millions of dollars of agricultural loss.

The white ant or termite is a pest found throughout the low altitudes in the Islands. He operates from underground, finds his way through crevices in hard wood or cement, bores his way through soft wood, builds for himself a covered pathway of mud under which he crawls over cement posts or foundations to the soft wood of which the house above is too often built, and makes his silent, destructive way into the interior of furniture, even books, in upper stories of houses. Constant vigilance is necessary to protect property from its ravages.

IFUGAO RICE TERRACES AT BANAUE

MAYON VOLCANO

The Philippine Islands are comparatively free from venomous insects and reptiles. Small fly-catching lizards, inoffensive to man, frequent the walls and ceilings of houses. Crocodiles are found in many of the streams and lakes. It is believed in the Islands that in only comparatively rare instances do crocodiles become man-eaters.

There are numerous varieties of snakes but they are seldom seen. About twenty-five kinds of venomous snakes are known of which the more dangerous are cobras, above all the king cobra, which attacks man, but fortunately is extremely rare. The comparative harmlessness of the snakes in the Islands is shown by the fact that apparently only about one hundred people die by snake bites each year. The pythons grow to very large sizes and are known to have swallowed whole full-grown deer. While small they are distinctly beneficial, as they live largely on rats.

The Islands are particularly rich in birds, of which there are more than 750 species, some of them peculiar to the Philippine Islands. This may be compared with 502 species in Japan, 290 in Formosa, 393 in the Celebes Islands, while the great continent of Australia has only 711. There are some unusually interesting birds: the monkey-eating eagle, one of the largest eagles known, of which very few specimens have ever been secured; the peacock pheasant of Palawan; the tiny curved-beak sunbird, the brilliant colors of whose plumage shine with a metallic gleam similar to that of our hummingbird. There are numerous other birds of brilliant plumage and some very sweet songsters. In September there is a great migration of snipe eagerly sought after by sportsmen, and some of the lakes are frequented by ducks, of which the commonest is the "wandering tree duck."

The scenic beauties of the Islands are little known, but whoever is privileged to travel about them will find vast volcanoes towering from sea level in majestic cones; great plains covered with waving coconut palms; dazzling coral beaches in little coves beneath towering cliffs of limestone which rise precipitously a thousand or more feet in the air, with strange tropical plants in every nook or crevice. The transparent sea enables one to see all sorts of marine growth, and corals; brilliantly colored fishes of fantastic shapes dart in and out among the coral, which can be seen clear to a depth of nearly fifty or sixty feet. Occasionally the eye catches sight of a huge turtle swimming about, or some monster shark, or perhaps some silvery fish gleaming in the sun, seemingly suspended in the air so invisible is the water which supports it. Under the island of Palawan runs an underground river which may be explored for four miles through long tunnels of rock and under great caves with vaulted domes, while all about chattering bats and swiftlets fly past the intruding boat. Bacuit Bay, the Pabellones Islands, and the island of Coron are startling examples of scenic grandeur. In some places continued action of the waves on the limestone rock has wrought shapes fantastic almost beyond description.

CHAPTER II

EARLY HISTORY

PHILIPPINE HISTORY may be said to have begun with the death of Magellan, who was killed in battle on the little island of Mactan near Cebu on the 27th of April, 1521, having espoused the cause of a native chieftain who had been baptized and who professed allegiance to the King of Spain. The survivors of this expedition and their captain, Magellan's successor, one Juan Sebastian del Cano, with the single ship Victoria, completed the epoch-making circumnavigation of the earth essayed by their leader. Of a fleet of five ships and two hundred and sixty-eight men but one ship and eighteen men returned to Spain.

Philippine history prior to this event is shrouded in obscurity, as there are no written records in Philippine or Spanish archives, and few prehistoric monuments with the exception of a few unpretentious tombs in the island of Sulu and burial caves occasionally discovered in the Visayan Islands. It is probable that the only documentary information that can shed light on these periods is to be found in the records of China, India, Japan, and Malaysia.

What are believed to be authentic sources indicate that the Islands now known as the Philippines were a dependency of successive Hindu-Malayan empires in Indo-China, Sumatra, and Borneo, from about the year 200 until 1325. Thereafter until 1405, they were subject to the Javanese empire of Madjapahit. During the next thirty-five years they were, under the Ming Dynasty, a dependency of China. Thereafter, from the year 1440 until 1565, northern Luzon was sometimes held by Japanese adventurers, and from Manila southward the Islands were dominated by Mohammedan Borneo. The Sultan of Brunei exercised a certain degree of authority over the southern islands and even as far north as Manila. There is evidence that trade was carried on directly between the southern islands and China and Siam.

In the early part of the sixteenth century the most active traders were the Portuguese. As early as 1498 they had extended their commerce and imperial domain to the coasts of India and a few years later to the Moluccas and other islands of the Indian and Pacific Oceans. They asserted and endeavored to maintain an exclusive right to the trade route from Europe southward around the Cape of Good Hope.

The Spaniards extending their empire and trade came into frequent conflict with the Portuguese adventurers. Several efforts were made to establish zones within which each empire should be free to extend its power and thus avoid conflict. In 1493, Pope Alexander VI fixed a longitudinal line in the Atlantic Ocean east of which all lands discovered should belong to Portugal and those on the west to Spain. In the following year the Kings of Portugal and Spain agreed upon another line further to the west. In 1529, a treaty-line was drawn east of the Moluccas which in effect was a relinquishment by the King of Spain of his claim to the archipelago later known as the Philippine Islands. For this the Portuguese paid a monetary indemnity of three hundred thousand gold ducats. This agreement did not endure.

The claims set up by the Portuguese for the trade route around the Cape of Good Hope to the rich islands of the East spurred the Spaniards on to an effort to find their way to these Indies by sailing westward, and it was this that led King Charles I of Spain to accept the proposal of Fernando Magellan, the Portuguese navigator, to seek a passage by the south of America. Magellan had achieved distinction in the exploration of the Far East, which he had reached sailing eastward, but, dissatisfied with his own government, he offered his services to Spain. These were accepted, and on the 20th of September, 1519, he set sail with his fleet of five vessels.

It must be remembered that at the time this voyage was undertaken there were few who believed in the theory of the spherical form of the earth. In this voyage Magellan discovered and successfully navigated the perilous strait which now bears his name, and, crossing the Pacific, discovered the Ladrone Islands, and reached what is now known as the Philippine Archipelago, to which, however, he gave the name of the San Lazaro Islands. Though he did not arrive at his point of departure, he had reached the same degree of longitude sailing westward that he had previously reached sailing eastward, so that in one sense he himself completed the circumnavigation of the globe.

Pigafetta, the historian of Magellan's expedition, stated that the natives appeared by their friendly attitude to welcome the Europeans, to whom, in return for presents, they brought food and furnished guides as well as giving general information. They were fond of music and dancing, alcoholic liquors, and cock-fighting. Merchant vessels brought trade from China, Siam, and Borneo. The people used weights and measures, lived in houses constructed of timber and palm thatch, and had boats like those of Europe, but marveled at the speed of Magellan's ship. The men wore only loin cloths, and they tattooed their bodies. The women wore skirts of bark and gold ornaments. The chieftains wore silk and cotton headcloths, and not only wore ornaments of solid gold and feasted from gold dishes, but had houses in part of gold. Gold was the principal trade product of the Islands. There were many petty kings or chieftains without any effective overlord. The King of Borneo exercised a certain supremacy through relations with the "King of Luzon," whose son was the commander-in-chief of the military and naval forces of the King of Borneo. In religion most of the people were heathen, some Mohammedans.

Magellan's discovery opened up visions of new empire to the Spanish monarch. New expeditions were organized, no less than four being undertaken in rapid succession, all ending in disaster. These expeditions found themselves in conflict with the Portuguese, who occupied the Moluccas and had established trading stations and even sent missionaries as far north as the Philippine Islands. The first was commanded by Fray Garcia Jofre de Loaisa, with whom Captain del Cano, the second in command to Magellan, sailed; the second was headed by Sebastian Cabot. The last two were fitted out from the Americas, then known as New Spain; the first of these under the direction of Saavedra, and the second under Villalobus.

These two expeditions did reach the Philippine Islands. Saavedra visited one if not more of the southern Philippine Islands and Villalobus reached Mindanao on the 2d of February, 1543. He was the first Spaniard to make explorations in that island and he gave to this and other islands the name of Filipinas (Philippines) in honor of the Crown Prince Don Felipe, afterwards Philip II. Besides Mindanao he visited the islands of Leyte and Samar.

The most notable name, however, connected with these expeditions was that of Andres de Urdaneta, who sailed with the first expedition as historian, returned to Europe after an absence of eleven years, was offered and declined the command of the Villalobus expedition, but later participated in the conquest of the Philippine Islands by Spain.

The conquest was the result of an expedition under the command of Don Miguel de Legaspi, who had distinguished himself in Mexico, as officer of the government, by gaining the good-will of the natives through forbearance and patience. Accompanied by his kinsman Urdaneta, who had meantime become an Augustinian friar, he embarked with a fleet of four vessels and three hundred and eighty men, took formal possession of the Ladrone Islands at Guam, and on February 13, 1565, anchored in the Philippine Islands near Cebu.

Legaspi decided to establish a settlement at Cebu in spite of the hostile attitude of the natives, whose weapons were bows and arrows, iron lances, and small cannon.

An image of the Christ child, perhaps that which Pigafetta described as having been given by Magellan to the Queen of Cebu, April 14, 1521, was found there by Legaspi's men April 28, 1565, and welcomed with all honors by the expedition as a good omen. It is still venerated in Cebu.

It was not long before the wise and considerate methods of Legaspi had gained the confidence of the natives. Tupas, who then had the title of King of Cebu, was baptized, and the work of conversion prospered. Urdaneta returned to Mexico and reported the success of the expedition, and reinforcements and supplies were sent to Legaspi, who moved his headquarters to Panay for greater security against the Portuguese. Spain soon began to receive cargoes of the rich "spices" of the Orient for the trade in which she had in large measure undertaken these expeditions.

Two other names illustrate the conquest of the Philippine Islands, those of Legaspi's grandson, Captain Juan de Salcedo, and of his general, Martin de Goiti.

Legaspi commissioned Salcedo to explore the islands to the northward and especially to punish the pirates who preyed upon the towns on the coast of Panay.

From his first arrival in the Islands, Legaspi had heard of an important trading point named Manila on the island of Luzon. For the conquest of that region he sent Goiti with Salcedo and a considerable force of Spanish soldiers and Visayan allies. This expedition found Manila — the fortified stronghold of the Mohammedan chieftain Rajah Soliman. On the opposite side of the river Pasig was the town of Tondo, whose chief was Rajah Lacandola. The Spaniards were given a friendly reception, but soon thereafter were attacked by a large force. They succeeded in occupying the fortification and driving out the natives, who set fire to the town. After some exploration the Spaniards returned to Panay, where they devoted themselves to strengthening their hold on the Visayas.

In 1571, Legaspi with a force of three hundred men, proceeded to Manila and in May of that year the establishment of the present city of Manila was begun. Legaspi laid out the settlement, reconstructed the fort, built a government house, and planned a monastery for the Augustinians, a church, and one hundred and fifty houses. The city was designated as the capital of the archipelago.

The Mohammedan rajahs now undertook to drive out the Spaniards, but they were repelled without difficulty and Rajah Soliman was killed, while Lacandola professed conversion to the Christian religion, was baptized, and made no further opposition to the Spaniards.

General Goiti and the young Captain Salcedo, by a series of masterly expeditions, explored and brought under Spanish control the entire island of Luzon.

Other detachments of Spanish troops secured the submission of the people on most of the inhabited islands lying between Luzon and Mindanao. On August 20, 1572, Legaspi died.

Thus, in seven years, with a very small force, the Spaniards had added to their empire the great island of Luzon and the Visayan Islands. Their main strength was the greatness of the leader, Legaspi. A keen student of human psychology, wise in the selection of his warriors, as the unbroken series of victories gained by Goiti and Salcedo proved him, Legaspi readily understood the native, whose confidence and loyalty he gained for himself and Spain. These achievements mark Legaspi as one of the world's great colonial pioneers.

With his handful of men, even Legaspi could never have accomplished what he did if at that time the Islands had not been much less populous than they are now. The natives were disunited; practically each village was an independent government. There was no great king or lord commanding a large force of fighting men.

A potent factor destined to be the controlling element in the development of Spain's colonial enterprise in the Philippine Islands was the missionary priest. The Spaniards found no powerful native priesthood, and but comparatively primitive religious observances. The ceremonial splendor of the Roman Catholic rites aroused the attention and won the admiration and awe of the Filipino. The soldier made his campaigns and withdrew to Manila or to some other military station. The Friars remained in the villages teaching the people the Christian religion, and new arts and sciences. The religion brought by the Spaniards undoubtedly met a need in the spiritual life of the people. Its truths appealed to their minds, and its pageantry to their love of beauty.

At the time of the arrival of the Spaniards in the Philippine Islands Mohammedanism had not been very firmly established. Mohammedan conquests in the Islands began about the middle of the fifteenth century from Borneo and Java, first in the Sulu Archipelago and the southern part of Mindanao, and later in the Visayas and Luzon, which had been reached not long before the middle of the sixteenth century.

Thus the original inhabitants that Legaspi found in Luzon, the Visayas, and northern Mindanao had no such deep-seated religious convictions as have the southern Mohammedans, else the labor of Christianizing them would have been much more onerous; for, in spite of the religious fervor of the Spaniards, they were never able to convert those of the inhabitants of southern Mindanao and Sulu whose forefathers had espoused the Mohammedan faith.

From early records it appears that the Japanese began trading in the Islands in the latter part of the fifteenth century for gold, pearls, and especially for a kind of rare pottery known as "Luzon ware," which was highly prized in Japan as receptacles for the leaves of tea used ceremonially by the Japanese nobility. If this pottery was made in the Philippine Islands, it became a lost art, as by the time the Spaniards arrived practically all of it had disappeared.

This Japanese trade increased rapidly during the sixteenth century, but came to an abrupt end early in the seventeenth century, at which time the Dutch occupied Formosa, while the Japanese expelled the Christian missionaries from their country.

An old Japanese book mentions an unsuccessful attempt to conquer the archipelago in 1540. The Spaniards on their arrival at Manila in 1570 found a small Japanese colony there, and the Japanese had maintained a settlement in northern Luzon until it was destroyed by the Spaniards in 1582.

The great Shogun Hideyoshi, ambitious to extend the Japanese Empire overseas, sent an embassy to Manila in 1592 and demanded formal submission and the payment of tribute by the Spaniards under threat of invasion and conquest by forces which had completed a successful campaign in Korea. The Spaniards, recognizing their inability successfully to repel such an invasion, resorted to dilatory tactics and actually paid tribute on several occasions.

Internal strife in Japan and the Dutch occupation of Formosa appear to have saved the Philippine Islands from further molestation, and shortly after this the Japanese government adopted a policy of isolation which lasted until Commodore Perry's visit in 1854.

During the early period of Spanish occupation the Philippine Islands were occasionally harassed by Chinese and Japanese adventurers. Only once did the Spaniards have serious difficulty in expelling these buccaneers, none of whom appears to have represented constituted government. The Chinese outlaw Limahong, a fugitive from the Chinese government, captured a Chinese merchant vessel off the coast of Luzon in 1574 and thus gained information about the wealth and military weakness of Manila due to the temporary absence of the Spanish forces on distant expeditions. He surprised and killed General Goiti, and was only prevented from capturing Manila by the opportune arrival of Captain Salcedo, who relieved the Spanish garrison besieged in the citadel. Limahong established himself in a fortified camp in the province of Pangasinan, but was driven out by Salcedo.

The Spaniards found trade with China so profitable that not only were merchant ships encouraged to come from China to Manila, but the Chinese were encouraged to settle both as merchants and as artisans. The excellence of the Chinese coolie as a laborer was early recognized by the Spaniards and it appears to have been their desire to encourage immigration of these laborers. However, the constant tendency of the coolie to develop into a merchant or a landowner created serious problems, especially in view of the Spanish policy of monopolizing commerce and limiting the ownership of land to themselves and the Filipinos. These circumstances contributed to strained relations between the Spaniards and Filipinos on one side and the resident Chinese on the other, with occasional clashes resulting more than once in massacre of Chinese.

The Chinese, as is their usual custom, came to the Philippine Islands merely to make their fortunes and return to China, and seldom brought their families with them. Continued residence, however, naturally resulted in the intermarriage of many Chinese with Filipino women and the resulting development of an increasing class of Chinese-Malay half-castes, or *mestizos*, as the Spaniards style people of mixed blood. There is a greater infusion of Chinese than any other blood in the Filipino.

The path of the Spanish empire-builder was not an easy one. There was bitter commercial antagonism between Portugal and Spain, but from 1581 to 1640 a temporary consolidation of the two kingdoms gave them respite. At the beginning of the seventeenth century, the Dutch began to take an active part in the Orient and harassed shipping and made prizes, not only of Spanish, but of Chinese merchant vessels, at one time even maintaining a temporary foothold on the north shore of Manila Bay. In 1624, the Dutch possessed themselves of the island of Formosa on the north. There were some notable naval battles, especially when the Spaniards destroyed the Dutch fleet. Eleven years later, another Dutch fleet was destroyed in Manila Bay. Other engagements followed in which the Spaniards were successful to a degree that assured their supremacy throughout the Philippine Archipelago.

The first appearance of the British in the Philippine Islands was in the year 1578, when the great English admiral Sir Francis Drake, the second circumnavigator of the world, having touched the coast of Luzon, engaged in friendly commerce with the Sultan of Ternate in the Moluccas in defiance of the Portuguese, and returned to England by way of the Cape of Good Hope.

About ten years later, the British began to harass the Spanish colonies, a practice which lasted for about one hundred years.

Spain was an ally of France during her seven years' war with England, and in October, 1762, Manila was attacked and occupied by British forces. The Spaniards, relying on the distance from Europe, had not planned the fortifications of Manila except as protection against Chinese and Moro raiders. At the time of this invasion there was no Governor-General present in the Islands and the Archbishop, acting in his stead, surrendered the city to the British. Local Spanish opinion was strongly opposed to this action. As in the case of the warlike Morga, a member of the Supreme Court, Simon de Anda, took the leadership, and withdrawing from the city, set up the Spanish government in the neighboring province of Bulacan. Anda limited the extension of British control, and succeeded in keeping the Spanish flag flying in the Islands.

The British overran southern Luzon and the Visayas, incited the Filipinos to rebellion against the Spanish in northern Luzon, liberated the Sultan of Sulu whom the Spaniards held prisoner in Manila, and developed friendly relations with the Moros in Mindanao and Sulu.

Upon receipt of notice from their government of a formal termination of the war in June, 1764, the British withdrew from the Philippine Islands, turning over the city of Manila to Anda.

The defeat of Spain by the British was a great blow to Spanish pres-

tige in the Philippine Islands and shattered the tradition of Spanish invulnerability which had been their greatest asset in dealing with the
Filipinos.

Another important result of this British occupation was the awaken-
ing of merchants of other countries to the possibilities of profitable
trade with the Islands, the Spaniards having theretofore maintained a
monopoly of all trade between the Philippine Islands and Europe, in
conformity with the prevalent conception of the use of colonial possessions. Their idea was to make of Manila a great trading center to
which they would gather, in the interest of Spanish merchants, as much
of the Oriental trade as they found it possible to obtain. During the
period of British occupation foreign merchants established themselves
in Manila. They were again excluded upon the return of the Islands to
Spain, but continued trade clandestinely or under special permits until
1814, when general permission was given foreign merchants to establish themselves in Manila. It was not until 1837, however, that the port
of Manila was opened to foreign trade.

Spanish control of the Philippine Islands was exercised through the
Viceroy of Mexico or New Spain and almost all the expeditions to their
East Indian possessions were fitted out in America. Upon the over-
throw of the Spanish power in Mexico by the war of independence in
1821, the Philippine Archipelago came for the first time directly under
the administrative control of Madrid.

Successive Governors-General continued the work begun by Legaspi
and exercised control throughout the archipelago, except in the mountainous interiors of the islands of Luzon and Mindanao and some of
the less accessible interior regions of the Visayas.

The Spaniards had never succeeded in establishing their sovereignty
over the Mohammedans and tribal peoples in the interior of Mindanao,
although there had been numerous expeditions following that of
Rodriguez de Figuroa in the year 1596, which ended in disaster.

At one time the Spaniards laid claim to the Moluccas and undertook
their administration from headquarters at Zamboanga.

In 1662, the Spaniards withdrew temporarily from Mindanao, and
finally from the Moluccas, fearing an invasion by the Chinese-Japanese
adventurer Koxinga, who, having succeeded in driving the Dutch out
of Formosa, demanded the submission of the Philippine Islands. Although Koxinga and his invasion never materialized, the Spaniards
limited their activities for the ensuing fifty years to Luzon and the

Visayas. The Moros took advantage of this respite to destroy the Spanish fort near Zamboanga and periodically ravaged the coasts of the Visayan Islands, southern Luzon, and even the shores of Manila Bay, in spite of repeated expeditions undertaken by the Spaniards in an effort to subdue them. Many stone watch-towers and forts which were erected by the people, generally under the direction of the Spanish mission fathers, as protective measures against surprise attacks by these pirates, still remain as monuments of this period.

In their efforts to protect their people against these raids the Spaniards re-established the *presidio* of Zamboanga in 1718 and in 1763 built the great stone fort which still stands.

In 1848, with the assistance of the first steam war vessels to reach the Islands, the Spaniards began a sustained effort to extend their government throughout southern and central Mindanao and the Sulu Archipelago, and undertook more vigorous operations against the Moro pirates.

Finally, in 1851, the Spaniards attacked and took the town of Jolo on the island of that name in the Sulu Archipelago. The Moro fortifications at Jolo were destroyed, and some months later the Spaniards concluded a treaty with the Sultan of Sulu. Among other provisions of the treaty was the pledge by the Sultan to fly the Spanish flag exclusively and to suppress piracy, and in return certain guarantees were given as to practice of religion, the succession to the sultanate, trading privileges of Sulu boats, the right of the Sultan to customs duties on foreign trading vessels in his ports, and an annual subsidy in cash to the Sultan and to certain of his advisors or principal retainers. Piracy continued, however, and Spain increased her fleet of small steam vessels and her military forces in a continuous campaign against them.

In 1865, an American company, under the name of the American Trading Company of Borneo, secured a large territorial concession in northern Borneo from the Sultan of Brunei. This company was shortly succeeded by the British North Borneo Company. This occasioned diplomatic negotiations between Great Britain, Germany, and Spain in 1876. Two years later, the Sultan of Sulu by treaty acknowledged Spanish sovereignty as suzerain. The diplomatic negotiations with the European powers were concluded in 1885, Spain relinquishing claim to the territory occupied by the British North Borneo Company, and Great Britain and Germany recognizing the preponderance of Spanish sovereignty in the Sulu Archipelago.

There can be no question of the greatness of Spain's earlier achievement in the Philippine Islands. The scattered, warring tribes were welded into a reasonably homogeneous people, and though they were not given one language they became fairly devout Christians. Travelers from different countries spoke highly of their progress. In 1787, the French explorer, La Pérouse, found the Filipinos in "no way inferior" to the people of Europe. Dr. John Crawfurd, who visited the Islands in 1820, was surprised to find them improved in "civilization, wealth, and populousness" under the domination of a European country regarded at home as backward. Sir John Bowring, Governor of Hong Kong, commented in 1858 on the advantages due to lack of caste; and Jagor in 1859 and 1860 said, "To Spain belongs the glory of having raised to a relatively high grade of civilization . . . a people which she found on a lower stage of culture distracted by petty wars and despotic rule." A present-day authority, Professor Edward G. Bourne, comments that Manila at the opening of the seventeenth century made provisions for the sick and helpless far in advance of any of the cities of the English colonies for more than a century and a half to come.

In 1859–60 a German traveler by the name of Jagor made a memorable journey through the Philippine Islands which he described in a volume published in 1873. His interesting account ended with an extraordinary prediction which events have borne out precisely as foretold. He spoke of the three powerful nations then bordering on the Pacific, China, Russia, and the United States, and found difficulty in forecasting the part that Russia was to play, but expected an interesting development between the United States and China, due to the fact that one had great undeveloped resources and extension of land, and the other a surplus population. He told how the Mediterranean had sufficed for the commerce of the ancients, how the Atlantic had then become the theater of the world's principal commerce, and he predicted that when the desert Pacific developed its potentialities one would "be able to speak truly of universal commerce." He also predicted that American influence would make itself felt over the Pacific and finally become the dominating one in the Philippine Islands. He drew an interesting comparison between American and Spanish methods and commented: "It seems that the North Americans have the mission of vitalizing the germ of the Spanish seed. As conquerors of the modern age, as representatives of materialism in place of the romanticism of the Spanish cavaliers, the American pioneers pursue their course wielding the ax and guiding the plow, a contrast to the Spanish method of colonizing, the outstanding features of which were raising the cross and thrusting with the sword."

The last century of Spanish control in the Islands was increasingly troubled. Controversies between Church and State grew more bitter.

The transfer of government supervision to Madrid and of trade to Barcelona and Seville when Mexico became independent in 1821, the opening of the Suez Canal in 1869, and the use of steamships, all facilitated communication and travel between Spain and the Philippine Islands. The Filipinos came into contact with the revolutionary changes which were then going on in Europe. For a time Filipinos were sent to represent their government in the Spanish parliament in Madrid.

The opening of the port of Manila to foreign trade in 1837 and the opening of other ports gave great impulse to the economic development of the Islands, which were soon exporting agricultural products, especially hemp, sugar, tobacco, and coffee in increasing quantities. The Spaniards, little inclined to engage in agriculture, left the land in the hands of the Filipinos, some of whom soon acquired relatively large wealth. Their sons, having completed the education offered in the colleges and University of Santo Tomas in Manila, began to travel and study in Europe. The monastic orders objected to this tendency and influenced the Spanish government to discourage it.

Many Filipinos embarked as sailors on foreign commercial vessels visiting Manila and other Philippine ports, and gained favor by reason of their excellent qualities. This also placed Filipinos, especially of the poorer classes, in contact with foreigners.

Until 1896, such uprisings against Spanish authority as had occurred north of Mindanao were local and in but one case had the Spaniards found serious difficulty in suppressing them.

During the reaction following the restoration of the monarchy at Madrid in 1871, the Spaniards degraded the Filipino clergy to the almost menial service of the friars in the parishes. The discontent this occasioned contributed largely to the mutiny of troops at Cavite in which two hundred Filipino soldiers conspired with Filipino troops stationed in Manila to revolt. The latter failed to move as planned, and the revolt was suppressed without difficulty. Many prominent Filipinos, known by the Spaniards to be advocates of reform, were arrested. Forty-one participants in the revolt were executed, others were sentenced to life imprisonment, and many to deportation. Three native priests were sentenced to death.

However, the disaffection which ultimately brought about the revolution of 1896 persisted and spread through the Tagálog provinces and to a lesser extent in northern Luzon and the Visayas. This manifested itself in a determined opposition to the friars and to the existing political administration of the Islands in which they exercised an influence amounting to virtual control. Spaniards of liberal ideas and European foreigners residing in Manila encouraged this disaffection.

The year 1888 witnessed the first great popular demonstration aimed against the friars, and a popular petition was addressed to the Queen Regent for their expulsion. This movement was partly inspired by orders of the Liberal civil authorities prohibiting, on the grounds of public health, certain funerary practices of the friars and curates. Agrarian troubles began to develop between the friars and their tenants on the rich lands. At the same time Filipinos living in Spain and other parts of Europe began a publicity campaign aimed against the friars.

Filipinos and Spaniards who sympathized with them formed a Spanish-Filipino association in Madrid in 1888 devoted to the propagation of liberal political ideas. This association did not set forth independence as an objective or an ideal, but confined its efforts purely to reforms in the administration of government and to transforming "an oppressed colony into a rich and flourishing province of Spain."

By far the most important of the Filipinos moving actively for reform was a young man, Dr. José Rizal, who was at that time completing his education in Europe. He became the most conspicuous figure in Philippine history. Born in the province of Laguna, in Luzon, in 1861, Rizal was a *mestizo* with Chinese, Spanish, and even reputed Japanese blood, although his prevailing ancestry was Malay and contained both Tagálog and Ilocano strains.

Extraordinarily proficient at his studies, both in Manila and later in Spain, France, and Germany, he obtained the highest honors in all his subjects, which included philosophy, medicine, law, and literature. He was fluent in no less than five languages: a Philippine dialect and four European languages; read easily four others, besides having an acquaintance with Greek, Latin, Hebrew, Sanskrit, Arabic, and three Chinese dialects, as well as being able to serve as interpreter in Japanese. By profession he was an oculist.

A deep student of Philippine affairs, he saw the backwardness and corruption of the priest-ridden Spanish administration of his country, and brooding over this, he brought forth a book which has been described as the "Uncle Tom's Cabin of the Philippines." It was called *Noli Me Tangere*.[1] In this he portrayed "the backwardness of the existing social and political régime in the Philippines, its stifling of thought, and its many tyrannies," and at the same time set before his people some of their own defects. Its circulation in the Islands was prohibited by the Spanish government. Four years later, he published his other novel, *El Filibusterismo*, in which he urged even more plainly the need for social and political progress among the lower classes.

Rizal never advocated independence, nor did he advocate armed resistance to the government. He urged reform from within, by publicity, by public education, and appeal to the public conscience.

In spite of grave danger to his life, Rizal insisted upon returning to his native country, where he underwent a variety of persecutions by the Spanish authorities. The following year, in July, 1892, Dr. Rizal inaugurated at his house in the city of Manila the Liga Filipina, a Filipino secret society. This organization brought together educated young men and representatives of the less educated classes. It was chiefly concerned with economic development and fraternal benefits to its members, and clearly did not contemplate separation from Spain. The League at once brought its members under grave suspicion by the authorities and its leader, Rizal, was finally sequestered in the little town of Dapitan on the northwestern coast of the island of Mindanao. Building a school in a lovely little nook near the town, he attracted to himself fourteen young disciples, and here undertook their education. When Spain found itself at war with Cuba, he volunteered to serve in the medical department of the Spanish army, but it was not in accordance with the ideas of those in authority in the Philippine Islands that he should be permitted to earn immunity from persecution by service to the mother country. He was taken off a steamer in the Mediterranean, brought back to Manila, subjected to inquisitorial proceedings, and finally executed on December 30, 1896.

It is fitting that Rizal should have become the acknowledged national hero of the Philippine people. The American administration has set aside the anniversary of his death to be a day of observance, has

[1] "Touch me not."

CHURCH TOWER

APPROACH TO A CHURCH CEMETERY

OLD CHURCH, SPANISH ARCHITECTURE

placed his picture on the postage stamp most commonly used in the Islands, and on the currency, and encouraged the erection of a monument in his honor on the Luneta in Manila near the place where he met his death. The Filipinos in many cities and towns have erected monuments to his name, and throughout the Islands the public schools teach the young Filipinos to revere his memory as a great Filipino patriot.

Weary of waiting for reform, the middle and lower class leaders in Manila decided upon more positive measures, and organized a secret society commonly known as the Katipunan, under the leadership of Andrés Bonifacio, with more or less socialistic ideas. The movement differed materially from the Liga Filipina founded by Rizal, in that it had for its object a complete reorganization of government and the social structure, the expulsion of the friars, and confiscation of their estates.

Bonifacio began his organization about the close of the year 1892. Although he had among his adherents some who had been members of the Liga Filipina, he found grave difficulty in securing active coöperation of Filipinos of wealth and standing. The appeal of the Katipunan to the masses of the people was so great, however, that at the peril of their liberty, their property, and their lives, they joined it in greatly increasing numbers.

It was not until four years later that rumors of the existence of a large secret organization planning rebellion became known by the Spaniards, and a member of the society was induced by his sister to disclose the secrets to the friar priest of the parish of Tondo, Manila, who immediately investigated the matter, and, finding undoubted evidence in a local printing establishment, informed the authorities.

Governor-General Ramon Blanco was strongly inclined to a policy of attraction rather than repression, but was unable to restrain the radical Spanish element which was determined upon drastic measures. There was confusion and great alarm among all classes, both Spaniards and Filipinos. A reign of terror ensued. Several lists of names of alleged members or sympathizers with the Katipunan, including Filipinos of the greatest prominence among the educated and property-owning classes, came into the hands of the Spaniards. There is good reason to believe that some of these lists had been fraudulently prepared with the object of impressing the lower classes with the abundant support of the movement by influential people. Numerous arrests were made, and, after trial by a special court, many persons were executed.

It was reported that Rizal without his knowledge had been elected honorary president of the Katipunan, and this fact undoubtedly contributed to the case against him which resulted in his execution.

On the exposure of their plans, Bonifacio and his associates fled from Manila, began the organization of their forces in the provinces in July, and, on August 17, 1896, formally decided to revolt against the Spanish government. Three days later, the Revolution of 1896 began with a declaration by the Katipunan which is now translated as "Long live the Philippine Republic."

Armed hostilities began. The rebellion spread from Cavite and Manila south to Batangas and northward as far as Ilocos. A number of Visayan sailors on shore in Manila were shot by the police, and an uprising followed in Cebu.

Meanwhile, summary imprisonments, executions, and deportations were carried into effect by the Spanish authorities.

Early in 1897, a new Governor-General, Polavieja, moved twenty-eight thousand troops, mostly Filipinos, against the insurgents, who had made successful attacks on several scattered detachments of troops and of organized police near Manila. The insurgents were driven out of the province of Cavite and from the lowlands generally in the other provinces and retreated to the mountains of Bulacan, making their headquarters in a natural stronghold known as Biac-na-bato.

Bonifacio, the founder of the Katipunan, lacked the qualities of military leadership, and, being unwilling to relinquish the management of the armed forces, was in course of time murdered to make way for the desired successor.

Early in the fighting, various insurgent leaders had developed, most prominent among whom was Emilio Aguinaldo. His inherent qualities soon made him the recognized leader of the revolution which thenceforward seemed to center in Cavite. He dominated the assembled leaders in their mountain stronghold at Biac-na-bato, and was elected head of the Katipunan. From Biac-na-bato he issued a proclamation in which he declared that the Filipinos wished to be free and independent. However, the Filipino insurgents, discouraged by reverses in the lowlands, wanted peace. So did the Spaniards. The home government needed troops and money with which to suppress rebellion in Cuba. The Spaniards made unsuccessful overtures to General Aguinaldo for peace.

In August, 1897, Pedro A. Paterno undertook to act as mediator. His services were acceptable both to the Spanish Governor-General and to the insurgent leaders, and he succeeded on December 14 in securing an agreement which has come to be known as the Pact of Biac-na-bato, thus making peace with Spain.

It is asserted, and is now generally believed by Filipinos, that the Governor-General agreed to:

1. The expulsion of the religious orders.
2. Philippine representation in the Spanish Cortes.
3. The equal treatment of Filipinos and Spaniards in the application of justice.
4. The employment of Filipinos in the high posts of the government service.
5. The liberty of the press, and the right to form associations.
6. The payment by the Spanish government of the sum of three million pesos, as an indemnity to those who had lost property during the war, to widows and orphans, and to the leaders of the rebellion who were to live in exile. This sum was finally reduced to eight hundred thousand pesos.

On December 16, 1897, General Aguinaldo proclaimed the restoration of peace, and very shortly thereafter left with some forty other insurgent leaders for Hong Kong, having been handed by a representative of the Spanish government a draft payable in that city in the sum of four hundred thousand pesos, which was honored upon presentation. A second payment of two hundred thousand pesos was made to these leaders and Paterno.

It is due General Aguinaldo and his immediate associates to state that the funds received by him were deposited in a bank in Hong Kong and kept practically intact until a portion was taken for the purchase of arms after Commodore Dewey's victory in Manila Bay.

The end of 1897 saw the principal leaders of the insurrection in exile, and the organized rebellion against Spain at an end, although peace was not fully re-established. But no reforms materialized, nor had the Spanish government made any appreciable change in the policy of its administration of the Islands when in February, 1898, the American battleship Maine was destroyed in the harbor of Havana, Cuba.

CHAPTER III

AMERICAN OCCUPATION

WAR HAS COMMENCED between the United States and Spain. Proceed at once to Philippine Islands. Commence operations particularly against the Spanish fleet. You must capture vessels or destroy. Use utmost endeavor."

These orders by cablegram from John D. Long, Secretary of the Navy in Washington, were received by Commodore Dewey at Mirs Bay, near Hong Kong, April 25, 1898. His squadron was in readiness to move immediately, but he waited two days for important information he knew to be en route from Manila. This arrived as expected. The squadron sailed, and with utter disregard of the fortifications and mines entered Manila Bay during the night of the 30th, circled past the water front of the city at daybreak of May 1, ignoring shots fired by the Manila batteries, and continued toward Cavite where the Spanish squadron was formed in battle line.

The engagement lasted from 5.40 A.M. to 7.35 A.M. and from 11.16 A.M. to 12.30 P.M., when the Spanish flag on the government buildings at Cavite was hauled down and, a white flag appearing in its place, the firing ceased.

All the Spanish ships that had not burned were sunk. "The order to capture or destroy the Spanish squadron had been executed to the letter."

The American casualties were none killed, and only seven men very slightly wounded. The Spanish casualties, including those on shore at Cavite, were three hundred and eighty-one men killed and wounded.

On paper the relative strengths of the two squadrons were not far different, somewhat inclining in favor of Spain with seven ships against six in the American squadron. The Americans, however, had greater tonnage and more guns, and their ships were of higher class and superior in armament. These advantages were more than offset by the shore batteries of seventeen heavy rifled guns at the entrance to Manila Bay and forty other guns in the fortifications at Cavite and Manila. None of the ships, either American or Spanish, was armored. Brown powder ammunition was used by both squadrons.

Dewey immediately informed the Spanish Captain-General at Manila that he would destroy the city if another shot were fired at the American ships from the Manila batteries, and that, if he were allowed to transmit messages by the submarine cable to Hong Kong, the Captain-General would also be permitted to use it. Assurances were promptly received that the Manila forts would not fire on the American ships unless it became evident that the latter were to bombard the city, and with this assurance, which placed him in virtual control of the situation, Commodore Dewey anchored his ships for the first time since they had entered the Bay.

The Spanish Captain-General refused the offer about the cable, and Commodore Dewey cut it.

It was not until May 4 that Commodore Dewey found it convenient to send to Hong Kong for transmission to Washington the complete news of what the squadron had accomplished three days previously. Various reports, however, of the battle had been dispatched before the cable was cut, including one by the cable operator at the Manila station. The American morning newspapers of May 2 were able to publish a brief account of the victory. At once the United States was ringing with Commodore Dewey's exploit.

Congress by joint resolution thanked him "for highly distinguished conduct in conflict with the enemy" and "the officers and men under his command for . . . gallantry and skill." He was immediately given the rank of acting rear-admiral, and later other honors were conferred on him, including that of the rank of admiral during his lifetime by special act of Congress.

Certain European countries, especially Germany, were more favorably disposed toward Spain than toward the United States during the events leading up to the war and until the conclusion of the Treaty of Paris in December, 1898.[1]

Neither Germany, Austria, nor Portugal had declared neutrality and

---

[1] It later appeared that all the principal European governments, especially Germany, Austria, France, and England, had given serious consideration to the relations developing between the United States and Spain, seeking to prevent the war and seriously concerned themselves as to the disposition of the Philippine Islands. The lack of definite policy at Washington in regard to the Islands, and other important features of this period, including the desire of Germany for territorial cessions in the Philippine Islands, are reviewed, in the light of authoritative material which became available in the archives of the German government following the World War, by Professor Lester B. Shippee in an article, "Germany and the Spanish-American War," in *The American Historical Review*, xxx, No. 4, July, 1925. (Hereafter cited, Shippee.)

there were rumors of intervention by one or another of these powers in the war between the United States and Spain.

From German archives evidence is now available that shows the extent of Germany's interest in the Philippine Islands. Unwilling to take action herself, her diplomats maneuvered to bring about the intervention of other powers.

Von Bülow, in a message to the German Emperor, said: ". . . in my humble opinion, the control of the sea in the end may rest on the question of who rules the Philippines, directly or indirectly." On the margin of his minister's letter, the German Emperor agreed with Von Bülow and expressed the opinion that the Philippine Islands, wholly or in part, must not pass to another power "without Germany's receiving an equivalent compensation."

Later these documents revealed that the least Germany expected to insist upon was a naval station in the Islands, and Baron von Richthofen reported that he was advised that the Germans would want "one or two positions in the Philippine group and the Sulu Archipelago. . . ."

The Honorable Andrew D. White, then American Ambassador to Berlin, took it upon himself to express his personal opinion that the United States would not annex the Philippine Islands, but that the extension of the German colonial system was desirable because it meant the spreading of civilization.

These revelations in a measure explain the activity of the German admiral in Philippine waters during that period.

Admiral Dewey's greatest, though less famous, triumph was as a diplomat after his naval victory. Within ten days of the battle, naval vessels representing foreign powers assembled in Manila Bay, including two British vessels, two German cruisers, a French and a Japanese cruiser. Other German naval vessels soon followed, including another cruiser, the Kaiserin Augusta, the flagship of Vice-Admiral von Diederichs, whose higher rank and offensively arrogant attitude greatly increased the difficulties of Acting Rear-Admiral Dewey's position. This was none too secure, as it was known that a Spanish squadron of armored cruisers and destroyers had left Spain via the Suez Canal for Manila, where the American squadron lay at anchor with but little ammunition and without access to any base of supplies. Moreover, the Washington government had as yet formulated no policy as to the Philippine Islands in the event of winning the war. Thus Admiral

Dewey was left practically to his own resourcefulness until the signing of the Treaty of Paris seven months later.

The Germans, meanwhile, had assembled in Manila Bay five men-of-war and a naval transport with fourteen hundred men, the latter a force in itself nearly equal to the total number of men in the American squadron, or a force strongly superior to Admiral Dewey's command.

The German admiral took occasion in the course of a conference with Admiral Dewey in which reference was made to the presence of so large a German force, to reply, "I am here by order of the Kaiser, sir."

Nations possessing commercial interests, according to international usage, had the right to have their interests protected by men-of-war whose duty it was to observe the operations of the belligerents, but such neutral naval vessels were expected to report their arrival to the commander-in-chief of the blockading forces, ask where they should anchor, and carefully abstain from interference with the course of affairs between the belligerents, especially in a way which could be helpful or prejudicial to either side.

Admiral Dewey reported that the British, French, and Japanese had conducted themselves throughout with obvious propriety. The Germans, however, insistently ignored the laws of blockade and the proprieties toward both belligerents. Their officers frequently landed in Manila. Admiral von Diederichs officially visited the Spanish Captain-General in Manila, who returned the call. No other senior foreign naval officer had exchanged visits with the Captain-General. German officers, including Prince Lowenstein, visited the Spanish troops and outposts, and also the insurgent Filipinos. German boats took soundings off the mouth of the Pasig River and German seamen for some days occupied the lighthouse at the mouth of the Pasig. The Germans "landed their men for drill at Mariveles Harbor . . . at the entrance to the bay and took possession of the quarantine station, while Admiral von Diederichs occupied a large house which had been the quarters of the Spanish officials." Early in July the German cruiser Irene visited the Spanish garrison at Subig, and interfered with the operations of the insurgent Filipinos at that point.

This conduct was so clearly in violation of international law and courtesy that Admiral Dewey, following the American naval victory at Santiago and the recall of the Spanish fleet to Spain, asserted formally by letter to the German admiral his rights in the blockade of Manila Bay. Admiral von Diederichs, denying these rights, notified Admiral

Dewey "he would submit the point to a conference of all the senior officers of the men-of-war in the harbor. But only one officer appeared, Captain Chichester, of the British Immortalité." He informed the German admiral that Admiral Dewey was acting entirely within his rights, and furthermore that the instructions from the British government were for him to comply with even more rigorous restrictions.

The German admiral, however, was not convinced and continued crowding until an American vessel found it necessary to fire a shot across the bows of a German cruiser which failed to stop when requested to do so by Admiral Dewey's dispatch boat. The following day Admiral von Diederichs sent a staff officer with a memorandum of grievances, to which Admiral Dewey replied so vigorously that, as he remarked later, "There was no further interference with the blockade or breach of the etiquette which had been established by the common consent of the other foreign commanders. Thus, as I explained to the President, after the war was over, a difference of opinion about international law had been adjusted amicably, without adding to the sum of his worries."

Captain Sir Edward Chichester, Commander of the British Naval Forces at Manila Bay at that time, is quoted as having said:

Your Admiral accomplished by tact, firmness, and good judgment in Manila Bay what many naval men would have thought only possible by war. Dewey is a natural fighter, but true fighter that he is, he prefers to win a peaceful victory. He is a great man.

The friendly attitude of the British authorities, in contrast to the repeated provocations of the Germans, was one of the bright spots in this period and showed how strongly the ties of blood relationships bind the American and British peoples. The British commander not only supported Admiral Dewey's interpretation of international law, but later placed his ships between the German and American squadrons when the latter took its position to attack the outer fortifications of Manila.

Of all the foreign naval commanders present, only the British, Captain Chichester, acknowledged by firing the national salute, with the American ensign at the main, receipt of official notification of the occupation of the city of Manila and the opening of that port.

Never were the evil effects of unpreparedness more abundantly exemplified than in the management of the Philippine campaign. Although the Spanish fleet was sunk on the 1st of May, it was sixty days before the first American troops arrived under General Anderson. The second expedition, under General Francis V. Greene, came about two weeks later. On the 25th of July, General Wesley Merritt, commander of all the expeditionary forces, arrived at Cavite; and six days later, General Arthur MacArthur came with the third expedition.

It then appeared probable that Admiral Dewey might be successful in negotiations for the peaceful capitulation of the city of Manila which he had initiated with the Spanish Captain-General.

On August 7, the American General and Admiral jointly served notice upon the Spanish Captain-General that "operations of the land and naval forces of the United States against the defenses of Manila may begin at any time after the expiration of forty-eight hours from the hour of receipt by you of this communication, or sooner if made necessary by an attack on your part. This notice is given in order to afford you an opportunity to remove all non-combatants from the city."

The Captain-General immediately replied acknowledging receipt of the notification, expressing his thanks "for the humane sentiments you have shown," and stating "that, finding myself surrounded by insurrectionary forces, I am without places of refuge for the increased numbers of wounded, sick, women and children, who are now lodged within the walls."

To this reply was made pointing out how helpless was the position of the Spaniards and how clearly it was the Captain-General's "duty to save the city from the horrors of bombardment."

Manila fell on the 13th of August, 1898, after a brief bombardment of the outer fortifications by the fleet, and attack by the troops. Almost simultaneously the United States and Spain had signed the protocol suspending hostilities.

At 11.20 A.M. Admiral Dewey made out "a white flag flying on the appointed place on the southwest bastion of the city wall." American troops then entered the city, the Spanish colors were hauled down, and the American flag raised over the walled city. "The guns of all our ships thundered out a national salute, while the band of one of our regiments played the 'Star-Spangled Banner,' the troops saluted, officers uncovered, and the Stars and Stripes, as it was raised for the first time over Manila, was greeted with all the honor so punctiliously given the flag on ceremonious occasions both by the army and the navy."

General Arthur MacArthur was appointed Provost-Marshal-General and civil governor of the city.

General Greene was charged with affairs pertaining to captured public funds and property, and the administration of public revenues. Other officers of notable experience in private business were assigned as his assistants.

The conduct of the American troops in their occupation of the city of Manila was admirable and greatly to their credit and that of their commanders.

The American casualties of August 13, incident to the occupation of the city of Manila, were four men killed, and three officers and thirty-two men wounded; also, in the course of the investment of the city the American forces had suffered losses of thirteen men killed, and seven officers and fifty-seven men wounded.

The total casualties in killed and wounded in the Spanish forces are stated as forty-nine killed and three hundred wounded.

Notwithstanding the efforts of the commanding generals, there had been spirited exchanges of shots between the American trenches and near-by Spanish fortifications.

The American army forces which had arrived in the Islands prior to the occupation of Manila comprised 470 officers and 10,464 enlisted men.

Filipino participation in the siege of Manila will be considered in subsequent pages.

In the occupation of the city 13,000 prisoners of war, 22,000 arms and $900,000 public funds were taken by the American forces.

On the following day formal articles of capitulation were arranged and signed. Of especial and immediate importance, as will be seen, was the final paragraph, or Article 7, of this protocol:

7. This city, its inhabitants, its churches and religious worship, its educational establishments, and its private property of all descriptions are placed under the special safeguard of the faith and honor of the American army.

Due to this provision, upon which the Spanish authorities had insisted, there could not be joint occupation of Manila by American and insurgent Filipino forces. The exclusion of armed Filipinos from within the American lines, and the extension of these lines to include the suburbs of Manila, met with protests from the Filipino leaders.

On August 29 General Merritt, who had been ordered to the United States, was relieved by Major-General Elwell S. Otis as Military Governor of the Philippine Islands.

The part played by General Aguinaldo and the insurgent forces he organized to attack the Spanish army on land before the United States troops could arrive was recognized by American military and naval commanders. Admiral Dewey in his "Autobiography" stated:

> The insurgents fought well. Their success, I think, was of material importance in isolating our marine force at Cavite from Spanish attack and in preparing a foothold for our troops when they should arrive. By the end of May they had entirely cleared Cavite Province of the enemy, and had so nearly surrounded Manila as to cause a panic among the inhabitants.

General Merritt reported:

> The Filipinos, or insurgent forces at war with Spain, had, prior to the arrival of the American land forces, been waging a desultory warfare with the Spaniards for several months, and were at the time of my arrival in considerable force, variously estimated and never accurately ascertained, but probably not far from 12,000 men. These troops, well supplied with small arms, with plenty of ammunition and several field guns, had obtained positions of investment opposite to the Spanish line of detached works throughout their entire extent. . . .

In the final period of the operations leading up to the occupation of the city of Manila, the American forces occupied the line from the beach south of Manila eastward and northward as far as Singalon. The Filipinos' longer line, on the east and north of the city, held the Spaniards from escaping from Manila during the advance of American troops after the reduction of the southern fortifications by the navy.

The peace protocol signed at Washington, August 12, 1898 (August 13, Manila time), suspending hostilities between the United States and Spain and contemplating the formal treaty which eventually was signed at Paris, December 10 following, provided among other things that the United States should "occupy and hold the city, bay and harbor of Manila, pending the conclusion of a treaty of peace which shall determine the control, disposition and government of the Philippines."

Meanwhile, with Cavite and Manila occupied by the Americans, and central, western, and northern Luzon by Filipino insurgents, the Spanish authorities endeavored unsuccessfully to maintain a *de facto* government elsewhere in the Islands.

General Diego de los Rios, governor of Mindanao, became Spanish Military Governor of the Philippine Islands with headquarters at Iloilo, and continued under appointment as Acting Captain-General until June, 1899. Thereafter, until December, 1900, a commission under General Nicolas Jaramillo remained in Manila to conclude the repatriation of Spanish officials and troops and the shipment of war material to Spain in accordance with the Treaty of Paris.

The pressure of popular revolt and lack of supplies soon forced General Rios to withdraw outlying garrisons and other government personnel in the Visayas and Mindanao, concentrating gradually all his forces at Iloilo and finally at Zamboanga. No American troops were available to replace these garrisons, and Filipino insurgents occupied the rich seaport city of Iloilo on its evacuation by the Spaniards.

At the end of 1898, all Luzon, except the post at Baler, which was held by a small Spanish garrison, and all the Visayas, had been evacuated by the Spaniards and government assumed by Filipinos. And by the end of May, 1899, all Mindanao had likewise passed to native control.

The loyal efforts of the Spaniards, unsupported from Madrid, to maintain the dignity and fulfill the obligations of their government during this long period of national humiliation merit the highest praise. The severe fighting at both Iloilo and Zamboanga to hold those important base points against insurgent Filipinos, and the fatal wounding of General Montero while embarking his troops in the evacuation of Zamboanga in May, 1899, after vainly awaiting relief by American forces, are but incidents of the efforts made by Spain honorably to carry out her undertaking of cession of the Philippine Islands to the United States. Nor was this the only example of the sacrifice of life and property to a high and chivalrous sense of honor, the extent of which few Americans know.

The heroic defense of its post by the Spanish garrison at Baler on the Pacific coast of Luzon aroused the admiration of both friend and foe. In April, 1899, at the request of the Spanish Acting Captain-General, Diego de los Rios, Admiral Dewey sent the gunboat Yorktown to endeavor to rescue the garrison of three officers, eighty soldiers, and two priests, who for many months had been besieged by several hundred insurgent Filipinos. The landing party was overwhelmed by the insurgents and the survivors were held as prisoners until, many months later, a vigorous pursuit by American troops caused their abandonment by their captors in the mountains of northern Luzon. The siege of Baler was raised and the Spaniards permitted to go at liberty by an order signed by the insurgent General Aguinaldo at Tarlac, June 30, 1899, in recognition of the display by the garrison of "valour and constant heroism worthy of universal admiration."

Meantime public sentiment in the United States was greatly divided in regard to the Philippine Islands. The idea of a dependency on the farther side of the Pacific was wholly new to the majority of the American people and to many of them repugnant. It was obvious from the beginning that they did not want to give the Islands statehood with a vote that might hold the balance of power between their own parties in the United States and thus enable the Filipinos to wield an undue influence in affairs with which they had little concern. Moreover, the government in Washington was poorly organized for the care of dependencies. There was no trained personnel able to administer the Islands, no department of the government to which dependencies naturally pertained, the word "colonial" was abhorrent to the American people due to their own unfortunate history as a colony, and many thoughtful people viewed with grave concern the entrance by their country upon a policy, the liabilities attaching to which they could not foresee, but which might involve them in political entanglements and possible wars with which otherwise they would have no concern.

President McKinley looked with serious eyes on all aspects of the problem, and was reluctant to embark upon the policy of expansion.

The protocol of August 12, 1898, suspending hostilities between the United States and Spain, provided that the two belligerent governments should "appoint not more than five commissioners to treat of peace, and the commissioners so appointed shall meet at Paris not later than October 1, 1898, and proceed to the negotiation and conclusion of a treaty of peace, which treaty shall be subject to ratification according to the respective constitutional forms of the two countries."

On October 28, 1898, the Secretary of State cabled to a member of the American peace commission in Paris outlining President McKinley's views as to what should be done with the Islands:

. . . The sentiment in the United States is almost universal that the people of the Philippines, whatever else is done, must be liberated from Spanish domination. . . .

Consequently, grave as are the responsibilities and unforeseen as are the difficulties which are before us, the president can see but one plain path of duty — the acceptance of the archipelago. Greater difficulties and more serious complications — administrative and international — would follow any other course.

After protracted negotiations, the terms of peace were definitely settled upon and the commissioners reached an agreement embodied in the document executed at Paris, December 10, 1898, known as the Treaty of Paris.

By the terms of the treaty, Spain, besides relinquishing her West Indian possessions, ceded to the United States the island of Guam in the Marianas or Ladrone Islands, and by Article III ceded "to the United States the archipelago known as the Philippine Islands." Article III further provided: "The United States will pay to Spain the sum of twenty million dollars ($20,000,000), within three months after the exchange of ratifications of the present treaty."

By Article IV, it was provided: "The United States will, for the term of ten years from the date of the exchange of the ratifications of the present treaty, admit Spanish ships and merchandise to the ports of the Philippine Islands on the same terms as ships and merchandise of the United States."

"The civil rights and political status of the native inhabitants" of the territories ceded to the United States were left to determination by the Congress.

The free exercise of religion was assured to the inhabitants of the territories over which Spain relinquished or ceded sovereignty.

Appropriate provisions were made as to the jurisdiction of courts and the conclusion of judicial proceedings pending at the time of the exchange of ratifications of the treaty.

On February 14, 1899, the United States Senate passed the following resolution:

RESOLVED that by the ratification of the treaty of peace with Spain it is not intended to incorporate the inhabitants of the Philippine Islands into citizenship of the United States, nor is it intended to permanently annex said islands as an integral part of the territory of the United States; but it is the intention of the United States to establish on said islands a government suitable to the wants and conditions of the inhabitants of said islands, to prepare them for local self-government and in due time to make such disposition of said islands as will best promote the interests of the citizens of the United States and the inhabitants of said islands.

The American Consul Williams at Manila reported to the Secretary of State on February 22, 1898

. . . War exists, battles are of almost daily occurrence, ambulances bring in many wounded, and hospitals are full. Prisoners are brought here and shot without trial, and Manila is under martial law. . . .

A republic is organized here, as in Cuba. Insurgents are being armed and drilled; are rapidly increasing in numbers and efficiency. . . .

Three reports in March gave additional details, in one of which Consul Williams said:

> . . . Rebellion never more threatening to Spain. Rebels getting arms, money, and friends, and they outnumber the Spaniards, resident and soldiery, probably one hundred to one.

General Aguinaldo himself had started for Europe and had gone as far as Singapore at the time war between the United States and Spain broke out. United States Consul-General Pratt at Singapore arranged for a secret meeting, at which he urged General Aguinaldo to proceed to Hong Kong, telegraphing Commodore Dewey:

> Aguinaldo, insurgent leader, here. Will come Hongkong arrange with Commodore for general coöperation insurgents Manila if desired. Telegraph.

Commodore Dewey replied:

> Tell Aguinaldo come soon as possible.

On the strength of this telegram General Aguinaldo proceeded immediately to Hong Kong, but arrived too late to see Commodore Dewey before his departure. General Aguinaldo impressed the Consul "as a man of intelligence, ability, and courage, and worthy the confidence that had been placed in him."

Consul-General Pratt further reported that he had enjoined upon General Aguinaldo the necessity "of exerting absolute control over his forces . . . as no excesses on their part would be tolerated by the American Government. . . .

"To this General Aguinaldo fully assented," giving assurance that he was perfectly able to hold his followers in check "and lead them as our commander should direct." He spoke in this interview of expecting to establish a government of their own.

There is no doubt that General Aguinaldo felt entirely free to take up arms again, as he felt the conditions of the Peace of Biac-na-bato had not been complied with on the part of Spain. There is also no doubt that General Aguinaldo hoped to establish his own government with the assistance of the United States. Filipino political exiles in Hong Kong issued a proclamation, a copy of which was supplied to Washington by Consul-General Pratt, in which they said:

> Compatriots: Divine Providence is about to place independence within our reach, and in a way the most free and independent nation could hardly wish for.

They called upon their companions to assist the Americans.

The State Department was evidently skeptical of the wisdom of these activities, and on June 16, 1898, Secretary of State Day cabled to Consul-General Pratt: "Avoid unauthorized negotiations with Philippine insurgents." Consul-General Pratt made all haste to deny he had carried on any negotiations. The Secretary of State in a letter dated the same day made the direct statement that the Philippine insurgents had "neither asked nor received from this Government any recognition."

These official records establish the fact that a state of insurrection against the Spanish government actually existed in an important portion of the Islands, especially the vicinity of Manila, at the time that war broke out between the United States and Spain, and that General Aguinaldo, after representing that the aim of the Filipinos was their own government, was invited to proceed to Hong Kong for conference with Commodore Dewey. Having failed to get to Hong Kong in time, by Admiral Dewey's orders he and thirteen companions were given transportation on a United States naval vessel to Cavite, where General Aguinaldo arrived on May 19, and established himself under the protection of the American squadron.

On the 26th of May, the Secretary of the Navy by telegraph advised Admiral Dewey that he was expected to exercise full discretion in all matters, and be governed according to circumstances, but that it was desirable, so far as possible, "not to have political alliances with the insurgents or any faction in the Islands that would incur liability to maintain their cause in the future."

In acknowledging receipt of these instructions, Admiral Dewey replied that his action from the beginning had been in accord with the spirit of those instructions, and that he had "entered into no alliance with the insurgents or with any faction."

The Secretary of the Navy, in a dispatch dated, Washington, June 14, 1898, called on Admiral Dewey for a full report of "any conferences, relations, or coöperations, military or otherwise, which you have had with Aguinaldo."

Admiral Dewey replied that he had refrained from assisting the insurgent leader in any way with the force under his command, stating that "the squadron could not act until the arrival of the United States troops"; that Aguinaldo had "acted independently of the squadron," but kept him advised "of his progress, which has been wonderful"; that he had allowed Aguinaldo to "pass by water recruits, arms and am-

A GATE IN THE OLD MANILA WALL

A BRIDGE OF SPANISH DESIGN

A BRIDGE OF AMERICAN DESIGN WITH MAYON VOLCANO IN
THE DISTANCE

munition, and to take such Spanish arms and ammunition from the arsenal as he needed. . . . My relations with him are cordial, but I am not in his confidence. The United States has not been bound in any way to assist insurgents by any act or promises, and he is not, to my knowledge, committed to assist us. I believe he expects to capture Manila without my assistance, but doubt ability, they not yet having many guns. In my opinion, these people are far superior in their intelligence and more capable of self-government than the natives of Cuba and I am familiar with both races."

On May 24, General Aguinaldo issued a proclamation addressed to the Philippine people, in the course of which he referred to the "North American nation" as "considering us as sufficiently civilized and capable of governing for ourselves our unfortunate country." On June 18, General Aguinaldo proclaimed dictatorial government; on June 23, he proclaimed the establishment of revolutionary government; and on August 6, he appealed to foreign governments to recognize the independence of the Philippine Islands.

Under instructions from Washington, Admiral Dewey, and subsequently General Wesley Merritt, commanding the United States land forces in the Philippine Islands, refrained from official relations with General Aguinaldo, who did not call on General Merritt on his arrival.

Although requested by General Thomas M. Anderson in a letter dated July 4, 1898, to coöperate with the American authorities, General Aguinaldo in his reply said nothing about coöperation and conducted his operations independently. Although he drove out the Spaniards from many of their posts, his armies were not well organized and it was hardly to be expected that they would be trained in what modern civilized people regard as the ethics of war.

The pride of the Filipino soldiers was deeply hurt when the American generals, upon the capture of Manila, declined to allow them to enter their own capital city. As before mentioned, the Spaniards in surrendering Manila had expressly stipulated that the city was to be under the protection of the American army, and with a large Filipino population within and a soldiery without, expecting, as the American officers had reason to believe they did, to loot the city, the situation would very quickly have come beyond the control of the meager United States forces, and it is questionable if the insurgent leaders themselves could have restrained their men.

There is no doubt that the course taken by the American generals was required by prudence and humanity, although it aroused resentment and hostility which presently led to actual warfare.

By December 21, 1898, relations had become so strained that President McKinley felt it incumbent to issue a proclamation, which with certain softening modifications was published by General Otis, the military governor, January 4, 1899.

General Otis, reporting on the attitude of the mass of the people, wrote: "Even the women of Cavite province, in a document numerously signed by them, gave me to understand that after all the men were killed off they were prepared to shed their patriotic blood for the liberty and independence of their country."

In the words of Admiral Dewey: "Mr. McKinley's proclamation of 'benevolent assimilation' fell on ears which had long since learned to distrust the beneficent and grandiloquent proclamations of which the Spanish were masters. It was a time for statesmanship if we were to avoid a conflict. As Washington seemed to be in the dark about the real situation on shore, I cabled on January 7, 1899, stating that affairs were very disturbed and that a small 'civilian commission composed of men skilled in diplomacy and statesmanship should be sent to adjust differences.' "

Admiral Dewey, in a private letter at the same time, expressed the fear that despite General Otis's forbearance the United States was drifting into a war with the natives, and that the occasion appeared to be one "for a triumph of statesmanship rather than of arms."

Although the President acted promptly on Admiral Dewey's advice and announced within a week the appointment of an investigating commission, as will be seen later in the chapter, yet before the civilian members of the commission could arrive in Manila war with the Filipinos had broken out.

During the period of peace negotiations resulting in the Treaty of Paris, the ill-feeling between Filipinos and Americans increased. General Aguinaldo's emissaries sought official recognition, appealing without success not only to the Washington government, but also to foreign powers.

Meanwhile General Aguinaldo and his associates organized a government with headquarters at Malolos, twenty-five miles to the north of Manila. There on September 15, 1898, the Congress of the revolutionary government began its sessions. The occasion was one of great festivities;

the town was thronged with thousands of people from the provinces and large numbers also from Manila, including prominent lawyers and merchants of the city.

As President of the revolutionary republic, General Aguinaldo named as cabinet officers and councillors many of the ablest Filipinos of the day. The brilliant and irreconcilable Apolinario Mabini exercised a predominant influence in determining the policy pursued by his chief leading up to and following the rupture of friendly relations with the Americans. Dr. Trinidad H. Pardo de Tavera, later member of the Taft Commission, and Don Cayetano Arellano, who became Chief Justice of the Philippine Supreme Court, were named by General Aguinaldo in the department of foreign affairs in his first cabinet. Don Gregorio Araneta, who was Secretary of Justice in the Malolos cabinet, was later appointed by General Otis Associate Justice of the Supreme Court. All of these, with the exception of Mabini, withdrew from the Malolos government prior to the outbreak of hostilities with the United States. They represented the conservative, well-educated class, and following them many others in minor posts also withdrew from the Malolos government and brought their families within the American lines at Manila, as they saw the unfortunate trend of insurgent organization toward armed resistance to American sovereignty.

Negotiations were carried on and efforts made by the leaders on both sides to avoid resort to arms, but in spite of these efforts on the night of February 4, 1899, American troops opened fire upon a Filipino patrol which had approached within the lines and this fire was returned. Armed conflict ensued, and the war continued with varying degrees of intensity for the ensuing two years and a half.

It was not practicable to exclude noncombatant Filipinos from Manila, and it soon became known to the American authorities that there were secret hostile organizations planning to burn and sack the city while American troops were engaged on the lines of defense. At least three thousand effective troops, therefore, were required as provost guard for police duty. On February 22, 1899, a concerted rising of Filipinos occurred within the city, under instructions to massacre all Americans and Europeans. Due to the precautions which had been taken, this attempt was promptly suppressed and the 300,000 Filipinos residing within the American lines were placed under strict police control.

At the beginning of armed hostilities the total effective land forces of the United States at Manila were about 14,000 including the provost guard of 3000. It is apparent that the troops available could make but a very thin line of defense against the force of armed insurgents, which, according to the best sources of information, greatly exceeded the American forces in number of rifles, a yet greater number being armed with bolos. The Filipino forces included several thousands of former native militia, volunteers, and regular troops of the Spanish army, and of these a large number were veterans of campaigns against the Moros in Mindanao and Sulu.

In the engagement which began on the night of the 4th of February, 1899, the Filipinos were driven back and the American lines extended on an arc surrounding the city.

Matters were further complicated for the American commanders by the early expiration of the term of enlistment of many of the volunteer troops, who had enlisted for the duration of the war with Spain and became entitled to discharge upon the exchange of ratifications of the treaty of peace on April 11. Practically all these troops, however, showed their patriotism by consenting to stay in the field until replacements should arrive.

On February 11, the city of Iloilo, then the second port of importance, was occupied by American troops, but before they landed the insurgents withdrew, setting fire to the city.

The navy occupied the city and port of Cebu which was garrisoned February 28 by United States troops.

Government was at once re-established by the military authorities and commerce resumed upon occupation of these cities.

On March 4, 1899, a battalion of California Volunteer Infantry occupied the city of Bacolod, capital of the provisional republic of Negros, which had been organized by the natives of that island in opposition to General Aguinaldo, and had sought the protection of American authorities.

While these extensions of American occupation had been going on in the Islands to the south of Luzon, Congress on March 2, 1899, authorized an increase in the regular army to 65,000 enlisted men and a force of 35,000 volunteers to be recruited for the suppression of the Philippine insurrection. Three regiments of these volunteers were organized in the Islands, chiefly of officers and men from the State volunteers who decided to continue in the military service. Volunteer regiments recruited in the United States did not begin to arrive in the Islands until October, 1899.

Major-General Henry W. Lawton, with the 4th Regiment and one battalion of the 17th Regiment of Infantry of the regular army, arrived at Manila March 10, from New York. These were the first United States troops to pass through the Suez Canal. Other reinforcements soon arrived from San Francisco. With these additional forces the American troops in the Islands, constituting the Eighth Army Corps, were reorganized. The First Division, General Lawton commanding, and the Second Division, General MacArthur commanding, were to operate out from Manila on the Island of Luzon. The troops at Cebu, Iloilo, Jolo, and elsewhere south of Luzon, operated as a separate brigade.

American lines were advanced eastward along the Pasig River and to the Laguna de Bay district, cutting off movement of insurgent troops and material. General MacArthur's troops entered Malolos, the insurgent capital, March 31.

A general movement northward was begun April 22, jointly by Generals Lawton and MacArthur, and the insurgents driven back. Among other noteworthy achievements, Colonel Funston, with his Kansas men, swam a rapid river to secure boats from the northern bank for the immediate transportation of additional forces to hold the position, the insurgents having dropped into the river one span of the only bridge.

Many State volunteers mustered into the Federal service for the war with Spain, in spite of the expiration of their term, had elected to continue to serve their country.

No less heroic though less spectacular work was done by an American scout organization composed of men from North Dakota and Oregon State volunteers and the 4th United States Cavalry.

Hard campaigning during the extreme hot season had severely tried the physical stamina of the troops, and almost constant exposure to enemy fire, together with the delay in arrival of reinforcements, had proved an exhausting strain for the State volunteers. The surgeon of one of these regiments reported thirty per cent of its officers and men sick in Manila hospitals, thirty per cent sick at station at San Fernando, Pampanga, and of the entire regiment only ninety-six were fit for duty.

At the battle of Zapote Bridge which began in the morning of June 13, and at close range, the Filipinos came boldly into the open ground and advanced to within one hundred yards. Shortly after three in the afternoon General Lawton reported to General Otis: "We are having a beautiful battle. Hurry up ammunition; we will need it"; and at four o'clock: "We have bridge. It has cost us dearly. Battle not yet over. It is a battle, however." The American loss was reported as some forty killed and wounded; the insurgent loss was over one thousand in killed, wounded, and captured.

The exigencies incident to the return of volunteers after the expiration of their enlistment and the substitution of newly enlisted forces delayed operations. The insurgents in northern Luzon were believed then to have perhaps twenty-five thousand rifles, and their plan was, if worsted in the lowlands, to retire to the mountains, where they believed they could prolong the war indefinitely. Pending the arrival of additional troops, it was deemed by General Otis unwise to pursue the insurgents, as territory gained could not be occupied nor could public order be maintained.

While armed hostilities in Luzon continued, insurgent organization in Cebu, Panay, and other Visayan islands increased. It appeared that the situation in Mindanao and the Sulu Archipelago demanded immediate attention. The Sultan of Sulu was reported as having gained the impression from the Spaniards that they were turning sovereignty back to him upon the withdrawal of their garrisons there, although that at Jolo had been relieved by American troops. It was also reported that the Sultan had been placed in possession at Siasi when the Spanish post was evacuated. However, the American troops had been able to enter upon friendly relations with the representative Moros whom they had placed in charge of local affairs on the island of Jolo.

A definite and amicable agreement in writing with the Sultan of Sulu was deemed of urgent importance. Brigadier-General John C. Bates was sent by General Otis early in July, 1899, to accomplish this difficult mission, which he did and placed American garrisons at Siasi and Bongao. This agreement, which came to be known as "The Bates Treaty," and the development of relations with the Sulu people and other Mohammedan Filipinos will be discussed in a later chapter.

On the arrival of the new volunteers from America, in October, the general movement northward in Luzon was resumed, General Lawton again advancing through the eastern part of the central plain and foothills and General MacArthur along the railway.

The insurgents were driven northward until, on November 12, 1899, American troops entered Tarlac and the insurgent organization dissolved. General Aguinaldo, retiring with his bodyguard into the mountains of Benguet, narrowly escaped capture by the advance point of General Lawton's column.

General Aguinaldo with a very few companions crossed slowly through the extremely mountainous country to the Pacific coast, his whereabouts being unknown until a short time before his capture in March of the following year.

The field operations necessarily were carried on during the extremely hot season and continued during the season of torrential rains. The American troops were not acclimated to the tropics; many regiments had but recently arrived from America. There was no practicable means of transportation after the heavy rains, when the roads became quagmires, rivers overflowed their banks, and much of the central plain of Luzon, which was the main theater of operations, became a morass. Bringing supplies to troops at a distance from the railway was a superhuman undertaking, and the Filipinos felt confident of their advantage. American troops on both the east and west flanks and General Lawton's headquarters were often beyond reach of supplies, except ammunition, and were compelled to subsist on buffalo meat and rice. Clothing and shoes could not withstand constant marching through the swamp jungles and fording the swollen rivers. Many officers and men, both from the regular regiments and the new volunteers, were disabled by malaria and other diseases due to exposure, exhaustion, and lack of wholesome food as well as from bites of insects and skin abrasions becoming infected, and many had to be invalided back to America. But all important points in central and northern Luzon had been occupied by American garrisons, and more than three thousand Spanish prisoners liberated.

The most important task remaining was the capture of General Aguinaldo. The campaign had succeeded in breaking up the central organization of the insurgents, leaving as the only forces of consequence those south of Manila in the provinces of Cavite and Batangas. Against these a vigorous campaign was directed early in January, 1900. Following these operations American troops drove out the insurgent garrisons and occupied towns in the remaining southern provinces of Luzon, releasing about one thousand two hundred Spanish prisoners.

The only point to the south of Manila where strong resistance was met was at the port of Legaspi in the province of Albay, but there the insurgents were thoroughly defeated, and surrendered. Little resistance was then offered by the insurgents in the Visayan Islands or in the occupation by American garrisons of the more important coast points in Mindanao.

After the occupation of the southern provinces of Luzon, American garrisons were placed in Samar, Leyte, and other islands of the Visayan group and in Mindanao. Cebu and Iloilo, as has been seen, had been previously occupied.

By the end of March, 1900, the occupation of all large towns in the Islands had been effected and the important ports opened to commerce. On May 5, 1900, General Otis was relieved at his own request and returned to the United States. General MacArthur was designated to succeed him in command of the Division of the Philippines and as Military Governor of the Islands.

In his annual report of 1900, Secretary of War Root stated:

> . . . formal and open resistance to American authority in the Philippines terminated, leaving only an exceedingly vexatious and annoying guerrilla warfare of a character closely approaching brigandage, which will require time, patience, and good judgment to finally suppress.

In this unequal warfare between the Americans, well commanded, energetic, well armed and equipped and amply supplied, though young in warfare, and the Filipinos, comparatively without leadership, resources, and equipment, the inevitable had occurred, the Philippine organization had been defeated and the pacification resolved itself into an endeavor to infuse order into a hostile-minded and suspicious people, told they had been misled as to the intention of the United States and believing that the Americans were acting in bad faith. The guerrilla bands mentioned by the Secretary of War hid in the outskirts of the populous areas and subsisted on the people by forced contributions. They attacked American scouting parties or supply trains when favorable occasion offered. In view of the large number of islands, their area, and the fact that the Americans were dealing with a population amounting to over six millions, it is surprising that the progress made was as great as it was. But, as a result of the fighting, mutual recriminations and misunderstandings and much racial animosity were engendered, which took long to abate.

One of the most daring exploits was that of Frederick Funston of Kansas, who effected the capture of General Aguinaldo. This he did by entrusting himself and a group of his officers to the good faith of a body of Filipinos, principally Macabebes, who brought them bound hand and foot as though captives to the insurgent general's camp. At the appointed time General Funston and his officers were freed of their bonds, given their weapons, and enabled to surprise and capture the Philippine leader. On being taken back to Manila, General Aguinaldo took the oath of allegiance to the United States, April 19, 1901, and by proclamation advised his people to stop fighting the Americans. Since that time as a distinguished private citizen he has coöperated in the further pacification of his country and adherence to the American régime. Although in his early environment a man of limited opportunity, General Aguinaldo is a remarkable character, and since taking the oath of allegiance to the United States he has supported measures looking to the economic development of his country. He has stated that he regarded the problem as an economic one, and that he hoped no further recourse to violence would occur. It was an interesting coincidence that Aguinaldo's son, Emilio, entered West Point in the same class with the son of his father's captor, Frederick Funston.

The cost of the Philippine campaign in American lives was small as compared with that of the Filipinos, but included very gallant men, the most noted of whom was General Lawton, who on the 18th of December, 1899, fell pierced by a bullet from the insurgent lines, while leading his troops near San Mateo in the island of Luzon.

Great as was the loss of General Lawton to the military service, even greater was the loss of his capacity for sympathetic administration, which would have been invaluable in the establishment of civil government. His is the credit of having organized the first municipal government with the exercise of popular suffrage by Filipinos on May 6, 1899, at the town of Baliuag, Bulacan.

General Lawton had the vision to see the necessity of coöperation between the army in its civil administration and members of the Schurman Commission in the effort to conciliate the Filipinos and end hostilities by the policy of attraction.

In coöperation with the Honorable Dean C. Worcester, of President McKinley's investigating commission, General Lawton rapidly organized municipal government with Filipino officials in all towns occupied by his troops, and at the time of his death was planning more general organizations. This plan was subsequently followed by the military government.

The protection of peaceful and unarmed inhabitants from guerrillas, and the re-establishment of local civil government, necessitated the distribution of the United States forces until there came to be in the year 1901 as many as 639 garrisoned towns and stations. As a matter of policy, people contributing to the support of guerrillas were rarely interfered with by the Americans, and even members of the bands were often released immediately after being disarmed. This, instead of inducing a friendly attitude on the part of the Filipinos, was regarded by them as a sign of weakness. "It was therefore," as the Secretary of War reported, "decided to apply more rigidly to the residents of the archipelago, the laws of war touching the government of occupied places." This decision was announced in a proclamation by the Military Governor (then Major-General MacArthur) December 20, 1900, "fully explaining the law, supplemented by letters of instruction, and followed by more vigorous field operations. It was followed immediately by the deportation to the island of Guam of about fifty prominent Filipino insurgent army officers, civil officials, insurgent agents, sympathizers, and agitators."

The army continued its vigorous field work until all prominent insurgent leaders with their commands were captured or surrendered.

The Secretary of War, in his report for 1902, mentioned "the important bearing which the continuous offer and bestowal of civil rights and local self-government as the result of pacification had upon the attitude of the people toward the insurrection." The report continued:

It is evident that the insurrection has been brought to an end both by making a war distressing and hopeless on the one hand and by making peace attractive, through immediate and present demonstration of the sincerity of our purpose to give to the people just and free government, on the other. . . .

There was at one time in the public press and on the floor of Congress much criticism of the conduct of the army in the Philippines, as being cruel and inhuman. All wars are cruel. This conflict consisted chiefly of guerrilla warfare. It lasted for some three years and a half and extended over thousands of miles of territory. Over 120,000 men were engaged upon our side and much greater numbers upon the other, and we were fighting against enemies who totally disregarded the laws of civilized warfare, and who were guilty of the most atrocious treachery and inhuman cruelty. It was impossible that some individuals should not be found upon our side who were unnecessarily and unjustifiably cruel. Such instances, however, after five months of searching investigation by a committee of the Senate, who took some three thousand printed pages of testimony, appear to have been comparatively few, and they were in violation of strict orders, obedience to which characterized the conduct of the army as a whole. . . .

Governor Taft, in his testimony under oath before the Philippine Committee of the Senate on the 4th of February last, said:

"After a good deal of study about the matter (and although I have never been prejudiced in favor of the military branch, for when the civil and military branches are exercising concurrent jurisdiction there is some inevitable friction), I desire to say that it is my deliberate judgment that there never was a war conducted, whether against inferior races or not, in which there was more compassion and more restraint and more generosity, assuming that there was war at all, than there have been in the Philippine Islands."

From May, 1900, to June 30, 1901, there had been more than a thousand contacts between the American troops and the insurgents, in which the insurgent casualties were:

Killed, 3,854; [ascertained] wounded, 1,193; captured, 6,572; surrendered, 23,095; with a total of 15,693 rifles and nearly 300,000 rounds of small-arms ammunition captured and surrendered. Our casualties during the same period were: Killed, 245; wounded, 490; captured, 118; missing, 20.

During 1901, pacification of the Islands progressed at a rate that made it evident in Washington that civil government could be established. Although the army felt that the time had not arrived, by the end of June, as will be seen, executive authority was transferred from the military to a civil governor in the greater part of the Islands. On July 4, Major-General Adna R. Chaffee relieved General MacArthur in command of American troops and as military governor of the territory not yet organized under civil government.

The United States Army, after having reached a maximum strength in the Islands of 2367 officers and 71,727 enlisted men, was reduced to 1111 officers and 42,128 enlisted men, by the latter part of 1901, through the return of the United States Volunteer regiments to America for discharge.

The United States regular army underwent a general reorganization in 1901 with provision for a permanent force of not to exceed 100,000 men. In the act of Congress authorizing the reorganization provision was made for a body of Filipino troops not to exceed 12,000, which was given the designation of Philippine Scouts, with Filipinos as non-commissioned officers and other enlisted men, under the command of American officers.

In Mindanao the situation in the Lanao region which had never been brought under control by the Spaniards required extensive field operations, the most important of which was the assault on May 2 on the *cotta*, or fort at Bayan. All Mindanao, except the north coast provinces of Misamis and Surigao, together with the Sulu Archipelago, continued under purely military government until given a special form of provincial organization as the Moro Province, June 1, 1903, and thereafter until December, 1913, the commanding general of army forces stationed in those regions was also provincial governor.

Public opinion in the United States was divided as to the wisdom of extending sovereignty to the Philippine Islands. The uncertainty in the public mind was manifested in the discussions leading up to the ratification of the Treaty of Paris, February 6, 1899, in the public press, and in the clause in the platform of the Democratic Party in the presidential campaign of 1900 that imperialism was regarded "as the paramount issue." These, together with public utterances of partisans during that campaign, encouraged the Filipino leaders to believe that the stronger the demonstration they made of opposition to the United States continuing in the Islands, the greater the certainty of American public opinion insisting upon withdrawal of sovereignty.

Abundant documentary evidence of this was found among captured insurgent documents and records. An interesting document of this class was cited by Secretary of War Elihu Root in his address of October 24, 1900, at Canton, Ohio, as follows:

General Order to the Philippine Army, No. 202

As I have in previous letters directed that all Commanders of Guerrillas are free to attack any detachment or post of the enemy, and continually molest the same: I reiterate the order the more strongly, because its fulfillment just now is very necessary for the advantage of the cause of independence of the Philippines in the approaching Presidential election in the United States of America, which takes place in the early part of the coming month of September [2] of the present year; on account of which, it is imperative that before that day comes, that is to say, during the months of June, July, and August, we give such hard knocks to the Americans that they will resound in our favor in all parts, and set in motion the fall of the Imperialist party, which is trying to enslave us.

Date, 27th of June, 1900.

Signed by the Captain-General,
E. Aguinaldo

Following that order and before October 15, eighty-nine American officers and men were killed and many more seriously wounded. General Lawton said of the anti-imperialist activities in the United States:

If the so-called anti-imperialists would honestly ascertain the truth on the ground and not in distant America, they, whom I believe to be honest men and

[2] General Aguinaldo was undoubtedly misinformed as to the month. The election was held in November.

misinformed, would be convinced of the error of their statements and conclusions and of the unfortunate effect of their publications here.

If I am shot by a Filipino bullet, it might as well come from one of my own men, because I know from observations confirmed by captured prisoners that the continuance of fighting is chiefly due to reports that are sent out from America.

The success of the Republican Party in the election in 1900 did not end opposition in Congress to the Philippine policy. In an address delivered by Secretary of War Root at Peoria, Illinois, September 24, 1902, he said:

The principal, indeed almost the sole attack by the representatives of the Democratic party, which occupied the greater part of the last session of Congress, was violent denunciation of the Administration's policy in the Philippines, and of the execution of that policy.

It was not surprising that the Filipinos, who had never had any experience of freedom of speech, should attach undue importance to these partisan utterances during the election campaign. There is little doubt that the result was a prolongation of the struggle and much suffering and loss in lives and in money both to the Filipinos and to the United States.

Some of the bitterest opponents to American acquisition of the Philippine Islands organized the Anti-Imperialist League, with headquarters in Boston, which raised money and undertook an active campaign, even going so far as to send representatives to the Islands. The men selected for this service were not trained administrators nor were they disposed to give fair consideration to the difficulties of the situation. They looked for things which they could criticize, and returned extremely bitter reports of the conditions they found, which were published and given wide circulation, sometimes in pamphlet form, by the Anti-Imperialist League. American troops operating in the field against insurgents captured papers which proved that some of this literature had found its way into the hands of the Filipinos and was giving aid and comfort to those bearing arms against the United States.

There is no doubt that these misguided activities, which added to the length and costliness of the insurrection, were undertaken with the loftiest motives and by men of the highest standing, and it was a curious anomaly that they and the representatives of the beet-sugar States and the tobacco interests should be found side by side opposing the continuance of American administration in the Philippine Islands — the one on the ground that they were champions of the Philippine people, and the other frankly taking the position that they did not care to have their own interests jeopardized by Philippine competition.

Bishop Charles H. Brent, the lofty-minded and able Episcopal Bishop of the Philippine Islands, who devoted so large a part of his time and energies to the welfare of the Filipinos, stirred by some fulmination of the Anti-Imperialists, wrote on March 29, 1913, to the Secretary of the Anti-Imperialist League, in the following terms:

I have received your appeal to me to support you in a movement which, after more than eleven years of experience in the Philippine Islands, I am convinced is faulty in its conception, unfair in its methods, and disastrous in its consequences.

Civil administration by Americans under direction of military commanders began in the Philippine Islands immediately following the occupation of the city of Manila, August 13, 1898.

Under instructions from Washington the civil and criminal laws of the Spanish administration were continued in force, amended from time to time by order of the Military Governor as was necessary.

As the Washington government did not contemplate permanent nor long-continued occupation of the Philippine Islands, there accompanied the army no civil personnel for these administrative duties. Army officers with business experience proceeded, however, to organize the important functions of police, revenue collection, and other essential administrative activities of government.

For the security of life and property and the maintenance of good order, police service was provided by a provost guard, with the result that within four days after the occupation of Manila, commercial houses and even the banks were open for business with the public.

The custom house and related duties with reference to regulation of commercial shipping and the harbor were organized under military officers as Collector of Customs and Captain of the Port, the navy taking charge of the lighthouse service.

The collection of internal revenue, with the incidental regulation of commerce and industries, was placed under an officer detailed as Collector of Internal Revenue.

The officer detailed to take over from the Spaniards the funds and other valuables in the treasury became the Treasurer of the government.

The public schools in Manila were reopened within a month after the occupation of the city, and other public schools were reopened as American military occupation extended to other cities and towns. By July 1, 1900, one hundred thousand pupils were attending primary schools established by the army.

The surrender of Manila brought into the possession of the United States for control not only the municipal affairs of the city, but to a great extent the commerce, shipping, and a large share of the trade revenues of the entire archipelago. As to foreign commerce, immigration, and the persons and properties of foreigners in the city of Manila, the United States stood in place of Spain during the period of occupation until the ratification of the Treaty of Paris. The remainder of the archipelago was in part controlled by Filipino insurgents and in part the machinery of government still remained in the hands of the Spaniards. Spanish sovereignty continued *de jure* throughout the entire archipelago until the exchange of ratifications of the treaty in April, 1899.

American and foreign observers have found much to commend in the civil administration of the Philippine Islands by the military authorities. Senator Sergio Osmeña, who at the time of the insurrection was a newspaperman ardently hoping for the ultimate independence of his country and who for a time was within the insurgent lines, made the following comments in regard to this period in an address in the United States in 1925:

. . . In the midst of war the government necessarily had to be of a military character, in which executive, legislative, and judicial powers were concentrated in one head, although the exercise of his functions could, if he so desired, be delegated to different persons or entities.

It is to the credit of the American military commanders of the time that it is possible to say of them that they considered extremely dangerous a government of concentrated powers without the intervention of the people and that they desired to establish, even in the midst of armed resistance, the foundations of civil institutions. The Filipinos will never forget the inspiring spectacle of American soldiers leaving their guns and, as emissaries of peace and good will, with book in hand, repairing to the public schools to teach Filipino children the principles of free citizenship.

Meantime the administration in Washington had not been idle in regard to the civil aspects of their problem. The investigating commission, previously alluded to, which President McKinley had appointed comprised five members. The chairman was Jacob Gould Schurman. As colleagues he had Admiral George Dewey, Major-General Elwell S. Otis, and, from civil life, Charles Denby, and Dean C. Worcester, who had twice visited the Islands on expeditions in the interests of science.

The Schurman Commission arrived at Manila March 4, 1899, just one month after the beginning of the insurrection. Insurgent troops everywhere faced American lines on the outskirts of the city, and, as the Commission reported, "the sound of rifle fire was frequently audible at our house. A reign of terror prevailed. Filipinos who had favored Americans feared assassination, and few had the courage to come out openly for us."

There appeared before the Commission representative men who were prominent as bankers, merchants, lawyers, physicians, shipowners, educators, and public officials, Americans, Europeans of various nationalities including Spaniards, also Chinese, as well as Filipinos.

The Commission dealt with all subjects touching the Islands and their people. It made efforts to conciliate the Filipinos and terminate hostilities. These efforts, however, were subordinated to the military authority, the supremacy of which was constantly recognized.

On April 4, the Commission "issued a proclamation setting forth the principles by which the United States would be guided in exercising the sovereignty which Spain had ceded to us over the Philippine Islands, and assuring the people not only of their rights and privileges, but also of the largest participation in government which might be found compatible with the general welfare and reconcilable with the sovereign rights and obligations of the United States."

The Commission, in its preliminary report of November 2, 1899, stated that the public sentiment of the native population in Manila which "had been strongly anti-American, underwent a palpable change, and currents of peace and conciliation were set in motion until they found a response in the ranks of the insurgents themselves." The report continued:

Aguinaldo sent a delegation to Manila to confer with the Commission, and while the commission steadfastly refused to discuss his proposal to suspend hostilities, as being a military matter, assurances were given of the beneficent purposes of the United States and the President's readiness to grant the Philippine peoples as large a measure of home rule and as ample liberties as were consistent with the ends of government, subject only to the recognition of the sovereignty of the United States. . . .

The so-called congress of Aguinaldo voted for a peaceful settlement on the basis of the commission's proclamation; and Mabini, the irreconcilable head of the so-called cabinet, was replaced by Paterno, the former mediator between the Spanish Government and Aguinaldo. But nothing came of negotiations, as Aguinaldo's emissaries were without powers, and merely came and came again for information.

After conferences between the Commission and representative Filipinos, and communication with the authorities in Washington, a proposed plan of government was authorized by the President to consist of an appointed Governor-General with cabinet, an elective advisory council, with independent judiciary of Americans or Filipinos appointed by the President. The President expressed the desire that the Filipinos "shall have the largest measure of local self-government consistent with peace and good order."

While military operations were still in full swing—although the back of the insurrection had been broken—the Commission returned to Washington, where, on January 31, 1900, they rendered their final report, in which they discussed at length existing conditions, and gave in detail the organization and administration of government under the Spanish régime.

The Commission reported: "While the people of the Philippine Islands ardently desire a full measure of rights and liberties, they do not, in the opinion of the Commission, generally desire independence." Further: ". . . it would be a misrepresentation of facts not to report that ultimate independence—independence after an undefined period of American training—is the aspiration and goal of the intelligent Filipinos who to-day so strenuously oppose the suggestion of independence at the present time."

The Commission reported that "it will be safe and desirable, in the opinion of the commission, to extend to the Filipinos larger liberties of self-government than Jefferson approved of for the inhabitants of Louisiana."

The conclusions of the Schurman Commission as to government were as follows:

1. The United States cannot withdraw from the Philippines. We are there and duty binds us to remain. There is no escape from our responsibility to the Filipinos and to mankind for the government of the archipelago and the amelioration of the condition of its inhabitants.

2. The Filipinos are wholly unprepared for independence, and if independence were given to them they could not maintain it.

3. As to Aguinaldo's claim that he was promised independence or that an alliance was made with him, Admiral Dewey makes the following communication to the Commission:

"The statement of Emilio Aguinaldo, under date of September 23, published in the Springfield Republican, so far as it relates to reported conversations with me, or actions of mine, is a tissue of falsehoods. I never, directly or indirectly, promised the Filipinos independence. I never received Aguinaldo with military honors, or recognized or saluted the so-called Filipino flag. I never considered him as an ally, although I did make use of him and the natives to assist me in my operations against the Spaniards."

4. There being no Philippine nation, but only a collection of different peoples, there is no general public opinion in the archipelago; but the men of property and education, who alone interest themselves in public affairs, in general recognize as indispensable American authority, guidance, and protection.

5. Congress should, at the earliest practicable time, provide for the Philippines the form of government herein recommended or another equally liberal and beneficent.

6. Pending any action on the part of Congress, the Commission recommends that the President put in operation this scheme of civil government in such parts of the archipelago as are at peace.

7. So far as the finances of the Philippines permit, public education should be promptly established, and when established made free to all.

8. The greatest care should be taken in the selection of officials for administration. They should be men of the highest character and fitness, and partisan politics should be entirely separated from the government of the Philippines.

Even before the publication of this report, President McKinley had in his message to Congress on December 5, 1899, said:

. . . As long as the insurrection continues the military arm must necessarily be supreme. But there is no reason why steps should not be taken from time to time to inaugurate governments essentially popular in their form as fast as territory is held and controlled by our troops. To this end I am considering the advisability of the return of the commission, or such of the members thereof as can be secured, to aid the existing authorities and facilitate this work throughout the islands.

Carrying out his policy of transferring authority gradually from military commanders to civil officers, he then appointed a second Commission, which was, in his own words, "to continue and perfect the work of organizing and establishing civil government already commenced by the military authorities, subject in all respects to any laws which Congress may hereafter enact."

Beginning with the first day of September, 1900, all legislative power of the government was to be exercised by this Commission, all of whose actions were subject to approval by the Secretary of War, and it was to report to the Secretary of War when conditions in the Islands were such that the central administration could safely be transferred to civil control.

President McKinley used great care in the selection of its members. As President he selected the Honorable William H. Taft, of Ohio, a federal judge, who gave up his judicial duties with much reluctance to accept the trying task that confronted him in the Philippine Islands.

Judge Taft's second in command and Vice-Governor was the Honorable Luke E. Wright, of Tennessee, a Democrat, and ex-Confederate soldier. He was appointed later by President Roosevelt to be Civil Governor, then became the first Governor-General of the Islands, later still was appointed by President Roosevelt Ambassador to Japan, and subsequently Secretary of War. When Colonel Roosevelt was seeking the presidency on the Progressive ticket, ex-Governor-General Wright was asked by him to take the position of Vice-President and to be his running mate on that ticket. The other members of this Commission were the Honorable Dean C. Worcester, the Honorable Henry Clay Ide, of St. Johnsbury, Vermont, and the Honorable Bernard Moses, professor of the University of California.

The Commissioners, with their secretarial staff and families, arrived in Manila June 3, 1900. Military operations in the field were still actively in progress. From a military point of view their advent was unquestionably premature. From a political point of view it was wise; and the result soon proved its wisdom.

The Military Governor after consultation with the Commission and with the President's approval issued a notice of amnesty June 21, 1900, with a supplementary public statement July 2, 1900, in accord with instructions to the Commission. More than five thousand persons who had participated in the insurrection presented themselves and took the prescribed oath of allegiance. Among this number were many of the most prominent officials of the former Malolos government.

The Taft Commission began the exercise of its legislative powers on the first day of September, 1900, with a published statement in part as follows:

> The policy of the Commission will be to give the fullest opportunity for public consideration and criticism of proposed measures of legislation affecting the people of these islands. . . .
>
> The Commission will hold public meetings at its offices . . . for the consideration of proposed bills, and at such meetings citizens of the Philippines and others interested will be given opportunity to make suggestions and criticisms in respect to the proposed measures if, upon the day previous to the meeting, application be made to the president for assignment of time.

WM. H. TAFT
DEAN C. WORCESTER
LUKE E. WRIGHT
HENRY C. IDE
BERNARD MOSES

A. W. FERGUSSON, *Secretary*

Almost immediately followed acts for the establishment and maintenance of an honest and efficient civil service; appropriations for public instruction, for the relief of widows and orphans of Filipino civil officials who had been assassinated because of loyalty to American sovereignty, $1,000,000 for the improvement of the port of Manila, and other sums for current governmental purposes, including many expenses of the army of occupation. Acts also were passed for the organization of the bureaus of audits, education, forestry, health, mines, statistics, supply, treasury, and weather; for the better administration of justice and public revenues; and for the simplification of regulation of commerce. Organic laws or general charters were enacted for municipal and provincial governments, and most of these governments had been organized before the executive authority in the insular government was relinquished by the Military Governor July 4, 1901, pursuant to the President's order. In all one hundred and fifty-seven acts were passed by the Commission during the few months it exercised legislative powers under military government.

Friendly relations were soon developed with representative Filipinos of all classes. An organized movement for peace was undertaken by the formation of the Federal Party in November, 1900, and through its local organizations most of the important insurgent leaders still in arms became convinced of the beneficent purposes of the United States government and the futility of continuing armed resistance.

As has been seen, the army late in 1900 entered upon more vigorous enforcement of "the laws of war touching the government of occupied places." The masses of the people less willingly gave supplies and protection to guerrillas. General Aguinaldo was captured and on April 19, 1901, issued his peace proclamation. The army offered a cash bonus for each insurgent firearm brought in; deported a number of prominent irreconcilables to Guam; released large numbers of political prisoners in recognition of the surrenders of insurgent leaders of especial prominence; and otherwise encouraged the acceptance of American sovereignty.

Congress, by what is known as the Spooner Amendment to an act approved March 2, 1901, authorized the President, who up to that time had acted under his war powers, to proceed with the establishment of civil government. By the following June conditions in Luzon and the Visayas and in the northern part of Mindanao were deemed by the President to be such as to justify the transfer of the executive authority in pacified territory from the military to a civil governor. An order was issued directing that this transfer be made July 4, 1901.

A year later military government was terminated by the executive order which ended as follows:

The general commanding the Division of the Philippines, and all military officers in authority therein, will continue to observe the direction contained in the aforesaid instructions of the President, that the military forces in the Division of the Philippines shall be at all times subject, under the orders of the military commander, to the call of the civil authorities for the maintenance of law and order and the enforcement of their authority.

By the President: ELIHU ROOT, *Secretary of War*

On the same day (July 4, 1902) President Roosevelt issued his proclamation of peace and amnesty.

CHAPTER IV

CIVIL GOVERNMENT

ON JULY 4, 1901, the Honorable William H. Taft was inaugurated Civil Governor of the Philippine Islands, and the administration of the executive functions of government was taken over by the Civil Commission.

President McKinley's letter of instructions for the Commission is a model of constructive statesmanship, and vitally important in its bearing on Philippine history.

When Governor-General Forbes asked President Taft, in 1912, what the history of the formation of the Philippine policy was, who it was that had written the instructions by President McKinley to the Taft Commission, he informed him that this was the work of Secretary Root, who wrote the letter of instructions, after which he had read them over to him (Judge Taft) and other members of his Commission, and that some suggestions and modifications were made but that the main work was intact.

After naming the members of the Commission and designating Taft as president, the letter read:

> You will instruct the Commission to proceed to the city of Manila, where they will make their principal office. . . . Without hampering them by too specific instructions, they should in general be enjoined, after making themselves familiar with the conditions and needs of the country, to devote their attention in the first instance to the establishment of municipal governments in which the natives of the Islands, both in the cities and in the rural communities, shall be afforded the opportunity to manage their own local affairs to the fullest extent of which they are capable, and subject to the least degree of supervision and control which a careful study of their capacities and observation of the workings of native control show to be consistent with the maintenance of law, order, and loyalty. The next subject in order of importance should be the organization of government in the larger administrative divisions, corresponding to countries, departments, or provinces, in which the common interests of many or several municipalities falling within the same tribal lines, or the same natural geographical limits, may best be subserved by a common administration.

The Commission is given powers in regard to revenue, civil service, etc.

In the distribution of powers among the governments organized by the Commission, the presumption is always to be in favor of the smaller subdivision, so that all the powers which can properly be exercised by the municipal government shall be vested in that government, and all the powers of a more general character which can be exercised by the departmental [provincial] government shall be vested in that government . . . following the example of the distribution of the powers between the States and the National Government of the United States, . . . [retaining for the central government] only such supervision and control over local governments as may be necessary to secure and enforce faithful and efficient administration by local officers.

. . . .

In all cases the municipal officers who administer the local affairs of the people are to be selected by the people, and that wherever officers of more extended jurisdiction are to be selected in any way natives of the Islands are to be preferred, and if they can be found competent and willing to perform the duties they are to receive the offices in preference to any others. It will be necessary to fill some offices for the present with Americans, which, after a time, may well be filled by natives of the Islands. As soon as practicable a system for ascertaining the merit and fitness of candidates for civil offices should be put in force. An indispensable qualification for all offices and positions of trust and authority in the Islands must be absolute and unconditional loyalty to the United States, and absolute and unhampered authority and power to remove and punish any officer deviating from that standard must at all times be retained in the hands of the central authority of the islands.

In all the forms of government and administrative provisions which they are authorized to prescribe, the Commission should bear in mind that the government which they are establishing is designed not for our satisfaction or for the expression of our theoretical views, but for the happiness, peace, and prosperity of the people of the Philippine Islands, and the measures adopted should be made to conform to their customs, their habits, and even their prejudices, to the fullest extent consistent with the accomplishment of the indispensable requisites of just and effective government. At the same time the Commission should bear in mind, and the people of the Islands should be made plainly to understand, that there are certain great principles of government which have been made the basis of our governmental system, which we deem essential to the rule of law and the maintenance of individual freedom, and of which they have, unfortunately, been denied the experience possessed by us; that there are also certain practical rules of government which we have found to be essential to the preservation of these great principles of liberty and law, and that these principles and these rules of government must be established and maintained in their islands for the sake of their liberty and happiness, however much they may conflict with the customs or laws of procedure with which they are familiar. It is evident that the most enlightened thought of the Philippine Islands fully appreciates the importance of these principles and rules, and they will inevitably within a short time command universal assent. Upon every division and branch of the Government of the Philippines, therefore, must be imposed these inviolable rules:

That no person shall be deprived of life, liberty, or property without due process of law; that private property shall not be taken for public use without just compensation; that in all criminal prosecutions the accused shall enjoy the right to a speedy and public trial, to be informed of the nature and cause of the accusation, to be confronted with the witnesses against him, to have compulsory process for obtaining witnesses in his favor, and to have the assistance of counsel for his defense; that excessive bail shall not be required, nor excessive fines imposed, nor cruel and unusual punishment inflicted; that no person shall be put twice in jeopardy for the same offense or be compelled in any criminal case to be a witness against himself; that the right to be secure against unreasonable searches and seizures shall not be violated; that neither slavery nor involuntary servitude shall exist except as a punishment for crime; that no bill of attainder or ex post facto law shall be passed; that no law shall be passed abridging the freedom of speech or of the press or of the rights of the people to peaceably assemble and petition the Government for a redress of grievances; that no law shall be made respecting an establishment of religion or prohibiting the free exercise thereof, and that the free exercise and enjoyment of religious profession and worship without discrimination or preference shall forever be allowed.[1]

The letter goes on to direct that "the principle of our Government which prohibits the taking of private property without due process of law, shall not be violated; that the welfare of the people of the Islands, which should be a paramount consideration, shall be attained consistently with this rule of property right. . . ."

Religious freedom is assured in the following words:

that no form of religion and no minister of religion shall be forced upon any community or upon any citizen of the Islands; that, upon the other hand, no minister of religion shall be interfered with or molested in following his calling, and that the separation between state and church shall be real, entire, and absolute.

Education and the provision for English as the language of the Islands are dealt with as follows:

It will be the duty of the Commission to promote and extend and, as they find occasion, to improve the system of education already inaugurated by the military authorities. In doing this they should regard as of first importance the extension of a system of primary education which shall be free to all, and which shall tend to fit the people for the duties of citizenship and for the ordinary avocations of a civilized community. This instruction should be given, in the first instance, in every part of the Islands in the language of the people.[2] In view of the great num-

---

[1] This letter contains the first bill of rights given to the Philippine people. These rights were given legislative sanction by Act of Congress of July 1, 1902, and were repeated and amplified in the Jones Law (Act of Congress, August 29, 1916).

[2] The Americans began giving instruction in English almost from the beginning. Very little instruction was given in the native dialects, as even if it had been desired, it would have been difficult owing to the non-existence of textbooks or literature.

ber of languages spoken by the different tribes, it is especially important to the prosperity of the Islands that a common medium of communication may be established, and it is obviously desirable that this medium should be the English language. Especial attention should be at once given to affording full opportunity to all the people of the Islands to acquire the use of the English language.

In any changes which the Commission may make in taxation they are charged "to bear in mind that taxes which tend to penalize or repress industry and enterprise are to be avoided; that provisions for taxation should be simple, so that they may be understood by the people; that they should affect the fewest practicable subjects of taxation which will serve for the general distribution of the burden."

The Commission is enjoined to maintain with as little interference as possible the main body of the laws which regulate the rights and obligations of the people.

And toward the end of the document is this final injunction:

Upon all officers and employees of the United States, both civil and military, should be impressed a sense of the duty to observe not merely the material but the personal and social rights of the people of the Islands, and to treat them with the same courtesy and respect for their personal dignity which the people of the United States are accustomed to require from each other.

It is believed that a study of the performance of the members of the Philippine Commission will prove that they lived up to the spirit of these instructions.

Congress by Act approved July 1, 1902, confirmed the action of the President in creating the Philippine Commission.

The powers of the Governor-General were extremely wide, much more so than is usual in democratic countries where the power is derived by delegation from the people. The Organic Act of Congress of 1902 granted the Governor-General certain powers in addition to those remaining in the Military Governor after the transfer of the legislative power to the Commission September 1, 1900. Except as otherwise provided by Congress, these were the powers of the Spanish Governor-General, of which the United States Supreme Court decided that an act was legal unless there was a law or order specially prohibiting it, and held that "the existence of power, being usual, will be presumed, and the absence of it, being exceptional, must be shown."

The Philippine government found its Washington home in the War Department.

The Islands were most fortunate in the character of the men chosen to hold the position of Secretary of War. President McKinley's appointee was the Honorable Elihu Root, who was succeeded in President Roosevelt's day by the Honorable William H. Taft, fresh from the governorship of the Philippine Islands, and who in turn was succeeded, for only a brief term, by the former Governor-General Luke E. Wright.

The need for an office within the War Department with machinery to care for the interests of this far-flung dependency was recognized by Secretary of War Elihu Root almost immediately following his accession to office in 1899. He organized a "Division of Customs and Insular Affairs" in his office under the direction of the Assistant Secretary of War. Captain John J. Pershing assisted in its organization before he went to the Philippines as a Major and Assistant Adjutant General.

Lieutenant Colonel Clarence R. Edwards, 47th U. S. Volunteers, a staff officer of the gallant General Henry W. Lawton who had been killed in action in the Philippines, was detailed early in 1900 in charge of the Division of Insular Affairs and was on that duty when, on June 25, 1906, it received legislative recognition as the Bureau of Insular Affairs. The position after that carried with it the temporary rank of Brigadier General.

General Edwards proved himself fertile in expedients and of tireless energy.

The bureau actively participated in the preparation of important acts of Congress affecting the insular government. It has done noteworthy work in connection with Philippine trade relations with the United States. It contributed constructively to important Philippine tariff legislation until unlimited free trade between the United States and the Islands was secured in 1913. Since then, it has effectively brought influence to bear to prevent legislation either in Washington or Manila adverse to these favorable trade relations.

To avoid confusion and to assure a successful government of the Philippine Islands, it was essential that general laws passed by Congress for the United States should not be made applicable to the Islands. The Bureau of Insular Affairs acted as the watchdog for the Philippine Islands, and vigilantly guarded against the frequent thoughtless as well as occasional insistent efforts of Senators and Congressmen so to word general legislation as to extend its operation to the Philippine Islands. So effective was the work of the bureau in this respect that no Congressional legislation has been enacted carrying clauses that were seriously embarrassing to the Philippine administration. Whenever it seemed desirable, as in the case of the Pure Food Law, the Philippine Commission enacted appropriate legislation, practically identical with that passed by Congress, but adapted to the existing machinery of the Philippine government.

Among other valuable and varied services of the bureau have been the advantageous sale of short-time notes of the Philippine government for the purchase of silver bullion, arrangements for minting the new Philippine currency and engraving and printing the paper currency, internal revenue and postage stamps, advertisement and sale of Philippine government bonds, delicate negotiations for interesting capital in the construction of railroads, the maintenance of a purchasing agency in New York, the securing of new employees, especially teachers, and filling requisitions for experts required for every class of service.

The twelve years 1901–1913 may properly be characterized as the period of the Taft policy. As Civil Governor of the Islands, then Secretary of War, and finally President of the United States, he was in a position to formulate and direct policies and insure their continuity. Associated with President Taft's name, however, in this period are those of other men whose impress upon world history has been great. Theodore Roosevelt was President for seven and a half years of the time; Elihu Root was Secretary of War and Secretary of State for an important part of the period; and Luke E. Wright was a member of the Commission, and later Governor-General — the first to hold that title — and Secretary of War.

In the words of President Theodore Roosevelt, it was a programme of changing a government of Americans assisted by Filipinos into a government of Filipinos assisted by Americans, or, as expressed by Governor Taft, a policy of making a government which was at the beginning strongly paternal as rapidly as possible less so. The creation of the Civil Service Bureau was one of the first constructive acts of the Commission, and examinations were given to qualify Filipinos according to modern practice. The steady and continued Filipinization of the service from the bottom up was regularly practiced; men were promoted as a result of proved efficiency though this was not rapid enough to satisfy the ambitious young Filipino impatient for advancement.

The policy of drastic retrenchment of expenditure could not be carried on without arousing antagonism, particularly among those who came out with the army, and later went into business, some of whom were dependent quite largely upon army patronage for their success. The feeling against the civil government was bitter. An American commercial firm in Manila even inserted in a Manila paper a large-sized advertisement consisting of Governor Taft's picture and below it the words: "This is the cause of our leaving the Philippines." The firm, however, continued profitably in business in the Islands.

Governor Taft's greatness of heart, true sympathy with the Filipinos and with their aspirations, his affection for them, and his unselfish devotion to the cause of good government assure him a high place in the affections of the Philippine people.

During his administration the débris of what was undesirable in the Spanish system had to be cleared away.

The Commission, with their American sense of justice and dislike of delay, were turned loose upon a world of medieval mismanagement and abuse like a group of knights-errant looking for wrongs to right and abuses to end. They found plenty to do.

With three lawyers on the Commission, it was natural that much of the time of the Commission should have been devoted to early revision of the codes, but financial matters were not neglected. Currency was in a condition of chaos, and until it had been entirely reformed little economic progress could be made. This knotty problem was tackled with conspicuous ability and solved. The assumption of the duty of maintaining order was ably cared for by the establishment of the insular Constabulary; beginnings were made in fighting epidemic diseases, and organizing a comprehensive system of education.

Another one of the "palpitating" problems, to use an expression common among the Filipinos, was the ownership of the lands which had been acquired by the friars in Spanish days, and the right of the friars to these lands which was disputed by the tenants, who had almost risen in rebellion against them and were declining to pay the rent demanded by the religious orders. This question became so acute that it was the occasion of a special trip on the part of Governor Taft to Rome, where he entered into negotiations which resulted in the acquisition by the government of most of these lands.

By September 6, 1901, the Commission had organized. Several bureaus reported directly to the Civil Governor, the remainder to the four departments of Commerce and Police, Finance and Justice, the Interior, and Public Instruction. The grouping of bureaus assigned to these departments was done with a view to meet the preferences and abilities of the secretary assigned to the head of the department. Bureaus formerly created by the military authorities were carried on and, as needs arose, new bureaus and offices created to take on new activities.

Some of the first legislative acts of the Commission have been mentioned. New laws came in rapid succession, organizing the different offices, bureaus, and courts, and appropriating moneys for current expenses, and gradually a more orderly and better articulated governmental machine was introduced.

Shortly after the arrival of the Commission in 1900, Governor Taft was of the opinion that it was extremely important that there should be grouped together in the form of a political party those who favored the American régime in the Islands. His idea was to create a Filipino medium of attraction and more amicable contact with the insurgent leaders outside, as well as the unreconciled within, American military lines. This was accomplished by bringing together, among others, a number of Filipinos who had participated in organizing General Aguinaldo's Malolos government and for various reasons had withdrawn and taken up residence in Manila within American lines. These included Dr. Trinidad H. Pardo de Tavera, and Don Benito Legarda, both of whom later were appointed members of the Philippine Commission; the Honorable Cayetano Arellano, Chief Justice of the Supreme Court; Felipe Buencamino, afterward first Director of Civil Service; Luis Yangco, a wealthy merchant of Manila; and Arturo Dancel, afterward Governor of the province of Rizal. Others were Florentino Torres, later a Justice of the Supreme Court, and José R. de Luzuriaga, a citizen of the Island of Negros, later appointed to the Commission. Some of these men had lived in foreign countries and most of them had held offices under or otherwise identified themselves with the Spanish government. Generally they were accredited members of the learned professions, or large property owners, or both. These, under the auspices of the American authorities, organized the Federal Party, late in 1900, with a platform in which the principal planks were peace and annexation, the immediate acceptance of American sovereignty in perpetuity, with increasing autonomy leading up to admission as a state.

The Americans associated with the army generally viewed with alarm or contempt this "playing at politics," but had been able to devise no other method than an appeal to reason capable of overcoming Filipino hostility.

Organizers and members of the Federal Party, at no small risk of life and property, personally urged upon the leaders of guerrilla operations, as well as upon influential unreconciled leaders in the cities and regions under control by Americans, termination of hostilities and acceptance of American rule. General Aguinaldo after his capture was influenced by Chief Justice Cayetano Arellano to take the oath of allegiance to the United States, and many other leaders undoubtedly discontinued active opposition because of the efforts of the Federal Party.

Secretary of War Elihu Root reported: "The organization of the Federal Party in the Philippines, which has extended throughout the provinces, loyally accepting the sovereignty and asserting the sincerity and beneficent purpose of the American people, has been of the utmost value."

Many of the party gained the Commission's confidence, and recognition was given by appointments to public offices in the several branches of civil administration. Generally these appointees continued faithful to their new allegiance and endeavored to acquit themselves well in the performance of their official duties. Naturally they incurred the stigma of being unpatriotic among the unreconciled Filipinos, and of place seekers among Americans not versed in the realities of practical politics. Commissioner Worcester wrote from personal knowledge of the facts:

The organization of the Federal Party caused an outburst of fury among the Insurgent leaders beside which that aroused by the organization of municipal governments was mild.

Throughout the islands the murdering of officers, members, and agents of this party was ordered and even those who sympathized with its ends were to be shot.

There is little evidence that many Filipino leaders really wanted permanent American sovereignty, but there is no doubt that all of them were actively interested in an increasing measure of participation in their government.

Philippine property owners and conservatives were inclined to accept permanent American sovereignty, not only because they feared continued danger to life and property under a weak government, but also because the idea of nationalism was new. There was no general demand for independence among the common people. Irreconcilable Filipinos kept up the cry of independence, which was picked up by the leaders of the bandits who were only too glad to cloak their depredations under the high name of struggling for independence. These elements were in sufficient force in some regions to make it actually dangerous to avow sympathy with the objects of the Federal Party. In this they received direct encouragement from the activities of the Anti-Imperialist League in Boston.

As the platform of the Federal Party asked for permanence of American rule, the political opponents of this party were certain to take up the increasingly popular slogan of nationalism when the time came to ask for votes. When this time finally arrived in 1907, the result of the first general elections proved conclusively that nationalism was the popular cry, and all parties found that if they were to maintain their numbers it was necessary to include it in their platforms. No general elections were held during Governor Taft's incumbency.

When Vice-Governor Luke E. Wright succeeded to the Governor-Generalship, he had had time to familiarize himself with conditions and no more admirable choice could have been made for the position. Impartial and far-seeing, he endeared himself especially to the Americans in the Islands. In his trips around the Islands he preached practical common sense. Apropos of Governor Taft's slogan of "the Philippines for the Filipinos," Governor-General Wright said with his usual directness that, while he believed in the policy of the Philippines for the Filipinos, "our job just now is to make the Philippines worth something to the Filipinos." On another occasion he said, "You have discovered the great truth that a government to be successful must be supported by the people, and not the people supported by the government."

One of the Spanish-owned newspapers, usually critical of Americans, especially as orators, took occasion to publish the following eulogy:

We know very few orators who excel Mr. Wright in depth, clearness, and connectedness of ideas, in propriety of language, in the marvellous art of hinging his thoughts together in such a way that from any point of view they shine splendidly and in all their roundness. Never like last night did he use his synthetic power to greater advantage, depicting in ten minutes a picture so grand and full of colors and figures; a complete program of government worthy of his elevated views, and bound as a whole to the aspirations of the country.

Governor-General Wright continued Governor Taft's policies with one very important modification. He recognized in his appointments of Filipinos men of both political parties, not confining himself to those who professed to belong to the Federal Party. He wanted the best man he could find for each place.

This period was notable for the ending of the guerrilla warfare which followed the insurrection, and of brigandage, and for a complete reorganization under which the government took on form, cohesion, and efficiency. At this time also an internal revenue law and a law imposing a land tax were passed.

The following two administrations were periods of steady progress, such as the further extension of autonomy to the provinces, establishment of the metric system and reform of the weights and measures, which had been in a condition prolific of abuse, and most noteworthy of all — the inauguration of the Philippine Assembly. At this time also a contract was entered into with a representative of the Hawaiian Sugar Planters' Association which resulted in the beginning of an important movement of laborers to Hawaii.

In 1909 an event of far-reaching importance occurred, namely, the passage of the so-called Payne Bill granting practically free trade between the United States and the Philippine Islands. The effect of this upon industry was magical and the resulting stimulus to business and the continuing annual increases to the revenues made the work of the administrators much easier.

By the wise and patient work of the earlier Governors and members of the Commission the foundations of progress had been laid and at last the American achievement began to rise as a distinct structure. Many observers seeing this later progress were inclined to forget that most of the credit for the structure they saw growing up was due to the painstaking wisdom of the early pioneers in American government in the Islands. They saw the roads being rapidly pushed out from the provincial ports and capitals to the producing areas that lay behind them in the provinces throughout the archipelago. They saw hundreds of permanent concrete bridges and culverts erected in all directions, and buildings of concrete for provincial administration purposes, hospitals, schools, and municipal markets erected throughout the length and breadth of the land. They saw aids to navigation constructed, buoys set out and lighthouses built, rivers dredged and wharves constructed; telegraphs and telephones extended, systematized, and organized; artesian wells by the hundreds rapidly being made available in the most populous centers, bringing health and strength to the people who had before become diseased and fever-ridden from drinking polluted waters; and finally they knew a comprehensive system of irrigation was being studied and the first beginnings of construction undertaken.

Through all this period it is not to be assumed that the path of American administrators in the Islands had been an easy one. It was beset with difficulties. The overworked members of the Commission one by one fell sick. In the United States the leaders of the Democratic Party did not let this great altruistic experiment remain outside the domain of politics. Misled in part by the campaign of misrepresentation conducted by the Anti-Imperialist League in Boston, they seized upon a few authentic instances of maladministration or errors committed by the sorely pressed American Commissioners, and, especially at the time of the presidential campaign, launched on the floor of Congress, from the platforms of public speakers, and in the press, extremely unjust denunciations of the work being done on behalf of humanity and civilization by their fellow-countrymen in the Orient.

For example, the Honorable Alton B. Parker, Democratic candidate for President of the United States running against President Theodore Roosevelt, erred in making virulent charges against the American Philippine government, in the course of which he quoted a "student of conditions" in the Islands as follows:

Of the character of many in office too little cannot be said. At the best they have been inefficient, at the worst dishonest, corrupt and despotic. The Islands seem to have succeeded in getting the very dregs of our people.

This description of men like Taft, Wright, Wood, Bliss, Pershing, and Harbord provoked from Governor-General Wright, himself a Democrat, a devastatingly complete answer which ended:

All these statements are the veriest nonsense without a scintilla of fact to support them. . . . Judge Parker has evidently been grossly deceived.

President Roosevelt remarked to a visitor that Wright's answer had been worth a million votes to him.

In compliance with President McKinley's instructions to give autonomy in the cities and rural communities, the earlier organizations set up by Americans were those of the municipalities. A municipality comprises not only one city or other principal center of population, but also whatever villages, hamlets, and scattered habitations occur within a given geographical district corresponding in area to a township or even a county in the United States. These municipalities are divided into districts, in charge of each of which is a member of the municipal council. These districts in turn are subdivided into *barrios*, in charge of each of which is a lieutenant, or *teniente*. He is in a way the successor of the *cabeza de barangay*, whom the Spanish system had taken over from the organization found on their occupation of the Islands. This local chief or headman is the first point of contact of the people with the government and it is to him they appeal in case of emergency as to public order, or, if they wish, in any other matter.

Already, even in the days of insurrection while military operations were in full swing, a start had been made in organizing municipal governments.

In August, 1899, the Military Governor promulgated in general orders a plan of municipal organization. Under this plan the military authorities organized municipal government in the towns along the railway northward from Manila and in the vicinity of Manila in the provinces of Cavite and Laguna, and, as fast as military stations were established, throughout the provinces.

In January, 1900, the Military Governor appointed a board comprising Chief Justice Arellano of the Philippine Supreme Court as chairman, and Attorney-General Torres and three American officers as members, to formulate a plan of municipal government which should be "as liberal in character as existing conditions permit." The plan recommended was promulgated by the Military Governor in March, and all municipalities occupied as military stations and others, aggregating perhaps two-fifths of the total number of organized local governments under the Spanish régime, were reorganized under this plan, which placed the administration of local government in the hands of elective officials.

In January, 1901, the Commission passed the Municipal Code, which served as a charter or general organic act for all local governments in the Philippine Islands except those regions inhabited chiefly by tribal peoples and Mohammedans, and the cities of Manila and Baguio, for which special charters were provided.

Under the Municipal Code, the chief executive officer, termed "municipal president," and the members of the municipal council, or legislative branch of government, were elected by popular vote. Office-holders have been limited to Filipinos and American citizens.

The Code defined the powers of the municipal council and of its president, similar in many respects to those exercised by town and city governments in the United States, and vested power to remove municipal officials at first in the Commission and later in the Governor-General.

Provision was made for municipal revenues, and the collection of these and preparation of municipal budgets were left in the hands of the municipal authorities. Subsequently, however, it became necessary to provide for the intervention and approval of the provincial authorities.

All municipal ordinances were subject to review by provincial boards, out there was a right of appeal to the Governor-General. The executive bureau called the attention of the proper officers to those ordinances which were contrary to law or beyond municipal jurisdiction. It was found that the municipalities, left to their own discretion, would almost immediately establish a salary list that would take up the whole of the revenues of the city, leaving nothing for public works and little for the purchase of supplies and material. It eventually became necessary to fix by law a percentage of revenues which could not be exceeded for salaries and wages in each class of municipality. Through the provincial boards the Executive Bureau investigated complaints against municipal officers and justices of the peace, and the officers complained of were given hearings, and suitable disciplinary action taken toward the guilty. The necessity for this work is well shown by the fact that during the years 1903 to 1913 no less than 2315 cases were tried, and in 1490 cases penalties inflicted ranging from reprimands through fines and suspensions to actual dismissal from service and disqualification from holding public office. This supervision prevented much undue infringement of personal liberties, as the municipal council not infrequently undertook to regulate matters of personal behavior in a manner not consonant with American ideas of freedom of the individual.

The municipalities varied in number, as they were from time to time annexed to each other or subdivided, during the first twenty-five years of American administration.

The municipal presidents who undertook the civil organization of their towns while lawlessness still prevailed often sacrificed life or property, and occasionally showed a fine spirit of service and sacrifice. At the little town of San Francisco in the small group known as the Camote Islands, near Cebu, the president and other officials voluntarily donated their salaries to the construction of a gravity water system, and labored with their own hands towards this construction.

The municipal president of the town of Jaro in the province of Leyte, upon assuming office, found the municipal treasury, "the larder of the people," empty owing to the then low price of hemp and the effects of a previous typhoon. His people were facing hard times. Instead of taking the usual view that taxes were excessive, he reached the conclusion that they could be paid if the people were shown how to plant to advantage and to work intelligently. Feeling that it was his duty to act as their counselor and to treat them in a kindly, paternal way, he spent most of his time going from farm to farm throughout the municipality,

which was largely agricultural, returning to his office but once a week
He instituted public meetings, had all the work animals listed, explained to the people that there must be a plow for every work animal,
brought about the passage of vagrancy ordinances, applied the gambling
laws to discourage idleness, and formed his people into plowing groups
He encouraged them to plant corn so that there would be an abundance
of food in case the hemp crop failed, and soon had everybody method-
ically plowing and planting. The result was amazing. His people had
provisions, fared better than before, were better satisfied, paid their taxes
more readily, and found that even so the burden was less than it had
been before. In addition, he macadamized the public roads, put in permanent concrete culverts over all waterways and at street crossings,
obtained money enough to build a new school, and a market partly of
concrete. This active president, by name Francisco Lastrilla, believed
in the gospel of work both for himself and others.

Under the Spanish rule Manila had had a special organization known
as an *ayuntamiento*, or "city corporation." After the surrender of the
city by the Spaniards, the American military authorities accepted the
existing organization as they found it, substituting selected Americans
for the supervisory positions and department chiefs. In June, 1901, General George W. Davis, Provost Marshal of Manila, concluded the preparation of a draft of a proposed charter for the city which was enacted
into law.

Under this charter the executive and legislative functions were vested
in a board consisting of the mayor as president, two members, and a
secretary, who had the supervision of the heads of departments of the
city government. In order to give Filipinos participation, the charter
provided an advisory board of eleven members, one representative for
each of the districts or wards into which the city was divided following
the subdivisions existing under Spanish administration. The government also adopted the practice of appointing a Filipino to the position
of president of the municipal board, or mayor, who retained the Spanish title of *alcalde*. City ordinances enacted by the municipal board were
subject to review by the Governor-General, under whose executive control the city government was placed.

The charter was revised by the Legislature in 1916, the mayor continuing to be an appointive officer but relieved from his duties as president of the municipal board. The board was reorganized to consist of
ten elective members and the advisory council discontinued.

The city of Baguio under its special charter had a mayor who was appointed by the Governor-General and a city council whose members were in part elected by popular vote and in part appointed by the Governor-General.

For purposes of coördination and supervision, municipal governments, except chartered cities, are grouped in provinces. President McKinley's instructions left the form in which the provincial governments were to be organized discretionary with the Commission. During the period of American military control, no formal provincial organization was attempted, but the supervision of local government was exercised by the nearest military station commander.

On February 6, 1901, the Commission enacted the Provincial Government Code, which provided for a provincial governor as chief executive of each province, to be elected by the councilors of the municipalities in the province, and a provincial board of three, with purely legislative functions, composed of the elected provincial governor and two appointed officers, the provincial treasurer and the provincial supervisor (engineer) in charge of public works. Provincial governors were responsible for the maintenance of public order in coöperation with the Constabulary. The provincial board had power to legislate for the province and had administrative supervision of municipal governments.

Following the passage of this code provincial governments were rapidly organized by the Commission, which visited the capitals of most of the provinces, appointed the first governors, and launched the new governments with appropriate ceremonies.

First elections for provincial governors were held in February, 1902, and the good judgment shown by the Commission in its first appointments was demonstrated by the fact that many of the appointees were elected by the voters. Among the provincial governors elected were three Americans, former officers in the army.

This organizaion endured till January, 1906, when the supervisor's place on the provincial board was taken by the appointive division superintendent of schools. He in turn gave way in the following November to an official, known as the "third member," elected by popular vote.

These changes gave the Filipinos political control of the provinces, and this concession was hailed with a great deal of satisfaction by the Filipino press and the Philippine public generally. They felt that

Americans meant their promise to grant increased autonomy to Filipinos by successive stages.

One of the duties of the provincial treasurer was to review the municipal budget and pass upon the estimate of receipts and the legality of the objects of expenditure as well as the amounts it was proposed to spend. Provincial budgets were subject to review by the Executive Bureau. The results were eminently satisfactory and served to train a large number of Filipinos in good government and in up-to-date financial procedure.

As in the case of municipalities, the Executive Bureau at Manila also maintained a careful supervision over the administration of the provinces and watched all the legislative and executive acts of the officials. Provincial governors approached the central government through this bureau, and under the wise and sympathetic direction of the two successive Executive Secretaries, Arthur W. Fergusson and Frank W. Carpenter, provincial officials realized that they had not a master but a friend at court when they brought their problems to Manila.

The experience gained in administering provincial governments proved helpful to the Filipinos who later reached high public office. Some of the provincial governors were very able men. The Honorable Sergio Osmeña, later for fifteen years Speaker of the Philippine Assembly, completely cleared his province, Cebu, of the organized bands of fanatical outlaws which had infested it.

On the destruction by fire of a portion of the city of Cebu, Señor Osmeña, not yet governor, but provincial attorney, laid out the area with new and wider streets adapted to the commercial requirements which he had the vision to foresee, and adopted the most modern requirements for fireproof construction. The delicate matters of settlements of property rights, exchanges of land, and assessments for betterments were adjusted with masterly skill. Señor Osmeña himself set an example by ceding to the city for street-widening his rights to valuable city property — a fine example of unselfish, constructive statesmanship.

Governor Manuel Quezon of Tayabas, who achieved distinction as floor leader in the Philippine Assembly, Resident Commissioner, and President of the Philippine Senate, was later first President of the Philippine Islands Commonwealth. He also assumed the initiative and used his official position beyond the legal powers of a provincial governor in requiring citizens to improve their own property by planting great areas of coconut and hemp. This extra-legal performance resulted in much greater prosperity in that region.

Many instances might be cited of provincial governors who sacrificed personal convenience and interests and showed great energy in carrying on the work of their provinces. Governor Bernardino Monreal, of the province of Sorsogon, was a conspicuous example of this sort.

There were also instances of misconduct on the part of provincial governors, chiefly as to the use of public funds and property. But in one instance only was the offense sufficiently grave as to seem to require removal from office and prosecution in the courts.

The Provincial Code contained a provision that an elected governor might not take office until his election had been confirmed by the Governor-General. The Governor-General could decline to confirm on the ground of unfairness in the election, ineligibility, or disloyalty. For eight years no man was elected to the office of provincial governor concerning whose loyalty there seemed serious question. Later, several provincial governors were elected whose antecedent record or campaign pronouncements raised serious doubt as to the sincerity of their allegiance to American sovereignty. In such instances a signed resignation with the date blank was required of the governor-elect. This given, he was confirmed by the Governor-General, but in each case he knew that the least evidence of disloyalty would result in the acceptance of his resignation. One of the important provinces on one occasion returned the election as governor of a former insurgent general, who, during the insurrection, was reputed to have permitted notorious atrocities. Once in office, however, he gave no reason for suspicion as to his loyalty and was fairly efficient during his period of service.

The system of privilege which the Americans found and set out to break up was well manifested in the community life in the municipalities and provinces. So many devices were employed by the unscrupulous and grasping *cacique* to mulct the poor man of his profits that there was little chance for a man, even of more frugality and diligence than the average, to save anything and better his condition.

American officials, insular and local, by precept and example taught the principle, new to the Filipino, that a public office was a public trust, that a government officer was to labor for the welfare of his community, and that the public revenues were to be used for the public benefit and for no other purpose. These Americans lived honorable and upright lives among the Filipinos in the provinces, accounting for every dollar of government property they handled, and instilled the American spirit of service throughout the municipal and provincial governments.

After centuries of different practice, where the appointed officials systematically enriched themselves and rendered little service in return for their pay, it was not surprising that, wherever supervision was relaxed, the old order reappeared. Nearly sixty-five per cent of the complaints against local officers required punitive action, and without supervision many times that number of cases would have undoubtedly occurred.

Three Filipino members were added to the Commission on September 1, 1901, the anniversary of its first legislative session. Up to that time the Commission had sat almost continuously in session and had to its credit an immense amount of legislative achievement. In that period, although much time had been devoted to public hearings, it had passed two hundred and fifteen laws. But it had lacked the intimate touch with Filipino sentiment which could only be obtained by having representative Filipinos joining in deliberation and expressing themselves by argument and by vote. The three Filipinos selected for the Commission were: the Honorable Trinidad H. Pardo de Tavera, a distinguished and scholarly gentleman of largely Spanish blood; the Honorable Benito Legarda, who had large and important tobacco and distillery interests in Manila; and the Honorable José de Luzuriaga, a distinguished and cultivated landowner from the island of Negros, representing the Visayans, the second most important group in the archipelago.

The Honorable Bernard Moses resigned after a brief period of service and returned to the United States, his place being taken on January 1, 1903, by the Honorable James F. Smith, also of California, who had been a practicing attorney in San Francisco and had been elected Colonel of the First California Volunteers. He had served with distinction in the army during the insurrection, had received the rank of brigadier-general and had been made civil governor of the island of Negros, the only important region which did not join the insurrection against the United States. He later was called to Manila as Collector of Customs, and then appointed a member of the Philippine Supreme Court. A Roman Catholic in religion, he was a gentleman with the strictest sense of honor, always more than scrupulous of his duties and responsibilities in the public service.

In November, 1903, Governor Taft relinquished his post as Civil Governor and returned to the United States to take the position of Secretary of War, Vice-Governor Wright becoming Civil Governor and Commissioner Ide, Vice-Governor. The vacancy on the Commission was filled by the appointment, in February, 1904, of W. Cameron Forbes, of Boston, to be Secretary of Commerce and Police.

By act of Congress the title of the chief executive of the Islands was changed from Civil Governor to Governor-General, and Governor Wright thus became the first Governor-General of the Islands. The title of Governor-General usually connotes one who has other governors under him, and, as there were between fifty and sixty provincial governors and lieutenant or district governors in the Islands, the name chosen was technically correct.

In November, 1905, Governor-General Wright returned to the United States, and in February, 1906, he was appointed first American Ambassador to Japan. This followed a protest made by influential Filipinos interested in distilleries and tobacco factories, against a revision by the Commission of the internal revenue law by which increased taxation was imposed on alcoholic liquors and manufactured tobacco. The opposition of these interests to the measure became bitter, and, in fact, a cabal was formed against the Governor-General, who as president of the Commission strongly supported the new law as a just and necessary measure. After rendering a decision entirely upholding the action of the Commission in imposing increased taxes, Washington made what seemed the grievous mistake of relieving Governor-General Wright, thus giving the Filipinos concerned in the cabal what they felt to be a victory. Although they had lost in the matter of the tax, they had secured the removal of the American chief executive responsible for its imposition. Thoughtful Americans felt that this was likely to result in similar attacks on future Governors-General as well as other high officials, as the success of one such campaign of unjust vilification was quite sure to encourage the local politicians to undertake others. The names of the Honorables Henry C. Ide and James F. Smith were sent to the Senate to be Governor-General — Vice-Governor Ide until the first of April and until his successor, Commissioner Smith, should qualify. The latter returned to the United States for a needed leave of absence and did not return to take up his duties as Governor-General until September 20 of that year.

On October 16, 1907, the first Philippine Assembly came into being and the Commission ceased to be the sole legislative body and became the upper house.

Further changes in the personnel of the Commission after 1913 are dealt with in a later chapter entitled "Later Régimes."

Widely divided as were the members of the Commission in race, traditions, language, religion, and views on public questions, their desire for coöperation made this heterogeneous group of men an extremely efficient legislative body. One member of the Commission during the Taft régime remembers only about three instances in a decade of legislative sittings when the Commission was divided on racial lines. Almost always on debated questions Americans and Filipinos were to be found on both sides. The decisions of the majority were usually accepted without bitterness, and, while debate sometimes rose to the point of heat, no ill-feeling resulted. Nine out of ten votes were unanimous. The sessions were usually conducted in two languages. If the discussion was in English, an interpreter sat beside the Filipino member who understood English least well and translated the debate as it progressed. Later, as the Americans became more familiar with Spanish, a very large part of the proceedings, including the debates, was carried on in Spanish. No instance is recorded of a vote later being repudiated or protested because of failure by one of the Commissioners to understand the issue on linguistic grounds.

The Commission was a group of honest, non-partisan, hard-working men, all imbued with a desire to serve the best interests of the Filipinos, without any selfish consideration, and no instance arose during that period in which any one of them could have been even remotely suspected of having used his public position for private gain. They spent many hours a day on legislation, and during the period preceding the creation of the Assembly (September 1, 1900, to October 16, 1907), when the Commission bore the entire legislative responsibility, they passed a total of eighteen hundred acts. This work, involving long public hearings and intensive study, included organic legislation necessary to set up the structure of government in its various branches, modification of existing Spanish laws to conform with American principles of justice, the careful enactment of customs tariff and other revenue legislation, and a well-considered programme for the organization of public schools, for the establishment of public order and public health, and for economic development.

Although the American forces operating in the field had never exceeded 70,000 men, expiration of the term of service, replacements, and other causes made the total number of Americans brought to the Islands in the course of the insurrection as high as 120,000. Among these there were many who were glad to leave the army and throw in their lot with the Philippine government service.

The usual complement of sutlers, hangers-on, and adventurers, and a fair sprinkling of the flotsam and jetsam of America and Europe, always are to be found wherever the elements of disorder prevail. Many of these were white men of a very low order, and did not tend to enhance the respect in which Americans were held either by the Filipinos or by foreigners doing business in the Islands. The least respectable degenerated into vagabondage, and, in the parlance of white men in the Orient, were commonly spoken of as beachcombers.

On the other hand, among the available Americans there was a large number of admirable men who were eager to enter the government service and who would have done credit to any government anywhere. The difficulty was to select the good material from the bad, and then to train it for the work in hand, for many of these positions required the services of highly specialized assistants, and, except for the doctors and army engineers, most of the Americans who came out had had no experience in the kind of service to which they were to be called in civil administration. Particularly was this the case in matters relating to the business of government. A good many years were to elapse before the United States could claim to have trained a force of highly efficient public servants. That time, however, came.

Conspicuous figures of those early days were the Fergusson brothers, Arthur and Rupert, brought up in California, Mexico, and South America, where their father served for many years in the American diplomatic corps. Arthur W. Fergusson, who held the position of Executive Secretary, had a fluent and exquisite command of both Spanish and English, great oratorical power in both languages, and such genius in their use that he was constantly being called upon to act as official interpreter. It was amazing to hear the stilted and awkward addresses of inexperienced, partially tongue-tied speakers transformed by the magic of Fergusson's eloquence into fluent Spanish, the resonant tones, rolling periods, and beautiful imagery of which he alone could impart to ideas uttered in halting English. The marvelous part of his achievement was that his interpretation was always absolutely true. He never changed the essential meaning intended. He died in the fullness of his power and usefulness and was so highly thought of that a monument has been erected and a plaza named in his honor in an important and distinguished part of Manila.

Another conspicuous name is that of Frank W. Carpenter, who came to the Islands with General Lawton, became private secretary to the Military Governor, and after the organization of civil government was appointed Assistant Executive Secretary. He became proficient in the use of Spanish, spoke Tagálog fluently, and so won the hearts of all Filipinos with whom he came in contact that he became an invaluable interpreter of private sentiments and of the trend of public opinion among the Filipinos. Into his willing and confiding ear were poured the grievances, personal bitternesses, hopes, fears, and confidences of the hosts of provincial officials who were constantly visiting Manila. They were often too much in awe of the Governor-General and the Commissioners to speak freely to them, but, when they had something deep in their hearts that they wanted to pour out, Frank Carpenter became the spokesman and champion. He succeeded Arthur Fergusson as Executive Secretary, and, still later, in December, 1913, succeeded General Pershing as Governor of the Moro Province. In all these posts he did great service.

The list of able and competent men who served the government is too long to give in detail. Many men come to mind: Major James F. Case, an engineer who built the water and sewer works of the city of Manila and later became Director of Public Works; Warwick Greene, son of Major-General Greene, the first Governor of Manila, who, though trained as a lawyer, proved himself great as an engineer, and as Director of Public Works planned and carried through the scientific road-building programme that has become so great a feature of American success in the Islands; Dr. Victor G. Heiser, who, from the position of Director of Health, carried through a comprehensive health programme with pitiably small resources and during his incumbency decreased the Manila death-rate from 42.28 per thousand in 1903 to 24.66 in 1914, and practically eliminated from the Islands the scourges of smallpox, cholera, and bubonic plague; Captain Charles H. Sleeper, who organized the Bureau of Internal Revenue, served well in the administration of the city of Manila, and later did fine work as Director of Lands; Major-General Henry T. Allen, who organized and trained the Philippines Constabulary and with his successors, Generals Harry H. Bandholtz and James G. Harbord, put an end to banditry and maintained good order in the Islands for fifteen years; and Drs. Paul C. Freer and Richard P. Strong, who organized the Bureau of Science, Dr. Strong later winning world fame in a series of extraordinary medical achievements.

Among those who rendered great service and died in the Islands the names of Ellis Cromwell, a Southern gentleman, Collector of Internal Revenue, John C. Mehan, Superintendent of Transportation for the City of Manila, a loyal public servant and fine executive, and Frank R. White, Director of Education, come conspicuously to mind.

On Thanksgiving Day, 1906, one of the Commissioners wrote down among the things he was thankful for: "The men throughout the service are clean cut, able, industrious, and in earnest, and a set of men with whom it is an honor to serve."

In spite of the adverse circumstances under which the Americans entered the Philippine Islands, those who liked the climate and the service found a charm that was most appealing to them. There had been nothing in the experience of the Americans to equip those who came to the Islands to meet the dangers carried by the climate and they had to learn how to live in the tropics by dint of costly experience. This cost included the lives of many young men and the health of more, but little by little the medical department of the army and the health organization of the civil government learned to meet these difficulties, and life in the Philippine Islands became as healthy, judged by the mortality statistics, as the average life in the States.

It also took a little time for Americans to accustom themselves to living among alien people of a different color and race from those to which they had been accustomed, and to adapt themselves to these conditions. A certain percentage of Americans were so constituted that they never could find happiness in this association, but the great majority did adapt themselves to the new conditions and learned to like them, and to many Americans their tour of service in the Philippine Islands marks the happiest time in their lives. This applies not only to the administrators connected with the civil government and others in civil life, but also, to an important degree, to men who came out with the army, not only as officers, but enlisted men as well.

There was an immense amount of constructive work undertaken by the various members of the Commission in connection with the work of their departments. In the hurly-burly of throwing together civil government many bureaus were created, and their duties hastily defined. They began working without cohesion, without any definite relations being established as between bureaus, and with no clear definition of where the responsibilities of one bureau should end and those of the next begin. In April, 1905, Governor-General Wright appointed a committee, one Commissioner and three others selected from the insular bureaus and from the government of the City of Manila, to formulate a plan for the complete reorganization of the government, reassignment of bureaus in the departments with proper consideration of their inter-relationships, reassignment of duties as between bureaus, and reduction of expenses to the lowest possible limit. After seven months' intensive work, a bill embodying their recommendations was enacted into law, and the new order of things went into effect.

The Committee had found in each bureau a tendency to be a complete unit, with its own transportation, machine shops, drafting room, scientific staff, etc., the chiefs apparently being unwilling to trust any of their work to an agency not under their own direct control. The Reorganization Committee insisted upon having the best-equipped bureau for each class of service do that service for the whole government and charge for it, thus eliminating free service of all sorts except the work done by police and Constabulary in guarding, which was construed to be their first business and not to be charged for. In all other respects every bureau paid for all service rendered to it by other bureaus. Surprising economies resulted. For example, when the bureaus had free telegraphic service, the amount of telegraphing they thought necessary clogged the wires, cables, and personnel. As soon as they had to pay for it, the officials reduced their telegraphing sixty per cent. As government business had had precedence over commercial business, commerce sometimes had had to wait days to get clear lines. As soon as this new rule went into effect, it was found that the plant and staff were ample for the needs of the country and commerce could be handled as rapidly and expeditiously as was the government service.

Those bureaus having inspection work or branch offices in the provinces had always insisted it was necessary that a special boat should be maintained for their service, and bureau chiefs and their assistants did not feel it possible to take an inspection trip unless a boat was detailed for the purpose. It was surprising to find how differently these same men felt about having a ship when the cost of it was to be deducted from their own appropriations, and after this reform it was found the government could operate with five steamers less than before had been believed to be necessary.

In the course of the work of the Reorganization Committee some fundamental problems of government were discussed at great length. For instance, the Committee had at first favored placing in one department the Constabulary, Bureau of Justice, and the Bureau of Prisons, the first of which was charged with the maintenance of public order throughout the Islands, the detection of crime, and apprehension of criminals; the second with the supervision of the courts wherein persons charged with crime were tried and either convicted or acquitted; and the third, the Bureau of Prisons, with the punishment of the convicted. More mature thought, however, convinced the Committee that these three activities should pertain to different departments to avoid the possibility of persecution. If one person supervised the maintenance of public order, and, convinced of a man's criminality, brought him before the courts, it was just as well that the accused should be tried in a department under the supervision of somebody who had nothing to do with his arrest and therefore could have no preconceived notions as to whether or not he was guilty; and the punishment of a person once proved guilty should be left to a third department, the head of which was equally unbiased. The prisons were placed by the Reorganization Committee in the Department of Public Instruction to emphasize the educational character of their work.

The Committee reduced the number of bureaus from thirty-four to twenty-five and would have reduced it further but that laws of Congress made the maintenance of certain lesser bureaus imperative.

Another policy enunciated by the Committee which was put into effect was the abolition of all board organizations. Every governmental activity was to be managed by a single responsible head, who had as many assistants as conditions seemed to make necessary, but there was to be no division of ultimate responsibility. This was found to make for efficiency in the government service, and is a good rule for executive efficiency wherever applied.

Besides the increase in governmental efficiency, the savings effected by this reorganization were estimated to reach a million dollars a year, or about one tenth of the then annual cost of the government.

Other problems besides the reorganization of the machinery of government challenged the attention of secretaries of departments. The condition of the inter-island merchant marine was pitiable. The ships were old and ill-found; they gave execrable service, had unclean and scarcely habitable staterooms; and it was unsafe to drink the water or eat the food served on the ships on account of danger of infectious diseases. The boats ran on no regular schedules, charged exorbitant prices, and, whenever rumor got about that freight was waiting at some port, there would be a race for it between two or more steamers and the lucky boat would get the business and the others nothing. When only one steamer was on hand to take perishable freight, the captain of such a ship often declined to receive the freight on the pretense that he had no room for it. The despairing owner would sell his produce at a fraction of its value to the captain, who would then take it aboard, carry it off, and reap the harvest which should have been the producer's. Of course, this choked agriculture at its source. Planters were not going to put forth their energies only to be deprived of the fruits of their labor.

Action was taken to remedy these abuses and defects. On September 19, 1904, Governor Wright appointed a committee to look into inter-island transportation. One result of the work of this committee was to bring about the organization of the owners of ninety per cent of the ships engaged in coastwise trade from Manila, who grouped themselves together under the title of the "Asociacion de Navieros," and appointed a directorate. This gave the committee an agency with which to deal. A schedule of specifications was drawn up by the government under which inter-island ships should operate. Routes were planned covering the whole archipelago and giving each port periodic visits at stated intervals, arranged so that enough ships visited each place to care for its normal produce at the proper season. The government paid a subsidy to ships undertaking these routes and promising to live up to very rigid specifications in regard to cleanliness, quality of food and water, and life-saving and other devices, and agreed to give all of its business to these vessels and take off any government ships which had previously been running to these ports. The steamship companies were slow in taking advantage of the offer of these subsidies and it was a matter of pleasant surprise when it was found that the first corporation to agree to these terms was a Spanish one, which made its bid in the kindest spirit of coöperation with the American government. So immediately beneficial were its results from this action that other companies made haste to follow its example.

The contracts also provided that, in case any vessel refused to take a shipment of freight at any port, the owner of the freight could telegraph that fact to the next port of call of the vessel, whereupon a government inspector would ascertain whether or not that ship had been in fact too full safely to take on the refused freight. If the freight space had not all been taken, the captain of the ship was fined double the amount of

THE HONORABLE LUKE E. WRIGHT, GOVERNOR-GENERAL

THE HONORABLE WILLIAM H. TAFT

the freight charge. This effectively checked the practice of refusing freight in order to buy it.

Meanwhile the government utilized its own steamers, which would otherwise have been idle under the new arrangement, to make regular commercial trips to outlying points and ports where the volume of business had not been enough to justify commercial vessels undertaking it. The result was magical. Business increased by leaps and bounds, and before many months had passed practically all the routes undertaken by the government vessels were eagerly sought for by commercial companies willing to put on their own steamers and to agree to the government specifications, schedule, and supervision without other subsidy than the withdrawal by the government of its own boat from the route.

With the increase in agricultural production following the assurance of dependable transportation to the larger markets and the consequent good prices to producers and profits to the local dealers, freight and passenger business increased. The subsidies were gradually withdrawn, until in 1925 they appear to have been practically discontinued.

Except as modified from time to time by sundry laws, enacted first by the Commission and later by the Philippine Legislature, the structure of government remained practically unchanged until the passage by Congress in 1916 of the act known as the Jones Law, which then became in effect the constitution of the Philippine government. It seems appropriate to outline here the structure of the central or insular government as then put into effect and continued, without great modification, until the independence of the Commonwealth.

General legislative power was vested in a Legislature composed of two houses — a Senate and a House of Representatives. Members of both houses of the Legislature were elected by popular vote, except two senators and seven representatives who were appointed by the Governor-General to represent the districts populated chiefly by Mohammedans and tribal peoples.

Laws amendatory to the tariff or to laws with reference to immigration, currency and coinage, the public domain, timber and mining, did not become operative until approved by the President of the United States.

The veto power was vested in the Governor-General, who might veto any particular item or items of an appropriation bill. There was appeal by the Legislature over veto by the Governor-General to the President of the United States. All laws enacted by the Philippine Legislature were required to be reported to the Congress of the United States, which reserved the power and authority to annul them.

The supreme executive power was vested in the Governor-General. He was appointed by the President, with the advice and consent of the Senate of the United States, and held his office at the pleasure of the President and until his successor was chosen and qualified. He received a salary of $18,000 per annum, and official residences in Manila and Baguio.

The Governor-General had supervision and control of all departments and bureaus of the government; was commander-in-chief of all locally created armed forces and militia; had the power to grant pardons; appointed all officers in the executive branch of the insular government; was "responsible for the faithful execution of the laws of the Philippine Islands and of the United States operative within the Philippine Islands, and whenever it became necessary he could call upon the commanders of the military and naval forces of the United States in the Islands, or summon the posse comitatus, or call out the militia or other locally created armed forces, to prevent or suppress lawless violence, invasion, insurrection, or rebellion; and he could, in case of rebellion or invasion, or imminent danger thereof, when the public safety required it, suspend the privileges of the writ of habeas corpus, or place the Islands, or any part thereof, under martial law."

The Governor-General was required to submit at the "opening of each regular session of the Philippine Legislature a budget of receipts and expenditures, which would be the basis of the annual appropriation bill." He was also required to notify the President of the United States at once in the event of his placing the Islands or any part thereof under martial law, and the President had the power to modify or veto the action of the Governor-General. Also, he was required to report annually the transactions of the government of the Philippine Islands to the War Department, by which the report was transmitted to Congress.

In addition to the Governor-General, the President also appointed a Vice-Governor, who was the head of the Department of Public Instruction, which included the Bureaus of Education and of Health. The Vice-Governor could be assigned other executive duties by the Governor-General and in case of the temporary absence or disability of the latter, or if the office should be vacant, had the duties and powers of the Governor-General.

The President also appointed an auditor and deputy-auditor who had "authority as that conferred by law upon the several auditors of the United States and the Comptroller of the United States Treasury."

The judiciary comprised the Supreme Court, Courts of First Instance, and Courts of Justices of the Peace. The Chief Justice and eight Associate Justices of the Supreme Court were appointed by the President with the advice and consent of the Senate of the United States.

In general the Americans found the Filipinos were very far from understanding the fundamental principles of a democracy. Their training, their habit of mind, had been all toward absolutism. It was present in the home and in the small community, where the *cacique* held sway. Their tendency was to look upon the Governor-General as a person of almost supreme power, and Governors-General traveling in the Islands were constantly having brought home to them the general supposition that they were given absolute power. It was very hard to make people understand the limitations to the power of the Governor-General imposed by the necessity of submitting certain matters to the courts and others to determination by local authorities or other governmental agencies, such as the Legislature.

It may fairly be said that the inauguration of civil government, the kindly spirit shown by the Commission, their laborious devotion to the service of the Filipinos, and the results they achieved brought about an early friendship between Americans and Filipinos which, in spite of misunderstandings and a natural impatience shown by the Filipino in pursuit of further concessions of political power, has persisted.

CHAPTER V

PUBLIC ORDER

As the fires of the insurrection died down and the civil government began taking over the administration of the public services, including the restoration and maintenance of order, the work of the army became less and the activities of the police forces in the provinces under civil control took on greater importance.

The executive authority in all organized provinces had been transferred to the President of the Commission, William H. Taft, as Civil Governor on July 4, 1901. Major-General Adna R. Chaffee had relieved Major-General MacArthur as Commanding General and as Military Governor of territory not yet organized under provincial governments, and shortly after issued an order directing that the troops should abstain from any interference with the administration of civil affairs unless requested by the civil authorities through army headquarters.

The situation was one of much delicacy and required great tact to bring about the necessary coöperation between the officers of the army and the civil officials.

The declaration of peace by no means ended active operations of the army in the Islands. American troops from the beginning of organized civil government, until 1906, were engaged in field operations of a dangerous and exhausting character against guerrilla bands in Batangas and other provinces of Luzon, and against similar outlaws and religious fanatics on Bohol, Leyte, Samar, and other islands of the Visayas.

In Mindanao and the Sulu Archipelago there were more extensive and prolonged operations, first against guerrilla bands and fanatics in northern Mindanao, and subsequently against recalcitrant Moros in the Cotabato Valley and in the course of the subjugation of the Lake Lanao region in central Mindanao and of the Sulu Moros on the island of Jolo and adjacent islands. The campaigns were hard, and the casualties many. In these field operations many officers and men revealed ability of a high order which marked them for later military leadership. Most noted of these is General John J. Pershing, who was promoted from the grade of captain of cavalry to brigadier-general on September 20, 1906, in recognition of his brilliant and successful campaign against the Lake Lanao Moros, previously unsubdued. Little by little most of the scattered army posts were withdrawn, and the forces gathered near the more active centers of population where transportation facilities were better, ships more frequent, and the cost of maintenance less.

The army selected strategic points which were set aside as reservations for permanent garrisons. The island of Corregidor became an important fortified post commanding the entrance to Manila Bay, all private rights to buildings and lands were extinguished by purchase, and extensive improvements and barracks for housing a large force were situated on these hills, which rise to a height of over six hundred feet.

The United States also spent sums of money running into many millions of dollars in additional fortifications at the entrance of Manila Bay, a small island by the name of Caballo and another called Carabao having been fortified, as well as an islet little more than a rock, known as El Fraile, not far from the middle of the southern entrance to Manila Bay, which is nearly seven miles wide.

In the city of Manila the army retained the old Spanish citadel, Fort Santiago, as military headquarters, also a water front and a number of buildings and tracts of land for barracks, officers' quarters, hospital, and supply purposes.

An extensive tract south of the Pasig River three miles from Manila, reaching nearly to Laguna de Bay and situated in the province of Rizal, was purchased for a large post named Fort William McKinley.

Seventy miles to the north a beautiful reservation, ultimately increased to over one hundred thousand acres for maneuver purposes, was set aside for a cavalry post and named Camp Stotsenberg.

At Baguio, the summer capital, a lovely tract of land was set aside as a military reservation, and temporary barracks constructed for a garrison of not more than two hundred men, with dwellings for a few officers. Later this was extended. Additional cottages, and hospitals, and barracks of concrete have been added, and it was named Camp John Hay.

The commanding general of the military district of Mindanao was also the civil governor of the Moro Province, which comprised in addition to the greater part of Mindanao the islands to the southward, including the Sulu Archipelago. As the inhabitants in that region were more turbulent and obdurate in arms than in any other region, the number of troops in the Moro country was comparatively great.

On the withdrawal of garrisons, the army generously turned over to the civil authorities such buildings as were not salvaged for use at permanent posts, and land for public schools, hospitals, Constabulary barracks, and other civil purposes.

The restoration of order was marked by the rapid withdrawal of American troops from the Islands during 1902 and 1903, until by 1904 the force had been reduced to 12,723, by 1913 to 11,655, and by 1926 to 4946.

Until the year 1906 the assistance of the army was necessary in Luzon and the Visayas to suppress outlawry and destroy armed bands, most of which had existed in the mountains and swamp jungles as far back as the Spanish régime. In the Moro country the army was more or less actively engaged until late in 1913.

It is impossible to assess and hard to overestimate the stabilizing influence of the army. Who can say how much of the stability of the institutions established by America in the Orient is due to their presence! When the Boxer War broke out in China in 1900, the first American troops to reach the scene came from Manila, and it is not too much to say that America's part in the Boxer War was largely borne by troops and supplies drawn from the Philippine Islands.

No account of events in the Philippine Islands would be complete without mentioning the fine service rendered by the United States Navy and Marine Corps, the former coöperating by sea with the army, and the latter on a few occasions taking active part in operations against outlaw bands, notably in Samar. The navy also has patrolled the Sulu seas against Malay pirates and has assisted the army in some of its storming operations against hostile Moros at Jolo and elsewhere.

Naval stations are maintained in Manila Bay at Cavite and in Subig Bay at Olongapo, both on the west coast of Luzon.

While the navy has generally maintained its Asiatic fleet in Chinese waters, the Admiral commanding has kept in touch with the Philippine situation through the commandant of the Cavite and Olongapo naval stations and by occasional visits of the flagship. One or more vessels, at times a squadron, were usually stationed in Philippine waters, and the Asiatic fleet cruised to the Islands for target practice and remained there for several months each year.

The Philippine Scouts were organized under Congressional authorization as a part of the military establishment of the United States for use only in the Philippine Islands. The creation of this body was recommended not only by army officers familiar with operations in the Philippine Islands, but also by the Philippine Commission.

Major General George W. Davis, United States Army, commanding the Division of the Philippines, in his annual report for 1903, said of the Scouts:

Fifty companies of scouts were fully organized, and all of the officers were commissioned provisionally for four years, while the soldiers were all enlisted for three years. Three natives of the Philippine Islands were appointed second lieutenants. The aggregate strength of the scouts on October 1, 1902, officers and men, was 4935. · · ·

From the first day of their use as auxiliaries to the United States Army the Philippine Scouts have rendered distinguished services. Throughout their history, there have been numerous instances of heroism and fidelity, sometimes under conditions involving hardship and temptation to disloyalty. One of the most distinguished was their loyalty to General Funston on the occasion of his heroic capture of General Aguinaldo.

Upon their organization as part of the regular army the practice was adopted of placing detachments of Scouts in the outlying posts and withdrawing the American troops to the more central garrisons.

To assist in the maintenance of public order, the civil governor was authorized to request the transfer of the Scouts to civil direction, and this was done during the development of the Constabulary.

An interesting early, and perhaps the first, instance of Filipinos in action under American military leadership was that of the "regiment" of "Manila men" chiefly from ships' crews at Shanghai, organized and led by "General" Frederick Townsend Ward, of Massachusetts, in the defense of that city against Chinese rebels in 1860. This force of American, European, and Filipino adventurers carried on the defense of Shanghai for nearly two years and in coöperation with British and French troops drove back the rebels for a radius of thirty miles around the city.

During the World War many spirited Filipinos served in divisions organized in the United States.

Many Filipinos naturally sought service in the United States Navy, as they had previously in that of Spain. During the World War, 4785 Filipinos served in the navy, of whom fifty-six were killed. Many other Asiatics formerly in the navy were replaced by Filipinos, until in June, 1926, there were 4240 Filipinos in the United States naval service.

The United States made provision for the training of a limited number of Filipinos at West Point. Some of these have graduated and received commissions in the United States Army.

The Philippine Scouts in 1926 numbered about seven thousand and have been assimilated fully by various branches of the military service but they are not subject to service outside the Philippine Islands.

The Filipino soldier in the United States Army, taught to use and equipped with the same firearms as the American, in marksmanship has excelled in relative number of qualified sharpshooters. The Filipino higher noncommissioned officers are given the same opportunity of learning military science as are Americans of similar grades, and are potential commissioned officers for time of war. The Secretary of War as of June 30, 1925, reported there were 1055 Filipino enlisted men rated as specialists in various branches of the army service.

Competent observers believe that the almost uniform loyalty of the Filipinos in the United States Army is due in large measure to personal attachment to their American officers.

Native auxiliaries were used more and more by the American army in Mindanao and Sulu, as they had been in earlier years in Luzon and Visayas, until, during the period of General Pershing's command of military forces and governorship of the Moro Province, as that civil jurisdiction was termed, American troops were utilized only as reserves and in the technical services. They were ultimately wholly withdrawn from the Moro Province, and the last important engagement under military direction against hostile Moros, in 1913, at Bagsak on the island of Jolo, was fought chiefly by the Philippine Scouts, who acquitted themselves most creditably.

The harsh measures practiced by the old *Guardia Civil* even against law-abiding citizens had aroused such bitter antagonism against an insular police as to make it especially difficult for American administrators to devise a working plan for such an organization with which to maintain public order when the army relinquished that duty.

The Philippine Commission, following the general practice in the United States, created municipal police, at first under the military authorities, and later under municipal presidents upon the organization of municipal governments. In creating provincial governments, the Commission made the municipal police subject to the provincial governor for service anywhere in the province that the public interest might require, and made it the duty of the governor to call upon the chief executive of the insular government, or the military officer commanding the district within which the province came, for the assistance of the army to suppress disturbance of public order when beyond the power of the local police.

As had been the case in Spanish days, the municipal presidents regarded municipal police very largely as their personal servants and used them as messengers and for menial duties, such as waiting on table. And under these circumstances it was not to be expected that they would be an efficient force in the maintenance of public order.

The Philippines Constabulary was one of the greater of Luke E. Wright's many statesmanlike contributions to the success of American government in the Islands. He recognized the fact that the army had neither the will nor the organization to do police service, or take part in the maintenance of order and suppression of crime, that its job was to put down armed insurrection that had got beyond the control of the civil authorities. A few days after the transfer of executive authority to Governor Taft the Commission, with the approval of the Secretary of War, enacted the law creating an insular police force which became known as the Philippines Constabulary. This force is similar in some respects to the mounted police of the British northwest territories of America, and it is interesting to note that it was organized in advance of the creation of any state police in any state of the Union, with the exception of the Texas Rangers. This example has been since followed, and several states, including Pennsylvania, New York, and Massachusetts, now maintain such forces.

Of this action in creating an insular police force, the Commission reported to the Secretary of War on October 15, 1901, in part as follows:

. . . The general scheme . . . is to create an insular force of not exceeding one hundred and fifty men for each province, selected from the natives thereof, who may be mounted in whole or in part, and who are placed under the immediate command of one or more, not exceeding four, provincial inspectors. The whole body is placed under the control of a chief and four assistant chiefs of constabulary. . . . Full powers are given to properly arm, equip, maintain, and discipline the force, which is enlisted for two years, unless sooner discharged. They are declared to be peace officers, and it is made their especial duty to prevent and suppress brigandage, insurrection, unlawful assemblies, and breaches of the peace. For this purpose they are given authority to make arrests, but are required at the earliest possible moment to bring the prisoner before a magistrate for examination.

General Henry T. Allen, of the regular United States Army, was selected for the work of organization. Four army captains were chosen to assist him, two of whom were Harry H. Bandholtz and

James G. Harbord. For officers General Allen selected Americans who had had some military training, some of whom had been volunteer officers, and a still larger number of whom were chosen from the non-commissioned ranks of the United States Army. Selected graduates of military schools in the United States were appointed junior officers, as also were Filipinos of proved loyalty and courage.

For administrative purposes the Archipelago was "divided into five districts each under charge of an Assistant Chief." These officials had "large freedom of action and were responsible for the condition of their districts as to law and order and for the administration of the force under them."

The enlisted men were taken from the province in which they served. Men so selected are more intimately acquainted with local conditions, and are more amenable to local public opinion and therefore less liable to commit abuses. . . .

. . . the following table is interesting and covers the four years up to the end of June of the present year [1905]:

Ladrones and insurrectos captured and surrendered	9155
Ladrones and insurrectos killed	2504
Arms secured	4288
Stolen animals recovered	5805

During the same period the Constabulary has lost in killed and wounded twenty-two officers and two hundred and ninety-five men. (From an article by Colonel W. C. Rivers, in the *Cablenews*, August 9, 1905.)

There was no intermediary force between the Constabulary and the municipal police, although provincial officials from time to time advocated a provincial police. The relation between the senior inspector of Constabulary and the provincial governor was a delicate one. While not under his direction, as the Constabulary officer had to take his orders from his own commanding officer — namely, the district chief — it was necessary to coöperate with the provincial governor and do nothing which would in any way lessen his dignity.

The Constabulary band, authorized by the Commission in 1903, won popularity with the Filipinos, who are fond of music and remarkably proficient in it. To organize and train the band the services of William H. Loving were secured, an American negro of exceptional musical talent and later given the rank of major. Major Loving and his band gave frequent concerts in Manila on public occasions and regularly on the Luneta, the principal park in Manila, where the crowds congregate in the evening to meet and enjoy the music. This band made several foreign tours, including an extensive one in the United States, and earned the highest encomiums by the excellence of its performances. At some of the world expositions, it won an enviable position in competition with some of the most noted bands in the United States.

The service of communication, including the telegraph and telephone, is one of the important agencies in the maintenance of public order and in prompt dealing with the movement of outlaws. For this purpose, the Commission, in September, 1902, authorized the organization of a telegraph division with personnel and equipment to take over and extend military telegraph and telephone lines.

There were then about eight thousand miles of telegraph and telephone land and submarine lines being operated by the army. Equipment and other material, and even personnel were generously transferred by the army to the Constabulary as rapidly as circumstances warranted. Great difficulty was experienced in securing operators. Filipino operators under the Spanish régime had used tape-recording instruments and their inability to handle messages in English was a great handicap. Moreover, it was necessary to be absolutely sure of the loyalty and disinterestedness of the operatives. American army signal corps operators were not all eager to leave the military service for prolonged residence in the Islands, and telegraph operators could not be secured from the United States except at comparatively high salaries. With the coöperation of the army, the situation was met and the service maintained. Schools for training Filipino operators were established at Manila and various important stations in the provinces. The schools were largely attended and within a year eighteen Filipinos had completed the course in telegraphy and English, enabling them to begin work as operators. From that time on competent Filipino operators became available in increasing numbers.

As an emergency measure the Constabulary was fully justified in taking over and managing the telegraph and telephone lines, but the time soon came when the emergency had passed and these services could be transferred to the Bureau of Posts, in which they properly belonged. This was done January 1, 1906. In most of the municipalities the same officer or officers could serve as postmaster and telegraph operator. There was marked economy and great convenience in this arrangement.

The lessened use by the police and other government agencies of the telegraph and telephone facilities resulted in a more adequate and better service for civil, personal, and commercial use.

The Chief of Constabulary had been given early certain powers of inspection and intervention in municipal police affairs. Later, to increase the efficiency of the municipal police, the Legislature enacted a law providing for their reorganization, management, and inspection by the Director of Constabulary under the general supervision of the Secretary of Commerce and Police.

This measure raised the standard of local chiefs of police, and reduced the influence of local politics in the service.

The Constabulary was charged with the regulation of the use of firearms. During the disorders following the insurrection, it was important to scrutinize the licensing of arms and to keep a record of the persons who held them. Landowners had to be in position to defend themselves, not only against outlaws, but against the depredations of wild animals, and at the same time it was vital that their firearms should not find their way into the possession of unauthorized persons or outlaws. The Constabulary were by law also required to keep a record of identification of all firearms distributed to provincial and municipal governments. Later the Chief of Constabulary had the duty of granting permits. Unauthorized possession of firearms was penalized by fine and imprisonment. By unremitting labor on the part of the Constabulary, most of the unauthorized serviceable firearms were brought in.

The Constabulary medical service was established at a time when there was a general lack of medical and surgical facilities in most of the provinces. Emergencies had been met in part by the army medical establishment, but upon the withdrawal of the army garrisons and the assumption by the Constabulary of their duties, the medical arm of the Constabulary service became more and more important to Americans stationed beyond reach of the larger centers of population. Small hospitals were provided at a few base points, and emergency hospital provision made at every Constabulary post.

In the care of the personnel of the Constabulary and in giving relief to sick and wounded prisoners, and to the general public in regions where the Constabulary doctor was the only person trained in modern medicine the Constabulary medical work was invaluable.

The Constabulary also was the reliance of the Bureau of Health for quarantine guards and assistance in combating epidemic diseases, especially cholera. It was also employed in the enforcement of measures by the Bureau of Agriculture in quarantines against anthrax, foot-and-mouth disease, glanders, rinderpest, and surra among domestic animals.

In short, the Constabulary at one time or another rendered service to practically every branch of government.

The tribal peoples in northern Luzon proved themselves excellent as enlisted men. It was found desirable to utilize in each region as insular police men who could speak the local dialect. In carrying out this policy, Bontocs, Ifugaos, and Kalingas were enrolled in the Constabulary. They quickly adapted themselves to the service and their loyalty, endurance, and marksmanship were remarkable.

In the Moro Province, under the control of the United States Army, the Constabulary was not organized until the latter part of 1903, when Colonel James G. Harbord undertook this duty. Colonel Harbord reported his results in 1904 as follows:

. . . Enlistments in the districts organized have been principally of Mohammedans and pagans. The illiteracy of these has made it necessary to secure a few Christians in each district, and in Zamboanga the Moslem and Christian have been enlisted in about equal proportions. For a time it was supposed that the well-known dislike of the Moro to eat with the Filipino, a feeling which is reciprocated with interest, was unconquerable, but the experience of eight months shows that Moslem, pagan, and Christian amalgamate with but little friction. Separate messes have been abolished. Tribal lines are disappearing, the loyalty to his new corps and white officers replacing the allegiance paid by the Moro to his hereditary dato for many ages. The objection of the Islam to a hat with a brim was met by the authority of the chief of constabulary for the use in the Moro Province of a red fez with black tassel. The Moro is proud to wear that, and the result is a very smart and attractive uniform.

General Tasker H. Bliss, who succeeded General Wood as governor of the Moro Province, and had abundant opportunity to observe the Constabulary, commended the organization as an auxiliary of the army and in its other varied duties.

The Constabulary continued to form its companies of mixed Christians and Mohammedans, and it is difficult to distinguish the average Christian Filipino from the Mohammedan soldier or Constabulary officer. The men of the Moro Constabulary soon distinguished themselves by gallantry in field operations against outlaws, and notably in leading the attack by American troops on Sulu outlaws in the fiercely contested battle at Bud Dajo in 1906.

Sometimes, in the regions occupied by tribal peoples where a very simple form of government was necessary, Constabulary officers were appointed governors of districts.

Official reports rarely portray the great constructive work, the thrilling experiences, and sacrifices of the men who gave the best years of their lives to this pioneer work. The roll of honor is a long one. In the

Moro Province, as the Constabulary gradually took over more civil duties, Constabulary officers were appointed secretaries of districts under army officers as governors, and replaced the latter in Lanao and Sulu on the passing of the Moro Province entirely to civil control in the latter part of 1913. Besides serving as governors these officers were also designated *ex officio* justices of the peace. This, while adding to their power, also added greatly to their burdens. In practice it worked well, and the officers, both American and Filipino, with rare exceptions displayed strength of character and a high sense of justice.

At first the army did not look with favor on this semi-military body under military direction, and with many military features in its organization and designations. Their attitude toward it varied from scoffing to resentment, particularly when a large number of Scout companies were detailed from the army to augment the commands of the Constabulary officers.

The path of the Constabulary officers was beset with pitfalls and difficulties. Filipinos were adept in the art of making counter-charges, and, if any young officer took action against a prominent Filipino, it not infrequently occurred that counter-charges were filed against him for shortcomings on his part, real or fancied. It behooved all young Constabulary officers to watch their steps very carefully in the performance of their difficult duties.

To raise the standard of officers and to assure their more thorough preparation before being assigned to duty, a Constabulary school for officers was established in Manila, and later moved to Baguio as soon as a site there was made available. Here all young men who had passed the necessary preliminary tests and had come to receive commissions in the Constabulary were required to take a course of special training under the direction of an experienced Constabulary officer before they were sent out to do responsible field work.

Little by little the Constabulary won its way into the confidence and esteem of the people of the Islands and early criticism gave place to general approval and applause.

In an address at the Lake Mohonk Conference, Colonel Rivers said of the Constabulary:

. . . Drunkenness and serious misconduct among the soldiers are rare. Smart in appearance and proud of his uniform and corps the Filipino makes a good soldier; he is susceptible through hard work and patience on the part of his instructors to thorough training in drill, discipline, and musketry and when so trained and well led by officers he respects and likes, he can be relied on to give an excellent account of himself. Sensitive to a degree to harsh words or conduct that cause him to be humiliated and lose prestige or face before his comrades, the Filipino should be dealt with patiently and justly. The men of the wild hill tribes, as is natural, make the best shots and sentries. The loyalty of all tends rather toward personal devotion to the officer who trains and commands them than attachment to the government that pays them. Once they know and understand an officer who, no matter how strict he may be, is just and sympathetic, their distress over a change is real, and they are liable to influence the community to send to Manila numerous pleas and protests.

. . . .

An oriental with an admixture of Latin blood in many cases, it is natural that the Filipino should have well marked temperamental peculiarities, yet it is not easy to see the great difference or gulf that some think so completely separates the East from the West. Certainly the inhabitant of the Philippines appears to be moved by much the same hopes and aspirations, the same fears and passions, as ourselves, and he is liable to respond to the same justice, kind treatment and sympathy that would win and interest one of us.

The story of the Constabulary is one of heroism, endurance, and loyalty to ideals under great difficulties, of which the American people should be very proud. The officers set painstakingly to work to learn one or more of the native dialects, and the best of them became the eyes of the government. Through their own enlisted men, whose confidence and affection they soon won, they learned what was going on among the people, and it was through their activities that the time soon came when good order prevailed throughout the archipelago.

The work of those officers often interfered with practices which local magnates had come to regard as perquisites of high place. These officers often found themselves in an extremely delicate position, beset with temptations and opportunities for abuses. In view of the number of young Americans brought out, the extent of their powers, and the widely scattered regions in which they operated, it was not surprising that abuses of various sorts occurred; the remarkable thing was that these were so few.

The Constabulary officer, speaking the local dialect, socially prominent in his province, and liked and respected by his men, was peculiarly in a position to feel the popular pulse. No secret organization was started in the Islands but one or more agents of the Constabulary enrolled among its members, and all its movements, views, and the persons concerned in the movement, whether its objects were lawful or not, were known to the authorities.

On one occasion, when General Harbord was acting chief, an organization which had been working for months planned an insurrection. The night before the outbreak was to occur, six Filipinos were invited to assemble in General Harbord's office, where they found six chairs placed in a row and upon which they were told to sit. He then informed them that an insurrection was planned to break out at ten-thirty the following morning, and that it would be the duty of the Constabulary to put it down; that there would be some loss of life attached to the process, and that probably a good many innocent lives would be lost because the real culprits in these movements usually acted under cover. He informed them that in this case, however, the real instigators of the insurrection were known to the police, and that they would be the first men shot. With this information he opened the door and told them they could go out and start their insurrection if they wished. Six badly frightened conspirators spent the next ten and a half hours in suppressing a movement they had spent as many months in fomenting. No blood was spilt, no arrests made, no harm ensued.

The secret service agents of the Constabulary frequently reported that some insurrectionary movements were in progress. All such reports had to be taken with a grain of salt. Many of these reports, for example, indicated that the friendly neighboring country of Japan was conspiring with Filipino agitators to foment insurrection, landing arms to equip the insurrectionary forces, and giving promise of actual intervention in favor of the Filipinos in case insurrection should break out. There was no evidence that the government of Japan gave any sanction to such movements, and the Governor-General in Manila and the Constabulary officers who advised him were convinced that these stories were all fabrications on the part of clever conspirators, who collected money from a credulous people desirous of an independence which they hoped to get and which they were led to believe could be obtained from these contributions. That these collections went into the pockets of the conspirators and were used for their personal needs goes almost without saying.

The romance of the work of the Constabulary can be told no better than in the words of one of the more conspicuous of its officers, Lieutenant-Colonel White:

. . . Bands of robbers [writes Colonel White] infested the jungles on the mountain sides and the sparsely cultivated lands outside town limits. Their rapid and rapacious raids spared none. A trail of blood and fire showed where they had

TYPICAL PHILIPPINE VILLAGE HOUSE

PHILIPPINE VILLAGE SCENE

passed. In different islands they went by different names: Ladrones, tulisanes, pulajanes, diosdioses or babaylanes. They are the counterparts of the dacoits of Burmah, India and the Malay States. Indeed banditry in some form or other has been for centuries a recognized, and almost tolerated, institution in Far Eastern countries and particularly in the Malayan possessions of European Powers. In the Philippines during the whole period of Spanish rule the "tulisanes" made travel unsafe even in the provinces nearest to the capital. Indeed Cavite Province was known as the "madre de tulisanes" (the mother of bandits). Today banditry is practically extinct throughout the islands.

Lieutenant D. H. Malone, commanding a station in the northern part of Mindanao, reported officially in 1913 a very extraordinary series of events leading up to the capture of the outlaw Taoidi in the province of Agusan. He told of the months of incessant campaigning in constant pursuit of the outlaws until they and their friends were worn out. The men were not given a chance to plant their crops, and the people who were called upon to guide the Constabulary, to assist in carrying supplies, and for other services, became very weary of it all. At length, certain of the leading men in the vicinity agreed to persuade the bandits to come in and surrender if this patrolling should cease, and, with the consent of the superior officers of the Constabulary, this was done. True to their promise these men brought about the surrender of Taoidi, who gave as his reason for surrendering that the soldiers had pursued him so closely during the last six months that he could not make any plantings and his people were about to starve.

The two organizations, Scouts and Constabulary, were kept very busy until 1906 by the irreconcilable elements of the various Filipino armies that had taken to the woods and continued their operations as guerrillas, and from fighting American troops had turned their attention more and more to robbing their own people. At one time, July, 1905, no less than thirty-five hundred Scouts, or about four-fifths of that body, in addition to seven thousand of the Constabulary, were actively engaged in the suppression of outlawry and the maintenance of public order.

Between the patriot fighting for his country and the bandit robbing for his private gain, the line is not hard to draw. Although claiming sympathy from their fellows because of having previously fought as soldiers, these outlaw bands levied tribute upon everybody of means in their vicinity, and having the guns and the power they did not scruple to use both for private gain long after all semblance of organized resistance to the American government had disappeared.

Even General Aguinaldo admitted in conversation with the Secretary of Commerce and Police that the ladrones were merely out for their pockets, that they were a low class of man, and that of those out, Montalan was the only one he knew personally and he was a poor grade of man of no particular intelligence, and couldn't even write his name.

In 1904 and 1905 the methods of the outlaws became fairly well systematized. Each leader of a band had his territory defined and had an understanding with other bandits that they were to keep out of that region. The chief levied tribute upon the property owners, so much per carabao, or other unit, per year. Sometimes the property owners connived at the maintenance of a band of robbers in their vicinity who, under their orders, were to keep other highwaymen out of their neighborhood. Those who refused to pay suffered, and some of the more terrible of the outlaws attained a very sinister reputation by their atrocities. It was wise for property owners who had beautiful young girls growing up in their families to send them away; otherwise they might be requisitioned to be sent to the outlaw camp. In case their terms and conditions were not complied with, some of the outlaws threatened fiendish retaliations. As one Filipino who had been found guilty of aiding outlaws said: "The punishment inflicted by Americans is merciful and slow. The punishment which we may expect from the outlaws is terrible and swift. We would rather take our chances with the former than with the latter."

General Bandholtz was able to return all Scout companies to army control and furthermore to reduce the Constabulary to nearly four thousand men.

In 1908 it was said with truth that "this year for the first time the army, including the scouts, has not been called on for aid in a single instance. The Constabulary has maintained peace and good order throughout the islands — a greater degree of peace and good order, it is safe to say, than has been known in these islands for more than twelve years."

With the appointment of a civil governor of the Moro Province, the Constabulary was increased to provide for police work formerly carried on in that region by troops. The number of Constabulary has been gradually increased to correspond with a general increase in population, until in 1926 it was over six thousand.

Filipinos are fond of organizing secret societies, and in some of these they have secret passwords, mystic emblems, and rituals. There was one society north of Manila, carried down from Spanish days, called the *Guardia de Honor*. It was not originally an insurrectionary organization but had certain highly improper ceremonies performed ostensibly in the name of religion.

Many of the outlaws liked to give themselves titles, particularly religious titles. Often one would declare himself the reincarnation of some other person known to Philippine or perhaps church history. At one time no less than three people calling themselves "Jesus Christ," and one, "God Almighty," were serving in a provincial jail, and several women styling themselves "Virgin Mary" found their way to jail on account of misdemeanors. More common among the real leaders as opposed to visionary fanatics was the designation of "Pope." A Manila paper in 1908 said:

> The great bandits of the island of Samar have been many, and all have called themselves popes — Pablo, Isio, Faustino, Tiducduc, and Otoy, only the last of whom roams the wild hills, the others having been shot or hanged, or are serving time in Bilibid for the murders and robberies traced to their doors.

Leaders of the outlaws sometimes claimed to be immune to bullets and to have the power to give immunity to their followers. This immunity was transferred by means of *anting-anting*, charms such as a little bottle or vial containing some liquid, or perhaps a package tied up and worn around the neck with a string. That invulnerability might not be questioned by their followers, they explained that people might seem to fall wounded or killed, but that in three days they would be resurrected.

Perhaps the most adroit of all the outlaws was one Felizardo, whose headquarters were in the town of Bacoor, about fifteen miles south of Manila. Here lived his family, here he came for supplies, and in the adjacent hills and fields he lived himself, and, when most of the other outlaws had been killed or captured, Felizardo still flourished, maintaining a successful protective organization. At length the toils were set, his band scattered, and it seemed practically impossible for him to escape the net. And then what seemed to be his body was found at the foot of a precipice. It was identified by certain scars and by peculiarities of the teeth, recognized by his mother and friends, the reward for his death was paid, and people he had long terrorized began to breathe freely. Later, the Constabulary were led to the conclusion that Felizardo was still alive and that a fraud had been perpetrated on them in connection with his supposed death. This time two pretended deserters from the Constabulary joined Felizardo's band, separated him from his followers, and succeeded in killing him and bringing in his body for a second payment of the reward.

Sometimes in the course of these operations, notably in the campaign against Felizardo, it was found necessary to resort to reconcentration, a practice much hated because, as carried out by the Spaniards, it involved a great deal of suffering. The Constabulary in each case made the recommendation to the Governor-General, who issued the order, and families were escorted, with such valuables as they could carry, to the reconcentration camp in which they were required to reside. They were allowed much freedom of movement provided they did not return to their *barrios*. The camps were under the direction of the presidents of the towns. The American officials were careful about the treatment of every one in such camps and complaints received prompt attention. The principal hardship of reconcentration lay in the fact that the farmers could not care for their crops. This, however, had the important effect of inducing the bandits to surrender when they saw that their continuance in the field was going to prove injurious to the interest of their friends.

No matter how popular a hero might be in insurrection, he could not turn to rapine and prey upon his more industrious fellow-countryman indefinitely without the sympathies of the people turning against him.

Instances were not unusual of private parties volunteering to assist the Constabulary in the suppression of outlawry and armed only with swords and spears joining in the pursuit of brigands.

It is not out of place to relate a few feats illustrative of the spirit with which the Constabulary officers and men, American and Filipino, were inspired.

The following account is taken from a report of the Senior Inspector of Nueva Vizcaya:

> Privates Domingo Tubag and Joaquin Otao, 1st Company, Constabulary of Nva. Vizcaya, . . . were returning from the road camp at Diadi at which place they had taken and turned over to the road foreman, twenty Igorrotes for road work. Near Bascaran they encountered Mandac's band of some 300 persons. Tubag immediately halted the band. Several of the members of the band then asked the two soldiers to join them, but Tubag refused, and seeing the people move out to the right and left of the road, indicating an attempt to surround himself and comrade the two men retreated to the rice fields on the side of the road and opened fire on the band from the shelter of the dividing ridges. In this matter [manner] they held the band off until the column under Colonel Taylor arrived.

One of the most conspicuously heroic men was a somewhat lethargic looking major of Constabulary named Harrison O. Fletcher. When riding a bicycle in the province of Albay on one occasion, he was attacked by about a dozen outlaws. He dismounted, threw the bicycle at his assailants, and, although wounded, drew his revolver and emptied it, and then unslung his rifle and finished the fight, after which he rode back on his bicycle to get bull carts to bring in the dead, numbering five, whom he laid in a row on the plaza, and four wounded whom he placed in the hospital. On another occasion the same officer boarded the Spanish steamer *Dos Hermanos* by climbing up the anchor chain, quelled a mutiny, and saved the lives of most of the officers of the ship. For this act of heroism he was decorated by the King of Spain.

Another daring exploit was that of Major Neville, who, with two of his men, walked into the camp of a band of fifty-seven armed outlaws. He was far in advance of his command and finding himself in the camp of the men he was pursuing, he engaged them in conversation, giving one or two sharp orders as though he were master of the situation, and thus held them for forty minutes until his supports came up, when he disarmed the whole band and marched them in.

Before the uprising in Samar and Leyte was finally put down, there was some pretty fierce fighting in which American army men took part. The following is taken from an officer's account of a fight at La Paz:

. . . His gun barrel was pierced by a bullet and had to be used as a club. Private Brennan was down and two men stabbing him in the back; the corporal strikes them off with the butt of his rifle, then runs forward to the assistance of Yates who was about to receive a second bolo thrust, bends his rifle barrel over a pulajan head and gets Yates and Brennan started for the rear in the lead of the enemy. He now struggled to save himself. His right arm is ripped open by a bolo but striking right and left with his rifle he succeeds in making his way to the rear preceded by about 30 pulajanes and followed by about 10 or 15 being jabbed at by spears and bolos at every step. The corporal passes in front of the company in the enemy's midst, when our volley crashes into them. He finally rolls in front of the company reaching our feet horribly cut and exhausted. How he escaped being killed by our fire may seem wonderful, but it only proved to me the excellence of our marksmanship. Each man must have picked his target.

There were a very few instances of mutiny, desertion, and of going over to the outlaws gun in hand. But such as occurred were less in number than might have been expected in view of the natural racial animosity following the insurrection, and the large number of men enlisted — nearly seven thousand at one time in the Constabulary only, which meant many more thousand passing in and out.

The wisdom used in the selection of those officers of the army who were detailed to the Constabulary was shown by the admirable results they achieved. But not only did the men make the service. The service made the men. They came with character, enthusiasm, and the usual military training. They learned in the Constabulary infinite patience; the necessity for a purely business management of their force; the knack of doing big work with small resources; and the versatility that comes from handling alien people, learning alien tongues, and accustoming themselves to the psychology of aliens. There is not one of the men whose experience was enriched by this service but will testify to its great value to him.

According to the latest reports available, the following were the organized forces of public order in the Philippine Islands in 1926:

Army:
Regular Army	4,601
Philippine Scouts	6,684
Philippines Constabulary	6,223
Manila City Police	713
Baguio City Police	16
Municipal Police	6,815
	25,052

The cost of the Constabulary has been borne wholly out of the insular treasury, no contribution being made by the United States toward it except the normal pay of the seven or eight army officers until 1917 detailed to its supervision.

The United States met from its own treasury all the cost of maintenance of the army and navy in the Philippine Islands, including the construction of buildings and improvement of the various posts and garrisons and the fortifications. Moreover, it paid all the cost of the Philippine Scouts, as a branch of the United States Army. The United States has not followed the practice of Great Britain, Holland, and other powers holding colonies, who deduct from the colonial revenue a certain sum which is paid into the national treasury so that the colonies shall pay their share of the cost of their own protection. In this respect, the United States has been generous to the Philippine Islands.

CHAPTER VI

FINANCE AND JUSTICE

FINANCE

THE CIVIL ADMINISTRATION of the Philippine Islands, contrary to a very prevailing misapprehension, has been self-supporting from the beginning of American occupation in August, 1898.

The revenues derived from taxes and incidental sources have been sufficient to meet all expenses necessarily incident to civil administration during this entire period, and to pay something toward public works.

The cost to the United States has been that of the army and navy during the insurrection and that which since pacification has pertained to the defense of the Islands. There have been large appropriations for fortifications and for the construction of naval bases in the Islands. There has also been an annual expenditure of about $150,000 by the United States government in coast surveys, toward which the Philippine government contributed about $100,000 annually. For civil purposes alone the surveys would not have been carried out so rapidly.

Costs of pacification of the Islands were estimated by the War Department to be $177,000,000 from May 1, 1898, to June 30, 1902.

The War Department also estimated that "the increased amount of expenditures made on account of the Philippine Islands by the War Department bureaus from United States appropriations over that amount which would have been expended if the Army had not been in the Philippines and an equal number of troops . . . had been maintained in the United States" amounted during the ensuing twelve years to $113,000,000, or about $10,000,000 a year. In the ensuing nine years, that is, from 1914 to 1923, the gross sum was $85,000,000, making a gross total for the army of $376,000,000 up to the 30th of June, 1923.

The navy's expense during the insurrection was $8,000,000, and since that time to June 30, 1923, $47,000,000.

It is to be noted that these amounts include the Pacific transport service and some other general expenses, portions of which were in fact chargeable to the Boxer rebellion in China, transportation and some of the expense of the garrison at Tientsin, and some pertaining to Hawaii, so that all of this money is not properly chargeable to the Philippine Islands. The War Department has given no estimate of the proper apportionment of these charges.

Contributions made by Congress from the federal treasury in aid of government and relief of distress in the Islands have been negligible as compared with the sums which have been donated to foreign countries.

Under the provisions of the Treaty of Paris, Spanish ships and merchandise were admitted during a period of ten years to the ports of the Philippine Islands on the same terms as ships and merchandise of the United States. In spite of the earnest efforts of the Philippine government to secure free trade between the Philippine Islands and the United States, it was not until 1909 that the Payne Tariff Bill was passed; at that time the period of ten years had elapsed, so that under the Spanish treaty it was no longer necessary to give free admission of Spanish goods into the Philippine markets. Newspapers owned by members of the Spanish community spoke somewhat bitterly when they called attention to the fact that the United States had deprived the Islands of access to the markets of Spain, without opening to them the privileges of their own.

In 1902 Congress reserved the power of regulating trade relations between the Philippine Islands and the United States. In 1916 this power was granted to the Philippine Legislature subject to approval by the President of the United States and with the usual right of review by Congress.

The coastwise shipping laws of the United States have not been extended to the Philippine Islands, although Congress passed a law authorizing the President to make such extension by executive order. The coastwise shipping laws apply to United States trade with Hawaii and Porto Rico, but it is believed that the extension of these laws to the Philippine Islands would prove to be a handicap to their proper commercial development and the President has wisely refrained from making such extension.

The revival of industry in the Islands which followed the restoration of peace, and the encouragement which came from the political and commercial association with the United States, can be best visualized by the following figures which show the receipts from taxation, the total annual revenues of government from all sources, the gross foreign trade, and the percentage the trade with the United States bears to the gross trade for the years 1899 and 1926:

Year	Insular receipts from taxation	Total revenue of insular government	Insular expenditures for public works	Gross foreign trade including that with the United States	Percentage trade with the United States bears to gross foreign trade		
					Import	Export	Total
1899	$ 3,328,865.53	$ 3,908,675.28	not segregated	$ 34,039,568	7	26	16
1926	29,615,935.54	39,808,463.48	3,771,021.45	256,183,311	60	73	67

The Payne Tariff Law, approved August 5, 1909, provided with certain limitations for free trade between the United States and the Islands. In the first year after the passage of this act the total Philippine trade increased nearly forty per cent to somewhat over $90,000,000. There was material increase in each of the two succeeding years, and in 1913, the last of the Taft régime, the total trade slightly exceeded $101,000,000.

In 1920, the high figure of $300,000,000 was reached. Thereafter a sharp drop occurred to $175,000,000 in 1922, from which there has been recovery to $256,000,000 in 1926. The following tables give the values of the principal exports and imports for selected years:

PRINCIPAL EXPORTS: VALUES FOR CERTAIN YEARS

[Sources: Reports of the Insular Collector of Customs for 1924 and for 1925; Statistical Bulletin No. 2 of the Bureau of Commerce and Industry, 1919.]

Article exported	Year				
	1925	1920	1913	1908	1903
Sugar	$45,514,002.50	$49,619,260.00	$ 7,032,889	$ 5,703,641	$ 3,325,234
Abaca (Manila hemp)	35,521,646.00	35,862,000.00	21,121,084	16,501,956	22,000,588
Coconut oil	19,820,188.50	23,268,886.50	1,146,339	342,280	81
Copra	15,868,702.50	3,716,870.50	9,545,724	6,058,886	3,819,793
Cigars	6,043,976.00	12,721,138.00	3,012,234	1,059,328	961,355
Cigarettes	80,919.50	169,785.50	47,915	46,054	22,194
Leaf and other unmanufactured tobacco	3,065,007.00	6,991,001.50	1,881,669	1,708,756	954,259
Embroideries	4,571,674.50	7,811,783.50	176,169	......	......

PRINCIPAL IMPORTS: VALUES FOR CERTAIN YEARS

[Sources: Reports of the Insular Collector of Customs for 1924 and for 1925; Statistical Bulletins Nos. 1 and 2 of the Bureau of Commerce and Industry, 1918 and 1919.]

Article imported	Year				
	1925	1920	1913	1908	1903
Cotton and its manufactures .	$27,598,309.50	$34,679,929.00	$11,844,301	$7,221,682	$5,068,788
Iron and steel and their manufactures	13,959,969.50	22,215,771.50	8,613,904	2,009,306	2,129,510
Mineral oils (kerosene, etc.) .	8,679,468.00	10,030,641.50	2,112,659	948,040	626,192
Rice	6,413,219.50	8,164,885.00	3,164,591	5,552,571	12,552,382
Wheat flour	5,606,675.00	4,721,757.50	1,898,954	943,022	807,854
Meat and dairy products	5,469,471.50	5,801,876.50	3,264,515	1,955,355	967,013
Automobiles, parts of, and tires for	4,606,156.50	7,460,683.00	1,263,402	......	......
Silk and its manufactures ...	2,807,903.50	3,018,255.50	836,322	511,780	534,818
Coal	2,142,013.50	5,396,038.50	1,584,067	597,507	618,078

The principal sources of revenue inherited from the Spanish administration were the poll tax payable in cash, customs taxes, an "industrial" tax of the nature of an income tax, documentary and other stamp taxes, lotteries, the opium "farm," the capitation tax on Chinese, a tax on the rental value of city real estate, and miscellaneous sources of revenues, including many provisional and transitory taxes. Municipal revenues were derived from public markets, pounds, slaughter houses, fisheries, fords and ferries, certificates of ownership and of transfer of property. A land tax, the imposition of which was optional with municipal governments, was authorized, but it does not appear that this tax was ever imposed.

In the year 1896, the year of greatest revenues preceding American occupation, the Spaniards collected $5,302,000 from direct taxation, and from all sources $9,332,000.

Government expenditures under Spanish administration for the year 1894–95, preceding the insurrection of 1896, allocated nearly fifty per cent to the support of the army and navy, nearly ten per cent to the support of the ecclesiastical establishments, and less than five per cent to public instruction, forestry service, lighthouses, and public works.

At the beginning of American occupation the instructions of the President to the Major-General commanding the army contained the following provision:

The taxes and duties payable by the inhabitants to the former government become payable to the military occupant unless he sees fit to substitute for them other rates or amounts of contribution for the expenses of the government.

The United States military authorities continued with some modifications the Spanish taxes. The poll taxes were reduced to the nominal figure of one peseta, or ten cents United States currency, to cover the cost of issuing receipts.

The Military Governor discontinued, as repugnant to American practice and theory of government, the lotteries, the vassalage tax or "tribute" which had been collected from tribal peoples, the compulsory fifteen days' labor requirement or *prestacion personal*, various provisional and transitory taxes, and also the opium "farm."

The system of revenue collections established by the American authorities from the beginning of the occupation of the city of Manila required that all moneys collected by government officials and employees should be deposited in the public treasury and taken up in accounts to be presented monthly or more frequently.

The management of the treasury was entrusted to a separate bureau known as the Bureau of the Treasury, the chief of which was known as the Insular Treasurer.

The Spanish customs tariff, including export duties, was continued in effect with minor changes until November 15, 1901, when the first Philippine tariff law became effective. This new tariff made a reduction of at least twenty-five per cent in the customs taxes, materially reducing rates on food staples and other necessaries chiefly imported from the United States, and increased the rates on luxuries. This law was confirmed by Act of Congress of March 8, 1902, which also provided that products of the Philippine Islands coming into the United States should pay but seventy-five per cent of the tariff charges on imports from foreign countries, and that revenue collections in the United States on imports from the Philippine Islands should be held as a separate fund and paid into the treasury of the Philippine Islands.

In March, 1905, Congress passed its first tariff act for the Philippine Islands. The average duty imposed was less than in the former tariff, important changes being reductions of about one-half in the rates on manufactured tobacco and gasoline, the placing of the duty on agricultural, electrical, and other machinery at the nominal rate of five per cent ad valorem, and the prohibition after three years of the importation of opium except for medicinal purposes.

Perhaps the most significant event affecting the revenues of the Islands was the provision for limited free trade with the United States contained in the so-called Payne Tariff Act, approved by President Taft, August 5, 1909. The bill had been bitterly contested by certain selfish sugar and tobacco interests in the United States, who maintained a virulent but ineffectual lobby, managing to delay the passage of the bill but not succeeding in defeating it. They did succeed, however, in securing for a few years a limit to the amount of sugar and tobacco admitted free of duty.

The result of this enlightened measure exceeded the hopes of its most sanguine supporters. Trade between the Islands and the States increased by leaps and bounds. From about four million dollars — the amount of this trade in Spanish days — it had gradually risen to fifteen million dollars in the year before the Payne Bill was passed. In the third year after free trade, it had jumped to forty-seven million dollars, or over three hundred per cent, and with the stimulus given to prices by the World War, it reached the high figure of almost two hundred million dollars in 1920.

While the customs revenue was responding to the new stimulus, the Bureau of Internal Revenue encountered greater difficulties.

The American Commission, in the Internal Revenue Act of 1904, levied its heaviest taxes on alcoholic liquors and tobacco products. It provided a percentage tax of one-third of one per cent on business, the remaining taxes being documentary stamps, licenses, charges on forest products taken from the public domain, and minor sources of revenues. The provisions for tax rates and methods of collection were simple.

The most radical change made by the new internal revenue law was the shifting of the burden of taxation on industries from articles of necessary consumption to articles of luxury or optional consumption, and the entire exemption from taxation by the central government of the multitude of small trades and occupations followed by the very poor.

It was estimated that the new taxes imposed by the Commission on alcoholic liquors, tobacco, and matches would produce an annual revenue of about $3,500,000.

Manila had long had an undesirable name in shipping circles by reason of the poor harbor, the long delays to which ships were liable owing to unfavorable weather for unloading in the open roadstead of Manila Bay, and the numerous feast days upon which no stevedore could be found willing to work. Ships were sometimes kept two weeks for work which could have been accomplished in favorable circumstances in two days. This resulted in a differential freight rate against Manila which amounted in effect to a tax on all goods going to and from the Islands and placed them at a disadvantage in marketing tropical products.

The American government had set itself resolutely to meet these difficulties, and with the improvement of the harbor and the construction of wharves, many of the causes of delay were eliminated. It was decided to go further. The Commission had imposed tonnage dues on all ships visiting Philippine ports. This is a customary and very proper tax. The yield, however, was small, and the government, desirous of holding out a welcoming hand and making Manila more attractive to shipping, passed an act in August, 1906, abolishing all tonnage dues. This action was extremely favorably received in shipping circles, and the customs agents of the Islands reported that they heard it most favorably commented upon in European ports as well as by the merchants in the Islands.

This tax was later reimposed in a period of comparative financial stringency in 1916.

The tax on real estate, or "land tax," as it came to be called, was an even more significant departure from Spanish revenue methods than the taxes on liquor and tobacco. Following American practice, the land tax was levied on the capital or market value as assessed against all privately owned land, buildings, and improvements. Real estate used exclusively for religious, charitable, scientific, or educational purposes was exempted, but the exemption did not extend to lands or buildings held for investment, whatever the use to which the income might be devoted. Real estate holdings valued at twenty-five dollars or less were exempt.

The land tax was an innovation and naturally unpopular among property owners, who were influential people and included or controlled most of the vocal elements of the population. The entire proceeds were required by law to be expended locally and for purposes approved by officials elected by the people, and, further, any increase above three-eighths of one per cent could be imposed only by these elective officers.

It was not burdensome to any landowner who made an appreciable effort to cultivate his land. Due to the low assessments, the average annual tax per parcel of land outside of Manila was sixty-six and one-half cents in 1908.

The collection of the land tax for a few years was more difficult because it came at the time of the loss of the customary foreign markets for sugar and tobacco through the change in sovereignty, the practical paralyzation of agricultural operations in many districts due to disturbed conditions of public order following the insurrection, and most of all to the loss of work animals by rinderpest. It was found necessary in some districts to suspend the land tax for one or more years.

In the year 1906 the Commission saw fit to remit the land tax for the year and appropriated money from the insular treasury to enable the provinces and municipalities to carry on. In the ensuing year the Commission again remitted the land tax, but in this instance only half the amount of the loss to the provinces and municipalities was voted from the insular treasury. The provinces, however, were permitted to impose this tax by vote of the provincial board and some of them voted to impose it in 1907. The following year the tax was put in effect, and has so continued except in cases of serious catastrophe or public calamity resulting in practical failure of crops.

There was general revision of assessment in 1913–14 and thereafter the assessment lists have been revised each year. At the close of the year 1925, the total assessed value of taxable real estate in the provinces was reported as $664,389,418, an increase of about $500,000,000 in twelve years. The public had come to approve this method of taxation, as the increases in assessment were made almost entirely by Filipino officials.

The two bureaus concerned with the collection of revenue from taxation are those of customs and internal revenue, both under the supervision of the Secretary of Finance. The Bureau of Internal Revenue is charged with the supervision of the collection by provincial treasurers, through their deputies, the municipal treasurers, of all other taxes accruing in part or wholly to the insular treasury, also, the cash poll tax, which is of general application, although the proceeds accrue exclusively to provincial and municipal treasuries.

The surplus and uninvested trust funds of government were carried on interest-bearing deposit with banks in Manila and in the United States which qualified as depositaries of public funds. Redemption funds covering the silver certificate paper currency, which on June 30, 1913, amounted to somewhat less than $16,000,000, were held in the vaults of the insular treasury. For storage of silver bullion and other treasure, bomb-proof vaults were constructed on the fortified island of Corregidor at the entrance to Manila Bay.

The municipal and provincial governments had their specific sources of revenue and a percentage of the internal revenue collected by the insular government. These shares in the internal revenue collections were apportioned by the Insular Auditor on the basis of population and were by law allocated to maintenance of primary schools, the construction and maintenance of public roads, and purposes in the discretion of local governments.

Unthinking or poorly informed Americans and Filipinos have charged the American administration with having taxed the Filipinos too heavily. This may be explained in part by the fact that Filipinos habitually complained of the high rate of taxation, while their orators eloquently pictured "the heavy burden" which was imposed on them, regardless of whether the tax was heavy or light.

Critics of America's course in the Islands were misled by these complaints into repeating and publishing the charge that the rate of taxation in the Islands was high, and Filipino politicians encouraged such misrepresentations. This was done without taking the trouble to make the simple analyses and comparisons which would have proved to them that the rate of taxation was lower than that of any other civilized country for which statistics are available.

This situation was summed up by the Governor-General, in a farewell address to Secretary Dickinson on the eve of his departure for the United States in 1910, as follows:

. . . We have talked so much of the calamitous condition of the country; we have gotten so used to using the word precarious in describing the affairs of the Philippines; we have said "crisis" so often, that we keep on saying it and saying it every time we get up to make a speech, in spite of the fact that there is no crisis, there is no precarious condition, and there is nothing to trouble us in the economic outlook of the country. The Filipino who thinks that his people can't pay the small rate of taxation that exists here, has a very poor opinion of their capacity. Why don't the orators who talk about the heavy rate of taxation tell us at the same time a thing they ought to know, that there exists here the lowest rate of taxation in the world when taken in relation with the power of the people to pay. What confidence in the possible development of his own people has a man who complains of this low rate of taxation? We of the insular government have often heard in our travels orators who coupled a request for lesser taxation with a request for additional expenditures . . .

PER CAPITA TAXATION FIGURES, COMPUTED AT PAR OF EXCHANGE, FOR CENTRAL GOVERNMENTS ONLY, FOR THE PHILIPPINE ISLANDS AND OTHER COUNTRIES IN YEARS SIGNIFICANT IN PHILIPPINE DEVELOPMENT

[Sources: Data furnished by the United States Department of Commerce, and Reports of the Auditor.]

Country	1907	1913	1925 or latest year available
Philippines	$ 1.32	$ 1.37	$ 2.56
Argentina	14.21	17.49	19.90
Australia	13.50	22.88	43.04
Canada	8.18	17.70	31.42
France	19.49	20.07	138.96(34.32)
Japan	4.48	4.98	6.67
Venezuela	3.52	4.44	6.84

A fair appraisal of the burden of taxation is found in the number of days a laboring man has to work in order to pay his tax. The total annual taxes of the Philippine Islands in the year 1908 amounted to $1.71 per capita. At the average rate of wages a laborer could earn thirty to forty cents a day, which meant he could meet his tax burden with about five days' work. If he were not the owner of real estate, however, the laborer was subject to no direct taxation except the possible maximum poll tax of one dollar per annum, which he could pay from his wages for two and one-half to three days' labor. This may be contrasted with at least twenty-one days for the poll tax alone under the Spanish régime, at which time there were the other prescribed taxes and a number of fees and personal perquisites collected by officials and employees and not entered on the official accounts.

Under American administration all moneys received from the Philippine taxpayer have been expended directly in the service of the Philippine people. No colonial department has been maintained in Washington, and the Bureau of Insular Affairs has been a charge on the federal treasury. Beside the cost of the army and navy, all expenses of the United States diplomatic and consular service in the Far East have, likewise, been met from federal funds.

In 1913, at the close of the Taft régime and after a period of five years during which no changes could be made in the tax laws of the central government without the concurrence of the elective Philippine Assembly, the per capita tax burden for the support of all branches of government was $2.08.

After 1914 the Filipinos, having come into control of both houses of the Legislature, increased the existing internal revenue taxation, trebling the "sales tax" or percentage tax on business, added the income, inheritance, and other new taxes, and brought into effect a general revision increasing the tax assessment of real estate to meet the increasing cost of government.

By 1920, the last full year of the Democratic régime, the revenue of the insular government from taxation had reached a total of $26,573,-262.36, an increase of more than one hundred per cent over that of the fiscal year 1913, which was the last year of the Taft régime. The per capita tax burden for all branches of the Philippine government had increased during that period from $2.08 to $3.525 for 1920. In 1925 it had reached $3.70.

In 1925, the total revenue from taxation in the Islands was somewhat more than $30,000,000.

After the inauguration of the Assembly in 1907, appropriations were made by the new Legislature, the Commission acting as the upper house. The Commission continued to make appropriations for the territory inhabited chiefly by the Moros and tribal peoples.

The organic law provided that, in case of failure on the part of the Legislature to pass appropriations for the support of government, the appropriation bill of the preceding year should automatically carry over. There were three years in which this occurred, but the law of Congress worked in such a way that there resulted no slowing up of the business of government.

The principal item of increased expenditure over Spanish practice was that of the salary list, the emoluments given to employees under American administration being made large enough to provide an adequate scale of living for the officers of the government. Except in a few isolated instances all fees were eliminated.

In the first years of American civil administration a large part of the revenues was necessarily devoted to the restoration of public order, putting down insurrection, and maintaining campaigns against the dangerous communicable diseases, cholera, plague, and smallpox, which raged through the Islands.

During the fiscal year 1903, the expenditures on account of the Constabulary amounted to nearly fifteen per cent of the total revenues of the insular government, in addition to the expense of the American troops and Philippine Scouts borne by the United States government.

As the public order situation improved and the ordinary revenues of the government increased, it was found possible to augment the expenditures for education, public health, and construction of roads.

A view of the movement upward of revenues for fixed charges and for expenses of government, exclusive of public works, is shown to have been:

Period	Average annual receipts of government	Average annual fixed charges	Average annual expenses of government
1910–1912 (Three years following free trade) ...	$18,132,673	$1,796,737	$14,681,502
1920	43,102,331	6,551,817	27,548,630

From 1909 to 1913, when the Philippine government was the target for very severe criticism, the administration in Washington having changed from Republican to Democratic, the financial situation may be roughly summarized thus: A gross revenue of $15,000,000 annually; expenditure for ordinary expenses of $9,000,000; leaving $6,000,000 to meet fixed charges for the service of the public debt, interest and amortization, amounting to about $1,000,000. This left a balance of $5,000,000 a year available for extraordinary expenditures and public works out of revenue. Most of these extraordinary expenditures were optional, as were almost all of the public works. With the reduction of revenue a lesser programme of public works was undertaken; with an increase of revenue a more ambitious programme ensued. Set forth in this way the course of the government seemed fairly simple.

It is most unfortunate that in preparing the Philippine Organic Act of 1902, Congress should not have had the vision to grant the Philippine government the right to borrow an amount bearing a fixed relationship to the value of the taxable property of the Islands or to the gross revenues. Such a provision would have given an automatic increase to the borrowing power, proportioned directly on the power to pay, and would have enabled the government of the Islands to forge ahead with much greater rapidity and with no conceivable disadvantage, except in the case of corrupt or grossly inefficient American administrators. This defect of law was remedied by the Jones Law in 1916.

Congress, in 1902, granted the insular government the right to borrow $7,000,000 for the purchase of friar lands; and later, in 1905, $5,000,000 for public works.

By Act of Congress of February 6, 1905, the Philippine government was further authorized to guarantee interest at four per cent annually on bonds issued for the construction of railroads, and this enlightened action on the part of Congress resulted in the expenditure of about $24,000,000 in railroad construction in the Islands, involving a potential expenditure for interest of $948,360 annually.

The first nine issues of Philippine bonds sold at substantially less than a four per cent basis at a time when the prevailing rate of interest in the Philippine Islands on the best commercial security, as also on mortgages on improved real estate, was about twelve per cent, or more, per annum. Sales of Philippine government bonds in the United States since that time have required a higher rate of interest, but seldom exceeding five per cent.

The low rate of interest which the Philippine government is able to command is due in an important degree to the fact that not only are its bonds by Act of Congress exempt from all taxation in the United States and in the Philippine Islands, but also, by order of the Secretary of the Treasury, bonds of the Philippine government are acceptable at par by the United States Treasury Department as security for deposits of public moneys. Likewise, the Postmaster-General has authorized the acceptance of Philippine government bonds at par as security for deposits of postal savings funds.

The payment of principal and interest of Philippine government bonds is not guaranteed by the United States government. However, as the bonds have been issued pursuant to authorization by Congress, the Department of Justice and the War Department have held that these bonds constitute a moral obligation of the United States. In the advertisements offering bonds of the Philippine government for sale, it is the practice of the War Department to quote an extract from an opinion by the Attorney-General of the United States, dated August 11, 1921, regarding the liability of the United States for a former issue of Philippine bonds.

The authorized borrowing capacity of the Philippine government in 1926 had reached $95,870,722.72. The total bonded indebtedness of the Philippine government, including municipal bonds, on June 30, 1926, was $81,815,000. The per capita bonded indebtedness for all branches of the Philippine government in 1913 was $1.29; in 1921, $2.95; and on June 30, 1926, $6.82.

Sinking funds adequate for the retirement of bonds issued by the Philippine government were established and due restrictions imposed regarding their investment.

One of the most important reforms achieved by American administrators was that of the currency. When the Americans arrived, there was in use a nondescript currency of fluctuating values, Mexican silver pesos, Spanish-Philippine silver pesos, silver subsidiary and minor copper coins, paper currency issued by the Banco Español-Filipino, by the British banks having branches in Manila, the Hongkong & Shanghai Banking Corporation and the Chartered Bank of India, Australia, and China, and some silver and copper coins of the Straits Settlements, Hong Kong, China, and Spanish governments. American gold and silver currency, and to a lesser extent paper and minor coins also, soon were used. Traders were by no means scrupulous about taking unfair advantage of these changes, while the money-lenders knew very well how to fix the rates of the day to suit their business. There was a multitude of money-changers and it was always the poor man who suffered. He found that his produce brought less than it ought and that his purchases cost substantially more. The early reports of the Commission speak of the bitterness with which the civil employees of the government, whose salaries were stated in gold — that is, United States currency — complained of the discrimination made against them in local currency exchange, which, they found, sharply reduced the purchasing power of their emoluments. This so-called "local currency" was on the silver basis typified by the Mexican peso coin or "dollar."

The importation of Mexican currency had been prohibited by the Spanish authorities for some years prior to American occupation, but it is alleged that with the connivance of the customs authorities it had constantly been brought into the country. The Military Governor, under the able guidance of Major-General Francis V. Greene, made an intelligent effort to establish a fixed rate of two Mexican dollars for one United States dollar, but this was only partially successful, as an increase in the bullion value of silver made it unprofitable to the banks to continue the arrangement.

Besides the difficulty of conducting business, that of keeping accounts in the fluctuating currency was extreme, and is noted in the early reports of the Secretary of Finance and Justice, who quoted the Auditor as saying: "At one time disbursing officers were handling two kinds of currency involving, in effect, five standards of value."

In 1901, an expert in banking and finance was brought to the Islands, and on his advice plans were completed for a new currency for the Philippine Islands on a strictly gold basis.

It was not until March 2, 1903, that Congress passed the necessary legislation to provide for a new coinage system in the Islands, the provisions contained in the organic act of July 1, 1902, being deemed inadequate.

The peso, equivalent in value to a United States half-dollar, was made the unit of value.

The silver coins authorized were the silver peso, half-peso or fifty centavos, the peseta or twenty centavos, and the media peseta or ten centavos, the centavo being the lowest unit of value and equal to one-half cent of United States currency. Minor coins authorized were the nickel five-centavo and copper centavo and half-centavo pieces.

This silver Philippine peso was made legal tender in the Philippine Islands for all debts, public and private. At the same time, the gold coins of the United States, at the rate of one dollar for two pesos, were also made legal tender in the Islands. Although it was not until 1904 that the new currency found its way into circulation, the good effects of the announcement were immediately felt.

The currency law provided for maintaining the parity of the silver peso and for financing the purchase of silver bullion for the new currency through the issue of notes or "certificates of indebtedness" for periods of not longer than one year and bearing interest at a rate not exceeding four per cent annually. These debentures were exempted from taxation in the United States and in the Philippine Islands. The Act of Congress also provided for the use of paper currency in the form of silver certificates in various denominations in exchange for deposits of standard silver coins of one peso. These deposits constituted a special trust fund for the redemption of this paper currency.

The period was one of radical changes in the currencies of the British government in India and in the Straits Settlements, the Japanese government, and the Dutch government in the East Indies, all of which then passed to some form of gold standard.

A fund known as the Gold Standard Fund was created for the purpose of maintaining the parity between the Philippine silver and the gold standard peso. This special fund was made up of the proceeds of the "certificates of indebtedness" already mentioned, the profits of seigniorage, the profits from the sale of exchange, interest, and incidental receipts. By 1911, or at the end of eight years, this fund had risen to over $10,300,000, at which time it was deemed unnecessary to add to the sum further. From that time on, the funds which had formerly gone to swell the Gold Standard Fund were covered back into the treasury to be available for general appropriation.

It was suggested from Washington that, rather than leave the whole of this sum of money in the banks in the United States drawing a low rate of interest, a portion of it could be safely brought to the Islands and utilized in loans to provinces and municipalities for income-bearing purposes. This was done.

This plan of investment was pursued with great advantage in the public interest. These loans hastened the completion of important sections of railways to the southward of Manila through the great coconut plantation regions of Batangas, Laguna, and Tayabas to an excellent harbor on the Pacific coast. The loans to provincial and municipal governments facilitated the construction of important bridges, roads, municipal markets, and other important permanent improvements. In no case did any of the provinces or municipalities default on payment of either principal or interest of loans from trust funds of the insular government.

The Americans found the prevailing weights and measures in use in the Islands to be even more chaotic than the currency. The picul — customary unit of weight in local as well as export trade in hemp, sugar, copra, and other products — varied in weight from one hundred and twenty-five to one hundred and forty pounds. The cavan, which was the customary unit of measurement of corn and unhulled rice, varied as much as ten per cent; the yard varied ten per cent, depending on which of various British or Spanish customary units were used. There was neither commercial standardization nor official verification of weights and measures. Besides this lack of standards, fraud was more or less generally practiced in the adjustment of scales for weighing and the use of different measures for buying and selling. The situation was complicated and the confusion was aggravated by the use of units of medieval origin which had come to have varying values in different localities.

In 1906, the Commission passed a law making the metric system legal for all weights and measures throughout the Philippine Islands, providing for inspection and sealing, and penalizing, after the end of two years, the use of fraudulent or unsealed weights and measures. It was specifically provided that the metric system only should be used in official documents and that no other weights or measures might be employed in contracts or other documents except those involving the ordering of commodities or articles from countries having other standards.

The Reorganization Committee, whose operations have been mentioned in an earlier chapter, had found the government suffering under an extremely backward method of auditing and accounting. It had been amazed to learn that the United States government at that time kept its books on a single entry basis under a system which ran back to the days of Alexander Hamilton. The Insular Auditor was appointed by the Secretary of War, and, although responsible to the Governor-General for the conduct of his employees, his judgment on accounting matters was final and no more subject to review by the Governor-General than were the judicial decisions of a judge subject to review by executive officers. There was no adequate distinction made between the duties of the Treasurer and the Auditor. The imperfectly trained Auditors who came to the Islands overstepped the limits which should have been placed upon their independence of action, and insisted in certain instances upon actually disbursing the departmental funds. The result was that whatever work of this sort was done by the Auditor became an unaudited function and deprived the government of the very check the Auditor's office was created to give.

The Reorganization Committee found the Insular Auditor arbitrary and autocratic in his rulings and it estimated his unnecessary requirements cost the government annually hundreds of thousands of dollars. Moreover, his system was so faulty that he could not give the chiefs of the bureaus usual business information as to their assets, liabilities, and costs. His audit was made, usually by correspondence, often a year or more after events had happened. Defalcations were usually detected by the organization within the bureaus, and if discovered by the Auditor it was usually too late for effective remedial action.

So strongly entrenched was the existing system that the Committee found itself unable to dislodge it; nevertheless, following the recommendation of the Committee, the Reorganization Act passed by the Commission placed nearly all the bureaus on a system of so-called "reimbursable appropriations," based on the principle that appropriations from general funds should be made only for the difference between the estimated receipts not derived from taxation and the estimated costs of each bureau. Under this plan all receipts of each branch of the government for services and supplies and other purposes not taxation, automatically went to the support of the office or bureau concerned,[1] and only the balance, if an adverse balance resulted from their operations, was appropriated. As most of the bureaus did services for other bureaus or offices of the government and charged for them, this device served a double purpose. First, it made the appropriations give the exact cost to the government of each bureau, and did not increase the apparent cost of government by the amount of inter-bureau charges. Where one branch of the government rendered service to another branch and received payment for it, the amounts thus paid across between bureaus did not appear as an added cost of government.

The second purpose which this device served was that it gave the bureau chiefs a direct interest in seeing that their earnings were maintained, bills rendered for all services performed, and the collections made, as they depended upon these revenues to meet their expenses.

Lest unrestricted use of receipts should lend itself to extravagance on the part of the bureau chiefs, an "allowance" was made for expenditure under each subhead and no bureau chief could spend in excess of that

[1] Act No. 1679, Philippine Commission, August 10, 1907, Section 10.

amount without the written approval of the Governor-General. Thus if a bureau by reason of its efficient operation should double its business but in doing so require increased expenditure, it could secure a suitable increase in its "allowance" by satisfying the head of the department and the Governor-General that the best interests of the government would be served by increasing the allowance. Some bureaus, like that of Printing, were wholly reimbursable and had no appropriation; in fact, turned back a small profit to the government. Some, like the Bureau of Posts, derived the bulk of the money for their expenditures from their own operations, requiring a comparatively small balance from the general treasury to bring them out even. Other bureaus, like the Constabulary and the Bureau of Civil Service, had practically no revenues at all, but had to depend wholly upon their annual appropriations.

The reforms instituted by the Reorganization Committee for the few years they were allowed to endure worked admirably. But the Filipino Assemblymen, perhaps influenced by the constant clamor of the newspapers against the cost of government, early developed a marked prejudice against the system of reimbursable appropriations under which the government was conducted. They felt that somehow these resulted in an undue latitude being given to the bureau chiefs to expend more money than they would spend were they limited by a fixed amount contained in the appropriation bill.

A very minor but typical illustration will show the advantage to the government derived from having reimbursable accounts. The government maintained in the Bureau of Science an ornithologist who could either remain at his desk working on accumulated specimens, or go out and get new specimens at additional expense. The Philippine Islands abound in rare specimens of birds, the skins of which are sought for in museums throughout the world, and it was found that the ornithologist could earn not only the cost of his own expeditions by sale to scientific institutions of the skins collected, but also enough to repay the Bureau of Science for the whole of his salary. He could in addition secure by exchange valuable skins of birds of other countries with which to enrich the museum in Manila. When the reimbursable feature of the law was later abolished and all revenues derived from the operations of the ornithologist were covered back into the treasury to be reappropriated by the Legislature, it was found that practically all incentive for these expeditions was lost, the revenues derived from sale of Philippine bird skins dropped to almost nothing, and further expeditions on the part of this ornithologist were discouraged because the cost had to be borne from the bureau's appropriations without any credit being given the bureau from his earnings.

The Legislature in 1914, the first which had a Filipino majority in both houses, insisted upon returning to the method of requiring that all receipts be covered into the general fund account of the government and including in the appropriation act the total amount that might be expended for operation, with the result, to take the extreme example of the Bureau of Posts, that they raised the appropriation for that year to $962,705, whereas the actual net cost to government of the bureau was but $118,632.23.

An analysis of the cost of government before and after these changes were made leads one to the conclusion that the reimbursable appropriation was more flexible and in the long run more economical. The increased expenses of the bureaus, however, cannot be attributed to the changed method of accounting, although there can be no doubt it was less economical than the former one. As additional revenues became available, it was inevitable that expenses should increase. All governments will spend their revenues as collected. All bureaus are desirous of extending their activities, and, with the extension of these activities, there is also necessary increased expense which will keep pace with the revenues. And so the explanation of much of the greatly increased expenditure of the government after 1914 is to be found in the fact that the Legislature found itself possessed of greatly increased revenue, and like all legislative bodies it had no difficulty in finding ways of disposing of everything it could get.

The Commission in 1906 enacted a corporation law based on laws in effect in conservative states. Conflicting portions of the Spanish code of commerce and other laws were repealed.

In 1906, also, the Commission created the Philippine Postal Savings Bank as a branch of the Bureau of Posts. Its success is proved by the remarkable increase in the number of depositors from 2331 in 1907 to 176,056 in 1925, and in amount of deposits from one quarter of a million dollars to nearly three millions in 1925.

This admirable institution, in which Secretary Taft personally took great interest, resulted in the deposit and use for income-bearing purposes of much of the hoarded savings which the people had been accustomed to keep buried in the ground or concealed about their premises. It is a noteworthy fact that the Philippine Postal Savings Bank was well under way and the Filipinos enjoying its advantages before the United States had made similar provisions for the convenience of its own citizens.

Congress, by Act of March 4, 1907, authorized the Philippine government to guarantee an income of four per cent upon the cash capital invested in an Agricultural bank. The Legislature in 1908 created the Agricultural Bank of the Philippine Government, and appropriated one-half million dollars for its capital.

The bank was authorized to "make loans only for the payment or satisfaction of incumbrances on agricultural lands, for the construction of drainage and irrigation works, and for the purchase of fertilizers, agricultural seeds, machinery, implements, and animals, to be used exclusively by the borrower for agricultural purposes. . . ." No loans were to be made by the bank to any person or corporation not engaged in agricultural pursuits.

In 1916, when the National Bank of the Philippine Islands was established by the Philippine government, all the assets and liabilities of the Agricultural Bank were transferred to it. The Agricultural Bank was thereafter "deemed abolished."

The Legislature passed an act in 1915 to encourage rural credit associations under government supervision. The purposes were to encourage thrift among the farmers, provide depositories for savings, make small loans at a low rate of interest for the purchase of seeds and work animals, to pay the expense of land titles, and for other agricultural needs. By 1924 there were 546 associations with 81,971 members and total assets of $1,326,890.94.

The Act of Congress approved July 1, 1902, authorized the government of the Philippine Islands to grant franchises, privileges, and concessions, including the authority to exercise the right of eminent domain for the construction and operation of works of public utility and service. This authorization contained various restrictions and safeguards. No franchise, privilege, or concession might be granted to any corporation except under the condition that it should be subject to amendment, alteration, or repeal by Congress. All grants of franchises and other concessions should forbid the issue of stocks or bonds except in exchange for actual cash, or for property of fair valuation, equal to the par value of the stocks or bonds so issued. The declaring of stock or bond dividends was also forbidden. In the case of public service corporations, it was required that provision be made for the effective regulation of charges, and for the payment of a reasonable percentage of gross earnings to the public treasury.

Congress by the same law provided that "no corporation shall be authorized to conduct the business of buying and selling real estate."

Franchises were granted for electric lighting, telephone, railway, and other public utilities with great benefit to the public interest, and provision was made for the regulation of rates.[2]

JUSTICE

The organization of the Philippine courts is simple and well suited to the prompt administration of justice.

1. Courts of justices of the peace have preliminary jurisdiction in all criminal cases, and are trial courts in minor civil and criminal cases much as in the rural districts in the United States. Justices of the peace also have powers to perform notarial duties and to solemnize marriages.

2. Courts of first instance are provided for the entire territory of the Islands. These are trial courts of record for all civil and criminal cases.

3. The Supreme Court of the Islands, the members of which were up to 1932 appointed by the President of the United States, was the court of appeals from decisions of the courts of first instance and orders by the Public Utility Commission. The Supreme Court has power to investigate the official and personal conduct of judges of first instance and recommend suspensions and removals of such judges when in its opinion there is sufficient cause for such disciplinary action. The Supreme Court also is charged with the admission to practice and the disbarment of lawyers.

4. The Supreme Court of the United States has jurisdiction "to review, revise, reverse, modify, or affirm the final judgments and decrees of the Supreme Court of the Philippine Islands in all actions, cases, causes, and proceedings . . . in which the Constitution or any statute, treaty, title, right, or privilege of the United States is involved" or in which the value in controversy exceeds twenty-five thousand dollars.

The Governor-General held no power of intervention in civil litigation, and in criminal cases only by pardon or commutation after final sentence.

[2] The number of cases presented to this commission for action during 1925 was 2493; and in that year the total number of public carriers and other enterprises falling within the jurisdiction of the commission was 2208.

The Secretary of Justice has administrative supervision over the Bureau of Justice, courts of first instance and inferior courts, the Bureau of Prisons, the Public Utility Commission, and the Philippine Library and Museum.

The principal law officer of the government is the Attorney-General, whose duty is to represent the government of the Islands in all civil and criminal cases to which the government or any of its officers in his official capacity is a party. It is also his duty to give legal advice to the government and various of its branches. The Attorney-General is the chief of the Bureau of Justice. A *fiscal*, or attorney, is provided for the city of Manila and for each province.

At least one notary public is required to be appointed for each municipality by the judge of first instance of the jurisdiction. Many officers are authorized to act as notaries *ex officio*, with duties and powers strictly prescribed by statute. Except in the cases of salaried officers acting as notaries *ex officio*, who are required to collect and account for the prescribed fees as for government funds, the office is one of the few compensated by fees.

When they came, the Americans found the prisons filled to overflowing with political prisoners and persons awaiting trial on more or less serious criminal charges. Provost courts were created for the trial of ordinary civil and criminal cases, and military commissions for the trial of civilians charged with serious crimes.

The civil courts were re-established by the Military Governor, beginning in May, 1899.

The codes of procedure and other laws had been framed to suit the Spanish colonial system. The practicing lawyers understood these codes, and to meet the new situation the military authorities appointed qualified Filipino and American judges on the re-establishment of the courts. It is noteworthy that the Supreme Court named by Military Governor Otis had a majority of Filipino justices — six Filipinos to three Americans. For Chief Justice the Islands were fortunate in the selection of Don Cayetano S. Arellano, a jurist of the highest character and the widest learning. He continued in office until his retirement April 1, 1920, after twenty-one years of service. His work was beyond praise.

In 1900, Colonel Enoch H. Crowder, then Secretary to the Military Governor of the Islands, reported that the "laws of criminal procedure contained harsh and oppressive features . . . in conflict with American standards." But he wisely saw that it was impossible without careful

deliberation to repeal the existing code and substitute a wholly new one.
Furthermore, it would be necessary to give the Filipino judges and lawyers time to learn the new order of things and adapt themselves to it.
In April, 1900, the Military Governor, having consulted leading Filipino lawyers, put into effect certain necessary changes, amending the
Spanish code of criminal procedure to conform more nearly with American practice and principles of justice.

The reforms effected by these changes included the requirement of a
specific complaint charging but one offense, in lieu of the Spanish practice which frequently was the prosecution for several distinct offenses
under one complaint; preliminary examination of the complainant and
his witnesses to determine whether arrest should be ordered; the extension of the rights of a speedy and public trial to include defense in person or by counsel; exercise of the right of the accused to testify in his
own behalf and exemption from testifying against himself; the right of
the accused to confront the witnesses of the prosecution; compulsory
attendance of witnesses for the defense; the right of appeal in all cases
from the decision of the trial court; the privilege of pleading a former
judgment or jeopardy; the right of joint defendants to be tried separately; the right of a new trial in certain cases; the right of providing
bail except in capital cases where the presumption of guilt is strong;
and the privilege of the writ of *habeas corpus*. Nearly one hundred
prisoners held over from the Spanish régime were liberated from un-
warranted detention.

One noteworthy reform brought about by the military authorities was
the legalization of civil marriage.

It remained for the Taft Commission to put into effect a fuller reorganization of the courts. The structure of the courts as held over from
the Spanish régime was continued temporarily, as the change to a new
system was too complicated a matter to be undertaken hastily.

Of the five alert and vigorous Americans who made up the Taft Commission, three, including Judge Taft himself, were lawyers, and set
themselves earnestly to reform the antiquated, corrupt, and inefficient
judicial system which they found in the Islands.

Judge Ide, Secretary of Finance and Justice, very vividly described the
evils incident to the challenging of judges in his report for 1901, in
which he said the system was found to result in "an absolute paralysis
of all the machinery of justice in certain cases. Aside from the ordinary
grounds of disqualification of judges which exist in the United States,

the Spanish law allowed a peremptory challenge of the competency of judicial officers on the ground of undue friendship or hostility to either party or his counsel." The attorney of either party to a suit, who imagined the judge or magistrate was liable to decide against him, could challenge him, and, thus challenged, the case could be referred to another judge, who could be challenged in turn; and so on indefinitely, even in criminal cases, until "the alleged criminal was able to hold the public entirely at bay and prevent all proceedings to secure his conviction."

On the other hand, decision in criminal prosecutions was sometimes delayed for years in spite of the efforts of the accused to secure speedy trial and determination of his case. One man in Spanish days languished nine years in jail awaiting trial for murder.

Beginning their work on the 1st of September, 1900, by the 11th of June, 1901, the Commission established "a complete system of civil tribunals for the administration of justice in every portion of the Philippine Archipelago." The Chief Justice has always been a Filipino and the majority of the justices up to 1916 under the new act have always been American.

Courts of first instance were established in each province, the Islands being divided into judicial districts, each of which had one or more judges. Additional judges, called at first judges-at-large, and later auxiliary judges, were appointed who were available for detail to assist in clearing up the docket where the work in any court exceeded the power of the district judge to handle. Within a month of the passage of this act six additional acts were passed by the Commission, for the need of which there was abundant evidence. For example, in the island of Negros alone the Commission reported that there were "in round numbers, 1,000 cases pending in the courts of first instance," and there were prisoners who had been waiting trial for nearly two years, some of them for offenses the penalty for which could not by law exceed a few months' imprisonment.

There was some bitterness of feeling among the Filipinos over the selection of so many American judges; Governor Taft appointed both Filipinos and Americans as judges of the courts of first instance. But the earnest and active manner in which the young lawyers set about their service soon silenced these criticisms. The exuberant energy which they brought to their work made them extremely efficient in the matter of keeping their dockets clear. Prejudice against them gave way to complete confidence, and not infrequently instances arose in which litigants on both sides requested that their cases be tried before an American judge, thus avoiding any possible family or partisan influence.

The first Filipino judges were chosen generally from an older class of men in more advanced stations of life, and, although not such rapid workers as their young American colleagues, in the main they performed their duties satisfactorily. "With perhaps one exception," wrote Vice-Governor Ide, "they have administered the law fearlessly and ably, dealing with their own people and with Americans with an even hand. It is believed that the wisdom of appointing a considerable number of Filipinos judges has been amply vindicated by experience and that in the process of time the proportion of Filipino judges may be increased without impairing the efficiency of the administration of justice." Further experience abundantly proved these words to be true. Filipinos made admirable jurists, and performed their duties impartially and fairly.

Having established the courts, the Commissioners immediately took up the revision of the codes with the same vigor and enthusiasm which had characterized their every activity. The new code of civil procedure was passed on August 7, 1901.

Significant legislation introducing American ideas and practice as to penology included amendments of the penal code making slander and offenses against chastity public crimes to be prosecuted in the same manner as other crimes; provision for the reduction of the term of imprisonment in reward for good conduct while serving sentence; the parole of convicts; and a vagrancy law which proved a most effective measure against vicious persons whose misconduct did not fall within other penal laws.

The question as to whether English or Spanish should be the official language of the courts was a difficult one. It was met by providing that Spanish should be the official language of all the courts until 1919, when the Philippine Legislature provided that until January 1, 1930, both English and Spanish shall be the official languages of all courts, it being at the discretion of the court to order its records to be made in either language as it may deem best for the public convenience and the interest of the parties.

The Spanish substantive law was admirable and in later years was to a great extent based on the Code Napoléon. The evils which had crept in were more in the nature of excessive technicalities or otherwise objectionable provisions in the codes of procedure, and in administration, rather than defects in the substantive laws. Thus, while the code of criminal procedure was modified, and a new code of civil procedure was enacted, the civil and penal codes inherited from the Spanish régime in the main continued in force, although from time to time somewhat amended.

In the re-establishment of the courts the Commission introduced the American office of sheriff as the instrumentality for service of notices, maintenance of order in the courtroom, and execution of court orders. In the provinces the governors were required to act *ex officio*, with the right, however, of failing to qualify, in which event the judge of first instance appointed another person.

Clerks of courts were charged with practically the same duties as are such officers in the courts in the United States. Appointees were Filipinos with the exception of the districts comprising the Moro and Mountain Provinces.

Governor-General Smith devised a provision of law calculated to expedite the work of the courts. Before any judge or justice of the peace could draw his salary he had to certify that all cases submitted to him for decision for a period of ninety days or more had been decided. Before the adoption of the law, judges sometimes had been known to delay as much as two years before handing down their decisions. This law, however, was not made applicable to Justices of the Supreme Court.

The Secretary of Finance and Justice had the power to detail judges to help clear up dockets in districts where the work became too much for the judge in charge. There were some provinces where, by reason of the unruliness or the number of the population, the courts were utterly unable to keep the docket clear. When an accumulation of cases reached a point that was considered serious, the Secretary of Finance and Justice detailed one of the judges-at-large, of whom up to 1914 there were two Americans and two Filipinos, to go to the place in question and clear up the docket.

During the period of early Commission administration critics of the government leveled many venomous shafts at this power, charging the Secretary of Justice with endeavoring to influence judicial decisions. It was implied that, by selecting judges with known leanings on certain subjects, verdicts could be secured of a sort desired by the administration. These charges were unjust; they were expected, and endured.

The spirit infused by the American administration into the whole

MANUEL QUEZON

THE HONORABLE CAYETANO S. ARELLANO
Chief Justice of the Philippine Supreme Court

judicial system was little short of marvelous. There was a change from lingering injustice to prompt justice in the courts throughout the archipelago. It was the expression of the spirit of the American administration by such men as Governor Taft and his colleagues on the legislative side, and by Chief Justice Arellano and his earnest and capable Associate Justices on the judicial side. From these men there radiated a spirit of fairness and of enthusiasm for the good of the service which became the dominant note in the courts throughout the archipelago, and reached even the justices of the peace.

Judge Gilbert had a very interesting experience. He was holding court in Cervantes when a young Igorot was brought before him by an old man at whom the youth had thrown a spear from ambush, wounding the man in the fleshy part of his arm and disabling him from work for twenty-one days. Judge Gilbert found the young man guilty and sentenced him to thirty days in jail, and, as required by law, to pay the injured party what he would have been able to earn had he worked during the period of his disability. This came to $1.05. The old man refused to accept the money, and launched into a speech translated to Judge Gilbert as follows:

I did not cause this suit to be brought in order to get money from the defendant. I caused the suit to be brought because it was the American law that a man shall not throw a spear at another and if he does he shall be punished for it; but I did not bring the suit in order to collect money from him. I scorn his money. We have methods for doing that better than any court. I have great respect for the court and I hesitate to fail to do what the court commands but rather than take the money I will go to jail myself.

A notable episode in 1910 was the deportation without notice of twelve undesirable Chinamen who had been leaders in a "tong" and had been terrorizing the Chinese community for a number of years. The more responsible and reputable Chinese merchants were very anxious that the situation should be cleared, as was the Chinese Consul, and they appealed for assistance and protection to the Governor-General.

The twelve men deported had a certain amount of prominence in the community, but there was no doubt that they were undesirable citizens and a menace to the peace of the community. They were summarily arrested and placed aboard a foreign steamer in the harbor chartered for the purpose and delivered to representatives of the Chinese government.

This action was very bitterly assailed by Americans and Filipinos. The right of the Governor-General was questioned, and a suit brought to determine it was carried on appeal to the Supreme Court of the United States, which confirmed the decision of the Philippine Supreme Court and upheld the Governor-General. Justice Holmes set forth that governments have the power to deport aliens; that this power may have to be exercised in a summary way; that the Philippine Bill of Rights cannot prevent such summary action, and that the action taken was not without due process of law.

Beginning with a larger number of American judges of first instance, the number of Filipino judges was greatly increased until 1912, when the proportions became half American and half Filipino. In 1914 additional Filipinos and but two Americans were made judges, and in 1926 there were two Americans and fifty-one Filipinos.

Judges of first instance were appointed by the Governor-General by and with the advice and consent of the Philippine Senate. Judges were removable from office by the head of the government at his discretion, upon recommendation by the Philippine Supreme Court, for serious misconduct or inefficiency.

Courts of justices of the peace, which had been established by the Spaniards in 1885, were re-established in every municipality upon the reorganization of the judiciary in 1901. They have exclusive jurisdiction in civil suits involving not more than one hundred dollars, and concurrent jurisdiction with the court of first instance when the amount exceeds one hundred but is less than three hundred dollars. Justices of the peace have jurisdiction for the trial of persons charged with misdemeanors and with other infractions of law for which the penalty does not exceed six months' imprisonment and a fine of one hundred dollars. Appeals in civil or criminal cases may be taken to the court of first instance and in any criminal case may be carried to the Supreme Court.

In the Moro Province there were created "tribal ward courts" having practically the same jurisdiction as the courts of justices of the peace in other provinces. In the Mountain Province the provincial officials and the lieutenant-governors in the sub-provinces were *ex officio* justices of the peace.

Justices of the peace and other minor officials, as well as employees of the judiciary, from the beginning of civil administration were with rare exception Filipinos.

The adjudication of titles to real estate soon became and continues to be a most important function of the courts.

The Spanish system of land titles, however admirable as provided by law, in practice was most unfortunate. Of some 2,300,000 parcels of land claimed to be privately owned relatively few were represented by title deeds acceptable for transfers of ownership, or mortgage purposes. Worse, there was no exact definition of metes and bounds, even in the instances of royal grants or other recorded titles, due either to vague description of natural boundaries or faulty surveys. The boundaries were sure to be disputed sooner or later and such disputes were likely to run for generations, giving ground for much ill-feeling, controversies between neighbors, and even crimes of violence.

It was early felt by Americans that no measure would make for better citizenship, economic progress, and contentment on the part of the people than one which would give them clear documentary titles, guaranteed by the government, to the land they, and in most cases their ancestors, had cultivated, improved, and considered their own. In November, 1902, the Commission enacted a law for the registration of land ownership under the Torrens system, which provides for the granting of titles to real estate, with government guarantee, after compliance with appropriate requirements as to surveys and proofs of ownership.

Inasmuch as the law was an innovation and did not make the registration of titles compulsory, landowners were slow to take advantage of its provisions, except the comparatively few who understood the use of first-class security in financing agricultural and other commercial enterprises. As a result less than four thousand land titles were registered during the first seven years of operation of the court, and these comprised almost wholly large private properties and lands purchased by the government. The titles to friar land estates purchased by the government were registered each estate as one case. As these were disposed of to tenants and others, these lands were subdivided and certificates of title were issued on about forty thousand parcels.

Upon investigation and check surveys by the Bureau of Lands, it appeared that fully eighty per cent of the early private surveys were seriously defective. To meet this situation the Legislature authorized the employment of a sufficient number of qualified surveyors to enable the Bureau of Lands to assist the court and imposed the requirement that private surveyors might not prepare cases for submission to the court unless they had qualified by examination for the civil service or by the Bureau of Lands.

The private surveyors had their permits from the Spanish government to practice their profession, and, partly as a matter of pride and partly with genuine apprehension as to their ability, resented the requirement that they should qualify by examination. They organized to secure a repeal of the law and used their influence to arouse antagonism to the Court of Land Registration and the Bureau of Lands.

Improved economic conditions stimulated agriculture to such a point that people began to take much more interest in the development of cultivatable lands. Gradually use began to be made of the privilege of homesteading, and many parcels were taken up by squatters.

The annual increase in the number of occupied parcels of land was estimated at twenty thousand. These, together with the more than 2,300,000 parcels occupied or claimed in private ownership at the time of the enactment of the registration law, became a major problem confronting the government. There was growing danger of conflicts between the rich landowners and the poorer people, increasing numbers of whom were asserting their claims to the ownership of lands they cultivated or were seeking homestead locations on lands they believed to be of the public domain. These homesteads often were later claimed by wealthy men as being within the boundaries of their holdings. Furthermore, it was found that the provincial and municipal treasuries were being defrauded of substantial amounts of tax revenue because of the failure of many landholders to declare more than a fraction of the areas they claimed. In some instances valuable parcels of land wholly escaped the assessment rolls.

It was necessary to devise a comprehensive measure which would assure justice to all interested, including the illiterate, small landowner and the local government treasuries, as well as the rich claimant of large areas of land. Such a measure was framed in 1910 in the form of a proposed cadastral law, under the operation of which the government was to undertake the survey of all the occupied lands in the archipelago, municipality by municipality. It proposed, just so soon as a sufficient number of parcels had been surveyed — say one thousand — to hold a special session of the Court of Land Registration in the municipality itself. The friendly object of the government was to be explained to the Filipinos through the medium of Filipino orators, and the Bureau of Justice was to detail and pay the salaries of two lawyers, one American and one Filipino, to defend the causes of the landowners. The government was thus to require all occupants of these parcels to prove their claim for ownership of the land they held. The landowner, through his attorney supplied by the government, would then bring his proof and, if satisfactory, the government would issue him a title for the land. It was estimated that an active judge could handle ten cases in a year, thus adjudicating the ownership of ten thousand parcels of land. The expense of these surveys, including the salaries of the law-yers, was to be advanced in the first place by the insular government and to be in part reimbursed in five annual installments in the follow-ing proportions: ten per cent by the province, ten per cent by the mu-nicipality, and seventy per cent by the landowners, leaving ten per cent as the ultimate net cost to the insular government. By this device the terms of securing title were made so easy that they were in no way burdensome to the landowner, and the increased tax revenue to the provinces and municipalities in most cases was found to be more than enough to cover their ten per cent of the cost.

The additional annual cost for the first few years to the Bureau of Lands was estimated to be something over $500,000, which would grad-ually diminish as the volume of repayments from previous surveys be-gan to roll up, until finally the necessity for further annual appropria-tions on the part of the insular government would practically disappear. It was not, however, practicable to put this system into effect imme-diately, as the government at that time had very little financial margin above the amount absolutely necessary to its existing activities. More-over, some years would be required for the training of the necessary number of additional surveyors. The Director of Lands estimated that it would take three years to reach the required rate of achievement.

A test was made of the operation of the principal features of the plan in the densely populated province of Pangasinan, where a block of 970 parcels of land was surveyed and carried through to conclusion, 906 cases being disposed of by one judge in three weeks at a net average cost of $3.75 per parcel. No effort was spared to inform the people in advance as to the purposes of the government, and the plan of having lawyers provided by the government to assist the landowners without charge in the preparation of their cases was found to work well. The people enthusiastically coöperated.

Opposition in the Assembly to the passage of the proposed cadastral act caused the Commission in 1911 to enact the law for the territory in-habited chiefly by Mohammedans and tribal peoples. A survey was then ordered of lands in Zamboanga, the capital of the Moro Province. More than two thousand parcels of land, valued at nearly $1,000,000, were surveyed in blocks and within less than two months titles of ownership determined by the court. The expense, apportioned on the basis of valuation, ran from $1.25 to $8.00 per parcel.

Finally, in February, 1913, the Legislature passed the cadastral act. A programme had been prepared contemplating the adjudication of cases involving one hundred thousand parcels per annum. At this rate twenty-five years would be required to conclude the work for the entire archipelago.

Surveys were immediately authorized in various municipalities and work begun in the province of Occidental Negros. The Bureau of Lands developed a staff of highly efficient, specially trained personnel, and the judges of the Court of Land Registration were selected for their ability to give prompt dispatch of cases with justice to interested parties.

The completion of a survey and the granting of titles under the Torrens system resulted in an average of a twenty-five per cent increase in the receipts from land tax, an important source of revenue to municipal and provincial governments.

On the whole, the policy of the registration of lands has worked well, and a summary made in 1927 indicated that in the towns in which the titles were earliest given to occupants of the land there was no general tendency revealed on the part of the occupants to sell their lands.

In 1914, the Philippine Legislature reorganized the courts of first instance. Although the number of judges of first instance was increased by twelve, the Court of Land Registration with six judges was abolished. This made a net increase of six judges, but the additional work of the cadastral cases added so much to the volume of the already greatly overburdened courts of first instance that land registration was seriously retarded as a result of the change. During the ensuing seven years, 1914-20, the courts decreed titles to less than one hundred thousand parcels of land, which did not cover the number of new parcels estimated to have been taken up during that period.

Under the Treaty of Paris, the United States acquired from Spain the public lands in the Philippine Islands. There has been no comprehensive survey of the public domain, but the most conservative official estimate of the area classifiable as agricultural is somewhat in excess of 16,600,000 acres.

Congress, in the first organic act for the government of the Islands, had placed the public domain under the control of the Philippine government to be administered for the benefit of the inhabitants of the Islands, and made detailed provisions for the acquisition of homesteads and sale of agricultural lands to individuals, limiting the areas to forty acres each for homestead entries under conditions which practically restricted such acquisitions to Filipinos. In the case of corporations, lease and ownership were limited to twenty-five hundred acres, thus, in effect, excluding any large enterprise which presumably would be financed by American or foreign capitalists. These and other restrictions, imposed by Congress ostensibly for the protection of the Filipinos, in reality were the results of a very powerful lobby maintained in Washington by the beet sugar interests, who looked with alarm upon possible Philippine competition and endeavored to cripple the Philippine sugar industry by preventing corporations from holding enough land to supply a modern sugar central. The machinations of the beet sugar interests were materially assisted by the activities of the Anti-Imperialist League, which, for wholly different reasons but with the same general effect, brought all the influence it had to bear to discourage American capital from going to the Islands. None the less, the centrals were built in spite of the limitation. The government-owned Philippine National Bank assisted in financing a number of these enterprises. The limitation, however, undoubtedly served as a deterrent to early private enterprise in sugar development and to the development of rubber and other industries requiring large tracts of land for economical operation.

Filipinos of means desiring to acquire large tracts of land were able to purchase holdings under former Spanish grants often very vague in their definitions as to metes and bounds, and frequently this very vagueness enabled holders of such grants to make good their claims to larger tracts than the grants ostensibly described. Many of these grants greatly exceeded the limit of twenty-five hundred acres placed by Congress on the acquisition of public domain as distinguished from private domain. In some instances these grants were found to include within their boundaries land occupied by small farmers who had believed the farms to be their own. The Filipino had been so long under a feudal system where the word of the local *cacique* was his law that often these small landholders were deprived of their property without realizing the possibility of recourse to the courts to assert their rights.

Many years elapsed before the Filipinos began to avail themselves in large numbers of the opportunity to obtain land through homesteading. That movement gradually gained headway and during the years 1913, 1914, and 1915 began to reach important proportions. The growth of the province of Isabela, following upon the opening of the new road from Nueva Ecija and Nueva Vizcaya, is perhaps the most striking evidence of the manner in which the Filipinos availed themselves of these opportunities once they came to understand them. In the year 1924, this road through the mountains was opened, and within two years the population of the province is reported to have doubled and its production to have trebled.

This is the more noteworthy as the Filipino is essentially a lover of his home and devoted to his native town and the inducement had to be very alluring to make him move.

By an act of the Legislature in 1924, approved by the President, more liberal conditions for homesteading were given, and the maximum area that may be purchased by an individual was increased to three hundred and sixty acres.

Unfortunately the situation was complicated by the ignorance of the average homestead applicant. Many of them got into the hands of unscrupulous land sharks or local magnates, who encouraged them to cultivate and improve lands other than those they had filed upon, so that, when the time came for them to prove up, they discovered to their dismay that the land they had improved did not lie within the lines of their homestead claim. Sometimes other means were used to drive them off land upon which they had planned to make their home.

Some shocking cases of abuse of power arose, violence resulting in a number of instances, even reaching to the extent of murder, or the filing of false charges resulting in the poor man being thrown into prison while his property and crops were taken possession of by the rapacious *cacique* of his region. Cases of this character came to the attention of the Wood-Forbes Mission in 1921, especially in the province of Nueva Ecija, in some districts of which homesteaders were terrorized by lawless landgrabbers with whom the government seemed unable to cope. These conditions were corrected by energetic action on the part of Governor-General Wood soon after his appointment.

In reviewing the homestead statistics, there are to be noted great discrepancies between the number of applications received and the number of patents issued, due to delays in surveys by the Bureau of Lands, cancellations of applications because of conflicting claims and protests, the inability or failure of the applicant to reside on and cultivate the homestead, and failure to pay the required fees, amounting only to ten dollars and payable in annual installments.[3]

[3] *Census*, 1918, III, 880, 881. Act No. 2874, Philippine Legislature, November 29, 1919, Sections 12–15.

A total of 11,088 free titles, covering an aggregate area of 87,560 acres, were issued by the close of 1926 to persons who, through ignorance and lack of money, had been unable under the Spanish government to secure documentary titles to lands they, and in many cases their ancestors before them, had improved and cultivated.

Foreigners, especially Japanese and Chinese, by organizing corporations under the Philippine corporation laws were able to acquire lands from the public domain, which otherwise were available to Americans and Filipinos only.

Up to December 31, 1926, under the various provisions of the public land laws, more than 550,000 acres of agricultural land have passed from the public domain to more than 21,000 private persons.

The determination of land titles has thrown a heavy burden on the courts, and careful observers believe that the problem would be more expeditiously and economically handled were the Court of Land Registration to be re-established with a sufficiently larger number of judges to care for its constantly increasing volume of business.

The number of judicial districts was increased during the period 1902 to 1926 from fifteen to twenty-seven, and the number of judges of first instance from sixteen to fifty-three. The work of the courts increased from 4194 civil and 6555 criminal cases presented in 1904 to 10,824 civil and 12,505 criminal cases in 1926. Nothwithstanding the increase in the number of judges, there were 18,510 civil and 4799 criminal cases pending at the close of 1926.

CHAPTER VII

HEALTH AND EDUCATION

HEALTH

AT THE TIME of American occupation the health conditions in the Islands were deplorable. Hygiene and sanitation were but little advanced from medieval days. Except as to vaccination against smallpox in Manila and to a limited extent in the provinces, there was little knowledge of the prevention of disease. The people of all classes, although living in the tropics, closed the windows of their houses and covered their heads against the night air, with the idea that it carried harmful properties. Dysentery, malaria, tuberculosis, and skin diseases were common. Vaccination was desultory, smallpox was endemic, and the deaths from that disease alone were often forty thousand in one year. There was no effective maritime quarantine. Bubonic plague was occasionally introduced, brought in by rats on ships from Oriental ports and transmitted to the people by fleas. Cholera repeatedly swept over the Islands, carrying off its victims by hundreds of thousands. No city had an adequate supply of potable water. Garbage and sewage disposal were primitive, even in Manila.

Perhaps the most prevalent and serious of all the evils were the insidious intestinal parasites, causing a reduction in efficiency and an incapacity for sustained physical effort which had much to do with the then prevalent unfavorable reputation of the Filipino as a laborer.

Before the Americans could begin their effective labors in public health, it was necessary to put down insurrection and establish public order; the close of hostilities left racial distrust, and it was obvious that some time must elapse before the Filipinos would subject themselves to the somewhat onerous health requirements which the Americans felt it necessary to enforce.

Before American occupation there had been a tendency to consider a pestilence, whether of cholera, plague, or other communicable disease, as an act of God sent in His inscrutable wisdom as a punishment for some lack of piety in the lives of the persons visited. Disease, according to this belief, was not to be combated by medicine, or by preventive measures, but by an increase in piety, which often took the form of liberal gifts to the church. A common method of combating pestilence was to form a procession to carry the image of San Roque through the village. Sometimes the result was the spread of disease and increase in deaths, as the people were called together to pray for cessation of cholera, thus bringing about a condition of crowding more likely to disseminate the germ of the disease.

From the beginning of American occupation, serious attention was given to the public health, first by medical officers serving with the troops, and, after the occupation of Manila, by army medical officers detailed exclusively to public health work and by selected Filipino physicians. Extension of this service went with the extension of military occupation throughout the provinces. Successive chief surgeons of the army of occupation directed public health work until a board for the whole archipelago was created by the Philippine Commission, in 1901. Officer after officer gave devoted service, and several lost their lives from exposure and overwork.

Major E. C. Carter, also of the medical corps of the army, served as Commissioner of Public Health, until, exhausted by his labors, he was relieved in April, 1905, by Dr. Victor G. Heiser, at that time Chief Quarantine Officer of the Islands, who took on, in addition to his quarantine duties, the direction of the Bureau of Health, as the public health service came to be designated. He came with a masterly grasp of his problems, great tact, infinite patience, and a mind of an extremely practical turn. An accomplished linguist, he soon learned how to deal with the Filipinos, discount their prejudices, and take advantage of their qualities to attain his objects, which were always directed with a single eye to the best interest of the Philippine people. Dr. Heiser developed the Bureau of Health to the marvelous degree of efficiency which it finally reached.

The death rate from all causes in this period was reduced from 27.46 per 1000 in 1905 to 18.82 per 1000 in 1913, and rose after he had left the service to 35.28 per 1000 in 1918. It was not until the later years of General Wood's incumbency as Governor-General that it was reduced to 19.94 per 1000.

Dr. Fulleborn of the Hamburg School of Tropical Medicine in 1909 wrote:

The Germans, and all other nations having colonies in the far east, will have to take lessons from the Manila sanitary authorities in dealing with the evils that beset us.

In regard to vaccination, I am sure many of our physicians will demand cold figures when I tell them that in the Philippines the Americans have vaccinated over six millions of people without a single death.

The revenues of the government were extremely small and not nearly enough to care adequately for the health needs of the people. With a gross population of almost ten million, about ninety-five per cent of whom came into the world, lived, and died without opportunity to obtain medical assistance, the total annual expenditure for the public health service during the nine years 1905–13 averaged less than seven cents per capita.

The work of the Bureau of Health was constructive and educational. The prejudices of the people against any health measures, against the use of hospitals, and against the Americans, had to be overcome. Popular interest, enthusiasm, and confidence once aroused, time was still needed to train Filipino doctors in modern methods, to train hospital and health nurses of both sexes, and get them at work. At the time of American arrival in the Islands, it was estimated that there was but one doctor for every twenty thousand people.

The cost of the quarantine service was defrayed from Philippine revenues although manned from the United States Public Health Service. It was conducted in the most modern and up-to-date manner without undue interference with commerce or with the movement of ships.

It was essential to teach the people generally the fundamental principles of hygiene. The matter of prenatal care for expectant mothers and the feeding of children had a direct bearing on infant mortality. The belief, to which allusion has been made, that all illnesses were acts of God, had to be combated and the people taught that most ailments were preventable and that an intelligent application of the laws of health would prevent them.

The fight against cholera was bitter and deadly. Officer after officer succumbed to the disease or to overwork. In the early military days the measures taken against the spread of the infection were drastic. Houses which had been occupied by the sick were burned, a measure, however, not so extreme as it sounds because most of these houses were built of bamboo, thatched with leaves of palm or with grasses, and could be rebuilt without burdensome expense. Later, Dr. Heiser was able to apply methods of effective disinfection without destruction of property. Americans soon learned to take precautions against infection; but even so, the death-roll among them was heavy. Preventive measures consisted mostly in the early diagnosis of the cases and their isolation, in the safe disposal of human discharges, the use of boiled water, sterilization of table utensils, washing hands in disinfectants before eating, and extreme care against flies in markets as well as in private places and kitchens.

This work against cholera was done by heroes, without fanfare, and never received the same degree of public attention as that of American administrators in dealing with yellow fever and malaria in other tropical countries. The sense of relief that came to the community when cholera was brought under control is keenly recalled by those who lived through the terrible days when a friend who might have been perfectly well at noon, was stricken ill by midafternoon, and died during the night; when burial forces could not keep pace with death, but could only throw a few shovelsful of earth upon the corpses, laid in trenches row upon row, cartload after cartload.

The bubonic plague was fought by an intensive campaign against rats brought into Manila by ships from certain foreign ports. The rats, destroyed by thousands, were sent in to the Bureau of Science from every part of the city, labeled with the names of the regions in which they were caught, and examined microscopically. Whenever evidence of infection of bubonic plague was detected, the region from which the rat carrying it came was immediately placed under suspicion, and the health authorities systematically killed all the rats in the immediate locality.

Bacteriological diagnosis and other studies were made by the Bureau of Science into the nature of the more dangerous communicable diseases, and in some instances vaccines or serums were devised for the production of artificial immunity. Very advanced work of this sort was carried on under the extremely able direction of Dr. Richard P. Strong.

In the Bureau of Science the specific and successful cure of yaws was developed and important advances were made in the diagnosis and treatment of the various forms of tropical dysentery and of cholera.

Smallpox was vigorously dealt with. Vaccination was compulsory and was extended to the whole population in spite of great difficulties, with results that left no doubt of its efficacy. It was not easy to make a start. There were vaccinators to be trained and they were not always reliable; and vaccine does not keep well unless maintained at a certain fairly cool temperature, a very difficult thing to do in the tropics. The result was that, although the sanitary officers learned the necessity and the means of keeping the vaccine cool, a good deal of it got into careless hands and became spoiled or rendered ineffective before use. Moreover, vaccinators were not always scrupulous about doing the actual vaccination. It was much easier to dump the vaccine in the wastebasket and report the people vaccinated, and in some instances health authorities found proof of this having been done. But despite all this the result of the fight against smallpox was little short of miraculous, reducing the number of deaths annually from this cause from forty thousand to but a few hundreds.

A very extraordinary instance indicative of the development of popular belief in vaccination against smallpox was reported by the Director of Health. On the little island of Caluya, just south of the island of Mindoro, a man arrived suffering from an illness which soon proved to be smallpox, and from which he died. An old woman, claiming to understand the matter of vaccination, took the contents of a pustule from the man shortly before his death and commenced to inoculate a number of the inhabitants. Nearly one thousand cases of smallpox resulted before the facts became known to the outer world. Vaccinators, properly equipped, were immediately sent to Caluya to vaccinate the remaining population, some of whom were found to have been vaccinated previously. Of a total population of two thousand about four hundred died from smallpox, all the deaths occurring among persons who had never been properly vaccinated previous to exposure to the disease. The epidemic was checked by proper vaccination.

With the passage of the Jones Law and control of both houses of the Legislature placed in the hands of elective Filipinos, there was a marked falling off in legislative interest in health matters, and a decrease in the appropriation available for vaccine and vaccination against smallpox. Dr. J. D. Long, of the United States Public Health Service, who was Director of Health in the Islands succeeding Dr. Heiser, is authority for the statement that the amount spent on vaccination was greatly reduced and the interest shown by vaccinators and the efficiency of their work were greatly impaired during the period 1916-18, and he handed in his resignation on account of lack of support.

The public health statistics reveal the immediate effect of this failure. The mortality from smallpox in the Islands rose from 4.77 per 100,000 in 1917 to 527.19 per 100,000 in 1919. In the city of Manila there had been no deaths from smallpox from 1909 until its reappearance in 1916; in 1918, as shown in the figures taken from the report of Governor-General Harrison, there were 869 deaths. The official figures for the whole archipelago reveal 16,147 deaths from smallpox in 1918, and 49,971 in 1919. Most of the deaths from smallpox occurred among children who showed no evidence of vaccination. It is probable the actual deaths from smallpox were much greater than shown in the official reports, as there was a tendency among culpable health officers who had not properly performed their vaccinations to fail to report smallpox as the cause of deaths occurring in their districts.

In the light of the foregoing it is curious that anti-vaccinationists have pointed to the Philippine Islands as proof of the ineffectiveness of vaccination. The cases cited by anti-vaccinationists of death or failure of the vaccine to protect, either were of persons not vaccinated, or were due to treatments now known to have been improperly administered, or to the use of deteriorated vaccine.

One of the most lamentable results of this failure properly to maintain vaccination manifested itself in a terrible calamity which overtook some Ifugaos who had been brought down by the Constabulary in 1918 to work on the construction of a necessary road from the province of Nueva Ecija into the province of Nueva Vizcaya. This road would have been of great benefit to the provinces of these people, but that did not justify fifteen hundred of these men being driven down against their will to work on the road, where they were exposed to contagion from smallpox. This disease was at that time prevalent owing to the failure of the health authorities to maintain efficient vaccination. So-called Spanish influenza was also prevalent at that time in the Islands and both diseases were contracted by the Ifugaos. The mortality was extremely heavy, and those who succeeded in returning to their province, where preventive measures were also lacking, carried with them the contagion, and the resulting mortality was appalling.

It is only fair to the Filipinos to say that this episode occurred largely under American direction. The governor of the Ifugao sub-province, the engineer who had charge of the road, and the chief foreman, all were Americans.

Leprosy is believed to have existed in the Philippine Islands at the time of the first Spanish exploration, and provision for the care of persons suffering from this as from other diseases was first made by the Franciscan friars in the sixteenth century by the erection of a shelter in front of their monastery, within the walled city of Manila, where the hospital of San Juan de Dios was subsequently erected. It was not until 1632, however, that there is authoritative record of the disease in the Islands and that provision was made for the separate hospital care of lepers. In that year the Japanese government was making a determined effort to drive all Christians from its empire. The Spanish records state that among the Christians deported to Manila by the Japanese authorities were one hundred and thirty Japanese lepers who had been converted to Christianity. After their arrival special provision was made by separate accommodation in the native hospital for their segregation, and later a special hospital was provided.

Aside from the San Lazaro Hospital at Manila, there were but two leper hospitals dating from Spanish days which merit mention, one at Cebu and another at Nueva Caceres, but these were little more than poor lodgings for lepers who cared to use them. The lepers of the wealthy families remained in private houses with or near relatives and friends, tending to infect those with whom they came in contact. The poorer lepers were more or less outcasts and sometimes lived segregated in little groups a short distance from the main towns, where they felt themselves neglected and often ill-treated.

When the American government organized the public health service, leprosy was found to be growing and to have reached formidable proportions in various provinces. By 1902 conditions were ripe for an intensive campaign to segregate the lepers, not only for the protection of the public against infection, but in order to give the lepers themselves better care and opportunity for modern treatment. A systematic investigation conducted by the Bureau of Health estimated about five thousand cases of leprosy in the archipelago. In 1904, the total number found was 3623, and an unknown, doubtless lesser, number not detected.

In 1902, the Commission appropriated fifty thousand dollars for the establishment of a leper colony, and the Governor-General in August, 1904, set aside the island of Culion for this purpose and the work of construction began. A coast guard ship was designated for the work of gathering up the lepers. Effective segregation began in May, 1905. The colony by 1913 numbered nearly 3500 souls and later reached 5400, and the arduous task of gathering the lepers and carrying them to Culion was undertaken largely by Dr. Heiser in person.

Culion, situated about a day's travel from Manila by steamer, has a beautiful harbor and high, rolling country. Here a concrete hospital

CARABAO AND CART

NAIC-INDANG ROAD, CAVITE, BEFORE IMPROVEMENT

NAIC-INDANG ROAD, CAVITE, AFTER IMPROVEMENT

was constructed, as well as other service buildings. An old Spanish church was made available and Jesuit priests secured to minister to the colony. It is typical of the Jesuits that, when the call for volunteers for this service went forth, every priest responded, including Father Algué, Chief of the Weather Bureau. Unselfish and high-minded clergymen attached to various Protestant missions, both in the Philippine Islands and the United States, also volunteered and some of them were rather insistent that they should be given the opportunity to join in rendering this self-sacrificing service. A corps of nurses was secured, mostly of the religious order of the Sisters of St. Paul de Chartres, who devoted themselves to this service with a piety and sacrifice that command the profoundest admiration. The lepers for the first time found themselves tenderly cared for, properly fed, and treated as human beings. The colony had a playground, and a band of its own; the patients were given an allowance of money, and they were permitted to marry if they desired, a priest performing the marriage ceremony. Children born of lepers are free of leprosy and likely to contract the disease only by contact later with those having it. Measures were taken to prevent this occurring.

Some years after the establishment of the leper colony, scientists announced that the disease of beriberi was the result of a prolonged diet too exclusively of polished rice. In government institutions, such as hospitals, sanatoria, prisons, and barracks, where polished rice was served, beriberi was often prevalent. Rice in its natural state carries a thin coating containing nutritive substances necessary for the maintenance of healthy human life. Polished rice is much nicer looking than the more healthful, unpolished rice, and people to whom it was served were apt to prefer it. The mortality in the leper colony due to beriberi was high. The government made early use of the new knowledge and substituted unpolished for polished rice, with the result that the death rate in the colony decreased sharply.

Leprosy is a disease which usually progresses very slowly. Many of the afflicted parts lose their sensibility and become painless. Lepers are very apt to die from some other disease than leprosy as their power of resistance is lowered.

Experiments with chaulmoogra oil were early undertaken in the treatment of leprosy. As first administered, the oil produced nausea and patients preferred the disease to the treatment. In later years methods were found by which the oil could be successfully administered without the nauseating effects. Until the arrival of General Wood as Governor-General in 1921, although there had been a number of cases and some reported cures, only ten per cent of the lepers had undergone this treatment and the Legislature had failed to provide funds for a more extensive use of the oil. General Wood's personal devotion to the cause of the lepers was such that during his administration a much larger proportion underwent treatment, reaching as high as seventy per cent. By the end of the year 1924, of these, seventy-five per cent were improved, four hundred and nine cases being "negatives" — free from evidence of disease — and one hundred and ninety-seven former lepers returned to their homes as cured. In 1927, Governor-General Wood in a cablegram to the War Department reported that nearly a thousand cures had been effected.

It was hoped that the establishment of the colony would result in the rapid elimination of the disease, but although more than twenty years have elapsed, reports received as late as 1926 indicate that the number of new cases admitted annually continues to be high. It is said, however, that in later years nearly all the new admissions are in the early stages of the disease, which proves that the carriers of infection are being more quickly discovered and segregated. The exact manner in which the infection of leprosy is communicated is not yet known, and as it may be communicable before its symptoms become manifest, and, moreover, years may elapse after the infection before such manifestations occur, the complete elimination of the disease may be remote.

It is interesting to note that in Dutch and British colonies, which have been under European rule in some instances for hundreds of years, lepers are still allowed at large and are not cared for at public expense.

The Philippine Islands were found to be particularly badly off in the matter of hospital facilities. There were two general hospitals in Manila under the charge of religious orders, but there were very few hospitals in the provinces. The United States Army maintains a military hospital in Manila, and also one at each military post in the provinces, in which emergency civil cases have always been given relief. Under the terms of the contracts entered into between the civil government and its employees free medical and hospital service was promised in all cases of diseases incurred in the service.

The Bureau of Health finally, in 1907, secured an appropriation of about four hundred thousand dollars for the construction of a general hospital in Manila. A well-designed modern hospital, with proper oper-

ating-rooms and wards for various purposes, was built; an adequate
staff secured; and an out-patient department opened. It was not long
before it was crowded.

In 1912, the Philippine Commission reported as to this dispensary,
which it stated ranked "among the principal clinics of the world," as
follows:

The growth of the Free General Hospital Dispensary has been phenomenal.
During the fiscal year 1911 it treated 24,335 patients and filled 39,178 prescriptions.
During the fiscal year 1912 it treated 64,673 patients and filled 83,517 prescriptions.
It is now treating patients at the rate of 80,000 per year.

By 1925, the capacity of the hospital wards had been increased to more
than six hundred beds without meeting the growing popular demands
upon it.

In another part of Manila there was built a group of hospitals for
plague, cholera, smallpox, tuberculosis, and other dangerous communicable diseases. It is a veritable triumph for modern science that no instance occurred of one of these diseases being communicated from one
patient to another.

It was not long before other Philippine regions began to demand hospitals. A well-planned institution was built in Cebu; another one in the
province of Bontoc for the savages in the hills; and another, including
cottages for tuberculosis patients, in the mountain capital of Baguio.
The ideal to be sought was a hospital in each sanitary district and provision for medical service at least in all the urban centers within reach
of the more accessible portion of the rural population. The scanty funds
of the treasury delayed the realization of this dream.

At the end of 1926 there were in operation 45 government hospitals
and 1028 dispensaries.

Tuberculosis was very prevalent in the Islands. In 1910, an American
woman, noted for her public spirit, had the vision and energy to take
the first steps toward organizing an association calculated to awaken the
Philippine people to a realization of the peril of tuberculosis, and under
her able direction an anti-tuberculosis league was organized. A hospital
for segregating cases in the vicinity of Manila was established, funds
raised, and an appropriation secured from the Legislature.

But in 1913 Acting Governor-General Gilbert reported that "Tuberculosis continues to be the most serious existing menace to the general
health and longevity of the people of the Philippines, and the existing

facilities for combating it, while productive of much good, are altogether inadequate. . . ."

Throughout the early days of American administration a crying need was for more trained personnel in the medical department of the government. Not only were doctors needed, but it was very necessary to have nurses, both male and female, and sanitary inspectors. The colleges carried forward from former days had neither the facilities nor the teaching staff trained in modern scientific methods. The Secretary of the Interior, the Honorable Dean C. Worcester, saw the need of a medical school established by the government, capable of educating high standard physicians and surgeons, and also in large numbers.

It was impossible to make a very early start because as a necessary preliminary there had to be potential students who had had an adequate academic education in intermediate, and part of the high school course. Candidates for this instruction had to have a two-years' preparatory course, which was given in the Normal School in Manila. Thus it was not until 1907 that the medical school was finally started. It later became a part of the University of the Philippines.

In order to assure a supply of young doctors well distributed geographically throughout the Islands, it was provided that there should be as many scholarships as there were regularly organized provinces in the Islands, such scholarships to be awarded after competitive examination in the provinces. It was stipulated that upon graduation the student should return to the province from which he came and there give his service to the people of his province for a number of years equal to those during which his education was paid for by the government. This assured the medical school a constant supply of carefully selected young students, and also tended to meet the need of the provinces for a properly trained medical staff.

The health officials gave special training courses for sanitary inspectors, and in 1909 adopted a novel method of improving efficiency and raising the standards throughout the force. They divided the sanitary inspectors into three classes or grades and limited the number in the highest grade. The doctor in charge of each inspector's service made a careful rating of his work each month. If any in a lower class had a higher rating than those in a higher class, the latter were transferred to the lower class and their successful rivals promoted to their places. The incentive for good work was very strong. It was not only necessary to do good work to reach the highest grade, but the standard of this grade had to be continuously maintained if the incumbent was to stay there.

Training classes for nurses were established in 1907 and met with a ready response from the Filipinos. In 1909 the Legislature recognized the success of the undertaking by providing fifty scholarships annually for candidates to be selected by the division superintendents of schools throughout the Islands. Thereafter the government training school for nurses developed into an institution of high standards and great usefulness. Young girls of the very best families came to Manila and devoted their lives to this service wholeheartedly. The fame of the school reached also beyond the boundaries of the Philippine Islands and girls came from China and even from Siam to take the course.

Training schools for nurses were organized also in connection with some of the larger hospitals supported by church missions and other private enterprises. Later it was deemed necessary to regulate the practice of the nursing profession by requiring registration, fixing standards of qualifications, and creating a board of examiners.

At the close of the year 1926 there were nearly two thousand registered nurses in the Islands.

Selected graduates of the schools of medicine and of nursing were sent on government scholarships to the best universities in the United States for post-graduate courses and training in special branches. Some of these distinguished themselves.

The general organization of the Islands into sanitary districts was a matter of somewhat late development because it had to wait for the availability of trained personnel. In February, 1912, however, an act was passed by the Legislature authorizing consolidation of municipalities into sanitary divisions, and it was provided by this law that each division should be in the charge of a duly qualified physician. The medical needs of the people had to be met from the scanty revenues of one of the lowest taxed countries in the civilized world.

One of the things which had to be postponed was the construction of asylums for suitable care of the insane. Hospital facilities in Manila were inadequate even for the dangerous and violent cases. It was estimated that there were four thousand insane people in the Islands, and it is obvious that without adequate and proper institutions built for the purpose and trained forces — not only doctors but nurses, matrons, and attendants — to care for them, these unfortunates had little chance of cure or proper care. In 1907, a new insane asylum was constructed in Manila which could care for two hundred and fifty of the most urgent cases. An adequate general institution, with proper wards and surroundings for each class of cases, was still needed.

One of the most potent means of improving the general health of the people was the installation of modern pure water systems, with necessary reservoirs, especially in Manila, Cebu, and some of the lesser cities. But that which contributed more than any other one thing toward improvement of the health conditions of the people was the supply of potable water obtained by boring artesian wells. In many parts of the Islands these wells provided a constant stream of pure water; and wherever bored the result, as manifested by the lowered death-rate of the people, was immediate and most gratifying. As a direct result of some of these artesian wells the death rate from water-borne disease was cut almost in half.

The following table presents for typical years the birth and death rates derived from available Spanish data and selected years since 1903:

Year	Birth rate per 1000 population	Death rate per 1000 population
1876	46.2	26.7
1885	50.5	28.9
1898	47.6	30.5
1905	40.32	27.46
1910	31.34	25.08
1915	38.61	20.94
1920	35.24	21.08
1925	37.42	19.94

The corresponding data for the United States for the year 1925 were: birth rate, 21.4; death rate, 11.8.

The principal causes of death among adults are tuberculosis and malaria. Against both these and other diseases campaigns of education have been carried on by the government through the schools and otherwise.

Scarlet fever and typhus are unknown in the Islands.

In 1921 the Rockefeller Foundation arranged a survey of public health conditions in the Islands and their representatives prepared a programme for more intensive work. The Foundation generously coöperated in putting this programme into effect by providing highly qualified specialists to assist as consultants and otherwise.

A systematic campaign against infant mortality was initiated in February, 1912, when a bill, passed by the legislature, created a committee of physicians for the purpose of investigating the excessive infant mortality. The rate in the city of Manila had been reduced from 811.35 per 1000 births in 1904 to 334.45 per 1000 in 1913, chiefly through strict inspection of milk supply and the enforcement of requirements that milk, whether fresh or canned, offered for sale should come up to certain standards not only as to purity but also as to content of butterfat and consequent nutritive value. This was reflected by a reduction in the infant mortality rate throughout the Islands during the same period from 224.40 to 152.91 per thousand.

The great problem of reducing infant mortality in the city of Manila was undertaken by the establishment in 1907 of a private institution popularly known as *La Gota de Leche*, to furnish pure sterilized milk to infants whose mothers were unable to nurse them. This enterprise, duly incorporated as *La Protección de la Infancia*, was continued with success from its small beginning in Manila and proved to be the nucleus from which has been developed a far-reaching organization with branches in most of the important centers of the population throughout the Islands, systematically coöperating with the government in its efforts to reduce infant mortality.

Due to the fact that army veterinary surgeons belonged in the medical department of the army, the eradication of dangerous communicable diseases of cattle and other domestic animals became one of the duties of the government health service at the time of its organization with an army medical officer as Commissioner of Health. The campaign against rinderpest was especially important because of the great losses of beef and work animals from that disease. In the reorganization of the government in 1905, this work was transferred, with its personnel, to the Bureau of Agriculture, and the most highly trained scientists available were secured to carry it on.

BUREAU OF SCIENCE

THE application of modern science was utilized from the very earliest days of the civil administration to solve many problems that were directly concerned with developing the natural resources of the Islands as well as to find means to control the diseases that were making such serious inroads upon the lives and happiness of the people.

There were assembled an able group of scientists to perform all the laboratory work required by the government. The Bureau of Science occupied a spacious new building and took over the government laboratories and performed most of the scientific work required by other bureaus. The number of uses to which these laboratories were put surprised even the most ardent supporters of the movement. Answers were available as to whether a curious mineral found was gold, whether a resin gathered in the jungle had commercial value, whether a food was adulterated or poisonous, or whether an illness was cholera or plague or leprosy or something harmless. The durability of road-making material could be tested, the possibilities of silk worm culture were worked out, the commercial value of many curious tropical products could be ascertained; in short, knowledge was to be had. If a photograph were needed, this bureau not only took it, but filed it away so that it might be available in the years to come. A great scientific library was assembled, covering not only the Philippine Islands but much of the East. Entirely new industries sometimes resulted from the researches. The scientific work was of the highest character. "The Journal of Science," published by the bureau, became a recognized source of authority.

In the early days a biological division in the Bureau of Science was set up under the able direction of Dr. Richard P. Strong. Thus was created one of the first large public health laboratories under the American flag. Since then laboratories doing similar work have been created in nearly every state and city of the United States and extensively emulated abroad.

United States Army boards on medical research and tropical diseases in the Islands have also carried on exhaustive studies, and missions, both Roman Catholic and Protestant, have contributed materially to the public health of the Islands by the establishment of hospitals and out-patient clinics not only in the city of Manila but at some of the more remote places in the provinces.

Private practitioners of medicine and surgery maintain a number of sanatoria on a small scale, which add to the available hospital facilities.

EDUCATION

IN accordance with the spirit of their institutions, almost the first thing to which the Americans turned their attention in the Philippine Islands was education.

The first public school opened by the American authorities was one on the island of Corregidor, at the mouth of Manila Bay, less than a month after the destruction of the Spanish fleet by Admiral Dewey. Less than three weeks after the occupation of Manila the following

August, seven schools were reopened and a teacher of English was installed in each.

These steps were taken before it was known that the Philippine Islands would pass to the sovereignty of the United States.

The Spanish government had not encouraged the general learning of Spanish, perhaps from a fear that general education and a common language would give the Filipinos too much cohesion. Schools had been directed by the Church; their curriculum was extremely limited, for they taught little beside the catechism, penmanship, and the rudiments of arithmetic. Teaching of science had been frowned upon. With rare exceptions, the few schools that had been established outside of Manila were conducted in the native dialects, nor had there been any effort made to adopt any one of these as a general language of the people. Spanish had been taught in a few schools attended mostly by the children of the wealthy and a few from the poorer classes selected for their exceptional ability, but the great bulk of the people scarcely knew it at all.

There were a few colleges and universities. That of Santo Tomas, established by the Dominican friars as a college in 1611 and erected into a university in 1645, is the oldest under the American flag.

The American Secretary of Public Instruction reported:

... It has been contended that the Filipino people had some educational advancement long before the first Spaniard set his foot in the Archipelago, but the proofs adduced to justify this conclusion rather prove the existence of relics of a decadent or dead civilization than the survival of a living and progressive one. ... From all the evidence at hand it seems no more than just to conclude that learning made no real progress among the peoples of the Archipelago until after Spanish occupation, and that the first Spanish explorers encountered on their arrival ... the inert remnants of a remote civilization of which the Filipinos may once have formed a part.

In addition to places of learning established for boys, schools for girls were established as follows:

Name	Year of foundation
Santa Isabela	1632
Santa Catalina	1696
Beaterio de San Ignacio	1699
Santa Rosa	1750
Escuela de Maestras	1864
Colegio de la Inmaculada Concepcion	1868
Colegio de San José de Jaro	1872

Asuncionistas, about 1890.

Beginning with 1872 and continuing until about 1890 seminaries were established for the education and training of priests in the archdiocese of Manila and the dioceses of Nueva Segovia (Vigan), Cebu, Jaro, and Nueva Cáceres. Schools of secondary lay instruction were also established at Guinobatan in 1890, and at Bacolod, Negros, in 1892.

. . . .

A study of the enrollment [for the year 1886–87] in the University of Santo Tomas, and in the colleges of Santo Tomas and San Juan de Letran, reveals the interesting fact that the total matriculation of 1,985 was made up of 123 peninsular Spaniards, 93 insular Spaniards, 180 Spanish mestizos, 1,381 Filipinos, and 208 Chinese mestizos.

In 1863 Spain recognized the urgent necessity of giving greater educational opportunities to the people of the islands, and by royal decree made provision for the development and perfection of a proper system of primary instruction. The decree directed the organization of a normal school in the city of Manila, and the creation of at least one primary school for boys and one for girls in every pueblo in the islands. Primary schools were placed under the inspection of a commission composed of the civil governor, the archbishop of Manila and 7 members, and the attendance of children between the ages of 7 and 13 was made compulsory.

The scheme of primary instruction provided by Spain was adequate for the purpose of furnishing a fairly good measure of preliminary education, but the want of proper administration by the local authorities, the lack of interest in primary studies not directly related to the moral training and religious instruction of the pupil, the ridiculously small salaries paid to teachers, the selection of instructors incapable of teaching Spanish and more in need of instruction than capable of imparting it, and the distance of the barrios and villages from the larger centers of population where the primary schools were usually located, all united to bring at least partial failure when complete success should have been the result of the well-intended efforts of the Government. In 1886, twenty-three years after the issuance of the royal decree directing the organization of the system of primary instruction, 1,052 primary schools for boys and 1,091 for girls had been established, an average of a little more than one school for each sex per pueblo. The enrollment was somewhere in the neighborhood of 200,000, but the attendance did not average more than 40 or 50 pupils to the school. Christian doctrine, reading, writing, some historical geography, addition, subtraction, and multiplication usually marked the limits of primary instruction.

There are no statistics as to the literacy of the Filipinos at the termination of Spanish sovereignty. The Schurman Commission found that ability to read and write a little of the local native language was comparatively common; and in 1903, of the native population ten years of age and over, 44.2 per cent were literate or instructed; that is, able to read some local dialect spoken in the Islands.

A normal school for the training of teachers had been conducted by the Jesuits at Manila since 1865, but had graduated only 1900, of whom less than half had pursued a career of teaching in the public schools. As a consequence many teachers in the public schools were without adequate training and unable themselves to teach, in many cases to understand, the Spanish language.

These schools generally throughout the Islands were under the immediate charge of the monastic orders, which during the last half century of Spanish administration pursued a reactionary and repressive policy and failed to carry out even the modest curriculum prescribed by the decrees and regulations of the Madrid government.

Beside the public schools there were about seventy private Latin schools under the immediate charge of secular persons, chiefly Filipinos, of which some twenty-five were located in Manila. All these schools, including those giving secondary instruction, were under the control of the Dominican friars of Santo Tomas University.

While attendance at public schools was by law obligatory, yet there were neither schools enough nor was the quality of instruction such as to render possible the enforcement of the law.

The Manila Ateneo, under the direction of the Jesuits, and a few schools in the provinces, together with the Dominican College of San Juan de Letran and the University of Santo Tomas, produced the comparatively small number of educated Filipinos found in the Islands at the time of American occupation. Some of these men had pursued studies in European universities, especially in Madrid; but these men were very few in number.

A military academy existed at Manila for the education of the sons of army men residing in the colony as well as for enlisted men who desired to fit themselves for promotion. Its graduates were admitted to the military academy at Toledo, Spain. The instruction in the Manila Military Academy appears to have been superior to that afforded in many other schools and colleges in the Philippine Islands. The annual attendance was about one hundred.

An institution of especial importance was the nautical school in Manila, which offered a course of three years' study and practical instruction in navigation, fitting its graduates for careers as officers of merchant marine. The work done in this institution is reported to have been very good.

There were also in Manila special schools giving instruction in engraving, painting, and sculpture, in agriculture, and in arts and trades.

Theological seminaries were maintained in Manila and other places by the Jesuits, Paulists, and Augustinians.

The Commission reported:

In view of the facts above set forth, it must be admitted that the average native has never as yet had a fair opportunity to show what he can do. The attainments of some of his fellows who have had exceptional advantages have been such as to dispose the commission to credit him with ability of no mean order. He is at all events keenly alive to the drawbacks under which he has thus far labored and strongly desirous of securing better educational advantages.

The government established in the islands should promptly provide for the fulfillment of this reasonable and most praiseworthy desire by the establishment of an adequate system of secularized and free public schools.

To this end the present number of primary schools should be increased as rapidly as possible until it meets the needs of the population. The course of study given should be revised and suitable buildings and equipment provided.

The standard set for teachers should be gradually raised, and additional facilities should be provided for their education.

Their compensation should be sufficient to enable them to live comfortably.

Instruction in the English language should be introduced as speedily as practicable into the primary schools.

Secondary education should be taken in hand, the course of study thoroughly revised, and a moderate number of new schools established at suitable points throughout the archipelago.

The establishment of good agricultural and manual-training schools is especially recommended, as it is believed that such institutions are peculiarly suited to the present needs of the people.

Thorough supervision of the schools of the archipelago should be provided for under a secretary or commissioner of education.

And the Secretary of Public Instruction reported that:

. . . Even after the insurrection broke out against the United States the plan of giving to the Filipino children the advantage of free public instruction was never abandoned, but was adhered to wherever circumstances permitted and conditions were at all favorable to the building up of a school. Of course, instruction in time of such great public disturbance was necessarily imperfect and desultory, yet it served the purpose in many localities of bridging the way to the hearts of parents and operated as a restraining influence to prevent them from becoming active participants in a movement with which many of them undoubtedly sympathized. The American soldier, acting in the rôle of an instructor of a people in arms against his country, was an object lesson which, while it did not serve to convince the insurgents of the error of their ways, at least caused many of the better element among them to soberly inquire of themselves whether, after all, the United States might not have the welfare and well-being of the Filipino people very much at heart.

General Otis, as Military Governor for 1899, reported:

... Parents and children are eager for primary-school instruction and are very desirous to acquire a speaking knowledge of the English language.

Except the salaries of officers and enlisted men who were for a brief period detailed for service with the schools, expenditures for public schools from the beginning of American occupation were paid from Philippine revenues. For books and other supplies for public schools the Military Governor expended more than $100,000.

Army chaplains and other officers especially selected for the duty were detailed as local superintendents of schools, and enlisted men, chiefly noncommissioned officers, were almost the only teachers of English outside of Manila until well into the year 1901. Sometimes American soldiers were teaching Filipino children whose brothers or fathers were fighting as insurgents.

General Arthur MacArthur, as Military Governor, in commenting to the Commission on a proposed plan for public schools, expressed the following opinion:

... I know of nothing in the department of administration that can contribute more in behalf of pacification than the immediate institution of a comprehensive system of education, such as recommended by the general superintendent.

The matter is so closely allied to the exercise of military force in these islands that in my annual report I treated the matter as a military subject and suggested a rapid extension of educational facilities as an exclusively military measure. ...

Public schools were opened by Americans among the Moros and the tribal peoples wherever garrisons were located, and as teachers became available additional schools were opened where the people desired them.

It does not appear that, except for the missions maintained by the friars and Jesuits, schools as such had ever existed among Mohammedans or among the tribal peoples prior to American administration. Some of these missions, especially those of the Jesuits among the tribal peoples of Mindanao, were excellent civilizing influences.

Very few of the tribal peoples possessed the art of writing.

The Moros, Mohammedans in religion, while not maintaining organized schools in the modern sense, had classes or "pandita schools" in which a "learned man" taught the boys to memorize passages of the Koran, religious history and observance, penmanship in Arabic characters adapted to Malay phonetics, rudimentary arithmetic, and a little general history and information. Girls, except those of the families of the sultans, datus, and other men of rank or wealth, rarely received such instruction.

One inevitable result of American occupation was an increase in the scale of wages throughout the Islands for all classes of service. The meager compensation given to teachers at the close of the Spanish régime was less than that which Americans were paying unskilled Filipino labor after the occupation of Manila. The Philippine Commission provided in one of its first acts for an increase in the salary scale of Filipino teachers in Manila and suburbs.

On January 21, 1901, the Commission passed an act creating a Department of Public Instruction in the Philippine Islands, and providing that all "primary instruction in the schools established or maintained under this Act shall be free."

The act further provided for the taking over by the civil government of all schools previously established under the auspices of the military government; the establishment of schools in every municipality in the archipelago; the division of the archipelago into school divisions; the necessary regulations as to authority to be exercised by division superintendents and principal teachers; a curriculum for public schools; plans for construction of schoolhouses; the areas of school sites and rules of hygiene and sanitation; the purchase of school supplies; the assignment of teachers of English to be paid out of the insular treasury, preferences being given to towns which showed their loyalty to the United States by their peaceful conditions and which constructed and maintained suitable schoolhouses by local taxation or contributions.

There were to be local school boards of not more than six members in addition to the municipal president, one-half to be elected by the municipal council and the remaining half to be appointed by the division superintendent of schools.

The act also provided: "The English language shall, as soon as practicable, be made the basis of all public school instruction, and soldiers may be detailed as instructors until such a time as they may be replaced by trained teachers."

Authority was given to the general superintendent of public instruction to obtain from the United States one thousand trained teachers; also to make plans and estimates for buildings for normal and trade schools with proper equipment, the cost not to exceed $400,000; and to purchase textbooks and other supplies not exceeding $220,000 in cost.

The same act authorized a normal school in the city of Manila for training Filipinos as teachers, and a trade school; also, in the island of Negros, a school of agriculture. Appropriations of public funds were made immediately available for the expenses of these institutions.

Under this authorization nine hundred and twenty-six American teachers were in service by May, 1902.

In an annual report the Secretary of Public Instruction said that the policy of attraction adopted by the Civil Commission "was brought home to the people in no inconsiderable degree by the disinterested devotion and unselfish work of the American teacher." He continued:

From the beginning the relations of the American teacher to the people have, as a rule, been pleasant and agreeable. Even in provinces where there was more or less disturbance and ladronism, the almost sacred regard in which the teacher was held exempted him from violence, and I know of none who came to grief except four teachers who were killed while traveling in the mountains where their status was unknown.

It was not only for his services in teaching the school curriculum that the American teacher was useful; in fact, seen with broader vision, that was perhaps a small part of his contribution to the Filipino. The American teacher brought with him the American spirit. He was the apostle of progress. He gave the children a healthy outlook toward life; he explained to them the principles of hygiene and sanitation. He brought with him the spirit of service. He inculcated into them a realization of the dignity of labor. And the children carried this spirit back into the homes, where it made its impress upon the parents.

The most difficult problem was securing a supply of competent teachers for the primary schools. There were no Filipinos properly trained according to American standards, nor could the finances of the Islands meet the expense of employing American teachers in sufficient numbers for much classroom instruction. At first the primary schools were manned by teachers ill-equipped for their work. While it was a matter only of months to give children a working knowledge of English so that they could get along in their daily contacts and have some facility in reading that language, it was a matter of many years so to train Filipinos in pronunciation, in grammar and idiom, as to make them competent teachers. In addition to normal schools for Filipinos, night schools were established, teachers' institutes, vacation schools, and special correspondence courses. Attendance at these was compulsory upon those desiring to continue as teachers.

By July, 1902, at the end of the first year of civil administration of the public schools, there were enrolled more than two hundred thousand in the primary schools with an attendance of about sixty-five per cent. The night school enrollment was about twenty-five thousand, and nearly twenty thousand pupils were enrolled in schools of secondary instruction, which had been organized especially for normal training and as assurance that opportunities existed for continued instruction following completion of the course in the government primary schools.

At this time the total number of teachers in the public schools was about four thousand, of whom more than nine hundred were Americans.

The following cogent clauses are culled from the second annual report of the Secretary of Public Instruction: "The ultimate character of the public instruction in the Philippines must depend on the character of the Filipino teachers which it will be possible to develop." He told of the insignificant salaries paid under the Spanish régime, about six dollars a month for women and eight dollars for men, the maximum being about twenty-five dollars a month and the minimum about one dollar, "which in some instances is for long periods withheld. It has happened that a teacher receiving a salary of $16.50 a month has hired a substitute for $4.50, and has lived as an independent gentleman on the remaining $12."

He pointed out the difficulties arising under a system in which the Director of Education appointed a teacher who was to be paid by a municipality. Some of the municipalities declined or delayed to pay; some wanted the right of appointment; and some made their payments otherwise than in money.

In the early organization of the public schools the term "primary" was used to designate all the grades below the first year of high school. Later the word "primary" was used to designate schools giving the first four grades, and the term "intermediate" those giving the three grades remaining to prepare for high school. As more and more students completed their primary course there arose a great demand for these intermediate schools.

The intermediate schools should properly have been maintained at municipal expense, but municipal school revenues were insufficient to meet the demands of their primary schools, and so the insular government necessarily bore the expense of the American teachers and superintendents while the provincial governments undertook to provide high schools from their general funds. Intermediate schools were organized only at the more important centers of population as feeders for high schools, of which for some years there averaged less than one per province.

The Secretary of Public Instruction in 1902 reported:

An important step in the development of the system of public instruction in the Philippines was the establishment and organization of the provincial schools of secondary instruction. . . . Prior to 1902 the Bureau of Education had been chiefly concerned with the organization of primary schools. As a consequence, many of the more advanced pupils in these schools, who had been taught English, began to entertain serious doubts respecting the possibility of continuing their studies in English in schools of a higher grade, and some of them thought it advisable to resume their studies of Spanish in order that they might be prepared to enter the Spanish schools of secondary instruction. This was particularly true in Manila, where there were several secondary schools which were maintained under the authority of the church.

The lodging and boarding of non-resident pupils at secondary schools in Manila was a serious problem, toward the solution of which Protestant missions and the Roman Catholics have made important contributions by maintaining dormitories for boys and for girls. The government built a fine dormitory in Manila where young girls from the provinces lived under American matrons and there many of them gained more from character-building advice than from their actual schooling.

At the close of the year 1925 there were one hundred and two high schools.

In 1925 a survey of the educational system of the Islands, authorized by the Philippine Legislature, was made by a board of distinguished educators, headed by Dr. Paul Monroe, of New York. The report of this board stated that in the year 1924, the latest for which comparative statistics were available, there were 47,419 pupils enrolled in the government higher schools, and 19,406 in approved private secondary schools; a total of 66,825, or 7.9 per cent of all the children of high school age. Corresponding percentages in other countries are as follows: in the United States 27.2, in Japan 8.4, in England and Wales 3.9, in Sweden 1.4, and in Spain 1.1.

These figures are of especial interest as indicating the progress being made in preparing the Philippine people for popular self-government. In a count made of some of the students in representative secondary schools outside the city of Manila, more than 72 per cent were the children of farmers, fishermen, artisans, laborers, and other wage-earners.

The ten years following 1898 were a period of organization and development. Beginning in 1909, public instruction entered upon the well-defined programme planned by American administrators and Filipino leaders.

It was difficult to secure adequate textbooks for the Philippine primary schools, as those prepared for use in American schools often dealt with matters outside the experience of children brought up in a tropical country. It was some years before appropriate textbooks, prepared by Americans and Filipinos in collaboration, were made available.

Economic and other considerations appear to cause the majority of the children to average less than three years in school. After extensive tests of school children the 1925 Survey found:

> The hopeful phase of the results is found in the success of a few conspicuous school systems. In these the high attainments of the children in reading give real promise that the graduates of the primary schools throughout the Islands can develop practical control of the English language.
> . . . In the primary school pupils develop marked ability to comprehend spoken English. Apparently this ability is sufficient to carry them through the ordinary language necessities of this generation of adult life in the Philippines. They learn to speak English with sufficient clearness to make themselves understood either by other Filipinos or by Americans, but with an accent, tonal expression and rhythm that are thoroughly Malay. . . . In receiving dictation and in spelling in English they almost equal American children.

"Grade for grade, Filipino children master the art of arithmetical computation as well as do American children."

Instruction in citizenship is given by a course in good manners and right conduct through the seven elementary grades, in civics, hygiene, and sanitation through the first six grades, and in Philippine history and government in the seventh grade.

The American government had no fear of danger arising from welding the Filipinos into a united people by putting them in understanding contact with each other. It was desired to fit the people to manage their own affairs, and as a necessary prerequisite, give them a common language with which they could communicate readily with each other. This was regarded as an essential step in making them capable of nationality.

The Americans encountered no difficulty in initiating instruction in English. Their efforts were met with enthusiasm and cordiality on the part of almost the whole population of the Philippine Islands. The young people generally were more than ready to learn it. In one of the provincial capitals the school children had an "Improvement Society" all the members of which entered into an agreement to speak nothing but English to each other at school or recess, and for each violation of this agreement a half centavo (equal to one-quarter cent United States currency) was paid as a fine.

It is unfortunate that, in reporting and publishing statistics of the proportionate number of Americans to Filipinos in the civil service throughout the archipelago, the number of Americans engaged in the work of education was not listed separately, as their work was on a wholly different footing from any other branch of the service. They pertained to a branch of the government in which Filipinization — that is, the substitution of Filipinos for Americans — should not have been on the programme, so that in computing the rate at which the government offices were being turned over to Filipinos the issues would not have been confused by large figures showing numbers of American teachers, and the salaries paid them, which had little bearing upon the general administrative work of the government.

Eventually, as Filipinos began to qualify according to American standards for teachers, a few of superior attainments having graduated from good normal schools and colleges in the United States giving courses in education, some of the Filipino leaders took the ground that more American teachers should not be brought into the service and vacancies occurring should be filled with Filipinos both in the teaching force and in the administrative positions. And, beginning with 1914, pursuant to this policy the number of Americans in the teaching service rapidly declined.

This desire of the Filipinos to work rapidly up through the educational department outran their good judgment and there was a steady diminution of the number of American teachers when, in the best interests of the Filipinos and their early acquisition of the accurate use and pronunciation of the English language, the number of American teachers should have been increased rather than diminished.

The introduction of English brought about some temporary inconveniences and some of the incidental problems raised difficulties that at times tended to strain the relations between the government and the people, as in the case of the judicial courts previously noted.

The matter was solved by the passage of a law which recognized English as *the* language of the courts and Spanish as *a* language of the courts. Apparently this satisfied both parties and enabled the Spanish-speaking judges and court officials to continue until they should be forced out by the pressure of the oncoming tide of English exerted by the younger Filipinos.

As a practical matter the prevalence of English was foreordained. There was no need for the Americans to endeavor to force its recognition. All that was needed was to extend primary education in that language as rapidly as possible, turn out by hundreds of thousands young potential voters who understood English and not Spanish, and these young people could be relied upon to do the rest. No intervention on the part of American administrators would have been necessary. Just as soon as the elective offices, executive and legislative, were filled by English-speaking Filipinos, there would be little doubt that they would take upon themselves the initiative of forcing the use of the English language in the courts. There was bound to be a period of temporary inconvenience to certain young men who had to acquire both Spanish and English in order to make themselves perfectly equipped for work in the courts or in the Legislature, but this was a difficulty inherent in the situation and impossible to avoid.

Since 1900, instruction in all government schools, from the primary through to the University, has been conducted in English, and latterly most private schools and colleges have taught in English. It has become the prevailing language in public administration and among the younger people in social and other relations between persons who use different local dialects.

At times schools are closed in order to enable the children to assist their parents in harvesting the crops. Such seasonal arrangements of the school year are not uncommon and are quite necessary in a country where agriculture is the principal source of livelihood. Americans have not made attendance at school compulsory in any part of the archipelago. Most of the difficulties were encountered in the Moro Province, where the Mohammedan parents feared that sending their children to schools conducted by Christian teachers might weaken their Mohammedanism.

It is noteworthy that the development of public schools has been continuous and steady through the period of military operations, civil control, the régime of the Democratic Party, the activities under the Jones Law, and throughout the incumbency of Governor-General Wood.

The percentage of school attendance to enrollment has shown a gratifying increase from year to year, and in 1923 reached the very creditable figure of eighty-five per cent.

The Bureau of Education laid especial emphasis upon practical subjects. Courses in agriculture, wood and iron working and other mechanical trades were given in both primary and secondary schools for the boys; care of the home, embroidery and lace-making for the girls; basketry, hat-making and other household industries; commerce and normal training for both boys and girls.

Industrial instruction comprises four principal lines:

(1) Household industries, utilizing the spare time of both men and women, which is especially valuable in the agricultural districts where field work is seasonal. The industries preferred are those using materials produced locally, especially fibers, bamboos, rattans, and timber, for making basketry, hats, mats, furniture, and fine cabinetwork. Embroidery, lace-making, and weaving are peculiarly household industries fitted to the spare time of the millions of women of all classes, not previously developed as factors in the foreign trade of the Islands.

The value of basketry, embroidery, and lace produced in the public schools in 1924–25 was $205,392.

In June, 1912, the Bureau of Education formally opened a School of Household Industries in Manila. Young women whose personality marked them as potential leaders were selected to organize and train promising workers in embroidery and other needlework.

(2) Mechanical trades — woodworking, etc. First introduced by the trade school in Manila and extended to provincial schools, commercial shop work has been extended to many municipal school shops. In the elementary grades especial attention is given the making and repairing of equipment and tools for the homes and to field work of the boys. The Insular Auditor devised a simple method of accounting for the cost of material and labor used in producing articles in the trade schools. Each student made out his work order, was allowed the necessary materials from the stock room, filled in time cards, and eventually turned in the product, the value of which was appraised. Besides making furniture for the school, some instances have occurred of school buildings being erected by boys in the trade schools. Apt pupils develop proficiency in fine cabinet work.

It was some time before teaching along these lines was really practical, but the government gradually developed a policy of teaching in the trade schools only things which were sure to be useful to the students. After they got to be skilled workmen the students were enabled to earn something by their labor.

By 1914 there were 19 authorized trade schools, 13 provincial school shops, and 267 municipal school shops with a total of 7774 pupils and a total output for the year 1914 valued at $98,274.

By 1925 industrial training had been extended to 356,043 pupils, of whom 3876 were in the provincial schools and shops; the value of the total products in that year was $492,532.

(3) Housekeeping. By 1914 plain sewing and garment-making was a prescribed course for all girls in the four primary grades. Instruction in cookery, intelligently using the foodstuffs and utensils customarily found in the average home, was being rapidly extended to the older girls in the elementary grades. Also, embroidery, lace-making, weaving, hygiene and sanitation were prescribed courses for the girls.

The courses in domestic science for girls proved to be one of the most popular and valuable services rendered by the schools. They were taught cooking, hygienic preparation of food, and the protection of food supplies from pollution, a very important thing in the tropics, as perishable articles deteriorate much more rapidly than they do in colder and dryer climates.

(4) Agriculture. As the Philippine Islands are essentially agricultural, proper training in agriculture was perhaps the most valuable economic service the educational department could render. The instruction, however, had to be practical and teach methods superior to those practiced by the parents of the children upon their farms. Competent teachers of tropical agriculture were difficult to obtain, and it was some years before really useful courses of instruction were worked out. This was ultimately achieved. Vegetable gardens on the school grounds and later at the homes of the pupils materially augmented the food supply produced in the Islands and often were sources of profit to the students or their families. Frequently vacant lots in the cities were brought into use as school gardens. The money value of the products of the students' school and home gardens in 1925 was about $450,000. The care of lawns and ornamental plants on school grounds was required of all schools.

For the older boys in the higher elementary grades and secondary classes, farm schools were developed in which general farming operations, especially the production of corn, rice, and other food staples, poultry breeding, and other appropriate forms of animal husbandry, have been taught with success among tribal peoples and Moros as well as Christian Filipinos. In 1925, there were 318 such schools with 23,779 pupils, nearly 7000 acres of cultivated land, and more than 18,000 domestic animals. The value of the products of these schools in that year was $194,174.

Instruction in seed selection, and the introduction of improved varieties of seeds of economic and ornamental plants and of pure-bred domestic animals, have been of great benefit to agriculture.

Nurseries have been maintained at many of the schools for propagating valuable fruit-producing shrubs and trees for distribution to the families of the pupils and other residents of the localities. There were 3557 of these nurseries in 1925, in which there were 282,588 such propagated shrubs and trees.

Boys' and girls' agricultural clubs have been organized through the public schools and are proving both popular and profitable. In 1925, there were 1766 such clubs, engaged in various activities, as gardens, fruit production, poultry, hogs, corn, and cooking, with a total membership of 30,578 and a total value of products from projects of $216,087.

The total value of the industrial products of elementary and secondary school activities, including agricultural, for the year 1925 was $1,352,400.

The Survey reported that:

> With a very few exceptions, these schools have failed to achieve their purposes. Although some of them have elaborate plants, they are ill attended and lacking in vitality. . . .
> The explanation of this situation is to be found in part in the prevailing social attitudes towards manual labor. . . . The crucial weakness is to be found in the educational organization itself.
> . . . Until adequate leadership is provided for the program for rural education and until the rest of the educational system is brought into harmony with this program, large results cannot be expected.

The Spaniards had made few opportunities for healthy participation in games available to the Filipinos. Cock-fighting was a national institution and the usual popular form of entertainment.

One of the most notable achievements of the Americans in the Islands has been the weaning of the young people from the cockpits, with their attendant vice of gambling, to the more healthful and vigorous competitive outdoor sports. There is nothing more important to the young man and woman of healthy mind and body than an outlet for the excess of physical vigor that normally surges within them.

A regular programme of school athletics was finally worked out consisting of group games, including baseball, basketball, track and field sports, as well as calisthenics. By the school year 1913–14 ninety-five per cent of the pupils were recorded as taking part in games and athletics of one form or another. And the Director of Education reported that year "a noticeable improvement in the physical development of the younger generation" and stated that "the moral influence of clean, healthy sports has been felt."

The young people turned with enthusiasm to baseball. Their elders neglected the cockpit to come and see the games of the young ones and cheer them on, and the terms incident to baseball were among the earlier English words which many of the older people acquired. Shouts of "Slide!" "Strike!" "Foul ball!" and "Rotten!" came readily from onlookers who knew few other words of English. Even in the hills the schoolboys took keenly to baseball and it was not uncommon to see an Igorot boy catching behind the bat, clad only in loincloth, baseball mask, and mit. The Filipinos, besides liking the game, became very expert. Baseball spread rapidly through the provinces and the schools to the hamlets. In 1913, a series of prizes was offered by some friend of sport to each of the provinces, to be given to the team which had the best record of victories in that province. No less than twelve hundred teams competed for these prizes, which means that something more than ten thousand players took part in the competitions.

There naturally followed the organization of a Philippine Amateur Athletic Association in which very careful rules to preserve the amateur status of the competitors in these games were adopted. This association looked largely at their problem, and before long initiated a movement that resulted in the formation of an Oriental Olympic Association with annual competitions between representatives of the Philippine Islands, Japan, and China. In these Filipinos have acquitted themselves with credit, and several times have won the largest number of points as against representatives of neighboring countries which drew from much larger populations.

The American army and navy introduced and popularized boxing, which, to the surprise of most Americans and Europeans and of the Filipinos themselves, has aroused widespread interest and remarkable participation, not only in Manila but in the provinces. The schools have not included boxing in their athletic programmes, but in some instances boxing was enthusiastically adopted by the pupils as a favorite sport and generally favored as the substitute for the customary Moro cutting weapons in the settlement of personal disputes, the rules of the game being strictly enforced by referee and popular school opinion.

The boxing contests of the soldiers and sailors were public and attracted increasingly large and increasingly keen audiences of Filipinos as the rules became generally understood.

Before the coming of the Americans, no girl in the Philippine Islands had ever engaged in athletics. The decorative dresses which were worn, not only by women but even by girls twelve years old, with a *panuelo* or stiff neckerchief round their shoulders, and their long skirts, quite narrow to the knees and flaring out in a long train, precluded any freedom of movement. The girls readily adopted middy blouses and bloomers and took up with enthusiasm tennis, basketball, and indoor baseball. The result was a more normal and healthy growth of the young people; and with the better physique came better morals.

In August, 1903, the Commission enacted a law providing for the selection by examinations of students "best qualified to receive and profit by a course of instruction and education in the United States. . . ." Candidates were required to be natives of the Philippine Islands, students in the public schools, of good moral character, sound physical condition, and not less than sixteen nor more than twenty-one years of age. A total of one hundred and twenty-five such students were authorized for appointment during the ensuing year.

Scholarship allowances adequate to cover all necessary cost of transportation, tuition, board, lodging, and other expenses were made from insular funds, and a superintendent of students, by frequent visits and correspondence with the students and the officials of the institutions where they were pursuing their studies, exercised supervision.

This practice has continued with the difference that scholarships were later almost exclusively given for advanced university work preparatory to assignment to duty of a scientific or technical character in the public service. Holders of these scholarships are required to return to the Islands in public service on such assignment as the government deems best in the public interest.

American universities have admitted Filipinos, not only those holding government scholarships, but those who have come at their own expense for residence and study in the United States. These young men and women have been treated with great consideration and have generally acquitted themselves with credit. Some have earned high scholastic honors.

The Philippine government has also provided scholarships for students to attend professional schools in the Islands. These scholarships have served a very useful purpose, particularly in bringing to Manila for advanced education representative Mohammedan and tribal young people. In the case of Mohammedan students care has been taken to avoid influencing them to abandon their religion, as this would deprive them of the influence which it was hoped they would exercise in their home communities upon their return.

Schools of Commerce and of Arts and Trades, and the Nautical School, have been included under the general head of secondary schools.

During the year 1907–08 the Bureau of Education opened in Manila a school for defectives, providing at first for a number of deaf children, and later for the blind. As the parents of these children were usually unable to pay the expense of maintenance away from home, the government made provision to subsist and clothe them, so that they were given a chance to develop into self-reliant and self-supporting members of society. Basketry, hat-making, and other handicrafts were taught, as well as academic subjects, the blind using the Braille system of reading.

By 1914 graduates of the school were engaged in remunerative employment as tailors, shoemakers, and seamstresses, and others were learning the printing trades. All the girls are taught the care of a home, plain sewing, dressmaking, and lace-making. The enrollment increased from forty-six pupils in 1913 to one hundred and three in 1925. In 1921 the government constructed for this admirable and popular institution a special building upon an adequate site in a suburb of Manila.

While the Filipinos were enthusiastic in their support of education for the people in general and for their own children and dependents in particular, the old system of privilege manifested itself in constant agitation on the part of the more influential classes for provision of intermediate and secondary schools even at the expense of primary schools. The American administrators with the limited resources at their command were compelled to insist upon maintaining the primary schools, which the Filipino political leaders seemed willing to close in order to give the children of their adherents the advantage of the higher education they wanted regardless of the welfare of the mass of the people. In this they ignored the fact that, as the stability of their institutions depended upon a wide extension of the suffrage, this action tended to postpone the time when they would be ready to maintain with a reasonable chance of success the nationality to which they aspired. Thus the curious anomaly was observable of the Filipinos proclaiming their adherence to the policy of early independence and taking a course inimical to their aspirations, and of the Americans, some of whom were supposed to oppose independence, steadily supporting the most important measure to make such independence possible.

During the temporary absence of the Governor-General in the United States, the Bureau of Education closed seven hundred and sixty-nine primary schools. The Governor-General upon his return early in 1913, recognizing the magnitude of this backward step, immediately ordered arrangements to be made for opening one thousand primary schools on the first of the succeeding July, and ordered that the Bureau of Education adopt a programme of five hundred additional schools to be opened in each of the succeeding two years.

The explanation given by the Director was that

The only logical relief obtainable was either through limiting to a considerable extent the amount of primary instruction by closing barrio schools, or by reducing the number of intermediate and secondary school pupils to the number enrolled during the school year 1909–10. The first was chosen for a number of reasons . . . the people who have had a voice in affairs have always been much more interested in intermediate and secondary instruction than in the extension of primary schools to the barrios. The Director of Education and his official superiors are constantly in receipt of letters protesting against the closing or demanding the opening of intermediate schools. During the past three years this Bureau has received more than six times as many communications asking for an extension of intermediate instruction as for an extension of primary instruction. Representatives of the Insular Government traveling through the provinces are met with requests from every section for the extension of intermediate instruction. *Their attention is very rarely, indeed, called to the desirability of extending primary instruction.*

The Filipino leaders later realized that the extension of primary education was of vital and fundamental importance, and in its session of 1918–19 the Legislature, elected under the Jones Law so that both houses were composed almost wholly of elected representatives, passed an appropriation of over fifteen million dollars "for the purpose of extending the facilities of free elemental instruction to all the children of school age of the archipelago." This was in addition to sums appropriated in the annual appropriations for the Bureau of Education.

There was at that time no such sum as fifteen million dollars available in the treasury for this purpose, and the bill was in one sense in the nature of a gesture, as only $367,500, or less than two and one-half per cent of the amount, was to be paid in the first year; $1,959,500, or about fourteen per cent, the second year; the balance to be paid in increasing proportions in succeeding years, spread over five years in all. The effect of this was to place the bulk of the burden of securing the money to meet this appropriation on the shoulders of a later American administration to be appointed after the ensuing presidential election.

The action, however, indicated a gratifying realization on the part of the Filipinos of one of the cardinal policies consistently urged by their American administrators.

In order to correlate the work of the Bureau of Education with the industrial markets of the world, the government determined to establish an agency whose business was the development of a market for Philippine articles and specialties.

One of the fundamental objects of the agency was to ascertain the probable market for each commodity the school children were taught to manufacture, and to make sure that articles for export were not being produced in excess of the probable demand for that class of product in the markets of the world. The Bureau of Education had nearly five hundred thousand children in school, many of them receiving instruction in embroidery, hat and lace making, basketwork, and other handicrafts. It was obvious that within a few years the schools would graduate young men and women skilled in making these articles for sale. It was most important that so many should not be trained in any one handicraft as to produce more than their potential markets could absorb. As most of these commodities were articles of general use, it was believed that the government should take the same care in providing a market for the potential product of the graduates of the schools as an industrial concern would normally take to provide for the sale of its own output. This meant a study of markets, careful advertising, and good salesmanship to make these articles known and properly introduce them to the consuming public.

The Sales Agency, as the new office was called, was directed to keep in touch with the big buyers of these products in the United States. Samples of all the products of the schools were displayed in its store, and it was also proposed that the office should keep a list of expert graduates in these industries and communicate with them through representatives in the different provinces, so that, upon receipt of an order for any one of these products, the agency could apportion the production to graduates of the schools and thus enable them to make use of the training which they had received.

The Governor-General in 1913 reported:

The term "sales agency" scarcely describes the most important work of the institution, for it has been found that it is the standardization of the product far more than the distribution that requires assistance and control. When the agency was founded, none of the handicrafts of the islands had been developed to the point of commercial soundness. Even embroidery, which appeared to be more advanced than any other, represented such a miscellaneous assortment of costs, materials, designs, and standards of execution as to be incapable of commercial classification. Due to the lack of uniformity in the different districts, the placing of orders for any considerable quantities was impossible. The state of affairs as regards other products was even worse. In this field substantial results have been accomplished during the year. In the case of embroidery, in place of 20 districts with at least that number of standards which formerly existed, there is now a single district whose product is fairly uniform, and large orders can now be placed with reasonable certainty as to prices, standards, and time.

It was not the intention of the government, however, to go permanently into business of this kind, or to compete with private enterprise in case this business proved to be profitable enough either for the big buying concerns or other private parties in the United States to establish their own direct connections with producers.

The Sales Agent having toured the United States reported:

There is no question as to the disposal of the handicraft output of the Islands. A single firm in Chicago — that of Marshall Field and Company — stated to me that they would gladly take the entire lace and embroidery output of the Philippines if they could get it. In New York, Philadelphia and Boston I found the same spirit. Philippine handicrafts are known in a small but extremely favorable way in these cities and dealers are so anxious to do business with the Islands that in a number of places importers are booking orders, delivery to be made three and four years from now.

Shortly after the Agency store opened the *Manila Times* said of it:

A "woman's Paradise," is the only possible way to describe the embroidery and lace department of the Sales Agency, the little concrete building on the port area, for (once inside) no woman ever leaves of her own accord. . . .

.   .   .   .

The Sales Agency is doing a wonderful work as regards opening up markets for the home products of the Philippines. Only with such a clearing-house as this could the home workers of the provinces, remote and near, be brought in touch with purchasers of their wares, at prices fair to both. By coöperation with the school of household industries, which is annually graduating women and girls as instructors and leaders in money making home pursuits, supply and demand are being brought together in a manner that was thought impossible several years ago.

The agency went out of existence in 1915 and the Bureau of Education established a general sales department "as a part of the industrial division of the bureau." Of this department it was reported that:

. . . in five months it had established 193 centers in 23 provinces, with 2,762 workers. . . . The purpose of the bureau in this matter is not to make profit, but to establish industrial centers, and when they are securely established in any community the bureau proposes to withdraw from that locality.

The agency had on its lists sixteen thousand embroidery workers in Manila and adjacent provinces, capable of turning out $480,000 worth of embroidery each year, provided a steady market could be assured. Their agents, working on a commission basis, came in contact with approximately twenty-five thousand handicraft workers, and the Secretary of Public Instruction reported that "sales of their products took place in more than one hundred of the smaller cities and towns of the United States." The work, however, was not in vain, for it was taken up by private parties who developed very profitable businesses, as is indicated by the growth of the sale of Philippine embroideries in the United States. Although these exports were not deemed of sufficient importance by the customs statistician to be separately mentioned before 1914, by 1920 they reached a value of more than seven and a half million dollars almost all of which was sold in the United States.

Little by little the government realized that one of the best ways of reaching the parents was through the schools. For example, when the Postal Savings Bank was started, the importance of thrift, the value of saving, and the use of the savings bank as a means of properly preserving their money was brought home to the parents through the medium of the children. Through the liberality of a visiting American gentleman and his wife, a sum of money was made available for prizes to be given in schools to those children who made the best showing in the matter of earning money and depositing their savings in the bank.

The importance of cleaning and beautifying grounds was impressed upon the children. Prizes were given for the best kept school grounds, and the orderliness taught at school was very apt to reflect itself in the appearance and sanitation of the home premises.

Perhaps the most important of the campaigns to reach the people through the children were those of hygiene and sanitation. The sanitary precautions against tuberculosis were systematically taught the children and through them carried to the attention of their parents. In order to make the best use of this power, a Junior Red Cross was organized, and through its agency much information was disseminated.

Publicity of preventive measures to combat dangerous communicable diseases, not only of human beings but also of domestic animals, has been given through the schools.

Popular movements to augment food production, including the planting of drought and pest resisting field and garden crops, have been in great part dependent for success upon school campaigns.

There was a curious anomaly in the use of corn as a staple article of diet in the Philippine Islands. In some provinces the people ate corn regularly, and in others they declined to touch it, even to the extent of suffering from famine in times of rice shortage. To remedy this, the Bureau of Education taught the children in their domestic science classes to make appetizing preparations of corn, and later conducted a campaign throughout the Islands, setting aside a corn-eating week. Corn cooked in many different ways was served free to the people by the children of the schools. As corn is successfully grown in most of the provinces, this campaign was of true value to the people, especially in years of partial failure of the rice crop.

Americans found the Islands poorly provided with schoolhouses. Many of the permanent buildings suitable for schools belonged to the Church, and in some cases the schools had been conducted on the ground floors of the so-called *conventos*, or residences of the priests. These buildings were no longer available for governmental school purposes, and a very general programme of construction was necessary to provide proper schoolhousing. Fortunately the climate of the Philippine Islands was such that it was not necessary to build a structure of permanent materials before a school could be started. Perfectly satisfactory results could be attained in an easily erected building of light materials, made of bamboo and roofed with grass. The instruction conducted in such a building was just as good and accomplished the same results as instruction given within concrete walls and under a roof of corrugated iron. It was therefore unnecessary for the school programme to be delayed even a week for lack of housing facilities. The interest in schools was such that every community, practically without exception, could be relied upon to put up the necessary temporary structure.

The Consulting Architect prepared plans for a series of schoolhouses of standard design to be built of reinforced concrete as the funds became available and the need arose. Several admirable buildings for normal and secondary schools and large numbers for elementary schools have been erected in Manila and the provinces.

By 1914 there were 748 permanent type school buildings containing 3950 rooms. Of these buildings, 275 were of concrete construction erected since 1907. In addition, there were 783 school buildings of semi-permanent and 1910 of temporary construction.

The Survey reported:

> . . . No other tropical country has attempted to build up a complete school system with a distinctive type of architecture. . . .

> . . . .

> A type of permanent, concrete school building has been evolved which is very satisfactory. These permanent buildings conform to the needs of the climate. Unless overcrowded with school children, they meet the standard set up by school hygiene in ventilation, lighting, and sanitation. They are simple and dignified in architecture. They are usually the most conspicuous, a well as the most artistically satisfactory, of the buildings in any community.

To provide ample space for future extension of buildings as well as adequate playgrounds, school gardens, and proper distance of buildings from public roads with their noisy traffic, the practice was adopted administratively of requiring wherever practicable areas of from one and a quarter to two and one-half acres for elementary school sites, and larger areas for secondary and agricultural schools.

Individual and collective voluntary contributions of land, labor, materials, and money have been made by all classes of Filipinos not only for the maintenance of schools but especially for school buildings and sites.

It is to be noted that the yearly expense of public instruction has increased from somewhat less than $2,000,000 in 1903 to more than $10,000,000 in 1923.

The Filipinos are in no sense apathetic toward education. They are enthusiastic. Nor is the desire for learning confined to any class. It has found expression in the voluntary contributions for support of additional teachers, purchase of equipment, in the gift of land for school sites, and of money, material, and labor for the construction of school buildings.

Tuition charges must have such prior approval and are allowed only in the cases of schools above the primary grades where instruction is provided as a result of popular demand beyond the limit of available government revenues. These charges run from one to two dollars a year.

With the graduation of the first classes from the high schools, the need for the creation of a university to be modeled upon the most approved American lines became manifest. Accordingly the government opened the University of the Philippines in Manila in 1909.

The government had established the Philippine Medical School as early as 1905, and had started schools in various professional and technical subjects, such as forestry, in order to train Filipinos to take on as many as possible of the government services. It was manifestly necessary to have all these schools belong to one university and their natural home was the University of the Philippines supported by the government. The University created or eventually took over the following schools:

College of Medicine established as the Philippine Medical School in 1905 became a college of the University in December, 1910; schools of dentistry, pharmacy and nursing were added later;

School of Fine Arts, created with the University;

College of Agriculture, established at Los Baños in 1909;

College of Veterinary Science, opened in Manila in 1910;

College of Engineering, opened in June, 1910;

College of Liberal Arts, opened in 1910;

College of Law, founded in 1911;

School of Forestry, established in 1916;

Conservatory of Music, established in 1916;

Junior College of Liberal Arts, opened at Cebu in 1918, became the Junior College of the University in 1922;

School of Education, organized as a department of the College of Liberal Arts in 1913, became the College of Education in 1918.

The University is shown by the survey to have increased from 1400 students in 1911–12 to 5993 in 1923–24. The teaching staff in the same period from 79 to 422.

By December, 1926, the enrollment in all colleges and schools of the University had reached 6464. At that time there were in the instructing force 44 Americans and foreigners and 419 Filipinos.

At first a very large proportion of the University students elected to take courses in the School of Fine Arts and it was difficult to get students who were willing to become veterinarians or to enter other schools of applied science. Scholarships were offered to attract the required number of students to courses necessary for filling technical posts in the government service.

The standards of instruction in the Colleges of Agriculture and Veterinary Science and in the School of Forestry are good and their graduates in great demand by private enterprises as well as for government service. The other schools of the University have healthy competition with courses in private institutions.

In 1898 libraries and museums containing volumes, manuscripts, and other material of historic and scientific value were to be found in the University of Santo Tomas and in some of the colleges maintained by the religious orders, especially those of the Jesuits. Also, there are in the libraries of the monasteries valuable manuscripts relating to the history of the Spanish administration of the Islands. Circulating and reference libraries open to the general public, however, do not appear to have existed before 1900, when the American Circulating Library Association of Manila, a private organization formed by Americans of the army and navy, opened to the public its library of books chiefly contributed in the United States. This institution was originally designed as a memorial to Americans who had given their lives in the service of their country in the Islands. A year later the Commission accepted the tender of the library and it passed wholly to the government, under the management of a board of trustees composed of Americans and Filipinos.

Also in 1901 the Commission established a museum of ethnology, natural history, and commerce.

To meet the need for an adequate scientific library provision was made in the Bureau of Science and an excellent reference and working library became available not only to government officials but also to the public.

In 1909 all libraries of the government were consolidated in an institution termed "The Philippines Library." In 1916 there was further consolidation by the addition of the archives of the former Spanish government of the Islands, the administration and records of copyrights, and all museum material owned by the government.

The demand for public libraries in the provincial cities and towns has been met as the revenues of the government permitted; by the end of 1925 branch libraries had been established at ten of the more important points outside of Manila, and a total of about 140,000 bound volumes and 300,000 pamphlets, besides the best current American and Philippine periodicals, were available to the public.

The public schools throughout the Islands have been encouraged to
orm libraries, and by 1925 these numbered more than 3800, with nearly
00,000 books.

The principal criticism which the Church leveled at the schools as
stablished by Americans is well expressed in *La Libertas*, the organ of
he monastic orders, in an editorial which praised the extension of pub-
c schools in all the municipalities but criticized the lack of religious
eaching in the schools, and objected to the fact that the schools were
oeducational. This latter reflected the belief brought down from Span-
sh times that girls and boys could not with propriety be educated to-
ether in school.

The Bureau of Education was very scrupulous in prohibiting the in-
erference of its teachers with the religion of their pupils. An effort
vas made to secure American Roman Catholics for the teaching service
n the public schools, but with little success. As most of the teachers
vere Protestants and almost all the children Roman Catholics, the
ntagonism of the Church and parents to the schools might have been
oused to a point that would have greatly lessened their usefulness had
ot the government made the rule absolute that no interference with
he religion of the pupils would be tolerated. In fact, the government
vent further and by law provided that a half hour of religious instruc-
ion, three days a week, could be given in the school building by the
arish priest or local minister to any child whose parent or guardian
lesired it.

The law establishing the public school system provided that nothing
n the act should "be construed in any way to forbid, impede, or obstruct
he establishment and maintenance of private schools."

In addition to the schools conducted under the auspices of the Roman
Catholic Church there were also schools carried on by Protestant mis-
ions of various denominations, and numerous private schools and col-
eges as lay enterprises.

The Church continued to maintain many of its former schools and
pened a number of new ones. These and some lay schools, in which
nstruction until recent years was usually conducted in Spanish, drew
heir patronage very largely from the wealthy families and were looked
pon by the families of social position as more select than were the gov-
rnment schools patronized by the children of people in all walks of
ife.

It was not long, however, before the results of the inferior teaching
vhich had been practiced in the private schools as conducted in Spanish

days, and which still persisted in many of the schools carried on into the days of American rule, began to manifest itself in the inability of the children educated in these schools to compete successfully for entrance to the University or professional schools, or for civil service positions — something very real to young Filipinos, particularly those who had political ambitions.

There was increasing criticism of the courses of study and instruction given in some of the private schools until, in the first session of the Legislature following the establishment of the Philippine Assembly in 1907, several bills were introduced looking toward governmental supervision of private schools. Such legislation was not viewed with favor by the government, as it was believed that the provisions of the corporation law accomplished substantially the results desired, in a more practical manner, and without arousing the opposition and friction which would undoubtedly follow the passage of a compulsory supervision law.

Some of the private colleges and schools had recognized the necessity of raising their standards of instruction, and when they applied for authority to grant diplomas and confer degrees it was found that their standards were sufficiently high to justify the government's giving them the necessary authorization. A large number of private educational institutions immediately applied for governmental supervision of their curricula, methods of teaching, textbooks, and equipment in order that they might receive similar governmental approval.

Private educational institutions under the auspices of both the Roman Catholic Church and Protestant missions, as well as lay schools undertaken as business ventures, are constantly increasing in numbers. They offer elementary and higher education, even university work, and are an important part of insular education.

In 1917, with Filipinos in control of both branches of the Legislature, a law was passed making the inspection of private schools and colleges obligatory for the Secretary of Public Instruction.

The Secretary of Public Instruction in his annual report for 1925 stated that the Legislature had provided for a private school commissioner and staff of twelve qualified assistants. This should make for more adequate supervision.

The following interesting summary of accomplishments of the Philippine public school system and the requirements for the future are given by the Monroe Survey:

Twenty-five years have witnessed the creation of an educational system in the Philippines that reaches into the most remote barrios and the most distant islands. Through this system the opportunities of elementary and secondary education are now extended to over 1,100,000 boys and girls. These children are housed in school buildings which compare favorably with the school buildings of wealthier countries. . . . The mere physical achievement involved in this development of an educational system is of great magnitude.

The Survey goes on to set forth that, creditable as the showing is, less than one-third of the children of school age were getting an education and estimates a further twenty million dollars a year as necessary to extend the benefits of education to all children of school age in the archipelago. American achievement in the extension of primary education has been notably greater than that of the British, Dutch, and other colonial administrations.

If the following words from the address of a schoolboy in Zamboanga could be taken as typical of the kind of spirit that American teachers have inculcated, one could look forward with confidence to a progressive regeneration of the Philippine people.

We have learned why the lands of the Filipino lie uncultivated, and why the people struggle against poverty, superstition and ignorance; that if our country would be free from this poverty we must cultivate our rich soil, for there lies our wealth. We must raise our own food and make our own clothes, must export more than we import.

If we would be free industrially we must raise up an army of workers who will be willing to work long at the same wages. The boys and girls of this country must learn to be proud of their ability to do things and not to be ashamed that they have to work. The long finger nails will have to go.

.   .   .   .

We hope to see every foot of tillable soil under perfect cultivation; to see these islands shipping rice to America or other nations of the world instead of importing it from China.

We hope to see Filipino merchants selling largely Filipino goods; to see the Filipinos rich enough to afford foreign luxuries but industriously producing their own necessities.

We hope to see the Filipinos eating good, nourishing food not only on fiesta days but every day, to see every window in every sleeping room wide open to the fresh air at night.

All this we hope to see, and more, because these are the ends for which we are striving.

CHAPTER VIII

PUBLIC WORKS

PUBLIC WORKS of the Spanish régime were to be found throughout the Islands in a number of dignified and some monumental edifices, usually built for church purposes or for use of the higher officials, some very fine bridges of stone, and the remnants of roads. Manila and Jolo are two fine examples of walled cities, and a number of forts which the Spaniards built — notably Fort Santiago, the citadel on the Pasig River; Fort San Antonio Abad, also in Manila; and the forts in Cebu, Iloilo, Zamboanga, and elsewhere — are instances of baroque fortifications scientifically planned. Other early constructions are the numerous towers along the coast for watch and defense against the marauding Moros. A short railroad, built by private capital under British control, ran from Manila northward. No port improvement of importance had been completed before the advent of the Americans, and there were but fifty-five lighthouses to light the eleven thousand miles of coastline of the archipelago.

A project of immediate necessity was the improvement of the port of Manila to provide safe anchorage and wharf facilities for freight and passenger shipping. A plan for this project had been made and construction begun by the Spaniards. This work was resumed in 1902.

In the days of the Spanish régime the public highways were maintained largely by forced labor. This practice came into odium because of fairly general administrative abuse. One of the early popular reforms of the Americans was the abolition of this requirement. As no substitute provision was made for road maintenance, the roads rapidly deteriorated until in the rainy season they became impassable on account of quagmires, and by the time civil government was established in the Islands, this process of disintegration had gone to the point of actually threatening the economic life of the people. Crops and supplies could not be moved during the rainy season, and at such times it was impossible to draw a loaded cart out of Manila in any direction. The handsome, arched Spanish bridges of stone were allowed to crumble and sometimes fall. What little money there was in the insular treasury available for road work had been used for new projects and not for road maintenance, which was deemed to be a duty of the provinces and municipalities, and the meager funds available for this purpose were too often used for such temporary expedients as corduroying the roads with coarse grasses.

Realizing the necessity of road construction, the Commission had, as its first appropriation, made available insular funds equivalent to one million dollars for road construction. The construction of a number of new roads and bridges was undertaken with the idea of opening up new territory.

Among the first measures adopted was the passage of a law which required every able-bodied man in the Islands to give five days of labor each year on road construction or maintenance, or in lieu of that to pay a sum equivalent to the local cost of such labor. In order to make this measure less offensive to the Filipinos and to give them popular participation in the matter of voting increased taxation, it was provided that the measure should not become effective until accepted by the provincial boards.

A campaign of education was undertaken which presently bore fruit. Delegations from the provinces began to besiege the government with petitions for the construction of roads.

Presently a new law was enacted authorizing the provincial boards to increase the cedula or poll tax to one dollar per annum, the proceeds of the increase being available exclusively for road construction and maintenance, and the Commission then appropriated over six hundred thousand dollars for roads, and authorized ten per cent additional participation in the proceeds of the internal revenue collections, the money to be expended in those provinces which increased the poll tax. Those who did not care to pay in money could work it out with labor. The law placed the additional revenue at the disposition of the provincial and not of the municipal authorities. The net result of these operations was to multiply the money available for roads in the Islands by about five, and change the grossly insufficient four hundred thousand dollars a year into something over two millions.

The road fund having reached suitable proportions, it was necessary to create an organization to expend it properly. The first organization of the provinces had provided an engineer, under the title of provincial supervisor, who was one of the three appointive members of the provincial boards. The Commission, in the fall of 1905, abolished the position of provincial supervisor and created that of district engineer, a subordinate of the Bureau of Public Works, to whom were transferred all the professional duties of the provincial supervisor. A general plan of road maintenance and construction was adopted. All the important roads in each province were laid out and the right of way enforced.

The construction and locality of new roads was left very largely for local determination, and all the funds secured by doubling the poll tax were covered into the treasuries of the provinces to be withdrawn and expended by their own legislative and administrative actions. The Bureau of Public Works retained control of the allotted money appropriated from the insular treasury to assist the provinces and municipalities on their road work. It was in the use of this part of the money that the general policies of the bureau found expression, rather than in the expenditure of the purely provincial funds.

In order to ascertain what roads were most urgently needed, computers were engaged to count the number of wheels which passed over each road in each province and report the result. The road carrying the greatest traffic received the first attention of the government, the policy being to facilitate the conduct of existing business first, leaving the creation of new business till later. Some amazing results were recorded, the traffic passing over one improved highway reaching a figure as high as one thousand per cent above that estimated. Each road was given a width of surface of broken rock, gravel, or coral, and a depth calculated to sustain the number of wheels known to pass over it. Cement or wooden boxes and other devices were adopted as places for deposits of approved road material, and great emphasis was laid upon the continuing maintenance of every bit of road improved and declared to be first-class. Roads were divided into sections and a laborer, known as a *caminero*, wearing a uniform, and provided with the necessary tools for his work, was employed to care for each section. It was found that it cost about one-third as much to keep the road in good condition by having the *caminero* constantly at work on it as it had to let the road go wholly unattended and later rebuild it.

The *caminero* exercised police powers to the extent of regulating traffic on the road, preventing the parking of bull carts or other vehicles in a way that would impede the progress of traffic, and he could also prevent abutters from misuse of ditches either for irrigating purposes or filling them up with refuse.

The use of motor vehicles in the Philippine Islands followed very closely that in the United States, and made it necessary to pass laws providing regulation of traffic, licensing of drivers, and registration of cars. A motor vehicle law, modeled on what had been found necessary in other civilized countries, was enacted in 1912.

While the maintenance of provincial roads was a provincial matter, within what the Spaniards called the *poblacion*, or what Americans would call the city limits, the maintenance of the roads was a municipal matter, and the exact line where the provincial maintenance left off and the municipal maintenance began was apt to be marked by a very notable difference in the condition of the road, a difference which made it inadvisable to pass the line in an automobile at a high rate of speed. The first automobiles to come to Manila arrived about 1903 and people skillful in their management were few. Mr. Warwick Greene, as Assistant Director and later Director of Public Works, used to take the governors of two neighboring provinces along, speed his car over the improved road of one province and then let it run at speed into the badly maintained road of the next province with a jounce that would cause a cry of consternation from the rear seat. The result was a rivalry between the governors of neighboring provinces and a great improvement of the roads.

It was a curious fact that the Filipinos could be much more easily induced to turn out and fix up their roads to make a comfortable trip for a visiting high official than in order to render the transportation of their own produce more economical. Often, in anticipation of such visits, the president of the town would call upon the citizens for "volunteer labor." The municipal police were freely used to induce the able-bodied men of the town to volunteer for this sort of service.

An obstacle to successful maintenance of roads was to be found in the form of the wheels with which the bull carts, carrying most of the cargo of the Islands, were equipped. These were made of solid wood, narrowing down to a little rim, sometimes shod with iron not more than an inch in width. A load of a ton or two on this narrow rim drawn over any road, no matter how strongly metalled, sooner or later cut its way through. As these narrow-tired wheels were fixed to the axle and did not revolve upon it, whenever the bull cart turned, there would be a leverage exerted on the road capable of prying a full-sized cobblestone out of place.

When the Commission in an effort to substitute a better class of vehicle prohibited the use of carts with fixed wheels and of less width of tire than two and one-half inches, there was a general protest.

The solution was finally found in the installation of cart-building machinery in the insular prison at Manila. Quantity production of wide-tired carts and their distribution to the provinces were soon in process, and provision was made so that anybody lacking funds necessary to purchase a cart outright could obtain one by giving to the roads thirty days' work of self and beast. Thus were the roads delivered from their worst enemy.

The policy adopted in the main was the construction first of the lines radiating from the port or railroad station through the most densely populated regions. The first step was usually the construction of concrete bridges and culverts, as these cost almost nothing to maintain and rendered the roads conveniently passable for heavy loads in the dry season. As funds became available and requirements for traffic grew, the required surfacing was put on, until little by little each province developed a more or less comprehensive system of scientifically constructed, strategically placed roads adequately maintained and capable of bearing the existing traffic.

TOTAL MILEAGE OF ROADS IN EXISTENCE

[Source: Report of the Governor-General, 1925, 42.]

Year	First-class roads Mileage
1907	303
1910	764
1915	1,906
1920	2,920
1925	3,520

Filipino support of the road programme was soon secured. Governor Tinio, one of the ablest of Filipinos, said that from what he could see of the road work, "it was the life of the people."

The installation of good roads also required the construction of good bridges. The engineers were ordered to bring in plans for bridges which were either frankly temporary or truly durable. Temporary bridges were to be built of soft wood with a surfacing of bamboo or matting; the permanent bridges and all culverts were to be built of reinforced concrete. The use of concrete reinforced with steel was introduced by American engineers and developed rapidly in the Islands.

This type of construction was remarkably successful, and the condition of both bridges and buildings after about twenty years indicates that the problem of permanent construction in the tropics was solved. At the close of 1913 there were nearly 6000 permanent bridges and culverts in existence, most of which had been constructed or reconstructed during the preceding ten years.

The policy was extended to the construction of all public buildings; nothing between temporary and permanent was permitted. As a result, all important structures built during this period by the insular government were of reinforced concrete, which, with a minimum of care, will last indefinitely and withstand the ravages of ants, earthquakes, rain, and vegetation.

Schoolhouses, provincial buildings, markets, port works, warehouses, libraries, and hospitals all sprang into being. Although the construction was slower than would have been the case had softer materials, easier to work upon, been used, everything that went up in this period was planned to endure and has endured.

By the construction of two breakwaters, Manila, formerly the worst major port for freight in the Orient, was transformed from an open roadstead into a closed harbor. Later, large and well-equipped wharves were built, with a depth of thirty feet at mean low water on each side, capable of loading and unloading with modern labor-saving devices the largest ships that then plied the Pacific.

An area within the breakwater was dredged, the refuse material being used to fill in ground for a new commercial district on what had been, before the arrival of the Americans, shoals in front of the shore-line of the former Manila. These new wharves jutted out from the tract of newly filled-in land on the south side of the Pasig River. Formerly commerce had been brought in lighters up the river and unloaded to wharves either on the river or reached by canals, or *esteros*, which branched off from it.

In 1910, fourteen thousand tons were unloaded at the new docks in five and a half days, in spite of bad weather, when the minimum estimate for handling this amount of cargo had been seven days. Manila began to have a reputation of being one of the best rather than one of the worst ports of the Orient.

Cebu, the second largest city in the archipelago, was given adequate wharves, and at Iloilo, the great sugar port, the river was dredged, straightened, and lined on both sides with piers at which shipping could load and discharge. Improvements were undertaken at several of the lesser ports, including Zamboanga, where ocean-going vessels could come alongside an excellent concrete wharf.

Many additional ports are capable of being developed to the advantage of the Filipinos. There are many deep rivers in the archipelago, scoured to considerable depths for miles inland, but closed to ocean-going vessels by shallow bars at the mouth. These could, without difficulty, be jettied, channels cut, and made into admirable ports and waterways.

The Division of Port Works undertook a "complete study of all harbors throughout the archipelago, to ascertain the cost of developing each one, the advantages which it presents, the movement of sand bars, tides, currents, etc., and to know where the greatest amount of benefit can be conferred upon commerce with the least expenditure of money."

The need for regulation of the use of banks of navigable rivers and foreshore of the harbors and other coasts was soon recognized. The old Spanish laws were of doubtful validity and long failure to enforce them had brought it to pass that not only along the banks of the river Pasig in the greater part of its course through the city of Manila, but also in many other places, unrestrained private interests had encroached until they claimed to have acquired vested rights. In May, 1907, the Commission enacted what became known as the "Foreshore Law," setting forth the conditions and terms upon which the government would permit use of foreshore and under-water lands elsewhere for wharves, docks, marine railways, and for other beneficial public or private purposes. This law also provided for the lay-out for industrial and commercial uses of the area reclaimed in constructing the port of Manila.

One of the earliest matters to invite the attention of the Americans was the need of railways in the Islands. The only railroad then in existence was antiquated in design, equipment, and methods of operation. It extended from the north bank of the Pasig River in Manila to the town of Dagupan, one hundred and twenty miles to the north. The territory traversed was densely populated, well cultivated, and gave abundant patronage.

Early steps were taken toward extension of the railroads. Ways and means of securing the needed capital occupied such national figures as the Honorable Elihu Root when he was Secretary of War and afterward, Secretary Taft, and Governor-General Wright. Engineers were secured, plans made, contracts called for, and finally, under authority of an act of Congress, the government guaranteed interest on bonds of railroads that agreed to build along certain routes believed to be those most likely to be profitable.

After months of negotiation, contracts were entered into between the Philippine government and the Manila Railroad Company by which an additional four hundred and eighteen miles of railroad construction was undertaken on the island of Luzon, including a number of branches and an extension north from Dagupan toward the rich Ilocano provinces on the northwestern coast of Luzon. The company further agreed to construct a bridge across the Pasig River and extend its lines through the populous and cultivated provinces of Laguna, Batangas, and Tayabas, to some port south of Manila, with branches to tap the most productive areas served. The contract also included the construction of a detached branch in the province of Albay to serve the rich hemp districts in that region. The company on its part agreed to release the government from claims arising out of the insurrection.

Later, the company requested and secured a modification and extension of their contract providing for additional construction amounting to some six millions of dollars, including a connecting link between the southern terminus of the railroad and the detached branch in Albay, a line to Baguio, and a line up the west coast of Luzon as far north as San Fernando in La Union Province. The company made progress in all this construction, but none of the branches projected in the later contract was completed by the company. Ultimately a contract was entered into by which the Philippine government purchased the railroad in December, 1915, and has since operated it as a government enterprise.

Another company accepted a concession with government guarantee of interest on its bonds for the construction and operation of nearly three hundred miles of railways in the three islands of Cebu, Panay, and Negros. The Cebu line was built, but has never been so successful as was hoped, being subject to competition of paralleling waterways and well-surfaced highways. The railroad built on the island of Panay was more profitable. That authorized for the island of Negros was never built.

Under the stimulus given by these contracts and agreements on the part of the government, the mileage of operating railways in the Islands has increased from 121 miles in 1898 to 792 miles in 1925.

The street railway in the city of Manila at the time of American occupation was an antiquated horse-car service that was very casual in operation. This connected with a steam-tram line to the populous suburban towns of Caloocan and Malabon.

As early as 1902, the Philippine Commission authorized a franchise granted on competitive bidding to construct and maintain in the streets of Manila and its suburbs an electric street railway and a service of electric light, heat, and power. This franchise was awarded to American capitalists, who acquired the existing antiquated plants and installed modern and highly satisfactory services which have contributed greatly to the industrial development as well as the comfort and economy of living in that city and its suburbs. The electric railways by 1913 reached a total of fifty miles. Electric light and power are supplied at reasonable rates.

In some of the larger cities and towns electric light and power have been provided by private enterprise and in a few instances, notably Baguio and Zamboanga, electric light and power plants have been constructed and maintained by the local governments.

The city of Manila in 1898 had an inadequate water supply and no modern sewer system. These two circumstances greatly increased the danger from cholera and other water-borne diseases. The construction of adequate modern services was early undertaken, and by 1909, the government had completed the installation of a successful potable water-supply service for the city of Manila, and sewer and storm-water drainage systems superior to those of any other city in the Orient. The government also encouraged the construction of water works in other cities.

In the city of Cebu, in Baguio, the summer capital, and in a number of other important towns wherever it could be afforded, the government provided gravity or pumping water-supply services.

Many districts of the archipelago produced an abundance of artesian water that flowed sometimes to a height of several feet above the surface of the ground. This has had a very important bearing on the health of those regions. It had always been the custom among the Filipinos to use the surface waters, regardless of pollution. Sometimes they drank the very waters in which they washed, not from the same household vessel, but from the same well or pool. It was difficult to make them understand the necessity of boiling the surface waters before use. Most of these waters carried infection of amoebic dysentery and other disorders, and in times of pestilence water was apt to be infected with cholera.

It was not long before these doubting people became ardent advocates of the artesian wells. "This water is as good as medicine," they were heard to say. Once they found that it was pure and salubrious, they came miles to get water for household use, and the difficulty first encountered in persuading people to partake of the water changed to a difficulty in explaining the impossibility of boring as many artesian wells as were insistently demanded.

In 1904 there was but one such well. Early in 1927 the Bureau of Public Works reported 1820, supplying approximately 2,700,000 people with potable water. In addition, there have been a large number of artesian wells opened by local enterprise.

There was little difficulty in interesting the Filipinos in irrigation. They knew its value. Their crops had been subject to the uncertainties of the season, falling off sharply in times of drought, and allowing only one crop a year, whereas two could have been obtained from the same ground and with little more work, had water been available. Extensive irrigation projects, however, involve years of preliminary study. The minimum flow of the rivers that supply a district must be measured. Without such observations it is unsafe to enter into expensive works of construction that may be useless much of the time. Thus, although money was early made available for irrigation and the department was prepared to go ahead with the projects, prudence dictated going slowly at first until the proper measurements of minimum flow could be completed.

But irrigation became a major governmental activity. In August, 1907, a continuing annual reimbursable appropriation of $125,000 was made. In May of the following year this was increased by $250,000. The sum of $375,000 was thus laid aside annually for irrigation projects. The reimbursable feature meant that all revenues derived from the sale of water or of completed projects to individuals or companies were to be added to the principal and available for later expenditure upon new projects or the extension and care of the old ones.

A division of irrigation was created in the Bureau of Public Works. It was soon evident that if the plans of the government were to be made effective, a new irrigation law was necessary.

In 1908 a committee of nine members was appointed, including three members of the Assembly and one Manila businessman, to make recommendations as to selection of projects for allotment, terms upon which allotments should be made, matters of administration, and the relations between the Bureaus of Public Works and Lands. In August of that year eighteen irrigation engineers were secured from the United States.

An expert was secured from the United States Reclamation Service and the needed legislation drafted. This proposed law was presented to the Legislature but failed of passage, at the cost of some delay. The Bureau of Public Works continued its investigations and by July, 1910, had reported on two hundred and sixteen projects, and begun work on three.

The reason for the delay was the insistence of the Assembly or lower house on granting to a committee composed largely of their members executive supervision over the expenditure of moneys for irrigation. This was opposed by the Governor-General and members of the Commission on the ground that it conferred executive powers on legislative officers. The compromise finally agreed upon provided for an irrigation council of which two out of five members were Assemblymen. The power to grant appropriations of public waters was vested in the Secretary of Commerce and Police upon the recommendation and approval of the irrigation council.

In February, 1912, the Legislature finally enacted an irrigation law providing machinery for the regulation of the beneficial use of public waters, and determination and registration of private rights, both for irrigation and water power.

All these delays resulted in comparatively little actual construction, and the work was further impeded when the sharp reduction of revenue in 1913, of which the causes will be set forth in a later chapter, made it incumbent upon the Governor-General to cover back into the treasury unallotted balances of this and other funds. Before the end of the year 1913 the Bureau of Public Works had, however, accumulated a valuable amount of irrigation data and work had been accomplished on a number of small projects, as well as reconstruction and extension of old systems and the settlement of many controversies in regard to water rights.

It was natural that the members of the Commission, seeing very large sums of money lying idle in the trust funds of the government, should cast eager eyes toward these, and a suggestion, emanating from Washington, that a portion of these funds could be used with propriety as loans to provinces and municipalities for needed public works, was warmly welcomed and promptly acted on. It was deemed wise to limit the use of moneys thus loaned to projects of a revenue-bearing nature.

A loaning system brought about the construction of municipal mar-

ZIGZAG ON BENGUET ROAD

BURNHAM PARK, BAGUIO

AMPHITHEATRE PLANNED BY GENERAL BELL, CAMP JOHN HAY, BAGUIO

kets to replace the unsanitary and antiquated structures, or meet the lack of structures, formerly designated as markets. Under the internal revenue law, the municipalities were entitled to a certain proportion of the internal revenue collected by the insular government. Under the new system, loans made to municipalities were limited so that the service of interest and amortization did not exceed the amount of internal revenue collected for that municipality by the insular government, and its share of the service of these loans was deducted by the insular treasurer. In this way the repayment of these loans was made entirely independent of the action of the municipal treasurer and required no annual vote of the municipal council.

The system worked well, and without exception the amounts loaned for the construction of these markets were reimbursed during the period allotted for payment, ordinarily five and never exceeding ten years.

By the end of the fiscal year 1913, loans to provincial and municipal governments amounted to $3,635,500. In the cases of markets constructed from insular loans, the rate of interest did not exceed four per cent per annum, and the increased municipal revenues were never less than six per cent on the investment, generally more than twenty per cent, sometimes as much as eighty per cent per annum. The increased revenues accruing to the municipalities put them in a position to render other municipal services.

The design and construction of public buildings for all branches of government were brought under the Consulting Architect and Bureau of Public Works, and have so continued. This arrangement worked well.

One of the earlier activities of the government was the careful planning of the cities of Manila and Baguio. Secretary Taft gave his personal attention to this, and it was through his good offices that the services of the eminent and patriotic architect, Mr. Daniel H. Burnham, of Chicago, were secured.

Mr. Burnham felt he was performing a patriotic duty and accepted merely his traveling expenses and the salary of one assistant. These two together laid out a comprehensive and excellent plan for the development and growth of the city of Manila and for the incipient city of Baguio.

The plan for Manila provided a site for a future government center with all the government buildings; it filled in the unsanitary moat which had surrounded the walled city, and made a park of the land which, for military purposes when the fort was maintained for defense, had had to be kept clear of trees and buildings. This preserved the beauty and charm of the walled city. At various places, the walls were pierced with openings for streets in order to let in the air and accommodate the traffic of the intramural district. The plan considered the future growth of the city, and made provision for wide, radiating avenues to reach all districts. All was done envisaging the possibility of great development.

The plan has been in the main adhered to. The central park was immediately begun, and with great benefit.

With the improvement of the port, and the anticipated construction of the new commercial city on the filled-in area outside of what had been the water front, the old Luneta of Spanish days was relegated to a position of diminished importance and greatly impaired beauty. Mr. Burnham's conception called for a park area of nearly thirty acres, which was laid out upon a new area reclaimed from the harbor by the construction of breakwaters filled in by dredging an additional section of the harbor. To this new land was moved the new Luneta or park, where the evening band concerts were held and the people took their evening stroll. A park was constructed in the center of this Luneta Extension, named Burnham Park, and a decorated flag pole has been erected there in Mr. Burnham's memory. There was abundant room for playgrounds, and this new area was flanked on either side by impressive semi-public buildings; on one side was the site for the new Manila Hotel, with its own separate landing, on the other side spaces were reserved for the construction of clubs, and these were used by the Army and Navy Club and the Elks Club.

It was long before the funds were raised for the construction of the new Manila Hotel, but by 1909 this project was well under way. The first participation of the government in this enterprise lay in purchasing the bonds of the hotel company at a reasonable rate of interest. But later the ownership of the hotel was transferred to the government.

Beginning at the Luneta Extension, the programme of municipal development called for a boulevard to be built along the water front of Manila Bay, with driveways, pathways, and parkways, and perhaps a bridle path, which ultimately it was expected would reach all the way to Cavite, twelve miles distant. The first mile was the most difficult and expensive portion of this tract, as it passed along the water front between some important mansions and the sea. The construction was authorized in 1909, and was gradually pursued in connection with the improvement of the port of Manila by extension southward of the retaining wall and the deposit behind this of material dredged in deepening the port. It has been appropriately named Dewey Boulevard.

These plans for Manila and Baguio awoke keen interest among provincial and municipal officers who came to Manila for information and advice. The more enterprising provincial and municipal treasurers subscribed for leading publications dealing with city planning methods, and sought advice and assistance of the government in the planning and ornamentation of cities and towns. The insular government contributed the services of a competent landscape engineer in many instances, and a contributory result of Mr. Burnham's services in the winter and summer capitals has reflected itself in real advances being made in many other cities towards the "city beautiful."

In September, 1905, the position of Consulting Architect to the Commission was created. Mr. William E. Parsons, a graduate of Yale and of the École des Beaux Arts in Paris, accepted the appointment and brought to the Islands a fine sense of proportion, thorough training, and unusual industry. The architecture of his time will stand as a permanent monument to the American administration of the Islands. His lines were always simple, proportions harmonious, colors agreeable, and the useful purposes of the building were never subordinated to mere architectural beauty.

No competent Filipino engineers were available at the time of the organization of the bureau, and it was necessary for some years to bring such technical personnel from the United States. Special effort was made to attract qualified Filipinos to the necessary studies. Such students, if without private means, were given financial assistance by the government to complete their professional studies in the United States. These young engineers generally acquitted themselves well and received rapid advancement. On June 30, 1913, of a total of one hundred and forty-five engineers in the bureau, eighteen were Filipinos and one hundred and twenty-seven Americans. At the close of 1925, of the technical force of one hundred and ninety there were sixteen Americans and one hundred and seventy-four Filipinos.

Under the régime of the Democratic Party, a Filipino, Mr. José Paez, was given the important position of Director of Public Works and brought to it real ability and technical training of a high order. At his own expense he had pursued advanced studies in engineering at the best universities in Europe and the United States. In 1924, he resigned to take the responsible position of president of the Manila Railroad Company, and his work was taken over in turn by an American.

In the main it may be said that of the many creditable and useful services rendered by Americans in the Philippine Islands that given by the Bureau of Public Works has been among the foremost. The engineers, from those in the highest positions down through the service, brought to their work true American enterprise and the will that succeeds.

BAGUIO

ONE of the Spanish traditions to which the Americans fell heir told of a "paradise" somewhere in the hills in northern Luzon, where was to be found a pleasing and temperate climate offering delightful conditions of life, not inaccessibly far from Manila and the populous regions of Luzon.

In July, 1900, two members of Judge Taft's Commission, Messrs. Wright and Worcester, undertook an expedition to search for this place. To their delight, they found the tradition more than borne out by the charms of the place. About one hundred and fifty miles north of Manila, five thousand feet above the sea, nestled among the mountains of the province of Benguet were the beautiful rolling hills of Baguio and the little plain of Trinidad. The situation and climate were ideal. The hills were covered with thick, rough grasses and great pines, interspersed in the valleys and along the watercourses with tree ferns. The soil, a reddish clay, was capable of supporting many varieties of vegetation; the average temperature was sixty-five degrees Fahrenheit, a relief from the heat of the lowlands, which averaged twenty degrees more. There were almost always breezes, and even in the heat of the day, with the tropic sun directly overhead, the air in the shade of the pines was pleasant and cool. The climate was invigorating, and, except in the rainy season, the days were generally clear, and outdoor life delightful, although there was always a likelihood of sudden and heavy showers. The temperature at night made a fire of pine logs most welcome.

At that time the trip was made by boat to San Fernando de La Union, and from there by horseback on a very fair trail known as the Naguilian Trail, involving nearly a day by sea before starting a ride of nearly thirty miles on horseback into the hills. Not only the time but the method of travel greatly limited the possible usefulness of Baguio, particularly as a health resort, presenting too many difficulties for invalids.

The Commission undertook to make Baguio available as the summer capital of the Islands.

The road as planned began near the foothills, to reach which one had to traverse thirty miles of poorly maintained provincial roads. The government made two unfortunate choices of engineers who grossly underestimated the costs and time required and it was thus involved in construction calling for unduly heavy expenditures.

As the Benguet Road began to creep up into the hills, a stage line was inaugurated from the northern end of the railroad at Dagupan through the province of Pangasinan to the end of the road, from which point the remainder of the trip was made up the Bued River trail. The great Chicago architect, Daniel H. Burnham, made a memorable visit to Baguio in December, 1904, the result of which was the preparation of a comprehensive plan for the development of the proposed new city.

The road finally — in January, 1905 — reached the site of the new summer capital, till then accessible only on foot or horseback.

In 1909, the Commission authorized a tax on all vehicles passing over the Road in order that the burden of its upkeep should be borne by its traffic.

The difficulties presented by this route to Baguio were abundantly demonstrated by the series of disasters which later befell the road from floods and attendant slides. The rainfall in Baguio sometimes reaches two hundred and fifty inches a year, and, while heavy typhoons are passing, it is not uncommon for the rainfall to reach as high as twenty inches in twenty-four hours. During a storm which took place July 14 and 15, 1911, there was a record fall reaching almost the proportions of a cloudburst, and the record showed the astounding figure of 45.99 inches in twenty-four hours. After such a deluge, it is surprising that anything was left of the road. At one point part of a mountain slid down and blocked up the valley until the Bued River rose to a height of one hundred and fifty feet and went roaring seaward, carrying with it that part of the mountain which had slid down, with numberless trees and, among other things, a number of the Benguet Road bridges, several of them recently constructed of steel, which had been expected to last for generations. These were left some miles down the river, rolled up into pitiful balls of tangled girders and trestles. Under the able management of the Bureau of Public Works the road was soon reopened.

The allocation of very large sums required to complete the Benguet

Road had not been made without arousing comment in Manila, and with each successive appropriation the Commission — not a popular body with those Americans who had come out with the army — was greeted with storms of abuse. The local American papers rang with scathing denunciations of the whole project, so that it was not a matter of surprise that the Filipino papers should have joined in the chorus, and habitual critics of the government were sure to bring in derogatory comments about Baguio and the Benguet Road.

The problem of the road, however, remained a constant one. Storm after storm made it temporarily impassable, but, despite gloomy prognostications on the part of the engineers, it was always restored.

Later, the Legislature appropriated $150,000 to improve another road to Baguio by way of Naguilian, and in 1927 both roads were being maintained and freely patronized.

In view of the almost universal condemnation of the venture, when the road was first opened, the Commission was unwilling to spend further money to develop the region then reached, and the government found itself in the unpleasant predicament of having spent something over two million dollars to build an unreliable mountain road to a place where the only accommodations for visitors were a so-called sanatorium with a few beds, built by the government, and about six poorly built houses.

Something had to be done, and it was decided to make a sale of lots with the condition that houses should be built on them within a reasonably short period of time. The money thus raised was expended in building the roads most needed to open up the parts of the proposed new city reaching such lots as were likely to be built on first.

A small additional fund was secured to put a thin layer of gravel over the surface of the roads, which made them safer for horses and possible for automobiles, which were just then beginning to be introduced into the Islands and to find their way up the Benguet Road into Baguio.

To those engaged in the development of the city of Baguio, the experience of city-planning was new and quite delightful. The reservation of the town site of Baguio was made by the Commission in 1903. The fourteen thousand acres which were later to be included within the city limits at that time had no vestige of a road, merely a few footpaths and only a half-dozen houses besides three or four little scattered groups of grass-thatched hovels occupied by Igorots. This tract was developed as a health resort. It was difficult to estimate the size which its growth might ultimately reach. The plans were made on the basis of a probable growth to twenty-five thousand. It was most fortunate that the Philippine government should have had the privilege and advantage of Mr. Burnham's vision in facing this problem, and the plan that he made has since been adhered to faithfully. The streets and avenues for the prospective city were planned, and districts set aside for the residence and business sections, for the service end, stables and garages, etc. Sites were designated for the government center, including the future capitol building, the provincial and municipal buildings, the Governor-General's residence, and other public buildings; reservations were indicated for an army post, a naval hospital, the railroad terminal, and a country club. Convenient sites were set aside for semi-public buildings such as churches, libraries, convents, hospitals, observatory, etc., and last but not least, a comprehensive system of parks and playgrounds connected by parkways winding in and out of the valleys and following the courses of streams, along which there were planned bridle paths, shrubberies, and driveways.

Having dreamed of the city to be, the American administrators and engineers set about to build it to fit in as nearly as possible with the form of the vision.

A country club was organized; a small amount of money was privately contributed and, wholly without recourse to public funds, a clubhouse, at first little more than a shack, was built, a steward employed, tennis courts built, and a golf links started. The United States Army also began developing its reservation. A hospital and a few residences for officers and barracks for men were built, which made the beginning of what has grown to be the very beautiful Camp John Hay. The Constabulary school for the training of officers was moved from Manila to Baguio. The government sanatorium which had been established at Baguio in 1902 was taken over by private parties and built into a rather extensive hotel, known as "The Pines." Another hotel was built on the other side of the town and called "The Hills."

A very modest beginning of a mansion for the Governor-General was made. To beautify and care for the grounds, a detail of fifty "trusty" prisoners was sent to Baguio, who lived there and arranged the terrace, parking, and ornamentation of the twenty-five acres set aside for the grounds of the official residence.

With a free hand and absolutely virgin territory to develop, it was possible to lay out the new city with an eye to harmony and beauty impossible in older communities encumbered with costly existing structures.

The Consulting Architect to the Commission, who had the duty of interpreting Mr. Burnham's plans, made the reservation for every road one hundred feet wide. The exigencies of the contours made it impossible to keep the road in the exact center of these reservations, but ample margin on either side was left for trees and shrubs.

First, there had to be implanted in the people a desire to use Baguio; secondly, there had to be a place there for them to stay in and something there for them to do; and thirdly, the transportation facilities must be comfortable and of moderate cost. From the railroad terminus at Dagupan, the stage line, which operated during the construction of the road, was continued direct to Baguio by means of four-mule teams with relays. The distance was fifty-three miles, twenty-seven over provincial roads, usually in bad condition, with two fords impassable in times of flood or high water. In 1907, the railway built a branch line to a point called "Camp One," at the foot of the mountains, and the stage line was thus shortened to twenty-four miles. The first trip over the railroad to Camp One was made by Secretary Taft when he came to inaugurate the first Philippine Assembly and spent a week in the hills at the summer capital which his vision had made possible.

Mr. Warwick Greene, later Director of Public Works, purchased for the government a number of big De Dion cars, and, in addition to performing his many important official duties, he demonstrated the operation of the cars himself until he could train a sufficient force of Filipino drivers to take over the service. Thanks to him the trip was made easy, safe, and popular.

The government decided to have a yearly convention of teachers in Baguio to which most of the Americans came, and, beginning in 1908, each year distinguished lecturers were secured in the United States to come to the Philippine Islands and give courses of lectures to the assembled teachers. The movement was a great success and made happier the life of the American teacher in the Islands.

In 1909, the government constructed a large group of buildings for its service in the hills, including one building for each of the five departments of the insular government. An adequate mess hall was constructed, so that the government clerks and employees in many of the bureaus could be moved bodily to Baguio for the hot season. An athletic director was secured and group sports carried on. The Filipinos took readily to this innovation, and a physical examination showed that there was a gain of weight on the part of the clerks who came up. The government built fifty cottages, which were leased, with preference to government employees, but to private individuals in case there were not enough official applications.

In the law creating the Assembly no place was mentioned at which sessions were to be called. The Governor-General, desiring to familiarize the Assemblymen with Baguio, on the occasion of calling the first session of the second Philippine Legislature made the rather bold move of summoning it to meet in Baguio. This was done after consulting Speaker Osmeña. No objection was raised; and a three weeks' session was held in Baguio in which a number of important measures, including the appropriation bill, became law.

The Roman Catholic Church was quick to appreciate Baguio. A dignified place was selected for the residence of the Archbishop and a cottage built for him, while a hilltop became the site of a modest church, later followed by a much more imposing one. The Jesuits secured another hilltop which they named Mirador, where they built an observatory and a monastery of stone, which they used for meteorological observations and as a health resort for their priests. The Dominicans crowned another hilltop with a fine stone monastery.

When General J. Franklin Bell became Commanding General, he became enthusiastic for Baguio, and began the structure of a series of cement buildings on the military reservation and personally designed and supervised the construction of an open-air amphitheater which seated a thousand people.

An American periodical published a discriminating article giving an interesting description of Baguio and the activities in connection with its use, ending with a remark that "even a brief period of usefulness has caused even its enemies to call it a 'glorious blunder.'"

The cloud-world at Baguio is something unforgettable. The moist, warm air of the southwest monsoon blown against the mountains piles up huge masses of cumulus clouds which come sweeping over the hills in an endless train of startling lights. As the setting sun shoots up through the cleft in the mountains north of the high peak of Santo Tomas, it plays on these cumulus clouds, kindling them to almost unbelievable brilliance. The air appears luminous with color, and one seems to be living in the sunset rather than as a spectator removed. There are times when one rides in an atmosphere permeated with orange-colored haze, seen through which the green of the pines is an almost livid blue. As one official described it:

Baguio has been . . . the most startlingly beautiful thing I have ever seen. We've had a full moon rising on the one side, and the late sun setting on the other, and the air so filled with luminous colors playing on the different piles and degrees of clouds that it all has seemed like a wonderland. . . . Night after night everyone gathers on some neighboring hill to see the colors. Last night it was as though the hills to the west were absolutely aflame under a sombre cloud cover.

"This is the place you always look for in the States and never find," said one army officer. An American visitor, with his wife, went up for a Sunday and stayed for a year.

Some prominent Filipinos came on a visit to Baguio. As a result, almost two dozen cottages were built and homes established in the hills. Those taking part in the movement included some of the best-known Spanish families and more important commercial and social leaders in the Islands.

Other Filipinos were not slow in appreciating the benefits to be derived from cooler airs. In May, 1909, General Aguinaldo visited Baguio as the guest of the Governor-General, had his first game of golf at the country club links, and took to that sport with enthusiasm. He made the pertinent comment that, in his opinion, Baguio ought to be the permanent capital of the Islands.

The potential economic value of Baguio to the Islands was something not to be ignored. Wealthy Filipinos had been accustomed to take their fortunes and set up residence in Paris or in Spain. Americans usually returned to the United States or for short vacations visited China or Japan. Many left their children in the homeland, and that fact alone made their stay in the Islands of uncertain tenure, the tendency being always to save their pennies and make plans to join their families at home. Bishop Brent, Episcopal Bishop of the Islands, had the vision to raise the money necessary to establish a school for American boys in Baguio, and a very successful school was started to which American and English boys were admitted. Many army officers brought out their sons and placed them in this school. The first headmaster was the Reverend Remsen B. Ogilby, later president of Trinity College.

With the growth of Baguio, transportation and accommodations had to grow. The shack which at first served as a country clubhouse gave way to a handsome building with porches, fireplaces, bedrooms, and gardens, and a series of cottages available for rent by club members. The original rough and artlessly planned golf course of nine holes little by little became smooth and perfected, and finally, by coöperation of the military authorities, who for a while permitted the use of a portion of the army reservation, it was extended to eighteen holes.

It was early evident that some special arrangement was necessary for the government of Baguio. The usual municipal government organization did not exactly fit the requirements of this hill station, where it was planned to house the higher officers of the government and many of the bureau chiefs, and during the hot season provide for Filipinos, Americans, and foreigners from the lowlands and from outside countries, and to which it was probable there would be a large number of army men and their families moved from the lowlands for health purposes. There was also a growing resident population of Igorots. In view of the exceptional circumstances surrounding its development, it was deemed wise to give Baguio a special form of city government, and in 1909, a charter was enacted which provided for an appointive mayor and council, the mayor being usually the engineer who already had charge of the maintenance of the Benguet Road.

In 1909, a new railway concession, agreed upon with the bankers who had undertaken the construction of new lines of the Manila Railroad Company, provided for an extension to Baguio.

By 1913 the success of Baguio was assured. The scant half-dozen houses had multiplied to several hundred buildings and the population of the city had increased with each season. The movement of the government to Baguio stimulated its growth very greatly. Following the construction of the government center, which was economically built of temporary materials around an open park or plaza, space was reserved for later construction of a permanent group of government buildings to be built on a larger scale around the temporary central group. Many Filipinos felt, as did General Aguinaldo, that Baguio ought ultimately to be the permanent capital of the Islands. A line down the main axis laid out by Mr. Burnham was cleared through the pines, the hills terraced, and an artificial lake constructed in the central valley. The park around the lake has been appropriately named for Mr. Burnham. Buildings and stores sprang up along the line of the main street, in the business center markets were built, and business grew so rapidly that the earlier buildings soon gave way to larger. On market days, the whole vicinity was thronged with people carrying their wares, some of whom had come in from many miles away. Playgrounds were built and regular sports indulged in.

With the ensuing years has come a growing and annually increasing popularity of Baguio. Governor-General Harrison, in his report for 1919, called it "the most beautiful hill station" in the tropical Orient of which he had knowledge. Filipinos especially saw the value of Baguio as a health resort. Tuberculosis was very prevalent in the Islands and the benefit of the cool air in the hills was early demonstrated. The government constructed a hospital with cottages for tuberculosis patients, and it was not long before the Filipino doctors began to prescribe a period in Baguio for their phthisis patients. Many notable cures resulted and a good many lives were saved.

Governor-General Wood wrote in 1926 of the service Baguio had come to perform for the Philippine people:

Baguio has fifty per cent more people here this summer than ever before and a good deal of building. . . . We had a good many conventions here this summer and a tremendously large attendance at Teacher's Camp; convention of Judges of First Instance, convention of fiscals, of provincial treasurers, auditors and of postmasters; also there was a large convention of public health officers . . . Camp John Hay is packed with people to the very limit. . . . I think we can count on Baguio as a real fixture. More and more Filipinos come here every year, and in fact it was almost impossible to house them all this year. The Government Center is now used for insular government employees and authorities and others who cannot find a place to stay in. I think as the years go on Baguio will be more and more a summer capital of the Islands.

The early criticism yielded to a general and cordial approval of the whole project on the part of the Philippine public, and words of contumely have given way to praise and appreciation.

CHAPTER IX

VARIOUS GOVERNMENTAL ACTIVITIES

PRISONS

IN THE MANY activities which absorbed the attention of the Commission in the early days of its labors, the especial attention of the officers of the government had not been directed to prisons beyond the adequacy and proper preparation of food, sanitation, and other obvious reforms.

Manila had a very extensive set of prison buildings, known as Bilibid, which served as a central prison for the whole archipelago, to which persons convicted of crime carrying a sentence longer than one year were committed. A high wall, commanded at intervals by stone towers, enclosed a tract of land, commanding which was a central tower mounted with a Gatling gun. From this tower radiated the prison barracks like the spokes of a wheel, each barrack having its own yard, the walls of which ran in a direct line toward the central tower, leaving no portion of the yards free from observation. This prison could accommodate about thirty-four hundred inmates, but it was inadequate to care for the numbers committed to it, which in 1904 rose above forty-four hundred. Overcrowding resulted in tuberculosis, the hospital facilities were inadequate, mortality of prisoners high, and insane and juveniles were herded with criminals.

To remedy these conditions tuberculosis patients were removed to a building outside the prison for special treatment, pending the time when an adequate modern prison hospital could be provided, which, when completed, included all essentials to modern hospital practice with separate departments for tuberculosis cases in an open-air ward on the roof, and for other dangerous communicable diseases, and also for women patients, with complete qualified staff.

Negotiations with the Archbishop of Manila resulted in his providing a separate institution to take charge of juvenile delinquents.

The insane were taken from Bilibid to the commodious buildings and grounds of the San Lazaro estate at Manila, upon the vacation of these by the transfer of lepers to the newly established leper colony on the island of Culion.

To further relieve overcrowding other devices were adopted, such as utilizing convicts on work of road building in the provinces, and in the construction and maintenance of fortifications at Corregidor. A penal colony on the island of Palawan also was established.

It was found in certain instances that transfers of prisoners to places far from home, or to very different altitudes, were injurious to their health. Igorots brought down from the mountains and imprisoned in Manila languished, and it was found necessary, in the interests of humanity and of justice, to establish a prison in the mountains so that the Igorots could work out their terms of imprisonment in their own climate and within sight of their own hills.

In 1905, the Bureau of Prisons was given general supervision over the administration of all insular and provincial prisons. In these, inspections had revealed a great many defects, some easily remedied and some not. Many were structural and required the erection of expensive new prisons. Proper care had not always been taken to see that there should be a free passage of air through the living and sleeping rooms, an important matter in all climates but essential in the tropics. Plans for a model prison were prepared by the insular government and distributed to provincial boards for their consideration and guidance in alterations of existing buildings and in new construction.

Municipal prisons were used for the confinement of misdemeanants, of persons sentenced to imprisonment for not more than one month, and for the temporary detention of persons charged with crime. These jails were generally located in a portion of the ground floor of the municipal office building or *presidencia*, and under the charge and immediate responsibility of the municipal president through his chief of police.

Provincial prisons were under the responsibility of provincial governors and provided for confinement of persons awaiting trial for alleged criminal offenses, and also persons tried and sentenced to imprisonment for periods not exceeding one year.

In addition to regular inspection by the Director of Prisons, provincial prisons were subject to inspection by judges of the Court and by the officers of the Constabulary, all of whom were required to report to the Governor-General faults in administration, alleged abuses, and other matters requiring corrective action.

The Director of Prisons standardized prison records and statistics and technical features of administration. All wardens were brought to Manila for instruction and proper training at Bilibid. They were supplied also with printed instructions, rules, and regulations for the government of prisoners, and a manual for the utilization of prison labor. In general, provincial officials responded well to these measures for increased efficiency.

It was customary for the Governor-General on his inspection trips always to walk unannounced into the local prison. Sometimes he found ugly abuses and sometimes such latitude and freedom that confinement was no punishment at all. Instruments of torture from former times were not unusual, and sometimes an inspection revealed ugly-looking whips, or heavy stocks and pillories in which unfortunate prisoners could be fastened by the legs, or hands and neck. Orders were issued that every instrument of torture, including whips, stocks, and heavy chains, be taken from the jails and destroyed.

Other abuses of a more subtle nature were discovered. In one province it was found that a little ring of rascals, including the provincial governor, the local justice of peace, and his brother, had grouped themselves into a closed corporation designed to utilize the machinery of the government for their private gain. People coming from the interior to the seaport and bringing their produce were compelled to sell their goods to the ring at prices fixed by it — a minor fraction of their fair value. Failure to do this resulted in charges being filed against the owner of the goods, perhaps for sedition, his goods "confiscated," and he himself thrown into jail to languish for months. The contract for feeding the prisoners had been awarded to the brother of the justice of the peace who made the commitments, and they were none too well fed, though a large part of the revenues of the province was supposedly used for that purpose. On the occasion of a visit by Governor-General Wright to this province, it was found that no less than one hundred and ninety people were confined in the provincial jail, without adequate air. Women held as witnesses were even detained in the same room with men convicted of crime. The Governor ordered a special session of the court to be held immediately in the province to give these people the privilege of an early trial under an American judge, and the delinquent justice of the peace found himself committed to the jail to which he had often consigned innocent persons.

On one occasion, when the Governor-General was walking along a street in one of the provincial capitals in northern Luzon, a paper was pushed into his hand by a woman as he passed. It proved to be a communication to the effect that her daughter had been seduced and later murdered by a young man of high family in the town, who had been convicted of the crime and sentenced to fourteen years of imprisonment at hard labor. The complaint went on to say that this man was not compelled to serve his sentence. Under pretense of being sick, he did none of the prison labor and, while nominally in prison, with the connivance of the warden and the provincial governor he had been living at home. Inspection of the jail proved this to be the case. The young man was then in the hospital of the prison feigning illness. The Director of Health of the Islands happened to be a member of the Governor-General's party and he examined the young man and found him to be in perfect health. It was pointed out to the warden that his prisoner's convalescence had now reached the point when it would be safe to move him, and so, duly manacled, the convict was transferred aboard ship and his period of immunity from punishment ended.

On another occasion an inspection of the municipal jail in a southern province revealed the fact that nine women, three or four of them with children at the breast, were confined in a little room, without furniture, where there was not space enough for all of them to lie down at once. There was no chance for admission of outside air or light, the only apertures being between slats in the door opening upon a corridor. As the Governor-General passed, one of the women prisoners burst into a flow of impassioned oratory, setting forth the evil conditions under which they were confined, and made so good a case that within half an hour all but one of the women were released by pardon on the ground that they had undergone cruel and improper punishment. The officials responsible for these abuses were called to account and vigorously reprimanded, and provision made for future adequate care of municipal prisoners. The evil in this case was all the greater because a commodious, well-aired room, suitable for women and children to occupy, stood empty at the time, but those in charge said it was reserved for the use of any of the police who happened to feel indisposed.

At the other end of the scale, it was sometimes found that the municipal prisons were mere lounging places. Upon the arrival of the Governor-General and party, unannounced, at a little town on the island of Mindanao, a visit to the jail revealed the fact that not one of the three prisoners was to be found. They were all out about their own

THE MANILA HOTEL

MANILA PIER NO. 7

affairs, reporting from time to time at the jail for their nominal confinement. In another jail, the guns of the guard were kept in a rack within reach of the prisoners.

Thus the administration of prisons ranged from extreme cruelty to careless good-humor. This was remedied when the Director of Prisons in Manila undertook the supervision of all jails. Through frequent inspection and prompt action, abuses in administration have been kept at a minimum and by 1910 the administration of the prisons was on the whole good.

Hard labor is required of convicts in the Philippine Islands as in the United States. In Manila the city repair shops were placed within the prison and all repair of municipal and insular transportation, automobiles, carts, and other vehicles, and of machinery used by the city and by the insular government was performed by prison labor. The government went further than this and selected certain specialties which were made in the prison and not elsewhere — certain types of furniture, silverware, and other objects which had not previously been introduced in the commercial shops of the city — and placed them on sale in the prison. In Bilibid and Bontoc Prisons about fifty per cent of the prisoners were constantly employed in the shops.

Thus, almost all insular prisoners serving sentences of more than one year had an opportunity to become proficient in woodworking, blacksmithing, or other mechanical trade as skilled laborers. Upon their release from prison they were able to devote their energies to their trades and served to fill in part the shortage of skilled mechanics throughout the country. Convicts upon release were found to be generally more robust than most Filipino laborers, who suffered from drinking the polluted waters and living the unhygienic lives common to the uneducated classes. Representatives of private enterprises were always on the lookout for released convicts, who were able to find immediate employment.

One practice that worked well was that of paying prisoners for their work. Only those rated as first-class were eligible and these were divided into first, second, and third grade laborers who received six, four, and two cents a day respectively. It did not matter what the nature of the work was so long as it was done in a first-class manner, and the janitor got his rating just the same as the silversmith or cabinetmaker. The prisoner was allowed to spend half of the money received for purchases of articles in the little prison store. The other half was paid to his family, if he had one, or laid aside to be paid him upon his release.

Another innovation was that of having all minor infractions of prison rules tried before a jury of first-class prisoners who assembled witnesses to testify, found the accused guilty or not guilty, and then recommended the punishment. It is noteworthy that these juries were disposed to be severe in their punishments, which however were subject to administrative scrutiny and approval by prison officials.

A former Assistant Director of Prisons is authority for the statement that the long-term prisoners in the Mountain Province proved to be reliable and when trusted on parole outside of the province uniformly returned on the day set.

A so-called "Good Time" law was enacted by the Commission providing under certain rules for an automatic reduction of the terms of sentences by reason of good behavior. The time deductions each prisoner might earn were five days for each month of good behavior during the first two years of imprisonment; eight days per month from the third to include the fifth year of imprisonment; ten days per month during the second five years of imprisonment; and fifteen days for each month of good behavior in execution of sentence after completing the first ten years. This law was applicable to all convicts sentenced to more than thirty days and less than life imprisonment. Detention prisoners who voluntarily offered in writing to perform such labor as might be assigned to them were entitled to similar credits to be deducted from the sentence which might be imposed upon them after conviction.

The Governor-General exercised the power of pardon of persons guilty of violation of laws of the Philippine Islands.

In July, 1902, President Roosevelt issued his proclamation of amnesty to all political offenders. This released from custody a very large number of prisoners who had been held for having participated in or aided the insurrections against Spain and the United States, and gave immunity to many more persons against whom charges were pending.

Pardons in the early days of American administration were granted with great caution. Applications were referred to the judge who had tried the case, to the Constabulary authorities, to the governors of the provinces concerned for comment as to the previous records of the applicants, and also to the warden of the prison in which the delinquent was confined, and recommendations sought as to what, if any, degree of clemency might be considered merited and opportune.

Prisoners were granted "conditional pardon," the conditions being good behavior following release, and a five years' requirement to report periodically, giving their places of residence and occupations. In case of violation of the conditions, they were liable to serve the unexpired portion of the sentence.

Continued good behavior was rewarded by complete pardon with restoration of civil rights on request.

The Commission found it necessary to enact a vagrancy law to provide a convenient method for handling cases of dissolute aliens who were to be found not only in Manila but throughout the provinces, especially in the seaport towns. The statute, however, was general and applied equally to Filipinos and to all who habitually consorted with criminals or with persons engaged in vicious or disreputable pursuits.

The vagrancy law not only proved an effective instrument for eliminating many vicious Americans and foreigners, but enabled local authorities to exercise a beneficial restraining influence on evil-minded Filipinos. Under the terms of the "opium law," foreigners convicted of a second infraction were sentenced to deportation by order of the court. This relieved the Islands of the presence of these undesirables. The Governor-General did not need legislative enactment to give him the power of deporting aliens. The right of excluding undesirable aliens either from entering or from residing within a country is inherent in sovereignty.

In 1906 the Commission enacted a law which provided that the Governor-General in his discretion could suspend the sentence of any person convicted of crime without granting a pardon, and prescribed the terms upon which it should be done. Failure on the part of the convict to comply with the conditions in the parole would result in his return to prison and the execution of his sentence without credit for the period during which he had been at liberty under parole.

Shortly after Governor-General Wood had entered upon the duties of his office in the latter part of 1921, he caused an investigation to be made and statistics compiled to ascertain the results of the pardon practice pursued during the preceding twenty years of American administration of the Islands. A new pardon policy was premised upon the results of this investigation. The Governor-General appointed a Board of Pardons of which two were Filipinos and one American, to take under consideration, without application from any prisoner, the case of each convict who because of period of confinement, good conduct, age, sickness, or other circumstance might deserve consideration for executive clemency.

Upon the recommendation of this board, during the year 1922, 1237 prisoners were pardoned conditionally on subsequent good behavior; nineteen were granted unconditional pardons; one hundred and forty-six were deported to China and eight to the United States; and three were paroled. In all 1413 prisoners were released by executive clemency. This resulted in a saving of more than $120,000 in the annual expense of maintaining prisoners.

In his report General Wood said of conditional pardons: "The system has been in operation for a number of years and has been very successful, and thousands of convicts have been returned to civil life as useful citizens." And in his report for 1924 he said: "There have been very few cases where prisoners granted conditional pardons have again been convicted. The practical efficiency of the method employed in granting pardons is demonstrated by the fact that during the past three years [1922–24] out of a total of 2384 granted pardons, conditional and unconditional, only 19 have again been committed as a result of offenses."

The Iwahig Penal Colony, which relieved the overcrowded condition of Bilibid Prison, was first conceived in the fall of 1904. The plan was to form an agricultural colony to which would be sent convicts selected from the so-called "trusties," or those who, at Bilibid Prison, had become accustomed to an orderly, industrious life, and had demonstrated capacity for good behavior. It was proposed to place these men practically on parole, without guards, on a location capable of extensive and profitable agricultural development.

Various sites were investigated and it was finally decided to place the colony in the neighborhood of Puerto Princesa on the island of Palawan, where is situated a fort in which the United States maintained an army garrison. The vicinity was inhabited only by a few very primitive tribal people known as Tagbanuas. A tract of 22,000 acres, later increased to 116,000, was set aside. The Iwahig River which flows from the mountains on the west through the reservation and empties into the bay is navigable for small launches for a distance of seven miles and served as an avenue of approach for the colony. Both banks of the river and most of the region selected for the colony were covered with rank tropical vegetation.

The idea of the colony was derived from a study of the George Junior Republic, an institution where boys and girls who had lived in crowded districts of large cities, under conditions which gave no opportunity for favorable environment, could be brought and given an opportunity to work at congenial occupations profitable to themselves.

It was believed that convicts not naturally depraved or criminal in their instincts, given a decent opportunity under favorable circumstances, would react in a satisfactory way. The first group of sixty "trusties" was selected and sent down to Iwahig to start the colony on November 16, 1904.

As is usual in tropical countries, the first clearing of the land was accompanied by severe malarial infection of many of the colonists, against which the superintendent in charge at that time had not taken adequate precautions. To meet this situation the Director of Health was given control of health conditions in the colony. "A mosquito brigade" was formed, and by the use of petroleum on breeding places that could not be drained mosquitoes and malaria were brought under control. An adequate hospital was provided and the health of the colonists brought to a satisfactory standard.

Additional colonists were moved down at varying intervals as the Director of Prisons and the superintendent of the colony judged best. It was thought possible that two thousand colonists might be the ultimate goal, but twelve hundred proved to be all the available prisoners that could be readily selected for the purpose and this figure finally became the regular number.

It was some years before the colony could be styled successful, owing to the incapacity of the first two superintendents, who proved to be poor selections. During this period there were one or two outbreaks and several attempts to escape into the hills, but invariably either the savage mountaineers or the colony police brought in the fugitives. The colonists soon learned that it was unwise to overstep the boundaries of their reservation.

At last in 1906 an able superintendent was secured in the person of Colonel John R. White, of the Philippines Constabulary. From the day of his taking hold, the colony was an assured success and astonished even its most ardent advocates. Colonel White vigorously opposed any plan of having a paid guard or of expressing distrust of the colonists in any other way. All needed protection was assured by the simple device of a telephone connection between the colony and the army post at Puerto Princesa.

The colony was made a sort of self-governing republic.

The colonists were started in the lowest grade without any special privilege but, as inducement to good conduct, an opportunity was offered of distinct improvement in their condition along various lines calculated to be attractive to men of different characters, so that within a few months by industry and good conduct they could find themselves moving up the scale. For example, when they first came they were dressed in prison garb. Upon showing enough devotion to their work to be rated as diligent workmen they were allowed to substitute ordinary headgear for the distinctive prison hat, and after a rather brief further period of good behavior they could wear the blue garb of the colony and dispense with the prison stripes. Different colored bands around their arms were worn as badges for various degrees of excellence in their work, and other insignia denoted the nature of the work to which they were assigned.

They were allowed a certain amount of freedom in choosing the kind of work to which they were to devote themselves, whether agriculture, fishing, forestry, carpentry, hospital attendance, clerical, or other work. On advancement to the higher grades a minimum amount of work was required and work in excess of this amount was paid for in the currency of the colony, made of aluminum and redeemable only at the colony coöperative store and bank. There was a better menu provided for those who wanted to pay for it from their savings. Also, the colony store had desirable articles which the colonists could purchase with their earnings. As a man advanced in grade and finally came to have his own house, the proportion of his time required by the government was lessened and the proportion he was entitled to use for his own benefit increased.

The colony president and council enacted colony regulations and enforced them through their appointees — judges, justices of the peace, prosecuting attorney, chief of police, and other officers. All these, however, were under the absolute control of the superintendent of the colony, who could veto any act of the council or of its officers or appointees, could issue any order, and intervene at his discretion in the operation of the colonists' government. The guards, selected from among the colonists, were armed only with bolos, to maintain discipline in the colony.

The convict judges were much more severe disciplinarians than the superintendent would have been. The colony jail was an open building with no walls but with a roof and a number of concentric fences of barbed wire, placed near the entrance to the colony plaza and where persons in confinement were exposed to the public gaze and ridicule. This proved a most effective support of the colony rules. The severest penalty meted to colonists was to return them to Bilibid in Manila, and the prison judges did not hesitate to inflict this penalty where it was felt that the presence of the culprit was injurious to the spirit of the colony.

The records of one year show that with twelve hundred colonists at Iwahig, penalties were meted out in only five hundred instances. As penalties were given for such lesser offenses as being out of bounds, loafing, being late at muster, dirty at inspection, pilfering fruit, etc., it can be seen that the conduct of the colony was in the main exemplary.

An inducement held out to the colonists was the privilege, after several years of continued good conduct, of having their own little farms on the reservation and of having their families come to Iwahig. When the time came for a colonist to be rewarded with this privilege, it was customary for all the colonists to turn to after hours and help him build his house, plow his field, and prepare for the maintenance of his household. The next step upward was a pardon conditional upon remaining at the colony.

In September, 1906, General Aguinaldo made a visit to Iwahig and was greatly impressed with what he saw. He asked if he might address the colonists and his request was cordially assented to. His speech was coöperative and a marvel of conciseness. He recommended the colonists to adhere to the rules and made the impressive statement that, if he had by force of circumstances been himself a colonist, he would have endeavored by good behavior to work himself up to freedom, and then ask nothing better than to have a plot of land given to him there and be allowed to remain on it.

Up to 1913 no colonist who had won his freedom upon recommendation by the superintendent had ever been returned to prison, a record indicating that the colony had been one hundred per cent effective in curing a tendency to lawlessness.

One of the most interesting individual cases was that of a citizen of the town of Balayan, in the province of Batangas, who had been sentenced to death for the murder of a neighbor with whom he had become embroiled over some land dispute. His sentence had been later reduced by the Supreme Court of the Islands to life imprisonment. This convict was sent to Iwahig in the ordinary course and there he made so good an impression that he was appointed chief of police. After earning a pardon, the man returned to his native town of Balayan. Here he volunteered to reorganize the municipal police, explaining to the town president that his men were not under proper discipline. His offer was accepted and this former convict made effective use of training received at the colony to better the public order of his native town.

It is believed that the success of the Iwahig Penal Colony points the way to a possible important advance in some of the fundamental principles of penology.

In an interesting magazine article entitled "A Prison That Makes Men Free," Mr. Lyman Beecher Stowe summed up the work of the colony in the following words:

> . . . The experiment of giving adult Filipinos, guilty of the worst crimes, a chance to develop the best that is in them under conditions approximating those under which they must live when released has proved a complete success. The ordinary prison cuts a man off from all opportunity for self-development just at the time when his only hope lies in such development. The ordinary prison is notoriously a failure. This colony gives full opportunity for self-development and has notably succeeded. The ordinary prison is constantly sending forth men who are dangerous enemies of Society. The men of this colony return to Society useful and friendly citizens. . . . Altogether, therefore, the colony at Iwahig is an important example of the possibilities that lie in giving convicts a chance to be men.

The colony has produced rice and beef for its own requirements, and in later years a surplus for shipment to Bilibid Prison. At the same time extensive plantations of fruit trees have been developed, including more than 145,000 coconut trees, which afford an income reducing the net cost of the insular prisons.

There were certain general principles in regard to treatment of prisoners which impressed themselves very strongly on those who were responsible for the direction of prisons in the Philippine Islands. At the beginning men and women committed to prison should be subjected to strict discipline and studied as invalids, and careful diagnoses made to determine whether or not they are defectives. All prisoners should have an abundance of air and sunshine and a hope of winning better conditions of confinement, if not of pardon, providing their conduct is good and they put forth their best efforts. In other words, the opportunity of bettering their own conditions should always be present for them. This was abundantly proved in the experience of the penal colony at Iwahig.

The insular prison system in the Philippine Islands was conducted in the belief that an opportunity to work in the open air, to care for animals or plants, or to give expression to inherent creative talent has a most important curative and helping influence. It gives to each prisoner an opportunity to develop his better self. The artisan learns to love the article he makes; the musician craves his music; the artist his art; the gardener his flowers; and the husbandman his crops. Without plenty of sun and air, and without proper psychological treatment, criminals become hardened, and when released are a greater menace than before commitment. Properly treated, a large proportion of them can become good citizens.

Civil Service

THE American administrators, acting in their executive capacities, had to meet the problems confronting them, and solve them as best they could, learning how to do much of the work by doing it. Many mistakes were made, and there was much duplication of labor, but little by little a strong, cohesive, effective government grew out of the somewhat chaotic beginnings.

The Commission enacted a civil service law, its purpose being to provide a system which would secure the selection and promotion of civil servants solely on the ground of merit, and would permit any one by a successful competitive examination to enter the service at the lowest rank and, by the efficient discharge of his duties and further examinations, to reach the head of any important department of the government.

They reported:

The difficulties are formidable. There are two classes of applicants, one the Americans and the other the Filipinos. The Filipinos have had no training except from being in the Spanish service or observing its workings. That service was notoriously corrupt.

. . . it is necessary, first, to banish all favoritism and political considerations from the selection of civil servants and rigidly to enforce the requirements of a competitive examination and a satisfactory showing by the applicant of his good moral character; second, to pay adequate salaries and to allow liberal leaves of absence, adapted to preservation of health in the tropics, thus securing that contentment with the service without which good work is not possible; and, third, to awaken an enthusiasm in the service by offering as a reward for faithful and highly efficient work a reasonable prospect of promotion to the highest positions in the Government. . . .

We are directed in our instructions to prefer the Filipino for office when other qualifications are equal, and we have by the act imposed this as a mandate upon the appointing power. We have also preferred in the same manner discharged soldiers and sailors of the United States.

The first problem was to secure a civilian personnel for the insular government to replace army men who elected to stay in the army rather than continue on civil duties, though many secured their discharge to continue in the Philippine service. There were very few Filipinos at that time who had sufficient knowledge of English to do even the simplest clerical work and none who could serve as stenographers or typists. Practically all technical and professional personnel had to be secured from the United States by the Bureau of Insular Affairs. The United States Civil Service Commission conducted examinations and helped otherwise.

Every encouragement was offered Filipinos to enter government service. Provincial and municipal governments as well as the courts were permitted to conduct their business and keep their records in the Spanish language. A consistent effort was made to give Filipinos preferential consideration in employment in the departments and bureaus. Examinations in the Islands for appointment to the classified service were conducted in both the English and Spanish languages. Large numbers of Filipinos took advantage of night schools and other opportunities provided for training in English, bookkeeping, stenography, telegraphy, and other subjects qualifying them for appointment or promotion in the service. Nor was there any aloofness on the part of the Filipino.

Considerations of economy as well as political reasons caused the government to proceed as rapidly as possible with the Filipinization of its personnel. From a total of 3307 in 1905 the number of Americans in the classified service was reduced to 2623 in 1913, 582 in 1920, and 506 in 1925.

The number of Americans brought from the United States to the Philippine service decreased from 338 in 1904 to 156 in 1913, 98 in 1920, and 48 in 1925. All but one appointee in 1925 were teachers.

LABOR

THE labor situation in the Philippine Islands is one about which very wide divergence of opinion exists among people supposed to be competent to judge. Sugar planters and other employers of labor complained of the shortage, and yet the Islands abounded with potential labor to the number of many millions, men and women. In some of the provinces the density of the population exceeded four hundred and fifty to the square mile.

Many did not hesitate to urge the admission of Chinese labor as a solution of the labor problem, and it was a common expression of those who employed labor, that "the Filipino laborer would not work." There were two principal reasons why the Filipino was not highly regarded as a laborer: the first was poor physical condition owing to his unhygienic manner of living, and the second was lack of incentive due to unfair treatment.

Numerous tests proved that the average Filipino was afflicted with one or more intestinal parasites that appreciably sapped his vitality. Potable water from artesian wells or carefully protected municipal systems was prerequisite to a condition of general health among the people. It was noted that the Chinese laborer was generally free from these parasites largely because his beverage is usually tea, to make which he boils the water.

As noted elsewhere, the long-term prisoners who served their term in Bilibid and were compelled to live and work under hygienic conditions in the prison, came out of it with a far better physique than most of their compatriots who lived according to their own light. Constabulary and Scout enlisted men showed similar evidences of development and indicated the lines along which improvement in the labor situation might be made.

Large employers of labor, especially of seasonal labor, had in too many instances failed to learn how to treat their employees in such a way as to inspire their confidence or their industry. This did not apply to employees who gave personal service in the houses or assisted landowners in small haciendas.

To some of the employers of labor who complained that the Filipino would not work, it was suggested that they add "unless paid." The various devices to which employers resorted to obtain work without properly paying for it were legion.

The prejudice against the Filipino as a laborer was not due to any essential disinclination on his part to work, but to known conditions which lay within the province of the government to remedy.

That the Filipino will work and work well if properly treated and properly paid has been abundantly demonstrated. This was proved over and over again at factories in Manila and elsewhere, and by many of the two million or more small landowners who diligently worked their fields and wrested a livelihood from the elements.

The Army quartermaster in charge of the transport service at Manila reported:

Chinese labor was formerly employed for the handling of coal, but has been abandoned and replaced by Filipino labor, which, by practical tests during several months, averaged more tons per day per man and at a much lower rate per ton.

The attendance of the Filipino laborer has been and is excellent. Their physical strength is much improved, and they are capable of doing as much and as hard work as any laborer we have in the Orient.

The manager of the Manila street railway gave further testimony:

The whole question can be answered in a few words. Filipino labor is entirely satisfactory if properly treated.

. . . .

. . . The labor is here in abundance and for quality and volume of work is equal, if not superior, to any in the Orient.

Perhaps the most emphatic proof of the capacity of the Filipino laborer was given in the course of a movement, which began in 1906, of Filipino laborers to the Hawaiian Islands, where the planters had become greatly disturbed about their labor situation which had grown far in excess of the laboring capacity of their natives. Japanese could come in, but it was a serious question as to how wise it was to bring in too many Japanese.

Unsuccessful efforts had been made by employers in Hawaii to bring in other kinds of labor. Finally, a representative was sent by the Hawaiian Sugar Planters' Association to the Philippine Islands to secure Filipinos. He entered into an agreement with the Philippine government and many hundreds of families moved to Hawaii. Those who returned gave such glowing accounts of the conditions under which they labored there that many more were sent, until by January, 1926, there were 26,283 Filipinos among a total of 49,155 laborers employed on plantations in the Hawaiian Islands, the Filipinos being seventy per cent of the field force.

One interesting and highly satisfactory aspect of this movement was that the sugar planters in Hawaii have given the Filipinos a high standing as laborers. They said that they were equal to the best they had been able to secure from any other country, and this was very high praise, as there were then about eighty thousand Japanese in the Hawaiian Islands, and the Japanese excel as laborers.

The first Philippine Legislature passed a law creating a Bureau of Labor, an action in line with modern enlightened legislative practice. The first Director of Labor, appointed in June, 1909, was General Manuel Tinio, an able young Filipino, who at the age of eighteen had held the rank of major-general in General Aguinaldo's army in the revolution against Spain, and in the insurrection against the United States, had held the same rank and commanded a corps which he had recruited.

This capable officer took over the direction of the Bureau of Labor at a time when labor unions had been newly formed. The leaders were not in every instance men of desirable reputation and many business and manufacturing concerns were placed under tribute, strikes being threatened if the exactions were not forthcoming. Every week or two a strike would be called to show what was likely to happen to those who did not accede to these demands, and the situation was rapidly becoming intolerable.

General Tinio set himself to rectify this abuse with the result that in a very short time the condition of labor and industry, in the region about Manila at least, was vastly improved.

In general it may be said that, as a result of General Tinio's management of the bureau, strikes ceased, laborers went their way contented, employers readily corrected abuses brought to their attention, and the leaders fell back into their proper rôle of caring for and representing the laborer instead of exploiting him wholly to his disadvantage and to the benefit of their own pockets.

That the Filipino laborer has not grasped the fundamental idea of the partnership between capital and labor is proved by one of the articles in the declaration of principles of a labor union, which the Bureau of Labor in 1927 characterized as "made up probably by the most intelligent of Filipino workmen, whose principles are typical of present day labor unions." The article reads as follows:

That, in case of an accident or misfortune, none of us has to help other than those who, like us, are slaves to capital, co-workers in shops, who have similar conditions of living as ours, and cherish the same ideals.

On the other hand, other unions set forth among their objects the maintenance of good relations between employers and employees, the promotion of the brotherhood of laborers whether members or not, and the improvement of their moral and intellectual conditions.

The Bureau of Labor extended its activities beyond those of conciliation between employers and employees and the compilation of statistics, to the inspection of factories, plantations, and other places of employment of laborers, especially those employing women and children, adjustment of compensation in industrial accidents, the maintenance of employment agencies, and intervention in the contracting of seamen and of laborers emigrating to Hawaii and foreign countries. The direction of homeseekers from the densely populated regions of Luzon and Cebu to locations on public lands in Mindanao was also added to its activities.

The impressive success of many of the homesteaders came to the attention of relatives and neighbors at their former homes with the result that applicants for transportation on government account exceeded the funds available, and many families went at their own expense to join those who had already migrated.

From the experience of the government in this movement, the fact emerged that the ordinary Filipino family does not cultivate more than ten acres of land, with the result that the homestead area of forty acres is usually excessive. The homesteaders were encouraged to bring onto their excess holdings other families of kinsfolk who later in turn could locate on homesteads surveyed from neighboring public lands if they became ambitious for independent holdings.

From these beginnings an inter-island migration has gradually developed of substantial volume, for which statistics are not available as it is in greatest part the movement of homeseekers at their own expense.

In setting forth the two reasons why the Filipino was reputed to be unwilling to work, mention has been made of the unfair treatment to which he had been subjected. The Filipino employer of labor often maneuvered his employee into a position bordering on peonage. He would lend him a small sum of money, or perhaps provide him with articles needed for wear or use, or desired for ornamentation. The "interest" charged on these loans was at the rate of ten and even as high as twenty per cent a month, and the unfortunate laborer would give many months of his work hoping to pay off a loan and at the end of the time find that the amount he owed to his employer was greater than it had been at the beginning. In other words, work as hard as he could, he was unable to work off the interest, to say nothing of being able to repay the principal. Once a laborer got into the toils of these unscrupulous persons his freedom was gone. He became little better than a slave.

It was no wonder laborers hesitated to put themselves into the hands of money-lending employers.

The Wood-Forbes Mission in 1921 reported the situation as follows: "A frequent cause of complaint is against extreme action taken under the provisions of act 2098," the operation of which it speaks of as resulting in a kind of legalized peonage. "During the fiscal year 1918 there were a total of 3266 cases of this nature, of which 1456 were convicted."

For some reason the Commission had never enacted a law providing a penalty for dealing in slaves. Although slavery was prohibited in the Philippine Islands under the terms of the organic act which rendered it impossible for "owners" of slaves to enforce their ownership if the slave chose to run away, there was no law providing a punishment for purchasing or selling a slave, or holding, or keeping him in captivity.

This defect in the law was developed by a decision of the Philippine Supreme Court of March 16, 1907. The Commission endeavored to correct this oversight by appropriate legislation, but the manner in which the matter was presented aroused the antagonism of the Assembly, for several sessions they declined to concur in the passage of the bill.

The Commission, however, acting in its exclusive legislative capacity for the tribal peoples, passed a slavery law in 1911 which "rendered immediately possible the release of a considerable number of Ifugaos held in slavery by Filipinos in Nueva Vizcaya."

The matter did not pass wholly unnoticed in Washington, for the United States Senate on May 1, 1913, passed the following resolution:

That the Secretary of War be, and he is hereby, directed to send to the Senate any and all facts bearing directly or indirectly upon the truth of the charge publicly made that human slavery exists at this time in the Philippine Islands and that human beings are bought and sold in such islands as chattels.

The Honorable Dean C. Worcester, Secretary of the Interior of the Philippine government, was stirred to activity in this matter and he prepared, printed, and sent out a pamphlet which he described as "arranging in logical sequence a small part of the written and signed testimony of Filipinos and Americans, declaring that slavery and peonage exist in the Philippines.

The basis upon which the Philippine Assembly declined to pass the law was on the untenable ground that slavery did not exist and therefore such a law was unnecessary.

They were perfectly right in representing that slavery did not exist as an institution. It was not recognized by law. There were no slave markets; no slaves working in the fields under the lash of an overseer's whip; nor was the mild form of unrequited service that existed accompanied with any of the horrors which are normally associated with a country in which forced labor exists as a recognized institution.

The problem was more complicated in connection with the Moros, who, as Mohammedans, looked upon slavery as an institution. There the whole system under which the sultans, datus, and headmen generally lived lent itself to a much greater control, even to the extent of life and death, exercised by the chiefs over the persons and liberties of their subordinates.

Governor-General Harrison secured action in November, 1913 and reported, "one of the first acts of the new Legislature was to pass, by unanimous vote, a drastic antislavery law, applying to the islands, as supplementary to existing law, the provisions of the United States statute against slavery and peonage."

BUREAU OF PRINTING

THE arts of printing and bookbinding had been introduced by the Spaniards in Manila before the end of the sixteenth century, and in 1898 there were various establishments which had been developed to meet both the commercial and government requirements. The methods employed were antiquated and the product poor. There were no facilities for quantity production; no modern typesetting machines; no means for the duplication and preservation of valuable forms of type; and no provision for the training of artisans in printing and its allied trades.

Moreover it was at the beginning impossible to secure Filipinos qualified as craftsmen in any of the printing trades. Typesetting machines, automatic presses, electrotyping, half-tone engraving, and the utilization of other than human energy in driving their machinery were industrial innovations.

The government was therefore compelled to secure an American contract printer, who installed the necessary equipment with American

COCONUT PALM AND MORO PROA

A TYPICAL GROUP OF MOROS

operatives.[1] As this expedient did not meet the requirements of a permanent service, the Commission organized a Bureau of Printing.

Specifications were drawn for all the equipment, materials, and supplies for a modern printing plant in Manila. The plant was purchased under competitive bidding.

A Bureau of Printing was created by act of the Commission. Its duty was to do all the work required by the government, and it also made these facilities available to the general public for services such as electrotyping, stereotyping, and photo-engraving, which no commercial establishment in the Islands then could perform. An efficient technical staff was secured in the United States to instruct Filipinos in all the specialties of printing and the allied trades. These trades were included in vocational training courses, and the Director proceeded "to instruct Filipinos in all the specialties of printing and its allied trades." True to the traditions of his profession that printing is a fundamental factor in the intelligent progress of a people, he trained Filipinos in all, even the most difficult, specialties of the art of printing, and advanced the more proficient craftsmen through the intermediate into the higher positions then held by Americans.

In effect the bureau became a thoroughly practical trade school in which the highest standards of workmanship were maintained. Apprentices were secured from the various provinces, one qualification being a high standard in school work to insure proficiency in English and other studies. The artistic inclinations of these young Filipinos and their natural aptitude for learning were quickened, their physical well-being assured by systematic athletic sports, and industry and thrift encouraged by a bonus plan and savings deposits. They responded with earnest enthusiasm, and, with their deftness, nervelessness, and patient industry, came in the course of time to approach the excellence of their instructors in most of the branches of the printer's art.

Through the craftsmen-graduates of the Bureau of Printing the commercial printing establishments in Manila and other cities in the Philippine Islands were able to introduce the use of typesetting machines and modern presses as well as photo-engraving and other advanced printing specialties.

The relation between the Director and his force, both American and Filipino, was one of friendliness and mutual sympathy. Within a dec-

[1] John S. Leech was the highly efficient organizer of the service.

ade a practically all-American force became ninety-four per cent Filipino, and at the time of the Director's resignation, October 21, 1913, all mechanical operations were being performed by Filipino workmen, one division was conducted by a Filipino graduate apprentice, all acting assistant chiefs of division were apprentice graduates, and Filipino craftsmen were being trained in positions requiring administrative and executive ability.

Bureau of Navigation

The Bureau of Navigation came into existence under the title of Bureau of Coast Guard and Transportation, primarily to assist in the maintenance of order, transportation of the Constabulary, and prevention of smuggling. It was also charged with the construction and operation of lighthouses. Prior to the war with Spain there had been fifty-five lighthouses in operation, but when the Americans reached the Islands Spain had, as a war measure, ordered these lights extinguished. When the American civil authorities took over the administration, they found not more than twenty-seven in operation. Under the direction of the American chief of the bureau, before many years the Philippine coast line was studded with lights, great and small, reaching in 1913 as many as 146. And in 1926 there were 193 lights, 146 buoys, and 77 beacons, a total of 416 aids to navigation, maintained by the government.

One extraordinary occurrence in connection with the lighthouse service deserves mention. The island of Balabac forms the southwestern extremity of the archipelago upon which the Spaniards had built a first-order lighthouse which was a most important aid to navigation for ships passing between the Philippine Islands and Borneo. It lay on one of the main trade routes of the Orient. The order of the Spanish government in April, 1898, to extinguish the lights failed to reach the light keeper at Cape Melville, and for a period of two years no attention was paid to the lighthouse by the government. The light keeper went two years without pay, and in the course of time his supplies — including his oil for the light — gave out. Yet he stuck heroically to his post, supplied himself as best he could from the natural resources at hand, and rowed out to passing ships and borrowed oil from them in order to keep his light lit. He may fairly be said to have carried the torch. Needless to say his sacrifices were recognized when the Bureau of Navigation was organized and he received his pay and allowances for the full time for services rendered, and later promotion.

For the government of this group of more than one thousand inhabited islands, it was obvious that marine transportation would be a primary necessity, and the government ordered a standard fleet of fifteen steamers built in China and Japan for the coast guard service. Three of these new ships were given the duty of inspecting, supplying, and maintaining lighthouses; four were transferred to the Coast and Geodetic Survey; one was equipped for special inspection trips of government officials; one was detailed to the Moro Province for the use of that government; one was used for picking up lepers and transporting them to the colony at Culion; while two or three were held in Manila for general service; some of them were laid up and at one time such of the remainder as were kept in commission were put on commercial routes to develop trade.

The high prices charged by private owners of marine railways practically forced the government to construct its own marine railway and repair shops. The site selected was a tract of filled-in land near the mouth of the Pasig River, known as Engineer Island. Here the fleet of government vessels were outfitted, repaired, and supplied.

A committee was appointed by Governor-General Wright to investigate and report upon arrangements that might be made to improve the passenger and freight services by commercial steamships in the inter-island trade. As a result the Commission authorized advertisement for bids from commercial steamship owners to take over the government passenger and freight services. Successful bidders were to be required immediately to bring their vessels up to modern standards of safety, sanitation, and comfort, to carry the mails, and to operate their ships on definite schedules. The law provided that vessels operated by the Philippine government should charge for services rendered, and that such charges should be as nearly as practicable the rates charged for the same services by vessels under contract with the government. There were other provisions calculated to assure as far as possible good and regular steamship service at reasonable rates to every port in the archipelago. Government vessels were to be taken off routes and commercial steamers substituted as rapidly as business justified a commercial line undertaking the service under contract. The Secretary of Commerce and Police advertised for bids on twenty-one proposed routes.

Contracts were awarded for a five-year period to commercial steamers for service on eleven routes; the total annual cost of government in the form of subsidies under these contracts, which included the free carriage of the mails, was somewhat less than $110,000. The immediate financial result to the government was the discontinuance of service of five vessels, representing an economy of $125,000 per annum. The contract rates for passenger and freight services gave an average reduction of about twenty per cent below that previously charged for like services. The coastwise merchant marine service was greatly improved, and, with dependable schedules for shipment of products and receipt of supplies, agriculture and commerce received a substantial stimulus.

Ships operating under subsidy contracts were required to have accessible to passengers a book in which complaints might be recorded. One extract, culled from the "Complaint Book" on board the steamship *Union* of the Tabacalera Company, read:

The undersigned consider it their duty to record their indignation at being unable to find anything to growl about during two days' voyage on this boat.

The shipping concerns were reluctant to enter into these contracts under the terms of which they necessarily relinquished much of their independence of action. Yet in practice they found to their surprise that adherence to the rules laid down by the government greatly enhanced their profits.

In 1905, Governor-General Wright named a committee to investigate "the whole subject of port dues and harbor management in the Philippine Islands, and to make recommendations looking to the removal of all unnecessary restrictions upon commerce entering and leaving the ports."

This committee, after months of frequent sessions, brought about the passage of a number of laws, one of which made commerce free within the Islands, discontinuing all customs inspectors and inspections at coastwise ports, and another abolished tonnage dues for foreign ships entering Philippine ports. The removal of these restrictions with their incidental expense was very well received by the merchants.

In October, 1905, the committee made a preliminary report in which it made a number of recommendations, including an interesting suggestion for the establishment of a free zone or free district in the port of Manila — which was never carried out.

BUREAU OF COAST AND GEODETIC SURVEY

No FULL and accurate survey of the harbors and waters of the Philippine Archipelago had been made before American occupation. The lack of reliable charts was so serious a handicap to the merchant marine, as well as to the navy and army transport service, that arrangements were made by the military government under which the United States Coast and Geodetic Survey in 1900 entered upon systematic coast surveys and the publication of charts and other aids to navigators.

These surveys had a military value and were made faster than if the civil government had undertaken the work for purely commercial service; the cost, therefore, was divided between the United States and the Philippine government. The technical direction and personnel and one survey vessel were provided by the United States, and one survey vessel, and later additional vessels, by the Philippine government.

On June 30, 1913, sixty-three per cent of the total length of shore line had been surveyed and the work was proceeding on a basis of somewhat more than five per cent annually. By the end of 1925 the major portion of the waters and islands of the archipelago had been surveyed.

BUREAU OF POSTS

THE Americans found a postal service almost medieval in character. The governors of provinces and the presidents of municipalities were charged with the duty of forwarding postal matter by land, while inter-island ships were required to carry it without charge. Post offices were not available very generally throughout the Islands and seem to have been limited to the more important commercial ports. There was no general organization or equipment outside of Manila which cared for the dispatch of postal transactions with foreign countries.

The American army and navy have well-established methods of handling postal matter in their own services, and in 1898 these were elaborated to meet the needs of the army of occupation. The postal service was carried on by the military authorities until May 1, 1899, as a branch of the post office at San Francisco. At that time the Philippine postal service was organized as a separate institution under American administration and under the general supervision of the United States Post Office Department as regarded postal relations with foreign countries.

The Bureau of Posts in the Philippine Islands was modeled on the United States postal service, and manned by experts especially detailed from that service who became officers of the Philippine government and responsible to the Governor-General and through the Governor-General to the War Department, in the United States.

With the extension of American occupation of Philippine territory it became necessary to develop the organization to meet constantly increasing demands. As more territory was occupied the postal organization was extended. During the period of active military operation the United States army and navy officers and enlisted men attended to transportation of mails and acted as postmasters except at Manila. An indication of the rapid development of the demands upon the postal service is to be found in the fact that during the year July 1, 1899, to June 30, 1900, a total money order business of more than one and one-half million dollars was reported.

United States postage stamps were used for a time on postal matter dispatched in the Philippine Islands. Later these stamps were surcharged with the word "Philippines"; and still later, in 1906, stamps of special designs were prepared at the United States Bureau of Engraving and Printing, bearing the portraits of men of Spanish, American, and Philippine nationality who had influenced Philippine history.

From the two post offices, Manila and Cavite, in August, 1898, the services were extended until, on June 30, 1913, there were 590 offices, and in 1925, 936.

The first telegraph line in the Philippine Islands was installed by the Spaniards in 1872 and extensions were made until there were three trunk lines and several branches on the island of Luzon. On some of the other islands telegraph facilities also existed. During the insurrection practically the entire system disappeared.

The early rehabilitation of the old telegraph and telephone services and the fairly comprehensive construction of a new service were regarded by the army as a military necessity, and during the period of the insurrection the whole service was in the hands of the officers of the signal corps under the direction of the commanding general.

During the period of gradual transfer to the Constabulary the telegraph, cable, and telephone lines were reconstructed on a more permanent basis, locations changed, and some new ones constructed.

On January 1, 1906, the telephone and telegraph service was transferred from the Constabulary to the Bureau of Posts. This proved to be a saving to the service, as it placed all communications under one bureau and made possible a helpful consolidation of offices. The military authorities finally transferred the remaining telegraph and telephone lines in October, 1907.

Upon the completion of this transfer, the army, which had maintained a cable ship for the purpose of repairing the marine telegraph lines, withdrew its ship and it became necessary for the civil government to undertake this service, as there was no ship maintained by any commercial cable company near enough to be ready in case of emergency. In 1908 the Bureau of Navigation purchased a three-thousand-ton ship in Singapore, which was named the *Rizal* and equipped for cable service.

In 1898 the telephone business in Manila was conducted by a private company, limited to the city, and had an antiquated installation. In 1905 a group of San Francisco people undertook the construction of a modern telephone system in Manila. They secured control of the existing company, obtained a franchise from the insular government, and put in an up-to-date system in the city of Manila, leaving the telegraph and telephone service throughout the balance of the archipelago in the hands of the government.

In lieu of trying to construct a highly centralized plant and service, it had been the policy of the government to operate the telephone lines outside Manila in conjunction with telegraphs by the army and Constabulary. When the Bureau of Posts took over these services in 1906, it pursued the policy of developing local government interest in telephone service, with the result that provincial governments generally took over inter-municipal telephone lines and the cities and larger towns installed local service or granted concessions to private enterprises. The army and navy maintained their own telephone service within their reservations.

Wireless telegraphy was first utilized by the army at stations in southern Mindanao and Jolo, where the submarine cables gave much trouble because of the sharp coral sea-bottom and strong currents. In 1908 the Bureau of Posts began wireless service with the station at Malabang, Mindanao, and the following year the army stations at Jolo and Zamboanga were transferred to the Bureau of Posts, which has further developed this service as circumstances required and funds were available. By 1913 seven stations were in operation and by 1927 there were thirty-eight in operation and three additional under construction. The navy constructed and maintained a powerful wireless station at Cavite near their local reservation.

Where there was no telegraph office the municipal treasurer was usually postmaster, and wherever there were telegraph offices, except at the larger ones, the chief operator usually acted as postmaster. The operation of the Bureau of Posts was exemplary from the standpoint of economy.

The personnel was largely Filipino. The bureau, upon receiving the transfer of telegraphs and telephones from the Constabulary and army, continued the school of telegraphy for the training of Filipino operators. During the year 1913, one hundred and fifty-seven Filipino students were admitted to the telegraph school, and ninety-one completed the course satisfactorily and were assigned to stations as junior operators.

Some idea of the magnitude of this service can be drawn from a few figures taken at random from the year 1913. At this time, June 30, 1913, there were a total of 2530 officers and employees in the Bureau of Posts, of whom 2343 were Filipinos. The American personnel was in large part the higher administrative personnel and radio and chief telegraph operators. The total number of post offices in operation on that date was 590, of which 440 were provided with free delivery letter carrier service. In the city of Manila alone, almost five million pieces of mail were handled in the course of that year, an increase of twenty-six per cent over the preceding year. In addition to the railway mail service, there were three hundred and twenty post routes, over which mails were carried variously by launch, automobile, wagon, horseback, and on foot. Two hundred and seventy-five post offices were equipped to transact money order business, nearly fourteen million dollars being handled annually. Domestic telegraphic transfers amounted to more than one million dollars.

During the fiscal year 1913 a total of 687,307 telegrams was handled by the Bureau of Posts, all within the Islands. The total mileage of land and submarine telegraph lines under civil control was nearly 5800. The number of telegraph offices in operation on the same date was two hundred and ninety.

In the fiscal year 1913 the expenditures of the Bureau of Posts, exclusive of the Postal Savings Bank, were nearly a million dollars, and the revenues $710,000, the deficit being covered by appropriations from general funds of the insular treasury.

An analysis of the receipts and expenditures of the bureau is most instructive and highly creditable, showing a surplus over the costs of operation every year since 1916, the surplus in 1926 amounting to over half a million dollars.

AGRICULTURE

ACCORDING to the census of 1918, seventy-two per cent of the men in the Philippine Islands were engaged in agriculture. The Philippine Islands are and always have been a distinctly agricultural community. The work of the Bureau of Agriculture was of prime importance, therefore, and could have been of incalculable benefit to the people. It was some years, however, before the right man was secured to direct the affairs of the bureau, and the early record of mistakes is a grievous one.

One of the greatest menaces to prosperity in the Islands was the prevalence of the animal disease known as rinderpest, which decimated the cattle of the Islands, made it necessary for the Filipinos to resort to new importations, and seriously threatened agriculture with shortage of draft animals needed not only to plow the fields but to carry farm produce to the points of shipment. The census of 1903 reported the total number of carabao and cattle as 768,430, and of horses as 144,171.

Many costly and some disastrous experiments were made by the government in its efforts to eradicate the disease. Yet it persisted. Two great difficulties lay in the way of combating it. The first was that the active period of giving the infection came in the early stages before the disease had manifested itself. The second was that rinderpest was carried by certain wild animals and thus a region might apparently be free from the disease and yet have reinfection by deer or wild carabao. Moreover, animal quarantine was an unqualified nuisance and most unpopular with the Filipinos.

When in 1911 Major-General J. Franklin Bell became Commanding-General of the Philippines Division, it was suggested to him that he do in the north what General Pershing had already done in the south, that is, use his troops to enforce animal quarantine. General Bell not only ordered to the service the requested number of Scouts with immediately beneficial results, but after personal investigation he multiplied by four the number of men so engaged.

Island after island, province after province, were quickly cleared of the dread scourge, and planters began to breathe easily as they saw their animals saved and the guards withdrawn. In 1913, the rinderpest had disappeared from the archipelago with the exception of one small district on the island of Luzon, consisting of eleven municipalities, divided among three provinces, but all adjacent to each other in one restricted area. More than eight hundred municipalities and all islands other than Luzon were clear.

This was the condition when the administration was changed in 1913. The new and inexperienced administrators saw fit to withdraw the quarantine guards and turn the rinderpest campaign over to provincial control with disastrous results. The direct value of these animals was about fifty dollars a head, and their incidental value as an aid to agriculture was many times that, so it is easy to understand the seriousness of the loss to the Islands involved by the destruction of their draft animals.

During the régime of Governor-General Wood the Legislature passed an act which authorized the Director of Agriculture to require that cattle be immunized; provided an appropriation of fifty thousand dollars; made obligatory coöperation by provincial governors and municipal presidents with the Director of Agriculture; and provided penalties of both imprisonment and fine.

As all commercial importations of beef and work animals from the continent of Asia were liable to bring in rinderpest or other dangerous disease, import quarantine stations were provided and great precautions taken at the ports of Manila and Iloilo, to which importation of cattle was limited.

Other dangerous communicable diseases, especially anthrax and foot-and-mouth disease, have been problems for the government and cattle owners. Until effective vaccines practicable for field use are perfected, quarantine will continue to be the main recourse to check the spread of these diseases.

The government encouraged the importation of the zebu of India, which has a high resistance to rinderpest and foot-and-mouth disease. This resistance was found to be transmitted to its progeny upon cross-breeding with Philippine cattle. The zebu was found to thrive in the Islands, and, since its introduction in 1909, there have been repeated importations.

Besides fighting animal disease, the government endeavored to promote agriculture by establishing experiment and demonstration stations at various points. Improved varieties of sugar cane, rice, corn, fruits, and vegetables were introduced from other countries. The breeding of better domestic animals was encouraged by the importation of pure-bred Arab and other selected stallions, Galloway and Hereford bulls, and several types of goats, poultry, and swine. The selection of superior native animals for breeding was also the subject of widespread instruction and demonstration. The improvement in horses, poultry, and swine is noteworthy.

For some years the government demonstrated the advantageous use of modern agricultural machinery. Commercial firms followed the lead of the government and obtained favorable results, especially with rice threshers, which in some districts, notably the province of Nueva Ecija, have practically replaced the ancient threshing floor. Also there has been great advance in the use of modern rice and sugar mills, motor tractors, and other machinery to render labor more effective.

Attention also was paid to seed selection, use of fertilizers, field methods, and the preparation of agricultural products for market, resulting in greater yields and improvement in quality of rice, corn, sugar, and vegetables.

Originally in the Department of the Interior, the Bureau of Agriculture was transferred in 1910 to the Department of Public Instruction for more close coördination with the public schools in the dissemination of information as to good agricultural practice, especially by the establishment of school and home gardens, school clubs for raising better poultry and swine, seed selection for field crops, and, through the domestic science classes, in popularizing the use of greater variety and better cooking of locally grown food products.

The problem of protecting field crops from destruction by locusts was a difficult one. The large areas of uncultivated uplands, especially in the sparsely inhabited foothills of the mountain ranges, were breeding places from which in the dry season great swarms of locusts might appear and devastate the rice and sugar cane fields, wholly destroying the crops and causing serious food shortage as well as financial losses.

It was found that the insects could be destroyed if attacked when they first emerged from the ground or soon after, while still in the "hopper" stage of development. In 1909 a plan was adopted which has since been pursued with good results wherever actively applied, the important features of which are to ascertain the places where the locust eggs have been deposited, place a watch to report immediately the first indication of hatching, and then require the services of all able-bodied persons from the nearest settlement to destroy the hoppers by fire or other efficacious methods. Provincial governors were placed in charge of local organizations to formulate and enforce regulations carrying the plan into effect.

In 1924 the Legislature made a continuing annual appropriation of fifty thousand dollars for use exclusively in combating locusts. In the same year the Legislature passed an act enabling the provincial boards to levy a tax of from ten to thirty cents on all grown men up to sixty years of age to assist in locust extermination.

FORESTRY

THE virgin forests covering much of the Philippine Islands are one of the most important of their natural resources. Something over forty-one million acres are commercial forests, heavily timbered, and their conservation early commanded the attention of American administrators. Some of the Filipinos, particularly the more nomadic peoples, had the primitive practice of making what was locally known as *caiñgin*; that is, they cleared a little area of forest land by cutting down the trees and burning them, planted a crop or two, and when weeds and wild grasses began to appear, they abandoned the clearing, moved on, and did the same thing somewhere else. This was prohibited by law.

A competent Director of Forestry was secured, and efforts made to introduce modern methods of conservation so that the trees ready for cutting could be taken out without depleting the forests. Also, careful rules were adopted for communal forests. The cutting of timber and firewood and the taking of rattans, resins, and other commercial products have been controlled by strict regulations. A schedule of charges was fixed and the collections were more than enough to defray all the expenses of the bureau.

No effort has been spared by the government to prevent waste in the exploitation of the public forests. The bureau has distributed seeds and rendered other forms of assistance to private landowners, and has encouraged reforestation of denuded areas. It has set out camphor, Para rubber, cinchona, and other trees of commercial importance as well as the best native woods, and has maintained forest reserves and botanical gardens.

The Bureau of Forestry also protects the sources of rivers which are of value for irrigation.

The use of modern machinery in the Philippine lumber industry was slow to develop. Gradually American, European, Chinese, and latterly Filipino capital entered the field until in 1925 there were forty-one mills in operation, the majority, however, of small capacity.

The production of lumber has increased from about 36,600,000 board feet in 1903 to 369,000,000 in 1925. Exports have increased from nil in 1903 to more than 52,200,000 board feet, having a value of more than $2,100,000, in 1925. During the same period the imports of lumber decreased from more than 7,600,000 board feet in 1903 to 4,300,000 in 1925.

A School of Forestry was established in 1910 and became a part of the University of the Philippines in 1916. Graduates of this school in an increasing degree have provided the technical personnel of the bureau, some of these Filipinos taking advanced studies in the United States. Borneo, China, and other countries in Asia have drawn on the American and Filipino personnel of the bureau for expert foresters, and natives of those countries have taken courses of study in the Philippine School of Forestry.

The bureau disseminates in the United States and in foreign countries correct information regarding the valuable Philippine woods, and cooperates with private enterprise engaged in the production of lumber for export. It also maintains helpful testing laboratories.

WEATHER BUREAU

THE story of the Weather Bureau is one of the most remarkable in Philippine annals, and like most great stories it centers about one extraordinary man. Father José Algué, a Jesuit priest, was so devoted to science that he made himself one of the foremost world experts in meteorology and seismology. With no lessening of his religious fervor, he had the mind of a pure scientist. He gave to the movement of typhoons in the vicinity of the Philippine Islands intensive observation and lifelong study, and the accuracy of his deductions was marvelous. It was told of him that in the early days he had gone to the Spanish government and asked for a modest appropriation to cover the cost of establishing a series of observation stations where readings of the barometer and other weather indications could be taken, to assist him in figuring the direction and speed with which areas of depression were moving, with the idea of giving notice to shipping and to the people generally of the approach of typhoons. His request went unheeded. Typhoons were an act of God, and it was almost impious to undertake to foretell what lay in the mind of the Deity. A little later, Father Algué announced the imminent approach of a destructive typhoon moving directly toward Manila, and urged that the police be sent out to give the people house to house warning to put away valuables, get out ropes to tie their roofs down, that all ships be notified to stay in harbor, steamers to get up steam, sailing vessels to lower their top hamper and get out extra anchors. Again his words fell on unheeding ears. Just as foretold, the destructive typhoon struck Manila and caused frightful loss running into millions of dollars. This object lesson opened the eyes of the Spanish authorities. The modest appropriation requested by Father Algué was granted him; the next typhoon advancing upon Manila found everybody prepared, and the loss was comparatively trivial.

The American officials were fortunate in being able to retain this superman and he remained at the head of the Weather Bureau. In March, 1899, two other Spanish scientists of the Jesuit order were appointed assistants. The remainder of the personnel was Filipino.

The accuracy with which Father Algué foretold weather conditions was so well known among shipping men that a ship seldom put to sea in the typhoon season without first ascertaining from Father Algué whether or not the way was clear and what might be expected during the course of the voyage. Ships proposing to carry cattle requested of Father Algué information as to whether or not the sea was to be too rough for transporting livestock.

Father Algué's scientific study of typhoons resulted in his invention of the barocyclonometer, an instrument that not only indicates the approach of a typhoon but also the course its vortex is taking. This instrument enables navigators to lay their courses so as to avoid danger.

Father Algué gave to the matter of earthquakes the same thorough analysis that he gave to typhoons. His instruments in the Weather Bureau were marvels of scientific accuracy.

The buildings and most of the scientific equipment of the Weather Bureau are the property of the Jesuits, the government paying a moderate rental.

In 1901 the Commission provided for seventy-two weather stations and these were increased as funds became available. These stations were equipped with the necessary apparatus for meteorological observations and at the principal ones trained observers were provided. By 1927 the records of rainfall and also of prevailing winds covered a period of about twenty-five years, and they are of great value to persons seeking advantageous agricultural locations. In the cases of the city of Manila and the few other points at which observations were recorded under

Spanish administration, rainfall and other meteorological data are available since 1865. Magnetic observatories are maintained at Manila and other selected points. The astronomical division at the central observatory communicates daily the correct time to all points connected by telegraph with Manila.

The Weather Bureau has published authoritative information as to Philippine climate and earthquakes, that on earthquakes and typhoons by Father Algué and his associates being especially noteworthy.

BUREAU OF SUPPLY

THE question of government purchasing was one of great delicacy and difficulty. The local merchants wanted the government bureaus to be compelled to buy from them, but the merchants had neither the capital to carry in stock the volume of material required by the government, nor the practice of making their prices reasonable. It took from four to six months to secure fulfillment of orders from the United States, and too often the articles when they arrived did not meet specifications and were useless. If they were held in stock by a merchant, the government often found itself obliged to pay many times the value. This penny-wise policy on the part of the local merchants resulted in the establishment of the government purchasing agency.

Management of a purchasing department of this magnitude requires a high order of business acumen besides special knowledge and unimpeachable integrity. It was difficult, within the range of the scale of salaries paid for bureau chiefs, to secure a purchasing agent fit for this work. It was fortunate that the agents secured both for Manila and for the New York office measured up to the standard of integrity required.

The government adopted more and more the policy of having the purchasing agent make his purchases wherever possible through the local merchants, thus decreasing the stock the government had to carry, encouraging private enterprise, and lessening to a certain extent the amount of business done by the government. This policy was pursued until, in 1913, the purchases locally amounted to 77.9 per cent of the total supplies for the government.

The annual expenditures by the government for supplies, excluding those purchased locally by provincial and municipal governments, increased from approximately $1,600,000 in 1903 to $3,500,000 in 1913, and to $9,650,000 in 1925.

The Bureau of Supply took over the management of the plant which was constructed by the military government in 1901 to provide cold storage for meat and other perishable foods necessarily imported at that time, and the manufacture of ice and distilled water for the troops, and for the hospitals. At that time none of these necessary provisions for the health of Americans existed in Manila, except a small ice plant which was inadequate to meet the requirements of the civil population.

The facilities of the government ice plant have been available to the public, but as a matter of good policy the establishment of similar services by private enterprise was encouraged, and Manila came to be well served in these modern facilities, which add greatly to comfort and health in the tropics.

CHAPTER X

TRIBAL PEOPLES AND MOROS

THE PRIMITIVE and semi-civilized peoples constitute about nine per cent of the total population of the Islands. These tribal peoples are the unassimilated descendants of aborigines and of immigrants in prehistoric times from the continent of Asia and the islands of the Indian and Pacific Oceans.

The aboriginal inhabitants were without doubt very primitive dwarf peoples of three distinct types: the Negrito, a pygmy negro with frizzled black hair and very dark skin; the straight-haired pygmy of Mongoloid type and brown skin; and the third combining characteristics of both the aboriginal Australian and the Ainu of Japan. These three aboriginal types long ago became mixed with each other, the Negrito being now the most easily recognized.

It is impossible to form any estimate as to the number of these aboriginal inhabitants at the time of the beginning of successive waves of Indonesian and Malayan invaders by whom the aborigines were gradually driven back from the coast to the comparatively inaccessible mountains. This movement continued during the centuries of Spanish domination until, by the time of American occupation, the aborigines were so few in number and so widely dispersed that they were not regarded as a menace to public order.

With the subsequent exploration and extension of government control throughout the Islands contact was gradually established with these small scattered groups of more or less nomadic peoples. Their customs and other characteristics have been studied and reported upon by ethnologists. The census of 1918 gives a total of somewhat less than fifty-six thousand persons who are classed as pygmies, of whom about twenty thousand were found on the island of Luzon, eleven thousand on the island of Mindoro, and the remainder in the Visayan Islands, and on the islands of Mindanao and Palawan.

These peoples for the most part live in wandering bands in the deep forests, subsisting on wild forest products, and building only temporary shelters of branches and leaves. Some, however, have assimilated customs of the civilized Filipinos, live in houses, engage in agriculture as well as hunting, and own domestic cattle.

The original languages of the pygmies appear to have been altogether lost. They speak dialects of the Malay type, with many archaic words and forms.

The largest number of aborigines in any single area are found in the southern Zambales mountains northwest of Manila. In these mountains there are Negritos of purest blood as well as mixed pygmy types. Negritos, more or less pure, are also found in the mountains near the eastern coast of Luzon and in several of the southern islands. In eastern Luzon and Mindanao there are also a few of a taller Negroid type who are thought to be descendants of people from New Guinea or the islands of the Pacific. In northern Palawan there is a remnant of a tribe of Negroid blood, known as Bataks, who are distinguished from others by the practice of polyandry and the use of the blowgun as well as the bow and arrow. They shave the hair from the front half of the top of the head.

In the island of Mindoro there is to be found an interesting tribe known as Mangyans, some eleven thousand in number, of whom it is estimated that about one-half are of the straight-haired pygmy type.

The Australoid-Ainu type is found among the pygmies living in the Apayao swamps in extreme northern Luzon and in some other localities.

While the pygmies are generally called savages as being very primitive in their customs of life, they are timid and often submissive when in contact with other races. In some localities they are definitely under the domination of the more civilized peoples.

While the descendants of the aborigines, notably the Negritos, are found in scattered recognizable groups, there has undoubtedly been extensive assimilation, especially of the straight-haired type, by subsequent immigrant peoples.

Almost as savage as the Negritos are the Ilongots, a semi-nomadic tribe living chiefly in the province of Nueva Vizcaya in central eastern Luzon. Their home is the dense forest, and they are timid, treacherous, and suspicious. When riding in on horseback to visit these people, through dense and seemingly uninhabited tropical growth, one hears in the forests the distant noise of voices, the weird cries of unseen people giving warning of the approach of a stranger. The men have long hair, rather effeminate and hairless faces, slight figures of small stature, and wear distinctive and striking costumes. They hunt with bow and arrow, and, although a few of them have been induced to live in permanent settlements, they prefer to move from place to place, staying only a short time in one locality.

The tribal peoples who are believed to be descendants of the earliest invaders of the Philippine Islands are those who appear to be related to the tall races of southern Asia and are termed by ethnologists "Indonesian." The general physical characteristics of this type are prominent and angular general features, straight black hair, light to dark brown skin, and an average height of about five feet seven inches, some attaining a stature of six feet or more.

Their early speech and culture have largely disappeared, although there is found in all Philippine languages some indication of an Indonesian element.

The Indonesian immigrants to the Islands are believed to have been followed by successive waves of Malay invaders who brought superior civilization and assimilated or drove earlier immigrants and aborigines back from the coast. Their descendants made up the great mass of the Filipino people at the time of the conquest of the Islands by the Spaniards.

There still remain four tribal groups of semi-civilized Malays. These inhabit the mountainous regions of northern Luzon and according to the census of 1918 numbered about 170,000.

All of these three racial types, pygmy, Indonesian, and Malay, are found in the interior of the large island of Luzon, where they constitute important tribal groups. In Mindanao the tribal peoples, Indonesians and pygmies, are numerous, aggregating about 187,000. On the islands of Mindoro, Negros, Palawan, and Panay there are groups of Indonesians and pygmies numbering about 45,000. While small numbers of aborigines are recognizable on some of the other islands, they are not so classified in the census enumeration.

It was with the group of savages in northern Luzon that the greatest advance was made in administrative achievement, and it was due to Commissioner Worcester that the interest of the American government was quickened and this work undertaken and carried through. The tribal groups varied greatly in their habits, degree of civilization, and the ease with which they could be won over to the arts of peace. The most highly civilized were the Tinggians, who inhabit the province of Abra. The others, who live principally in an extensive mountain region, which in 1908 was designated as the Mountain Province, and divided into sub-provinces each under a lieutenant-governor, were the Igorots of Benguet, Amburayan, and Lepanto; the Bontocs; the Ifugaos; Kalingas; and Apayaos.

It was a curious failure on the part of the Commission to live up to one of the main tenets of American government, that when dealing with these people legislatively they classed them as non-Christians and legislated for them as so designated. It would have been much more in accordance with American principles had they called them "tribal peoples," for in classing them as non-Christians they apparently made a religious distinction. The distinction, in fact, was not religious at all. These peoples might all have embraced Christianity without necessitating the change of a single word in the laws enacted in their behalf. The difference is one of civilization.

One of the early acts of the Commission created a Bureau of "Non-Christian Tribes" which was charged with the making of "systematic investigations with reference to the tribal peoples . . . with special view to determining the most practicable means for bringing about their advancement in civilization and material prosperity."

The Act of Congress of 1902, creating the Assembly, provided that it was excluded from legislating for the territory inhabited by Moros and other tribal peoples. Thus, upon the inauguration of the Assembly on October 16, 1907, the Commission became the upper house or senate for the regularly organized part of the Islands, but remained the sole legislative body for the tribal and Mohammedan part.

In this dual capacity there were many problems in which the Commission had to use discretionary judgment, as, for instance, deciding what proportion of the insular revenues it was fair for them to divert to the care of the tribal people, whose contribution to those revenues was insignificant. On the other hand, they were a potential source of trouble. Without proper administration by police, sanitary officers, teachers, and provincial governors, they might very easily have become an actual menace to the well-being of the civilized populations in the neighboring provinces.

The Commission met this difficulty by dealing with the problem with what seemed to them scrupulous fairness, and in no instance was their action in appropriating moneys from the general treasury for the territory over which they held exclusive control, the subject of bitter attack by members of the Assembly.

Another nice question arose in connection with the construction of the summer capital at Baguio. Located in the territory set aside to be under the exclusive legislative jurisdiction of the Commission, the city was to be built only incidentally for the benefit of the tribal residents and almost entirely for the benefit of the civilized Filipinos, to whom it became a place of popular resort in the hot season.

There were many laws passed by the Legislature, namely the Commission and Assembly sitting as upper and lower houses, which were of general interest, but under the terms of the act of Congress were not applicable to the territory inhabited by the Mohammedan and tribal peoples by reason of the participation of the Assembly in their enactment. It was deemed advisable for the Commission, acting in its exclusive legislative capacity, to scrutinize all these laws and if appropriate make them applicable to tribal territory in order that the Islands should have in so far as was possible a uniform set of laws. In several cases the Commission passed an act applicable to the territory over which it held exclusive jurisdiction before the Assembly could be induced to take this action.

Before the advent of the Americans there had been little pacification of these tribal peoples. They had lived practically uncontrolled and undirected for centuries, each town a unit in itself, with little intercommunication with neighboring towns except that of a hostile nature. The men, armed with head-axes, spears, shields, and sometimes bows and arrows, formed themselves into a guard and with a system of signals occupied points of observation to protect the aged, too infirm to fight, and women and children who worked the fields.

As there was very little level country within their reach, for purposes of cultivation the savages, most notably the Ifugaos, had terraced the mountains almost from bottom to top. In one place as many as three hundred terraces were to be seen one above the other. Often the acreage of wall built to protect these terraces exceeded the acreage of cultivatable land which they held. These people were very adroit in their use of water. Their manner of building a terrace was to build up the walls with stone, plaster the interstices with clay, then puddle mud into some brook from a high point in the mountain and let the water carry it down to the retaining wall, where in the course of time it would settle and little by little a cultivatable field would be built up. Very ingenious devices were invented to keep away the *mayas* or rice birds, which, unchecked, would have brought starvation to a village. Moving scarecrows worked by hydraulic power were to be seen waving about over the tops of the growing rice.

The people mostly wore almost no clothes, the men merely a loin-cloth and the women an extremely scanty skirt.

A sport of the men, if one might call it that, was head-hunting. Every town was intermittently at war with every other town, the young warriors of each village pitting their wits against their enemies of that neighboring town with which their feud was most active. According to the code in vogue, it mattered not whether the head of the person taken was that of a warrior or of some one entirely defenseless, like a little child; everything was fair game.

Commissioner Worcester chose as governors of the sub-provinces of the Mountain Province a number of active young Americans, sometimes selected from the Constabulary, and started out to win the confidence of these strangely assorted peoples. The savages were told they must stop their inter-village warfare and bring their disputes to the American governor for settlement. Those who put their cases in the hands of the governor would have all the forces of law and order to settle their questions; and the governor and his police dealt with those who failed to do so. Persons charged with criminal acts were required to be brought in for trial. The police at first were Filipinos; later men from the tribes were enlisted in the Constabulary until each tribe was policed by picked men from its own number. These enlisted men proved to be excellent soldiers, faithful to trust, tireless, courageous, and skillful.

The villages lying near the Constabulary stations were the first to give their allegiance to the government. Others a little farther afield followed; and gradually the people were won over to the new order of things. They found the Americans patient, honorable, fair, and diligent. They could get sympathetic attention to their grievances, prompt and just settlement of their disputes, and presently to their amazement they found themselves prospering as never before, for the energies of the able-bodied men could be taken from guarding and devoted to productive effort. Moreover, they were astonished to find that interest was taken in their well-being and that hospitals, schools, provincial buildings, and markets were all built for their service and were well run and sanitary. When Commissioner Worcester visited these provinces it was most touching to see the enthusiasm with which he was greeted. Crowds gathered literally in thousands, and the hillsides were black with leaping and shouting savages, waving large American flags, and cheering in a frenzied unison.

Trails were built throughout the Mountain Province with easy grades, which seldom exceeded six per cent and usually followed the contours of the hills. The trails were six feet wide, carefully drained. After these improvements were made one could ride for a distance of some two hundred miles over a mountain trail from Benguet to Apayao that, with occasional dips through the river valleys, continued at an elevation of well over four thousand feet, sometimes reaching a height of more than six. Rest houses were built at which travelers could lodge for the night. The diminutive Igorot horses, stunted descendants of the Arab brought in in Spanish days, were commonly used both by Americans and savages for their journeys in and about the Mountain Province.

When a law was passed compelling every able-bodied man among the tribal peoples to give ten days a year of free service to road and trail construction, the men were incensed — not because the work was required, but because it was limited to ten days. "How do we know," they said, "that ten days' work is going to be enough to complete the road, and what good is a road that is not completed and doesn't lead anywhere?"

The peaceable customs, religion, and prejudices of the inhabitants were respected. Besides schools, hospitals, and public order, they were given an opportunity to earn something for themselves and aspire to a better scale of living. The enthusiasm with which they grasped an opportunity to get an education was almost pitiful. It was interesting to enter one of the schools where some Filipino teacher, often a woman, was instructing a lot of little girls in the use of English. Visiting parties of inspection were likely to be greeted by a class of perhaps a dozen or two Igorot girls singing in unison, "In the Good Old Summer Time," or "Honey Boy," popular favorites of the day.

The Bureau of Health also did effective work for these tribal peoples, old and young, who quickly learned to appreciate the resulting benefits. Many prevalent skin diseases could be cured by cleanliness and simple remedies, and in this direction the work of the health officers in instructing the people generally in hygiene proved immediately beneficial. One of the more outstanding health achievements was the discovery by Dr. Strong, of the Bureau of Science, that salvarsan, or "606," as it is sometimes called, is a specific for the disease of yaws. Persons suffering from this disease were horribly disfigured, and there were numerous cases among the hill people.

It was provided that a certain number of girls from the tribal peoples should receive financial aid to take a nurses' training course. Selected residents of the Mountain Province, including Igorot girls, were brought to Manila, received their training, and returned to carry back to their people the torch of hygiene and sanitation.

The differences between these tribal peoples are very interesting. The isolation of village from village brought it to pass that each village has its own customs and codes. What is good etiquette in one village does not suit another. There have been cases of blood feuds handed down from generation to generation, and these presented great difficulties in the effort to bring about peaceful relations between towns.

How serious these feuds may prove to be is shown by something that happened in the central school at Bontoc. One little boy told his teachers that he was likely to be murdered. The peaceable Americans pooh-poohed the idea and took no precautions. Shortly afterward another small boy under orders drove a knife into the child's stomach, inflicting a wound of which he died.

The Bontocs were inveterate head-hunters and among the wildest and most intractable of the tribes, but they came at length to be very appreciative of what the Americans brought them.

The Igorots have certain virtues and certain defects common to savages. They are kindly, appreciative, truthful, and, to marked degree, faithful to trust. If one gives an Igorot an errand to do or message to carry and is sure he understands it, one can rest assured that that man will be faithful to trust even to the death. It is entirely safe to stop an Igorot anywhere and, without asking for his credentials, give him something to deliver. If he undertakes the task, the article in question is as good as delivered no matter how valuable it may be. During the construction of the Benguet Road hundreds of thousands of dollars were sent up on the backs of Igorots, and the only loss incurred was when one of the Igorots was stopped on the road and robbed by an American.

The Igorots of different localities differed from each other in many respects. Those of Benguet had no warlike proclivities, did no head-hunting, and were rather scorned in consequence by their more warlike neighbors in the north.

To the northwest of Benguet were two other peaceable Igorot subtribes, timid, patient, hard-working, and long-suffering, known as the Lepantos and the Amburayans.

In all these tribes the men wore nothing but a scanty loincloth called "gee string," but there were marked differences in the clothing worn by women of different tribes — in their manner of wearing their clothes, the colors they used, and in their ornaments and tattooing. The Benguet women were carefully and completely clothed from the neck to well below the knees in a distinctive garment, woven by themselves, of pleasing, quiet colors, reds, blues, grays, and whites, but they wore no shoes or stockings. Their long, straight black hair hung loose down their backs, or was sometimes wound partially around their turbans, a strip of white or red and white cloth wound once around, but never over, the head. Women as well as men carried heavy loads on their backs, and the women usually carried what they called an *anito* stick to keep away the evil spirits. This was a section of bamboo, open at one end and split up both sides, which they carried in one hand and tapped against the other forearm in such a way as to produce a musical note.

The Ifugaos were sometimes awkward in learning American customs. Handshaking, for instance, was very new to them, and their efforts at this form of greeting were sometimes quite uncouth.

The Ifugaos occupy a very extensive territory, all mountainous, in which the most remote town, that of Majayjay, was nearly three days' journey over mountain trails from the capital of the province.

North of Bontoc lies the territory of the Kalingas, a warlike people, with their own very strict moral code, unchastity in women, for example, being punishable by death. These people are most picturesque. Their warriors have a way of painting their faces red; they tie their long hair in a knot behind and decorate it with plumes made of the curling feathers of the tails of roosters into which little tufts of brilliant red feathers are tied at intervals. These plumes are fastened to a stick and stand high on either side of the head. Their ornaments and loincloths are red and yellow. Their skin shines like burnished copper, and they wear armlets of the curved tusks of the wild boar, and carry a head-axe tucked through the belt, the naked blade resting against the bare skin of the thigh. They carry light, graceful wooden shields decorated with a tasteful pattern of their own design, and their long spear handles are decorated with bands of brass or copper. Tradition has it that some time in the past the Spaniards transported a few Moros to the Kalinga country and the infusion of Moro blood has rendered them somewhat different from the neighboring tribes.

A contemporary description, as given in the journal of a visitor to the Kalingas, follows:

Kalingas

> Yesterday we had an exhibition of the ceremony incident to the taking of a head, with the same approach we saw at Kiangan, except that the shielded warriors were opposed this time in their advance by a single spearman who acted as a pretended enemy. A pig was killed as part of the ceremony.
>
> A piece of wood rudely shaped to resemble a head was stuck on a post, decorated with earrings, necklaces, and wreaths of flowers, and given the name of a man now serving in Bilibid for murder, and then the rites proceeded, different in detail but similar in appearance to the other, except that young girls joined the dances. One, who was very striking, danced most gracefully within a few inches of the so-called head. One peculiar thing about these dances is that they rob both the cradle and the grave — withered old dames well past sixty, and that is older here than at home, joined in the slow figures with frisky maids of sixteen, matrons of forty, or children of eight; similarly with the men. One robust and advanced dame performed her movements with a baby strapped to her back.

The journal continues:

> A dozen of the most brilliantly and gaudily got-up men took up their *gansas*, as the tom-toms are called in this country, and began their curious rhythmical beat standing; then, as the beat quickened, first one and then another would begin to move his feet till all were dancing up and down. One girl, a child of perhaps eight, would dance forward slowly, and presently another, till about twenty women were dancing in a group facing the men. They either move the feet slowly forward and back, holding their arms out with the palms of the hands upward, protruding their chests, or they put their hands on their hips and run forward or back with a graceful movement, always keeping the feet very near the ground. Presently the men turn and dance round the women, following the leader, winding in and out, putting their heels high and bending their bodies low. The women dress in light colors, with many beads, and skirts of a strip of cloth that barely meets at the side, hanging over a belt of many thicknesses of some woven stuff that makes a big and rather unsightly protuberance bulging all round just at the hips.

North of the Kalingas lies a mountainous territory, heavily forested with primeval jungle and watered by the Abulug, a large river flowing into the sea almost at the extreme northern point of the island of Luzon. On this river live the Apayaos, the last of the tribes of northern Luzon to come under the civilizing influence of the American government. Suspicious, wild in their habits, few in number, they dwelt in a region too difficult of access to give early contact with the Americans.

Like other mountain tribes, the Apayaos were head-hunters. One of their practices, on the return from a successful foray, was to chop up the head of their victim into as many pieces as there were members in the attacking party. Each man had a basket made by splitting the end of a bamboo cane, spreading the pieces, and then weaving other pieces of split bamboo around them, thus making a cone-shaped receptacle at the end of a stick. This stick was driven into the ground and a fragment of the victim's head was placed in each basket. These baskets lined the trail leading from the village where the head was taken. According to the traditions of the Apayaos, this practice kept the evil spirits from pursuing them.

With the appearance of an American provincial governor, it was not long before he was able to change the attitude of these people toward Americans and prove our good intentions, but it was necessarily a long, slow task to wean them from their savage practices and lead them into a more civilized mode of life.

The attitude of the Filipino toward the tribal peoples was very similar to that of the Spaniard, perhaps copied from it. It was one of entire indifference when the tribal peoples were at a distance; when they were close, the Filipinos wanted protection from them in case of warlike intent.

In one respect the Filipinos were deeply interested in the question of the tribal peoples, and that was in greatly resenting their exhibition in their natural state, especially in the United States or in foreign countries. While the exhibition of an Igorot village or a Negrito village, such as were shown at the World's Fair at St. Louis, was interesting from an ethnological and scientific point of view, it did the Filipinos a great social and political injustice, as it gave an utterly false impression to most people of the Filipino and his institutions. That the Igorots were mostly unclothed was heralded throughout the United States, in the course of a press discussion as to the propriety of the exhibit, to an extent that brought multitudes visiting the World's Fair to see this exhibit, each one desirous of determining for himself whether or not it was proper. The fact that these were inhabitants of the Philippine Islands was broadcast; the fact that they did not comprise more than five per cent of the population was not. The result was the dissemination of a totally false and objectionable impression about the Philippine people. Belated action was taken by the Legislature penalizing the exhibition of these tribal peoples.

One of the laws it was found necessary to pass in order to protect the tribal people was that providing against the importation and sale of spirituous liquors in their province. The Christian and civilized Filipino had seemingly little inclination to drink to excess. One seldom sees a Filipino intoxicated. The tribal people, on the other hand, often become ready slaves to the habit, and it was early seen that legislation on that subject was necessary for their preservation. They were not, however, prohibited from making their own wine from rice and sugar cane.

An interesting and picturesque part of the Philippine Islands is the great island of Mindanao, second largest of the group, which lies below the typhoon belt. It is sparsely populated, fringed with 488,000 Christian Filipinos, mainly in the north and parts of the east and west coasts, and with nearly 250,000 Moros in the south and on the Lanao plateau. The great interior is inhabited chiefly by tribal peoples of whom there are about 187,000. The density of population of the entire island of Mindanao and adjacent islands is less than twenty-five per square mile. Mindanao contains mountain ranges, beautiful upland lakes, great rivers, some of them navigable for one hundred miles, and watering level plains of rich soil capable of cultivation.

Various tribes of pagans, such as have been described elsewhere as tribal peoples, inhabit these interior regions, their villages sometimes reaching to the coast. Of these the most numerous are the Manobos, who live in the interior of the island on the headwaters and tributaries of the Agusan River. To the eastward of these are the Mandayas, who occupy the region on the eastern headwaters of the Agusan River. The Bukidnons, on the north and westward of the Manobos, live on a high, grassy plateau deeply creviced by cañons coursed by rivers. This region is well adapted for raising cattle, hemp, coffee, and fruits. On the west coast, but living mostly in the hills back from the sea, are the Subanuns, who in numbers are next in importance in Mindanao to the Manobos. On the southeast side, in the mountains forming the deep indenture in the coast known as the Gulf of Davao, are to be found the Bagobos, who dress in a homemade cloth of a handsome deep red shade, profusely beaded, and ornamented with bells which with each movement of the wearer jingle almost like sleigh bells.

In the same region of the Gulf of Davao, there are also Atas, Bilaans, Tagabilils, Isamals, Kulamans, and Tagacaolos. On the hills between the Cotabato River and the Celebes Sea is the small tribe known as the Tirurais.

These relatively primitive people generally retain their pagan cultures, except as modified on the north by contact with Christian peoples and missionaries, and on the south by their relations with the Mohammedans. The tribal peoples are distinguishable from their Christian and Mohammedan neighbors by their dress, and in some cases by disfiguration of the lobes of the ears for large earrings. There is no marked racial difference in physical appearance.

There seem to be no great differences in the dialects spoken by these various groups except in the cases of the Bilaans and the Tirurais. Both otherwise agree to a marked extent, in general type of life, with adjacent groups of Moros and of other tribal peoples.

A large proportion of Christian and Mohammedan inhabitants of Mindanao appear to be descendants of pagan tribal peoples who in other generations pertained to the groups the remainder of which exist today in the interior of the island.

The Atas, and in lesser degrees other groups of tribal peoples in Mindanao, give evidence of intermixture of aboriginal blood, and there still exist a few of these Negroid and pygmy elements, of whom three distinct groups are recognized. The Mamanuas, of whom there are about sixteen hundred living in the region adjacent to Lake Mainit in Surigao, northeastern Mindanao, are considered in part at least of Papuan origin. Some of these people live in more or less permanent villages founded by the Jesuit missionaries, and practice a certain amount of agriculture. The poorer types, however, continue to live in wandering bands without settled habitation. The second group of aborigines are of marked Negroid type, dwelling on the north and west slopes of Mount Apo among the Atas; and the third group is that of the Mangguáñgans, a very primitive, timid, wild people of the straight-haired pygmy type. Of these people there are about three thousand, many of whom live among or near the Manobos and Mandayas, whose culture and languages they have acquired. These aborigines are generally more or less dominated by chiefs of the Manobos or other tribal groups with whom they come most in contact.

Somewhat tardily the province of Agusan on the north, inhabited by the Mandayas and Manobos, and that of Bukidnon, adjacent to the province of Misamis, were put under the general direction of Mr.

Worcester and his bureau of "non-Christian" tribes. Their pacification and winning to the ways of peace was a much slower and more formidable affair than the winning of the tribes to the north. In the southern part of Mindanao the Subanuns, Bagobos, Tirurais, and other tribal peoples were under the administrative control of the governor of the Moro Province; and the province was divided into districts or sub-provinces, each with its appointed governor, in order to get a closer contact with the people. The tribes, however, in most cases were so far intermingled as to make it impracticable to designate one administrative head over each tribe.

On the occasion of a trip into Bukidnon with General Pershing in 1911, the Governor-General had an interesting experience when riding into the town of Tanculan. His party were greeted with most cordial demonstrations by the populace and a ceremonial dance by a warrior who danced backward in front of them, holding a spear with which he made pretended thrusts as he leapt backward purporting to prevent their advance. The party found the streets of the town scrupulously clean, the buildings neatly fenced from the road, and the yards planted with fruits and flowering shrubs, and in the public square the party were invited to play the newly introduced game of baseball with the young people of the town. Accepting this offer, the Governor-General occupied one base, General Pershing another, one of the secretaries caught, while the aides-de-camp were placed in other positions, and a few of the native boys of the town borrowed for fielders. The older people took the greatest interest in the contest.

The Bukidnons of that time were described as follows:

The native costume for women is a long black skirt, a jacket that does not quite reach the waist, which is bare. The jacket is of Moro cloth, red, white, and blue, in perpendicular stripes, but the tones soft and mixed with patterns and often some black. The hair is banged across the front and on either side there are locks left long that hang down in front of the ear. The hair behind is rather elaborately tied and greased, showing a couple of neat loops or bows of hair stretching out on each side, more Japanese in effect than anything else I have seen in the Islands. A cloth arrangement of red with white borders hanging down in four flaps, two to a side, serves as a cap on an old lady's head does at home, except that this cap arrangement is gaudy in color and hangs from the knot of hair at the back of the head. The toes are heavily ringed as are the fingers, the rings extending out over the several joints instead of ornamenting only the joint next the hand. The people are earnest, modest, quiet, and generally pleasing in spite of their ugliness.

One of the problems in the administration of the regions inhabited by tribal peoples was that of the development of commerce. The products of these peoples, in addition to honey, gums, rattan, resin, wax, and other jungle products, include coffee, Manila hemp (abaca), tobacco, native woven cloth, mats, and minor articles.

The Spanish government appears not to have succeeded in introducing the use of currency among these people, and trade with them was exclusively the barter of cheap distilled spirits and other merchandise for their products. This trade was in the hands chiefly of Chinese, a lesser number of Christian Filipinos, and a very few Spaniards. To remedy these bad conditions, and to give incentive to the people to devote themselves to productive labor, roads and schools were built, markets regulated, and care taken to avoid danger of food shortage.

Efforts were made by the government to regulate trade and induce greater competition, but without success. Local American administrators in trying to remedy these conditions carried paternalism to the point of putting the government squarely into business.

In the province of Agusan, on the island of Mindanao, the American governor in 1910 found the tribal peoples so exploited by traders that they had practically stopped planting and would not work. After vain efforts to induce the traders to modify their methods, the government put in small stocks of suitable trade goods in four out-stations and in the provincial capital. The use of currency was made compulsory for all transactions, and operations were on the basis of twenty-five per cent net profit. There was no authority of law at that time by which government funds could be used for financing these operations and consequently the provincial governor and his associates used their personal funds, under the supervision of the government auditor.

As it was not permissible under civil service rules for government officials to engage in trade within their jurisdictions, the Secretary of the Interior authorized these stores to be taken over on government account. To meet similar situations, similar measures had been tried in the Moro Province, and later this "trading system," as it was called, was authorized in the Mountain Province and the province of Nueva Vizcaya to encourage commerce among the tribal peoples in northern Luzon.

The Legislature, following its reorganization under the Jones Law, pursued the policy established by the Commission and made generous appropriations for the maintenance of schools and public health services and for the construction of roads in the territory inhabited by the tribal peoples. Funds were also appropriated annually for promoting good relations between the tribal peoples and the more highly civilized population, and groups of influential men and women were brought from the mountains and more remote regions to the large cities, including Manila during the carnival season, and on tours through the more advanced provinces.

The provisions of the special local government laws were extended to tribal groups located within the regularly organized provinces; the land laws were amended by the Legislature to protect the landholdings of the tribal peoples by requiring approval by the Director of the Bureau of Non-Christian Tribes to validate any conveyance or encumbrance of their lands. The Legislature also has made appropriations annually for the expense of educating selected young men and women from among the tribal peoples in the secondary schools in Manila and at other centers of the civilized population, and in other ways has endeavored to promote their assimilation.

With the establishment of civil order, the missionaries began to take great interest in endeavoring to convert these people to the Christian religion. Under the leadership of Bishop Brent, missions were established at Bontoc and Sagada by earnest and zealous ministers. They erected houses, opened schools, taught manual trades, converted some of the people to their religion, and endeavored to teach them the Christian spirit and civilized practices. The Roman Catholic Church also reopened a number of missions, notably in the towns of Bontoc and Bauco, where Belgian fathers devoted themselves unselfishly and without stint to the work of Christianizing the Igorots. Some of these men came from very wealthy families in Belgium, and brought, besides a thorough training and a very holy spirit, their own money to help a cause to which they were devoting their lives. To equip themselves for this service, in addition to their theological education, these Belgian priests had taken courses in engineering and agriculture, and thus were peculiarly fitted to serve in caring for the material as well as the spiritual welfare of those who came under their influence.

In Mindanao the Jesuit fathers returned to their missions, and later the Christian Missionary Alliance established a school and the American Board Mission (Congregational) a few schools and also medical work among the tribal peoples.

The government as such could take no part in the support of these missions, as its policy, fixed by law, was that of religious tolerance and of showing no favor to any one sect. The influence of the missions has not reached a very large proportion of the tribal peoples, and the great majority of them still entertain their former beliefs.

MOROS

It now becomes appropriate to deal with the Moslem inhabitants of a portion of the great island of Mindanao, the Sulu Archipelago, the small islands of Balabac and Cagayan Sulu, and southern Palawan.

Six of the twenty-three tribal groups inhabiting this region profess the Mohammedan religion and for this reason were termed by the Spaniards "Moros." The remainder are tribal peoples, among whom are to be found groups of Christians. All are of the same stocks as the natives of Luzon and the Visayas.

Mohammedanism in the Philippine Islands was introduced by adventurers who came to Mindanao and Sulu from Borneo and Malacca during the latter period of the Javanese empire of Majapahit, of which these islands were formerly political dependencies. After the fall of that empire, the Mohammedan states of Maguindanao, on the island of Mindanao, and of Sulu, in the islands to the southwestward, came into being about 1490 A.D., shortly before the discovery of the Philippine Islands by Magellan.

The first rulers of these states were Arab-Malay nobles, members of the royal families of Borneo and Malacca. They married daughters of the native rulers, and in emphasis of their religious affiliation arrogated to themselves the title of "sultan," as distinguished from that of "rajah," which had been used by the native kings. The families thus established have continued, in 1918 the Sultan of Maguindanao being the twenty-first, and that of Sulu the twenty-fifth, of their respective lines.

It is believed that one or two Mohammedan missionaries had preceded the arrival of those who made themselves the first sultans, and that their teaching had contributed to the ease with which the latter made their conquests. The Mohammedan missionary is self-sustaining, generally by trade, there being no organized financial support for foreign missions. Working among peoples of inferior civilization, and generally claiming to be an Arab and a descendant of the Prophet, he is accorded great respect. Missionaries, as early as the end of the fifteenth century, introduced the art of writing in Mindanao, adapting the Arabic alphabet to Malay phonetics. Arabic and Malay books on law and religion were translated into the native dialects and there are still extant manuscript translations of the Koran, books on law, magic, and other literature, as well as original writings in the major dialects of Mindanao and Sulu.

By 1565, which marked the beginning of Spanish conquest, Mohammedan adventurers and traders, chiefly from Borneo, had established themselves at points on the coast and had extended their religion as far north as Manila. While Mohammedanism had been established longer in the southern islands, it had not been generally accepted. The majority of the inhabitants of the great island of Mindanao were still pagan.

Even after the occupation of Luzon and the Visayas by the Spaniards, the Sultan of Borneo continued his efforts to maintain and extend Mohammedanism in those islands, until 1578, when the Spaniards made a successful military expedition to Borneo. The Spaniards eradicated Mohammedanism from all the Philippine Islands southward from Luzon through the Visayan Islands and from practically the entire north and east coasts of Mindanao, and also that part of Palawan north of Puerto Princesa. In the remainder of the southern islands and the Sulu Archipelago, for nearly three hundred years, the Spaniards made no sustained campaign against the Moros and permanently occupied no strategic places, except Zamboanga at the southwestern point of Mindanao.

At the time of the arrival of the Spaniards, the Malays were given to piratical raids not only on foreigners but even on villages of their own kindred. Sporadic expeditions, chiefly of a punitive character, by the Spaniards against the pirates resulted in nothing but the devastation of the Moro districts and reprisals against the Spanish settlements, until after 1850, when the use of steam vessels gave the Europeans a conclusive advantage.

Owing to the feeble control exercised by Europeans in the southern region, these notorious pirates ravaged the islands from Luzon on the north, southward through the Dutch East Indies, and to the westward the British possessions in Borneo and on the coast of the continent.

Sulu, because of its political independence and the advantageous geographical location of the island of Jolo, became the great mart for the pirates' booty, which included many human captives. The Moros took the women into their harems and kept the men as slaves. European and American shipping and trading posts in Malaysia suffered as well as the islands within reach of the fast vessels of the pirates, who moved northward into the Philippine Islands or southward into the British and Dutch possessions as the monsoon favored and the hope of plunder inclined them.

Sir James Brooke, who as Rajah of Sarawak added a portion of the great island of Borneo to the British Empire, and nearly wrested the domains of the Sultan of Sulu from Spain, took a prominent part in the suppression of Malay piracy. His vigorous operations were coincident with the beginning of a sustained campaign by the Spaniards.

With the extension of Spanish stations to south Mindanao and the occupation of the lower Cotabato Valley, and occupation of the town of Jolo, piracy in the Philippine Islands was reduced to occasional sporadic raids.

Although the Spaniards had never succeeded in converting the Mohammedans, they had checked the northward advance of Mohammedanism at the southern part of the island of Mindanao, except for a wedge thrust out through the island at its narrowest part to Lake Lanao, a beautiful mountain lake twenty-five hundred feet above the sea, surrounded by wooded slopes interspersed with cultivated fields and with distant views of lofty mountains. Upon the points and promontories of this lake, which is thirteen miles across, the Moros built their cottas or forts. In an effort to subdue these people the Spaniards had extended their lines from the north and south coasts of Mindanao and finally established a post on this lake, to which they had laboriously transported in parts several launches and barges which they put together and operated in the subjugation of that difficult region. In order to prevent these vessels falling into the hands of the Moros, the Spaniards, upon the advent of the Americans, took the precaution of giving the ships several coats of paint and grease to guard against deterioration by water and they were then taken out into deep water and sunk in the lake, the location of each sunken vessel being marked on a chart. In due course the chief of staff of the Spanish forces operating in Mindanao had the grace to deliver the chart and accompanying memorandum to the commanding general of the American forces operating in Mindanao. The boats were found some ninety feet below the surface. They were raised and the United States Army used them to great advantage in the pacification and administration of the region.

The Mohammedans may be divided generally into the following main groups: the Maguindanaos in the Cotabato Valley; the Maranaos in the Lake Lanao region; the Yakans on the island of Basilan; the Samals on the coast of the peninsula of Zamboanga and throughout the islands to the southward of Mindanao and of the Sulu Archipelago; and the Sulus, or "Joloanos," who are the ruling class generally in the Sulu Archipelago and in northeastern Borneo and southern Palawan. Although there is no recognized caste system among these people, the Samals are regarded by other Moros as of inferior standing.

There is a very extraordinary group of rovers, known as Bajaos, who move between Borneo and the Philippine Islands, living on their boats, and are in fact a sort of sea gipsy. They are timid, engage exclusively in fishing, and are pagan in religion, never having identified themselves with the Mohammedans, by whom they are held in utter contempt.

The Moro is hardy, self-willed, and a terrific fighter. General Pershing, in describing a battalion of Moro Scouts, said of them that every man in it could fight his own weight in wildcats. They were accustomed to the sea, skilled in the use of their weapons — the kris, barong, campilan, and the long-handled spear which they handle with great dexterity, protecting themselves with a large circular shield of light and rather soft wood.

The Moro wears distinctive and striking costumes. The favorite colors are red, orange, yellow, and all the intermediate shades, but they also use greens, blues, purples, black, and sometimes other dark colors. Some of the men wear their hair long and tied with a knot. They blacken their teeth, and the juice of the betel nut, which they constantly chew, stains their lips a brilliant vermilion, more vivid but less regularly applied than the colors in common use in civilized countries.

Under the Mohammedan religion plural marriages are allowed and to some extent practiced. The sultans, datus, maharajahs, pañglimas, and other petty chiefs support harems proportionate to their wealth.

In 1898 the government of Mohammedans presented problems for the solution of which there were no experienced American military or civil officials to be obtained. Few Americans had experience in governing dependencies and none of these had dealt with Moslems. Moreover, when the responsibility of the United States in the Philippine Islands began, there was little useful information available to American administrators in regard to the Mohammedans in the Islands as all military records were withdrawn by the retiring Spaniards.

In May, 1899, the fortified and walled town of Jolo, the Spanish capital of the Sulu Archipelago, was occupied by American troops. During the preceding months all other Spanish garrisons in Mindanao and Sulu, without awaiting relief by American forces, had proceeded to Iloilo and Manila. In the interim between Spanish and American control over the police force of the Islands the government necessarily reverted to the natives, Moros in Sulu and southern Mindanao and Christian Filipinos in the north. From December, 1899, as troops became available, American garrisons were placed at Zamboanga and other strategic points in Mindanao.

In August, 1899, General Bates negotiated with the Sultan of Sulu and certain datus of the vicinity an agreement, known as the "Bates Treaty," which established amicable relations between the American authorities and the Sulu Moros during the period of armed insurrection in Luzon and the Visayas. This agreement in effect defined the status of the sultanate as a protected sovereignty under the United States, and included the proviso: "The United States will give full protection to the Sultan and his subjects in case any foreign nation should attempt to impose upon them."

This "Treaty" was only with the Sultan and datus of Sulu, representing at most residents of the Sulu Archipelago. These were only about one-third of the total number of Mohammedan Filipinos. In the first two articles the agreement in terms specifically refers to the "Archipelago of Jolo and its dependencies," and thereafter reference is specifically to the "Archipelago of Jolo" and to the "subjects of the Sultan." Moros of Mindanao and adjacent islands do not acknowledge themselves to be "subjects of the Sultan" of Sulu.

Moros hold that the vernacular version of the agreement differs from the English, especially in Article I, which in the English is an unqualified recognition of the "sovereignty of the United States over the whole archipelago of Jolo and its dependencies," whereas it is claimed the vernacular version expresses merely recognition and respect to the American flag, but does not in terms relinquish sovereignty. The complete dependence of American and Moro negotiators upon interpreters and translators, not always trustworthy, made such misunderstandings possible.

The Sultan of Sulu claimed sovereignty, not only over the Sulu Archipelago, but also over an important part of British North Borneo, and he has been treated with more consideration by British authorities than by Americans. Upon arrival on British territory, he is received as a royal personage and given honors which Americans have not seen fit to accord him. Not only do the British ceremonially recognize a degree of sovereignty in the Sultan, but they pay annually a small sum which is in a sense a recognition of the Sultan's claim.

General Davis, who had been military governor of Porto Rico, relieved General Kobbé as military governor of Mindanao and Jolo. In 1901 General Davis made the first thoughtful and sympathetic study into the habits, conditions of life, and desires of the Moros, and the period during which he was governor was one of progress, peaceful except in Lanao, where the turbulent inhabitants of the lake region, who had defied the Spaniards, compelled the Americans to resort to military operations.

After peaceful overtures had failed and the Lanao datus had refused to surrender the murderers of Americans and to return a number of stolen cavalry horses, Colonel Baldwin, with a force of about one thousand American troops, moved from the south coast of Mindanao toward Lake Lanao, repeatedly attacked by hostile Moros. After a severe engagement the *cotta* of the Sultan of Bayan was destroyed and an American garrison established at Camp Vicars.

The main burden of these operations, however, fell upon the shoulders of an aggressive and capable American captain named John J. Pershing, who led his troops into the center of the island of Mindanao, underwent all sorts of hardships, and conducted his operations with such brilliant success that numbers of reinforcements were sent in to him until he had a command much larger than his rank as captain would normally have justified. In sending in these reinforcements it was occasionally necessary to find other duties to which to transfer officers who by reason of their seniority to Captain Pershing would automatically have taken command of his forces had they accompanied their commands. In recognition of his services, President Theodore Roosevelt gave Captain Pershing the unusual distinction of early promotion to brigadier-general from the grade of captain. It is fortunate for humanity that President Roosevelt had this degree of vision.

The organic act for the Moro Province was drafted by Governor Taft with the advice and assistance of General Davis and passed by the Commission in June, 1903. The province was given a special organization, differing materially from the thirty-one regularly organized provinces in which the Christian Filipinos enjoyed autonomy. It had an appoin-

tive governor and a legislative council which consisted of the governor
and five others: the secretary, the engineer, the treasurer, the superintendent of schools, and the provincial attorney, all Americans. This
council, subject to the approval of the Philippine Commission in Manila,
made its own laws except as to customs and forest revenues. The provincial treasury received the customs and internal revenues collected
within its territory. These, together with all other revenue collections,
were expended by the council at its discretion. Thus the governor of
the Moro Province enjoyed much greater freedom of action than any
other in the archipelago, and the power of supervision retained in Manila was used only very generally, owing in part to the confidence which
Governors-General in Manila always had in the capacity of the successive governors of the province.

Throughout the continuance of the Moro Province and its subsequent
reorganization as the Department of Mindanao and Sulu, the political
capital was at Zamboanga.

In July, 1903, General Sumner, who had succeeded General Davis,
was in turn relieved by General Leonard Wood, who had previously
won distinction as Military Governor of Cuba. He became the first civil
governor of the newly created Moro Province. In this capacity he was
responsible to the Governor-General for the civil administration of the
Moro Province and to the division commander at Manila for the conduct of military affairs in his department.

General Wood drew to himself a number of brilliant young men, the
most notable of whom was Captain Frank R. McCoy, a young cavalry
officer, who served both as engineer and secretary of the Moro Province,
and as governor in the absence of General Wood.

General Wood considered so unsatisfactory the situation created in
Sulu by the Bates Treaty, especially as to the powers of the Sultan and
datus in local government, that a few months after assuming the
duties of his office he recommended and President Roosevelt approved
the abrogation of the agreement. In 1904, General Wood notified the
Sultan to that effect.

Later in the same year, on the recommendation of the military authorities administering government in Sulu, the Commission authorized
a monthly payment equivalent to $250 to the Sultan of Sulu, and from
$37.50 to $75 each to seven of his datus, to "continue during the pleasure of the Commission." The total amount authorized was $6,750 an-
nually, and the Sultan's share is understood to be in lieu of revenues he

had formerly received as Sultan, with the understanding that he and his datus would "aid the government in every way possible when called on."

During the three years' incumbency of General Wood the province was organized; its administrators reached out into regions hitherto uncontrolled by central government; and important progress was made in the matter of public works and other developments. Public order was rigidly maintained, and when the Moro wanted to fight, he found he was up against foemen worthy of his steel. It was during this period that the engagement known as the first battle of Bud Dajo took place.

General Wood was succeeded by General Tasker H. Bliss, who was succeeded on November 28, 1909 by General Pershing.

Among the Mohammedans slavery was very generally practiced; datus and headmen felt they had the power of life and death over the people under their control and did not hesitate to put inconvenient persons out of the way without what the Americans held to be due process of law; and too many of them derived an important part of their revenues from depredations on their neighbors and from smuggling.

Some of the American administrators of the sub-provinces, or districts, were very adroit in following up the history of previous crimes and transgressions that had taken place in their regions. Many prominent Moros had placed themselves in positions of jeopardy through abuses committed. Although they had the justification of traditional practice, yet, under the American rule, these men were liable to prosecution. They were so numerous, however, that it was impracticable to bring them before the courts. American governors placed these men in a position practically that of prisoners on parole. If they behaved themselves and assisted the government in breaking up piracy, cattle thieving, and crimes of violence, they enjoyed in effect an amnesty for past offenses.

Left to themselves, the Moros would unquestionably have maintained a system purely feudal in its essence. The privileges claimed by the datus and other chiefs were such as could not be tolerated under the American flag. There is no question but that the action of the American authorities in breaking up these practices brought about the dissatisfaction and armed resistance with which the administration of the Mohammedan territory has been marked.

An example of the sort of abuse practiced by Moros upon their own people, and especially upon the pagans or tribal peoples in their vicinity, is well illustrated by the following statement from a Constabulary report:

> . . . This man [Datu Taog] was placed by the Sultan in charge of the pueblo of Dinas, and used his authority to abuse the Subanos. He forbade them to sell rice except to himself. He purchased cloth in Malabang, worth 40 cents Mex. (20 of our cents) a piece, which was sent into the hills and forcibly left in the houses of the Subanos; later his agents would collect as high as 47 cavans of rice (value $1.25 per cavan) for one piece of cloth.

It was natural that military officers with a force of troops at their command should set about remedying these manifest evils with a stern hand. In the opinion of some careful observers it is believed that progress would have been more rapid and these abuses could have been cured with much less bloodshed and open hostility had the early administrators made haste a little more slowly, won the confidence of the native rulers by first learning their language and dealing with them in their own tongue, and then explained the necessity for these reforms, perhaps one at a time. They could then have secured the assent of the leaders to them and their coöperation before promulgating hard-and-fast rules or laws which deprived the Moro chieftains of privileges which they had come to believe, according to religion and custom, to be the prerogatives of their position.

General Pershing as Governor of the Moro Province exercised the utmost patience in endeavoring to appeal to the reason of the Moro people and in avoiding a recourse to arms.

The successive administrations of the Moro province were marked with more or less fighting, usually with petty chiefs. The Moro was an eager fighter, and it is to the credit of the Sultans of Sulu and Maguindanao and of most of the important datus that they did not resort to arms against the government.

Many of the Moros had been allowed to retain their firearms and there had been so much lawlessness and so many murders, particularly of Americans and foreigners, that in 1911 it was felt that the time had come to put a stop to it and that the best way to do so was to take away their guns. This could not be done without bloodshed, and General Pershing cautioned Governor-General Forbes that disarmament would undoubtedly be resisted to the death by some of the Moros. But the necessity was palpable, and, regardless of the probable cost, the policy was definitely decided upon early in General Pershing's incumbency. A formal order was issued by the provincial governor September 8, 1911 "that it is declared to be unlawful for any person within the Moro Province to acquire, possess or have the custody of any rifle, musket, carbine, shotgun, revolver, pistol or other deadly weapon from which a bullet, ball, shot, shell or other missile or missiles may be discharged by means of gun-powder or other explosive, or to carry, concealed or otherwise on his person, any bowie knife, dirk, dagger, kris, campilan, spear, or other deadly cutting or thrusting weapon, except tools used exclusively for working purposes having blades less than fifteen inches in length, without permission of the Governor of the Moro Province as provided in said act, or unless otherwise authorized by law to possess and carry such weapons.

> "JOHN J. PERSHING,
> "*Brigadier General, U.S.A.*,
> "*Governor for the Moro Province.*"

Since the completion of disarmament it has been safe to travel unarmed and unguarded through territory that could formerly be traversed by others than Moros only when accompanied by troopers.

Poorly informed people have charged that the Moros were promised that if they delivered their weapons Filipinos should not take over their government. No such promise was made nor could have been made.

What remained of piracy was more difficult to suppress, and smuggling was almost impossible to eliminate. The sea was dotted with little islands and coral reefs; every coast Moro had his boat; Borneo was very near and very little inhabited, and such inhabitants as there were had similar proclivities. The ponderous government gunboats, of deep draught and none too fast, had difficulty in keeping up with the swift Moro boats which drew little water and could pass in over the shoals or hide behind an atoll anywhere in the Sulu Sea. The work of the Constabulary in that region was particularly trying, and a good many promising young Americans met their deaths at the hands of intractable and often treacherous Moros.

The religion of the Moros taught that, if any one of them were to meet his death as a result of killing a Christian, he would go to paradise. When a Moro became tired of life he could go *juramentado*. Such a Moro would shave his eyebrows, get blessed by a priest, done a white garment, and rush in to kill as many Christians as he could before meeting his death. He would make an especial effort to cut down an officer of rank.

The juramentado will steal up toward his intended victims, keeping as much as possible unobserved, until a chance arrived to rush in and start slashing with cold steel. One Moro was seen to seize the rifle of his opponent and pull the bayonet through himself so as to get near enough to reach his adversary with his kris before dying.

Perhaps the most notable outlaw among all the Moros was one by the name of Datu Ali, who in 1905 terrorized a region in the district of Cotabato. Crafty and cruel, unscrupulous, brave, and resourceful, Datu Ali eluded all efforts to capture him or bring him into open fight, nor could he be brought to terms by parley. Captain McCoy's expedition in search of Datu Ali is one of the most dramatic in Philippine annals. It began like Byron's "Waterloo" — "There was a sound of revelry by night." At a dance in Zamboanga, certain officers were touched on the shoulder and, none of them knowing to what they might be called, slipped silently out, and were taken to a steamer lying in harbor with no lights showing, which noiselessly made its way no one knew where. Effecting a landing at a distant part of the shore two days later, Captain McCoy ordered a trip overland in which the resourcefulness and endurance of his picked men were taxed to the utmost. One misadventure nearly ruined the success of the whole expedition. Before realizing where they were, the party entered a certain village around which they had intended to pass, and Moro couriers ran off to apprise Datu Ali of their approach. McCoy and his men followed so close on their heels that though Datu Ali was packed and ready for departure, the troops were upon him before he had time to start. He and his men were shot down in the course of a spirited battle, which lasted only a few minutes, as the troops were in sufficient force to overcome whatever resistance they encountered. With the fall of Datu Ali the district became peaceable.

The most severe opposition which the Americans had to encounter was that which resulted early in 1906 in the fight on Bud Dajo against the outlaws on the island of Jolo. Bud Dajo is an extinct volcano in the crater of which the Moro outlaws, with some of their women and children, took refuge and defied the authorities. The steep wild slopes of the volcano were fortified with a series of breastworks behind which the Moros crouched prepared to repel attacks. Besides their spears and shields they had an abundance of firearms and ammunition and their brass *lantakas*, or cannon, with which they commanded the narrow approach. Repeated efforts to secure the removal of the women failed, although some of them were persuaded to come out. They could not be distinguished from the men, as both were dressed alike, wore long hair, and fought side by side, so that it was impossible to spare the women in the bombardment and attack that followed. American and native troops fought side by side. Led by the heroic Captain John R. White, the Constabulary, largely Moros, proved their hardihood and fighting capacity by charging fifteen fortified positions one after another, overcoming them and reaching the top in spite of the loss of their gallant leader, incapacitated by a shot that shattered his knee. The fanatical outlaws fought until the last one was dead or wounded. More than six hundred of them perished in this fight, the news of which roused a storm of criticism in the United States, particularly among those who resented any effort on the part of the American people to pacify the Islands, and who looked upon the killing of women in battle as an unpardonable crime against humanity. It is easier for the ignorant to criticize than for the competent to achieve.

General Pershing had a crisis somewhat similar to that which General Wood met at Bud Dajo and in the same region during his incumbency as governor. It was a direct result of the disarmament order. In this case certain leading chiefs of the Sulu Moros retired to Mt. Bagsak with their followers and families and refused to give up their arms. To show that great pains were taken by General Pershing to avoid injuring the women and children, the following is quoted from his letter of February, 1913, to the Governor-General:

> The nature of the Joloano Moro is such that he is not at all overawed or impressed by an overwhelming force. If he takes a notion to fight, he will fight regardless of the number of men he thinks are to be brought against him. You cannot bluff him. There are already enough troops on the Island of Jolo to smother the defiant element, but the conditions are such that if we attempt such a thing the loss of life among innocent women and children would be very great. It is estimated that there are only about three hundred arms altogether in the Island of Jolo and that these are assembled in Lati Ward on top of Mt. Bagsak in fortified cottas. It is a common thing among these people to have the women and children follow them into these cottas so that we have there probably five or six times as many women and children as armed men. . . .

> . . . .

> While I do not believe now, nor have I ever believed at any time, that the Moros who are now opposing us will all yield without a fight, yet I am not prepared to rush in and attack them while they are surrounded by their women and children as I think most of the women and children can be induced to return to their homes. The situation, as I stated at the beginning, is a difficult one, but every official concerned is striving his best. Coolness and patience are the requisites

required. I fully appreciate your confidence in my ability to handle it, and you may rest assured that my best efforts are being put forth to carry out the purpose of our undertaking — disarmament with as little disturbance and as little loss of life as possible.

After some months of negotiation, General Pershing finally, in June, 1913, made a surprise attack at a time when most of the women and children were absent. This resulted in the extermination of all the Moros who had taken their stand on Mt. Bagsak. The attack was made almost entirely by Filipino and Moro Scouts; the American troops were kept in reserve.

The published account contained the following description:

Many cases of great bravery have been reported. A private in M Company, 8th infantry, rushed to a fortification through a shower of bullets, tore away a red flag from the top, started back, and was wounded. . . .

Another saw his brother killed at his side, rushed onto the fortifications, emptied his gun and killed five with his bayonet before he fell. And when the officer in command called for volunteers to crawl up and fire on a cotta, the entire company volunteered, so a choice had to be made by one of the first sergeants.

Another Scout during the advance had his bayonet shot off twice in fifteen feet; the third time it was hit it struck him across the side of the head, cutting an artery. At the same time another Scout was killed at his side. But as soon as the first recovered from the blow, he deliberately turned over, unfastened his dead comrade's bayonet, fixed it on his gun, and painfully though courageously started on his way up the hill, leaving a trail of blood. A colored hospital corps man named Mosely carried Lieutenant Rackley, who was wounded in the leg, 50 yards under fire to a place of safety.

As a matter of fact, General Pershing has reason to be proud of the conduct of all the officers and men under his command, who engaged in this short but terrific taking of Bagsak. He was on the spot from beginning to end and knows what they were up against.

Just as the confidence of the tribal peoples was won by justice and fair dealing, and by convincing the leaders among them of American interest in the welfare of the people, and of the fact that governmental measures were enforced for their own benefit, so was the confidence of the Moros finally won. Little by little they became convinced of the justice of the American rule.

The most picturesque of the latter-day Moro pirates was one by the name of Jikiri, who terrorized the Sulu Archipelago for a number of years. With his band he swooped down upon defenseless settlements, murdered and robbed them, and carried off their women. He was finally, in 1909, run to earth on Patian, a small island a few miles from

Jolo, where he took refuge, with eight male companions and three women, in a cave on a steep hillside, heavily wooded. On a ridge of the hillside before the cave he built a small parapet of stone, and here he was hemmed in by troops of the Sixth Cavalry. Cannon and machine guns were brought up, and the place was shelled after the usual requests for the withdrawal of the women and children had been refused, the women preferring to die with the men. The rainy season was on, the forests were infested with swarms of mosquitoes, and the besieging forces endured all kinds of hardships, but they held the cordon round the cave night and day until finally the captain commanding ordered the parapet charged, which was done with a small loss of life. Once within the parapet, the troops found themselves facing three openings. The cave was filled with smoke from the bombardment, which had been so heavy that trees as large as six inches in diameter had been cut right through by the bullets. Nothing could be seen within, and three officers of the Sixth Cavalry, Lieutenants Miller, Kennedy, and Wilson, charged into the cave at the head of their men knowing that they would be cut down by the cold steel of the lurking Moros, who could see them as they came in against the light. They were cut down, but fortunately survived their wounds, and Jikiri and his band were exterminated. The American loss was five men killed and twenty wounded. All three of the gallant officers received the Congressional Medal of Honor for their heroic action. This operation was wholly carried out by American troops, as at that time there were no native troops stationed in Jolo. The policy later adopted was to fight Moros with Moros and Filipinos.

It was much more difficult to win the confidence of the Moros and convince them of well-meaning than was the case with the tribal peoples. First they had to be assured that no ulterior designs were harbored against their religion. They suspected the schools and in some districts it was long before they could be persuaded to let any of their children, especially the girls, attend school. They were quick, however, to realize the advantages of agricultural and trade schools and very appreciative of the service rendered by doctors and hospitals, for they soon learned to come in to have their wounds bound and their ills treated.

Another thing they liked was the establishment of markets at which trading was carried on under government supervision and under sanitary conditions. To these markets, the Moros, Filipinos, and Chinese brought their wares for daily interchange.

One of the major industries was the development of pearl fisheries, and the Moro divers brought up many million dollars' worth of beautiful pearls to be traded at the wharf at the town of Jolo, which is the capital of the province of Sulu. Japanese pearl divers with modern equipment also operated in Sulu waters.

By 1912, the time seemed to have come when a change in the manner of handling the Moro Province was necessary. Good as had been the quality of the men selected for governorship of the province, a continued military personnel seemed to be inexpedient. Continuity of service was the most important lacking element. Where the positions of deputy-governors were held by army officers, it was found that just about the time they had held their positions long enough to learn their duties, the military requirements of the service resulted in their transfer. About this time the so-called "Manchu" law was passed, which required every officer in the United States Army to serve a certain proportion of his time with troops, and under the operation of this law even the most efficient army officers who had been detailed for service in the insular government had to return to their regiments and serve the required time before they would be available for a further detail. This made it all the more difficult for the army to govern the Moro Province properly, and General Pershing supported the recommendation of the Governor-General to Washington that the next governor of the Moro Province should be chosen from civil life. This was done in December, 1913, by the appointment, as the first civilian governor of the Province, of Frank W. Carpenter, who had served with striking ability as head of the Executive Bureau for many years. He was a notable success in his new capacity.

Shortly afterward the Moro Province was reorganized as the territorial Department of Mindanao and Sulu, and the adjacent province of Agusan with its sub-province of Bukidnon brought within that jurisdiction. The land area of the department was more than 36,500 square miles, or nearly one-third the total area of the Philippine Archipelago.[1]

Under this reorganization the customs and internal revenue collec-

[1] For the purposes of administration this territory was divided into seven provinces, five being the former districts of the old Moro Province — Cotabato, Davao, Lanao, Sulu, and Zamboanga — and the remaining two Agusan and Bukidnon. The Department comprised the Sulu Archipelago and practically the entire island of Mindanao except the two provinces of Misamis and Surigao on the northern coast, inhabited almost exclusively by Christian Filipinos, who, however, numbered in those provinces some 300,000, or about one-third of the population of the entire island of Mindanao.

tions which had accrued to the treasury of the Moro Province were taken over by the insular government as in the rest of the Archipelago, and larger amounts were appropriated by the Legislature from insular funds for grants in aid to the provincial and local governments, and for the development of roads and other public works, of public health, including a hospital at each provincial capital and dispensaries at outstations, public schools, and other services. The Legislature expressed as its object the complete unification of the inhabitants with the inhabitants of other provinces of the Archipelago.

The American troops had been withdrawn prior to the relief of General Pershing in December, 1913, and later the Scout garrisons, except that of four companies at Zamboanga, were withdrawn to replace American troops at posts in Luzon during the World War. The Constabulary was increased.

In 1916, the Jones Act reorganizing the Philippine government established a Bureau of Non-Christian Tribes to "have general supervision over the public affairs of the inhabitants of the territory represented in the Legislature by appointive Senators and Representatives." This territory included the Department of Mindanao and Sulu and the Mountain Province on the island of Luzon. Governor Carpenter was designated director of the new bureau in addition to his duties as department governor.

In February, 1920, the Legislature abolished the government of the department, placing the seven provinces directly under the Bureau of Non-Christian Tribes, and extending to that territory the jurisdiction of all bureaus and offices.

While the Sultan of Sulu apparently endeavored to maintain friendly relations with American administrators following the abrogation of the Bates Treaty in 1904, vexatious questions frequently arose by reason of the undetermined status of sovereignty in Sulu. The subjects in controversy were chiefly those concerning the administration of justice in matters arising between Moros. The American authorities had assumed jurisdiction and provided courts for the trial of both civil and criminal cases. In practice, however, the great majority of the people continued to recognize the customary jurisdiction in these matters of the Sultan and his subordinate chiefs. Soon after the appointment of a civilian governor of the Moro Province, the Sultan presented the matter to the Governor, alleging encroachments upon his prerogatives by government officials, especially in cases involving domestic relations, the partition of estates of deceased persons, and the collection of certain tribute. The Sultan claimed that, before American occupation of the Islands, he and his predecessors had always exercised sovereign powers at least as to internal affairs, and that under the Bates Treaty the American authorities had recognized his government and authority to administer justice in cases arising between Moros. He further claimed that the effect of the abrogation of the Bates Treaty had been to restore the situation existing during the Spanish régime, though he had been able to enforce his authority only in part because of encroachment by the American military forces. Many of the datus and a large proportion of the people looked to the Sultan as their ruler as well as their religious head, and in general among the Sulu people there were confusion and recurring unrest because of uncertainty as to the extent of the powers of government and the limitations of the Sultan's prerogatives.

It therefore seemed of fundamental importance that all pretensions of the Sultan to temporal sovereignty be terminated. Negotiations to that end were entered into by Governor Carpenter, of the Department of Mindanao and Sulu, and a formal agreement reached March, 1915. In this agreement the Sultan specifically and without reservation recognized the sovereignty of the United States of America in the Sulu Archipelago and over the Sulu people wherever located within American territory with "all the attributes of sovereign government that are exercised elsewhere in American territory and dependencies. . . ." The government for its part in this agreement recognized the Sultan of Sulu as the titular spiritual head of the Mohammedan Church in the Sulu Archipelago with all the rights and privileges of and subject to the same limitations as apply to the spiritual heads of all other religions existing in American territory, the Sultan, his adherents, and all Mohammedans being assured "the same religious freedom had by the adherents of all other religious creeds, the practice of which is not in violation of the basic principles of the laws of the United States of America."

Although prominent Moros when in Manila have shown a tendency to align themselves with the Nationalist Party there, and their representatives in the Legislature have cast their votes in favor of Nationalist measures, yet, in talking with Americans and disinterested parties, they frequently express a desire for separation from the rest of the Archipelago and a continuance of American rule in case independence is granted.

There was substantial progress in Mindanao and Sulu during the period 1914 to 1920 in the construction of roads and trails, improvement of ports, public health service, public schools, and public order. Following the publication of the abdication of sovereignty by the Sultan, additional local governments were organized with Moros as municipal presidents and councilors. For lack of American school teachers and doctors, such places were filled by qualified Filipinos. Dispensaries and schools were established in all important villages however remote from Constabulary garrisons. Filipino engineers, foremen of road construction, and land surveyors worked unmolested throughout the province. Upon the entrance of the United States into the World War, the greater proportion of American officials and employees in both Mindanao and Sulu resigned from the Philippine service to enter the army, and their places were filled by Filipinos, generally by promotion from lower grades. By 1920 the American governors of all provinces, except Sulu, had resigned either to enter the United States civil or military service or to engage in private business. These important posts were likewise filled by Filipinos.

There have been comparatively recent instances of Moro women who have held positions of the highest leadership, notably that of the Sultana Inchi Jamila, mother of the present Sultan of Sulu, who compelled the Spanish authorities to withdraw their candidate and recognize her son as Sultan of Sulu. This distinguished woman was visited by General Bates in the course of his negotiations in 1899. It is a matter of gossip among the women of the Sultan's household that his mother was the descendant of a beautiful Spanish girl taken captive in a raid on the coast of Panay, brought to the market at Jolo, and taken by the then Sultan into his harem. This captive woman, not only because of her physical beauty, but because of her intellectual superiority, became the controlling influence in the Sultan's household, and by heritage this superior ability reappeared in the Sultana Jamila. This heritage again appeared in the latter's granddaughter, the young Princess Tarhata, who has been educated under American tutelage at Manila and in the University of Illinois, in the hope that, upon her return to Sulu, her American training would be a valuable factor in her assumption of a position of leadership.

Another distinguished Mohammedan-Filipino woman of royal blood was the Rajah Putri, or "Princesa," by which title she was known at the time of American occupation of the Cotabato Valley. By reason of her ancestry and her personal wealth she exercised much influence, which is believed to have been in the main in favor of submission to American sovereignty.

Another Moro woman of the Maguindanao tribal group, and perhaps of greater personal abilities than the Rajah Putri, was the wife of Inok, a war leader of the well-known Datu Piang and a staunch partisan of Americans in the upper Cotabato Valley. Upon her husband's death, she became the acknowledged leader of his people, and on the organization of municipal government in her district of Buluan, Cotabato, she was appointed municipal president by the overwhelming popular demand of the men of that region. She became a vigorous partisan of public schools, especially for girls, and in other ways a valuable influence in the extension of American administration in Mindanao.

An interesting incident of the willingness of Moros to concede pre-eminence to a woman was the case of Panglima Fatima of Tandubas, one of the islands of the Tawi Tawi group of the Sulu Archipelago. It is said that during the latter days of Spanish sovereignty this woman accompanied her husband and his followers when they engaged in battle with a hostile neighboring group of Moros. In the midst of battle her husband was killed, and she immediately took his place and led his forces to victory. In recognition of her prowess she became the successor of her husband as the local dignitary and ruler. It is interesting to note that her attitude toward American authorities was one of friendliness and loyalty.

Among the Moro women who exercised decided influence in governmental affairs mention should also be made of the Dayang Dayang Hadji Piandao. The Sultan, having no child of his own, adopted Piandao, the posthumous child of his predecessor and half-brother. A woman of strong character, entirely without Occidental education, Hadji Piandao exercised her influence in favor of American sovereignty during the negotiations in 1915 which resulted in the renunciation of temporal sovereignty by the Sultan.

The Mohammedan Malays are inclined to religious tolerance.

Mosques are rarely to be seen in Mindanao and Sulu. Except for insignificant structures of inferior construction, the only mosques in Mindanao and Sulu in 1920 were that of the Sultan in the town of Jolo and that being built by Datu Piang near his home in the upper Cotabato Valley.

The pilgrimage to Mecca has been made by a few Mohammedan Filipinos. This journey, made in some cases on account of piety and in others because of the distinction which the pilgrimage confers, involves expense beyond the means or the willingness of the vast majority of the people.

Under American administration the Moros have shown an increasing disposition to fraternize with Christians, and in some communities, notably in the Filipino colonies in the upper Cotabato Valley, the Moros have contributed materials and labor in preparations for the celebration of Christmas and other Christian festivals. Reciprocally, during the period 1914 to 1920, Christian Filipino officials and private persons assisted in the celebration of the Mohammedan festivals, especially that at the close of the Ramadan, the annual fast. Moros rarely question food offered them when visiting, and the preparation and kinds of food offer no difficulties involving special kitchens in the Constabulary or in boarding schools.

Many American observers and writers have treated at considerable length the attitude of the Moros toward the Filipinos, and the prevailing impression which they give is that there is an innate and very general hostility on the part of the Moros to the Filipinos. The policy of the United States has been to promote friendly relations between all peoples of the Archipelago. To this end, for instance, scholarships were given to Moro boys and girls to pursue advanced studies in the schools in Manila.

It is unfortunate that certain Americans have not hesitated to discredit Filipinos. Especially humiliating was the frequent charge that the Filipinos were not courageous as fighters and compared unfavorably with the Moros in this respect. The record of the Filipinos in the ranks of the Scouts and Constabulary was good and did not justify this sort of comment. It is to be noted that some distinguished officers of the army and of the Constabulary, who had had experience with hostile Filipinos during the insurrection and later with hostile Moros in Lanao and Sulu, expressed the conclusion that in organized warfare or guerrilla operations the Filipino is equal or superior to the Moro.

There have been many occasions in which Moros have expressed emphatically their approval of American rule and they have often shown their preference for continued American administration and their hope that their people will not be turned over to Filipino rule.

The Governor-General wrote in his journal in 1913 of a gathering of Moros, including some thirty sultans and many datus, in Dansalan on the shores of Lake Lanao: "One recalcitrant datu was present for the first time in history; and finally one old hero said that one thing they were agreed on was that they didn't want anything to do with native [meaning Filipino] rule."

The Honorable Clarence B. Miller, a keen and critical student of Philippine affairs, journeying through the Islands not long afterward, reached the conclusion that the Moros would immediately take to arms if compelled to live under the rule of Filipinos.

This was further brought out most emphatically in the Wood-Forbes investigation, in the course of which a most impressive and dramatic meeting was held at Marahui, also on the shores of Lake Lanao, when orator after orator arose to express his resentment of Filipino rule, which had been by that time imposed upon them, and to ask for the return of an American governor. This in spite of the fact that the Filipino se-lected was a remarkably competent Constabulary officer, a fine athlete, who had made a splendid record in his position. One of the Moros pointed through the window to a building over which were flying side by side the two flags, the American flag and the Filipino flag, and said impressively: "What is that strange flag [meaning the Filipino flag] flying beside ours? Take it down."

When General Wood asked all of those present desirous of continued American rule to raise their hands, every Moro in the room threw up first one hand and then the other until pandemonium broke loose, the only unenthusiastic observers being a few representative Filipinos who stood looking on grimly with folded arms. The foremost datus began to execute a dance, and the cheering and stamping rose in volume until two sultans danced forward and each of them embraced one of the two members of the mission.

The idea of partially dismembering the Islands is not a new one and has been suggested many times by thoughtful persons concerned with the Philippine problem. It is an idea that is deeply resented by the Fili-pinos, and no solution of the Philippine problem involving the separa-tion of any part of the Islands has ever been met with favor by any of the political leaders in the archipelago. In fact, it has been met with deter-mined hostility. The Filipinos do not fear to face the problem of man-agement of the Moros or of the tribal peoples. They feel that the hostility which the Americans claim exists, and of which there is sub-stantial evidence, is one which they can allay by considerate treatment and by conciliatory methods.

When the reins of government were put very largely in their hands, the Filipinos did not show the same consideration for the Moros in granting them participation in the Moro government that they had demanded for themselves in the Filipinization of their own. It is, of course, true that fewer Moros were ready for the management of their affairs in a modern world, but there was a good deal of bitterness engendered none the less.

CHAPTER XI

INFLUENCES: RELIGIOUS, SOCIAL, AND POLITICAL

THE WORK OF THE Roman Catholic Church in the Philippines had been a potent factor for good in the history of the people. It dealt with the disunited, warring factions and tribes which the Spaniards found in the Islands at the period of their conquest and gave them that unity of thought which comes from a common religion to which they are devoted.

Up to the time of the arrival of the Americans the Roman Catholic Church had largely dominated the State, and, as usually happens, abuses ensued. But the magnitude of the service rendered by the Church should not pass unrecognized.

It is said of Urdaneta, who accompanied Legaspi at the time of the conquest, and his companion friars that "inspired by apostolic zeal and tolerance they labored in harmony with Legaspi, won friends, and checked the slowly advancing tide of Mohammedanism." Representatives of the various orders, Augustinians, Dominicans, Franciscans, Jesuits, Capuchins, and others, from time to time found their way to the Philippines and became established in the Islands. Public instruction was exclusively under the direction of the friars. Higher education at first was only for the sons of Spaniards, and the friars opposed teaching the Spanish language to the mass of the people.

To the lasting credit of the Church it can be said that they succeeded in developing a civilization in which woman took a high place in the community life. The women of the Philippines came to hold a position of responsibility in the management of the home and in the business of the husband.

The monastic orders in time secured the possession of large tracts of some of the best lands, which they leased to tenants on terms profitable to themselves. Little by little an antagonism to the orders grew, attributable in part to the control exercised by the friars over their numerous tenants.

The priests also in time came to exercise many functions of civil government within the limits of their parishes. Some idea of the extent of this intervention is seen in the following summary of the average priest's activities: He was inspector of primary schools; president of the health board and the board of charities; president of the board of urban taxation; inspector of taxation; honorary president of the board of public works; he certified the correctness of the cedula or poll tax; he was president of the census-taking of the town; he was president of the board of statistics; he was censor of the municipal budgets; president of the prison board and inspector of the food provided for the prisoners; and he was a member of the board for partitioning crown lands. In some cases, in the capitals of provinces, he acted as auditor. He was also counselor for the municipal council. He was supervisor of the selection of the police force; examiner of the scholars attending the first and second grades in the public schools; censor of plays (comedies and dramas) given in the language of the country. In some cases it appears that the friars in fact controlled the Guardia Civil, or insular police.

At the time of the American Occupation it is estimated that nine-tenths of the people were professed adherents of the Roman Catholic Church.

One of the early duties of the Americans was to bring about, without too greatly disrupting the local services, the complete separation of the parish priest from matters of civil administration; for example, civil marriages were immediately made legal, government schools were set up, and the work of educating the people was taken over from the Church. These schools were extended as rapidly as funds permitted. There was no interference by the Government in the proper conduct of Church schools, which in the main served as universities and schools of higher grades.

The problem of the Friar Lands was solved in large measure as a result of a visit to Rome by Mr. Taft, the President of the Second Commission and Civil Governor of the Islands, during which he arranged for the purchase of Friar Lands by the Government for something over seven million dollars, which were then sold to the tenants on long-term payments under the operation of which the Government recovered the bulk of the money advanced, and those who had been tenants found themselves with assured title to their land.

Another important solution which Governor Taft obtained during his visit to Rome was the withdrawal of the higher officials in the Church and the appointment of Americans in their places. The following declaration of policy was announced, that "It was not the intention of the Roman Catholic Church authorities to send back Spanish friars to any parishes in which the majority of the people were opposed to their coming." Three-fourths of the friars left in the next few years.

A considerable number of Filipinos, under the leadership of Gregorio Aglipay, who had been a priest of the Roman Catholic Church, organized a schism with nearly two million adherents, calling itself the "Independent Philippine Church." In many regions the Aglipayanos, as they came to be called, took possession of the churches on the ground that having been built with moneys derived from the people the people of each town could decide what denomination should occupy them. The matter, however, was settled peaceably by a decision of the Supreme Court of the Philippine Islands that these churches belonged to the Roman Catholics.

A number of other controversies between the Church and the American State were settled by wise statesmanship, forbearance, and considerate dealings between the heads of the State and the American hierarchy that came to take charge of the direction of the Church.

It was natural that with the new freedom and religious tolerance which accompanied American rule, a number of Protestant churches should establish themselves in the archipelago. The Episcopal Church, under the able and wise leadership of Bishop Charles H. Brent, erected a cathedral in Manila, started a hospital and training school for nurses, a club house for men, and a school at Baguio for American boys. Bishop Brent established missions, hospitals, and schools among the hill people and the Moros. The Methodists, Presbyterians, United Brethren, and Congregationalists also established missions in which hospitals and schools were noteworthy features.

According to the census of 1918 the adherents of the Protestant churches did not exceed one and three-tenths per cent of the population.

With the advent of the Americans and their taking over the control of government a new problem presented itself, namely, the attitude of Filipinos of all classes throughout the Islands, and the means of winning the confidence, respect, and ultimately the affection of the Filipinos.

The Filipino is impressionable, filled with sentiment for nationality and with genuine and justifiable pride of race. He is naturally friendly. He likes to be liked, responds quickly to signs of interest and affection, and to acts of kindness. He is particularly appreciative of acts of social recognition.

No matter how benevolent of intention and lenient, the invader inevitably arouses antipathy by imposing a system of government new to the people. While wiser heads were ready to concede that American tutelage for a while was necessary, there was the inevitable jingo element that became impatient of control and chafed at the delay in obtaining political preferment. The Filipino, or "tao," who owns and works a little farm is no fool, and represents the great mass of the people. He appreciates peace, justice, good roads, free schooling, efficient public health service, and assurance of good prices for his products. He can see the money he has paid in taxes being returned to him by the government-managed activities from which he benefits. He is contented, has no political aspirations, and is the backbone of the country.

The Americans from the very beginning began to win the confidence of the Filipino leaders by considerate social treatment. This was well expressed by General Aguinaldo in a public address in 1921. He said:

America came to the Philippines as the result of championing a cause in behalf of liberty. The independence of Cuba gave us the opportunity to know the United States, first as an ally, then as belligerent, and, finally, as tutor in our national edification. This tutelar rôle, undertaken by America with benevolence since the occupation of the Philippines by the United States, has served to efface all the ill-feelings created by the natural course of the war. . . . From the very moment that America and the Philippines joined hands to accomplish the restoration of our republic, Filipinos and Americans have been blended in one group as brothers guided by only one aim, a noble one, unmixed with egoisms of any kind. This example is unique in the history of weak peoples.

In view of the bitterness necessarily incident to the insurrection and the loss of lives on both sides, with the inevitable recriminations, it is little short of surprising that really friendly relations were so soon reached.

One handicap to a good understanding lay in the fact that the American army came with the inevitable accompaniment of undesirables, beachcombers, adventurers, and others, some of whom were of very low ethical standards and made an unfortunately bad impression upon the better class of Filipinos with whom they came in contact.

When the Civil Government took over the administration of affairs from the army, with limited funds, it enforced rigid economies in the administration. The result was the growth among Americans of a sentiment hostile to the reforms that the Government was establishing. Some Americans had started newspapers which fortunately did not last very long; but while they did, they lent themselves to sharp and sometimes vitriolic attacks upon the American Government of the Islands and in this way demonstrated to the surprised natives the extremes of freedom which the press was permitted under democratic guidance.

It was inevitable that both Filipinos and Spaniards should follow the example of these hostile papers and join what was aptly called the "anvil chorus." It was not surprising that some of them did not observe the fine line between license and liberty, and some of the native papers had to answer in the court for libel. If they had not been corrected when they exceeded the proper limits, the position of the American officials in the Islands might have become extremely difficult, perhaps impossible.

In spite of this unfavorable condition, in his trips of inspection the American Governor-General was always sure of extremely cordial reception in every region he visited.

The Filipinos, led in part by their shortsighted newspaper editors and in part by literature from America, became very apprehensive of an unknown creature which bore the terrible name of "Trust," and all movements on the part of Americans in the Islands looking towards physical and economic development were viewed with apprehension lest some terrible ogre with long tentacles, like their own devilfish, should be finding itself a way into the Islands to suck the lifeblood of the people and frustrate their movement towards independence.

There were not lacking, however, public-spirited Filipinos who believed in the necessity of bringing in outside capital and were not afraid to say so. Apprehension was successfully met by personal assurances and the evidence given by such enterprises as did come of the advantages they brought; the tide began to turn quite strongly, and the Filipinos, even those prominent in politics, began to express readiness to welcome American capital.

The following words of a Filipino orator may here be pertinently quoted:

If you ever stopped to figure the number of Japan's inhabitants and her available area, you would easily see that instead of howling for independence and wanting every American to get out of these Islands, you would feel like offering prizes for American settlers to come here and lend you that air of security and safety which are so essential to the upbuilding of the Philippines.

The Filipino is a natural orator, and he readily took to political activity. At the public or private sessions representatives, often very young, jumped to their feet and came forward with carefully prepared orations, not always wholly logical, as it was usual for them to inveigh against taxes which as a matter of record were extremely low,[1] and then go on to ask for additional costly favors in the matter of public works and improvements.

As indicated in an earlier chapter, the American Government was somewhat hastily organized. The positions were largely filled by men who had come to the Islands in the army, either as volunteer officers, noncommissioned officers, or enlisted men, and it was inevitable that there should be some misfits among these hastily assembled thousands. It was also inevitable that some should find that the enervating influences of the tropics weakened their moral fiber, and that they fell victims to temptations which they would have resisted in the environment of home and tradition, reinforced by the rigors of their accustomed home climate. The few who fell suffered the penalty of dismissal, deportation, or, in the worst cases, trial and imprisonment for crime. The number of the latter was extremely small but their punishment impressed upon the Filipinos in general the impartiality with which justice was administered in the Islands and the rigid attitude of the administration toward evil-doing by whomsoever done.

It was a matter of course that the Filipino papers should allege that too slow progress was being made in the appointment of Filipinos to government positions; they clamorously advocated more rapid "Filipinization." This was going steadily along carefully-considered lines up to the time of the change of administration in 1913 when the rate of Filipinization was accelerated.

One cause of irritation was the fact that Americans in some categories were paid at a higher rate than the Filipinos for the same class of work. This rule did not apply to lawyers, judges, Constabulary officers, doctors, etc., but did apply to clerical positions and others in the classified civil service.

For a long time and in various branches of government there were many jobs for which trained Filipinos could not be found. In most pursuits requiring scientific training it was years before young Filipinos could be brought through the different grades of schools, universities, and special training to give them the ability to deal helpfully with such matters as engineering, the veterinarian services, medicine, public hygiene, and the telegraph and telephone administration.

[1] With the gross public debt of only $1.26 per capita, the Philippine annual taxation was $1.82, which compares with $6.30 in Japan, $7.45 in the United States, and $17.87 in Great Britain. (The figures given are for 1908.)

Although bringing in American employees caused resentment in certain directions, this was not true in regard to schoolteachers; Americans were welcomed heartily. Almost all Filipinos wanted education; they liked the teachers and the teachers liked them. Scattered about in isolated towns and villages all over the Islands, these teachers became true crusaders preaching the advent of the modern era. They taught much more than mere book knowledge. They taught the American spirit, fairness in play, the dignity of labor, hygiene, beautification of home, and the spirit of democracy and progress. These brave American men and women gave the best that was in them; some of them lost their lives, and many gave the best part of their lives and their hearts to their work. They should be spoken of reverently.

One must also say a word for the fine work done by the Constabulary officers. Fewer in number but often no less in apostolic zeal were the doctors, engineers, and provincial treasurers.

The policy inaugurated by Governor Taft and followed by other civil officials in the Islands has been to treat the Filipinos as their social equals. Few, if any, important functions were held in the Governor-General's palace without an important representation of Filipinos. They were welcomed at receptions; they were invited to official banquets and unofficial meals; and the official balls participated in by high officials usually began with the *rigodon*, or dance of honor, at which the Governor-General took the ranking Filipino lady as his partner, and the wife of the Governor-General, or the highest ranking American lady present, went through the measured steps of this formal dance with the most prominent Filipino gentleman present.

In Manila, where society was large and very varied, it was natural that social groups should be formed and that the tendency of like seeking like should manifest itself in Americans forming most of their social contacts with people of their own race, as did the Spaniards, English, and Filipinos in their especial circles and clubs. In the provinces society was much more cosmopolitan; the Americans in each of the provincial capitals and in the outlying cities of importance were not numerous enough to form a society of their own and they were thrown into close social relation with the more prominent Filipinos among whom they lived. Warm, cordial, and lasting friendships were thus established.

A most potent influence for the establishment and maintenance of good relations between the Americans and Filipinos, after the Philippine Assembly came into being, was the wise and statesmanlike position of its leaders. The Honorable Sergio Osmeña, Speaker of the Assembly, believed so firmly in conciliatory and friendly dealing that he took occasion in the course of public addresses to give praise where he felt it could be given to the unselfish nature and efficiency of American work in the Islands.

Many years later, in 1944, Señor Osmeña outlined happily the growth of mutual good will and understanding between the Americans and Filipinos, in a speech before the Naval Academy Women's Club, at Annapolis, Maryland, from which the following excerpts are taken:

. . . the American soldiers are to be commended for their exemplary conduct during the military campaign in the islands.

Disregarding old colonial methods, America followed in the islands a policy that was humane, altruistic, and progressive. Her dealings with the people have been characterized not only by sincerity and good faith, but also by a spirit of liberalism, equality, and justice. She has complied with every promise made to them. She has administered the affairs of the islands as a true trustee not for her benefit but for the benefit and welfare of the Filipino people.

The Americans set themselves to put an end to certain established practices which they felt tended to social injustice. They had found a code of laws calculated to aid the privileged classes and hold the masses down; they found a general tendency among the leading Filipinos to protect men of wealth.

Native leaders showed more interest in the higher education of the few than in the general education of the masses. The rights of the laboring man had not been generally protected. It was this system of privilege which the Americans set themselves resolutely to bring to an end, and in that way to lay the foundations for a truer democracy.

While the Filipino proved himself an apt and adroit politician, it was natural that some time should elapse before he learned to submit to party discipline. There were at first some gropings and misunderstandings in regard to what platforms their political parties could adopt and permit while the country was under American control, but it was not long before it became evident that the desire for nationality was so strong in the Filipinos that the parties favoring nationality would get the majority of votes, and those standing for political affiliation with America would find themselves a hopeless minority.

The group of prominent Filipinos known as the Federal Party, whose early platform called for the continuance of American rule, had during Mr. Taft's term as Governor received many appointments to high places in the Government, among them three memberships of the Commission.

By act of the United States Congress it was provided that when the conditions of public order justified it a census of the Islands be taken, after which the Filipinos should be granted the right to elect an assembly which should act as the lower house. This house was to have legislative power over that part of the Islands occupied by the Christian and civilized Filipinos which, the census reported, came to 91 per cent of the total population, although, living as these did in regions with dense population, they did not occupy a proportionate part of the land, the amount being somewhat less than two-thirds of the Islands' area.

In 1906 a proposed law for the election of an Assembly, or lower house, of the Legislature was drafted by the Commission and submitted to a convention of elected provincial governors for suggested changes, after which it was offered for public discussion; and the resulting law was enacted by the Commission in January, 1907. General elections were called for July 30 of that year and the election held. Each of the 34 provinces was given at least one delegate, and for the larger provinces a delegate for every 90,000 population or major fraction thereof. The total number of representatives was 80.

As the time approached for the election, the partisans of immediate independence, whatever earlier party they had belonged to, were brought together to form the Nationalist Party under the leadership of Señor Sergio Osmeña, Señor Manuel Quezon, who later became floor leader, Señor Rafael Palma, Philippine Commissioner and later President of the University, and others.

In June, 1907, the elections were held, and were generally peaceable, the main issue being the future political status of the Islands.

The Federal Party changed its name to the Progressive Party with a platform calling for increased autonomy and eventual independence. The result was a decisive victory for the Nationalist Party.

Mr. Taft, Secretary of War, journeyed to the Philippine Islands to preside at the ceremonies incident to the inauguration of the Assembly, the date for which was set for the 16th of October, 1907.

Assemblyman Señor Sergio Osmeña, member of the Nationalist Party and only twenty-nine years of age, received the remarkable tribute of a unanimous election as Speaker, a position which he held by successive elections for fifteen years, during which period he guided the affairs of the Assembly. Señor Osmeña had prepared himself by a careful study of parliamentary law and procedure and brought to the position a pleasing personality, ready wit, great power of speech, and consummate tact. Throughout his long tenure of office he presided over the lower house of the Legislature with ability, impartiality, and great decorum.

The floor leader in that first house was Señor Manuel Quezon, also a Nationalist, a consummate orator, destined to play a very important rôle in the development of his country.

The first act of the Legislature was a resolution conveying to the President of the United States "their profound sentiments of gratitude and high appreciation of the signal concession made to the people of the Islands of participating directly in the making of the laws which shall govern them."

The Commission thereafter sat in the capacity of Senate, or upper house, in so far as they dealt with legislation affecting that portion of the territory occupied by the Christian and civilized peoples; and in its sole legislative capacity legislated and made appropriations, without concurrence of the lower house, for the regions occupied by the Moros and tribal people. This arrangement brought about some curious anomalies, but fortunately the Commission was able to smooth out difficulties as they arose and no insurmountable misunderstanding or controversy ensued. Where a proposed item of legislation was of general character the Commission adopted the practice of passing an identical law for the region over which they had exclusive control, and care was taken not to abuse the right to appropriate moneys from the general treasury for the benefit of the tribal peoples by appropriating disproportionate amounts. As at that time the Moro Province had its own revenues and sources of income no question about their use of public moneys was raised.

It was the policy of the American officials in the Islands, generally followed, to mix in no way with Philippine politics or local political parties, but to leave the Filipinos to direct from within the affairs of their own parties without interference and without advice except when asked. It was not long before a curious political situation developed. The Progressive Party, successor to the Federalists, originally organized with the approval of Mr. Taft and expected to coöperate with the American administration, now found itself with only a small minority of the delegates. As Señor Osmeña developed and pursued his policy of coöperation, the Progressives felt they must oppose his measures and gradually worked into the position of opposition to the Government their

MORO DWELLING

GENERAL JOHN J. PERSHING

party had been organized to support. And when, as was inevitably the case, in a party holding so large a majority, factions began to develop within the Nationalist Party, the Progressives were apt to side with the left wing or opposing element rather than to vote where they naturally belonged, namely on the right.

The Act of Congress had further provided that the two houses, the Commission and the Assembly, voting separately, should select two Resident Commissioners to the United States House of Representatives, where they were given the privilege of the floor with the right of debate but not the right to vote. The two first Resident Commissioners were the Señores Benito Legarda, a Progressive who had sat for many years on the Commission, and Pablo Ocampo, Nationalist.

Ensuing elections in 1909 and 1912 merely emphasized the strength of the Nationalist Party and the futility of any opposition party asking for votes that did not stand squarely for early independence. This was still further exemplified in 1916 when the Nationalists elected almost all their candidates and the Progressives lost all but one senator and seven assemblymen. At this time the Progressives gave up the struggle and a party known as the Democrata Party came into existence.

While it was inevitable that many measures originating in the Assembly should come up for consideration by the Commission carrying provisions which were not felt to be in the public interest and were struck out by the Commission, the matter was discussed amicably and the usual result was ultimate agreement. The Commission adopted the sympathetic practice of concurring in the passage of every bill desired by the Assembly which could be helpful to the situation or which in the opinion of the Commission would not be clearly injurious.

The rather irresponsible attacks of the native papers on the Government had often been leveled at the scale of expenditures which, as was easily proved, were extremely low when compared with the costs of similar items in other countries; but the delegates to Manila were quite generally convinced that the Government was extravagant and that one of their primary duties would be to reduce costs. The scale of wages necessary to lure Americans in one of the professions to the Islands was a natural object of attack, and the Filipinos generally failed to recognize that no fees, exactions, or extra emoluments attached to these positions, as had been frequently the case in the past. The call for reductions of costs finally came to a head in 1908 when the Assembly and the Commission failed to agree upon a general appropriation bill.

The Organic Act of the Philippine Government passed by Act of Congress provided that "if at the termination of any session the appropriations necessary for the support of government shall not have been made, an amount equal to the sums appropriated in the last appropriation bills for such purposes shall be deemed to be appropriated." Because of this provision, the failure to agree upon the appropriation bill in no way stopped or seriously hampered the existing operation of the government, though making extension and advances difficult. One vital question that arose in connection with the interpretation of this clause was whether the appropriation bills should be deemed to be reappropriated item by item, or as a lump sum, and whether or not it was discretionary with the Governor-General to reapportion these expenditures as between bureaus and offices and thus to change the purposes for which these moneys had been specifically allocated in the original bill. The decision of the Auditor, of the Attorney-General, and of the War Department, following a judicial interpretation of a similar clause in the organic act of Porto Rico, was to the effect that the total only was to be considered and that the Governor-General could allocate amounts in such proportions and for such purposes as seemed to him wise provided the total was not exceeded.

While the general appropriation bill failed of passage, there were numerous special bills enacted each carrying its appropriation and the development of government was not wholly retarded. The increasing revenues of the government were thus made available for the increasing needs of the people. There was never any difficulty in getting liberal appropriations for public works. Most of the provinces and municipalities had had projects more or less ambitious for local improvements; waterworks and other public utilities were in demand; highways, bridges, markets, school buildings, provincial offices, and irrigation systems were needed, and often profitable to build and operate.

Not only was the Assembly usually ready to concur in the appropriation for public works, but it frequently sent up to the Commission measures carrying large appropriations without due regard to available balances in the treasury. As this period (1908–1910) was one of rapidly expanding revenues the Legislature adopted the device of appropriating for public works a sum measurably in excess of the estimated balance of revenues available for such purposes, but with the conservative proviso that these appropriations were to be expended only when specifically released by executive order of the Governor-General. The revenues were watched from month to month, and whenever they exceeded the estimate for a safe balance in the treasury immediate release was made of sums for new public works.

An analysis of the labors of the Legislature reveals an impressive number of important measures which originated in the Assembly enacted into law. Among these are to be noted an insolvency law; employers' liability law; an act creating a code committee to revise civil, commercial, and penal procedure; the negotiable instruments law; an act providing for the exercise of eminent domain; an irrigation law; and the cadastral law.

The Assembly early showed its interest in labor by passing a bill creating a bureau of labor; in agriculture by a bill creating an agricultural bank; in giving women part in public affairs by making them eligible or mandatory in certain positions. It approved the establishment of nurses' training schools. Additional concessions were granted the railroad company, and interest was guaranteed on bonds of the same.

The Assembly was misled into making one rather serious error in 1909 when it passed unanimously a resolution opposing the extension of free trade between the United States and the Philippine Islands. This came at the time when the so-called Payne Bill in August of 1909 was under consideration. Congress wisely disregarded this vote of the Assembly which was in part due to a misunderstanding of the attitude of the Commission. The advantageous effect of this law in the Islands was abundantly proved by the results. The fall in customs revenue was soon more than balanced by the increased collection of internal revenue.

In certain instances measures desired by the Commission met with difficulties in the Assembly. In some such cases the Commission took action in its sole legislative capacity passing laws making them applicable to that portion of the country over which it held exclusive legislative control. Some of these were soon afterwards enacted for the whole country by appropriate Assembly action.

The character of the men elected to the Assembly was in large measure responsible for the good record of that body under the guidance of its Speaker, Señor Sergio Osmeña, who steered them away from petty politics and directed their energies towards matters of practical and economic value.

In August, 1916, the so-called Jones Bill became law, and provided for an elected Philippine Senate. This did away wholly with any difference in legislative control over the territory occupied by civilized people and tribal peoples and Moros, but gave the Governor-General power to appoint representatives of these latter in each of the houses. Up to the date of the passage of this bill (1916) the Governor-General had had no veto power; the Commission, however, acting as the upper house, could refuse a concurrence in Assembly bills; under the Jones law the Governor-General was given the right to veto and the Legislature was given the right to pass measures over the veto, but the President of the United States could approve or veto such measures. With the passage of the Jones law in 1916, elections took on even more significance because of the provision of an elective senate as the upper house of the Legislature in place of the appointed Commission. Special elections were held in October of that year, and of the twenty-two elected senators all but one were Nationalists. Of the two appointed senators representing the Moros and tribal peoples, one joined the Nationalists and one declared himself independent of either party.

In 1917, the Progressive and National Democrata parties agreed on a platform of absolute and immediate independence and united to form the new Partido Democrata. This platform, as revised in 1930, was profuse and very carelessly drawn. It covered fifty points and included many needed reforms, besides some very radical and occasionally socialistic matter.

The general elections in 1919 were held under the suffrage provisions of the Jones law, which reduced the age requirement from twenty-three to twenty-one years and the educational qualification by including men able to read and write a native language, whereas formerly the requirement had been ability to speak, read and write English or Spanish.

The new party succeeded in electing but one senator and four representatives.

Following 1919 the Nationalist Party suffered the result of too large a majority and split into factions, Señor Quezon setting up a new party under the title of Partido Nacionalista Colectivista, the platform of which declared for "absolute, immediate, and complete independence, and complete trade reciprocity between the Islands and the United States, before and after independence."

No party had a majority in either house of the Legislature; the Democratas made a distinct gain. Señor Quezon was elected President of the Senate, while his candidate, Manuel Roxas, was elected Speaker of the lower house. Before the elections of 1925, however, the Nationalist and Colectivista parties joined forces as the Partido Nacionalista-Consolidado under the united leadership of Señores Quezon and Osmeña. While repeating the demand for independence, among other things it stood for the adoption of English as the official language of the Government. In the elections of 1925 the Nationalists continued their unbroken record of electing a large majority of the Legislature.

Reviewing this period it can be fairly said that the two major parties, both committed to Philippine independence, had differences that were largely those of the leaders, and differences of platform dealing mainly with matters of minor significance so far as concerns the relations between the Islands and the United States.

One of the most significant incidents in the history of political parties in the Islands was the organization early in 1926 of the *Consejo Supremo Nacional*, or National Supreme Council, by the directorates of both the major parties, the Consolidated Nationalists and the Democratas, for the direction of Philippine policy "in all that concerns the campaign for independence, all matters which may affect the relations between the United States and the Philippines, and the administration of the interests of the country in general."

The Council as organized comprised ten members, five from each of the two parties. Señor Manuel Quezon as its presiding officer became the chosen leader of both parties for the purposes of the coalition.

The record of the conduct of elections from 1901 onward is remarkably free from acts of violence, and in no instance were the forces of the United States called upon to intervene.

Further evidence of this is to be found in a message to the Philippine Legislature sent by Governor-General Wood in 1922 as follows:

I congratulate you, and through you the Filipino people, on the orderly and lawful conduct of the recent elections, which, notwithstanding the keenness of the struggle and the appearance of a strong new party in the field, were conducted with due regard to the rights of the candidates and with an absence of fraud and irregularity which would be a credit to any people.

While the elections thus were orderly, the defeated candidates not infrequently charged fraud, corruption, and intimidation. The election law had to be changed more than once to provide new safeguards. There were numerous contests and some disqualifications of elected officers as a result of evidence of improper procedure.

CHAPTER XII

LATER RÉGIMES

THE INAUGURATION of President Wilson in 1913 marked the close of an era in Philippine history, the results of which it is appropriate to summarize. There had been sixteen continuous years of Republican administration in Washington, and during fifteen of these the United States had been responsible for the Philippine Islands. In this period the trade between the Islands and the States had increased by leaps and bounds, having jumped from some six millions of dollars in Spanish days to forty-five million dollars in 1913.

The Islands had been pacified, their laws reconstructed, and a very workable and economical government set up, of which Professor Albert Bushnell Hart, who held the chair of government at Harvard University, said after visiting the Islands:

. . . the government is brisk, novel and aggressive — a fine example of Western energy. In fact the régime of the Philippine Islands is one of the marked successes of the American people. It stands high among the tropical colonial governments of Christendom, for the skill with which it is framed and the efficiency with which it is carried on; it is immeasurably the best government that has ever been known within the Archipelago; furthermore, it is not too much to say that no territory, no city and no State within the United States has a system of government so carefully thought out, so well concentrated and so harmonious in its parts as that of the Philippine Islands.

People who had been out of work had returned to the soil and to such few factories as existed, and were industriously and profitably engaged. Successive steps involving increased autonomy had followed in orderly progression. The Filipinos had early been given the right to elect the officials of the cities and towns; soon afterwards they had been given the right to elect the governors of the provinces; then the majority of the provincial boards; and finally the lower house of their Legislature.

The policy of Filipinization of the service had been adhered to consistently by the succeeding Governors-General of the Islands, who had uniformly exerted their influence to have qualified Filipinos preferred in appointments.

By a process of careful selection, preparation, and supervision, the American administration had gradually built up a body of Filipino officials and employees who generally rendered good service and, by so doing, agreeably disappointed those who had opposed their appointment.

The following table gives more graphically than words an idea of the progress which had been made:

APPOINTED OFFICERS AND EMPLOYEES, PHILIPPINE GOVERNMENT SERVICE

Year	Total	Americans		Filipinos	
		Number	Per cent	Number	Per cent
1903	5474	2777	51	2697	49
1904	6605	3228	49	3377	51
1905	7330	3307	45	4023	55
1907	6518	2616	40	3902	60
1908	6559	2479	38	4080	62
1909	7056	2659	38	4397	62
1910	7272	2633	36	4639	64
1911	7614	2633	35	4981	65
1912	8713	2680	31	6033	69
1913	8986	2623	29	6363	71

Note: The increases in the number of Americans in the years 1904, 1905, 1909, and 1912 were due to appointments of civil engineers, surveyors, and other technical and professional personnel.

While this table speaks in numbers, it does not give the picture as it looked to the Filipino. He naturally wanted the place that carried the greater dignity and paid the highest salary. The policy of Filipinization from the bottom up — that is, by promotion from the lower positions as a result of proved efficiency — was all too slow for his humor. Filipinization of the positions of clerks, portmasters in small towns, and other lesser posts of the government interested him very little. Even the substitution of Filipinos for Americans as provincial treasurers to supervise the collection of internal and local revenues passed almost unobserved, as did the increase in the proportion of Filipino Constabulary officers.

Thus, when the percentage of Filipinos in the service moved in four years from sixty-two to seventy-one per cent, this fact passed almost wholly unnoticed, whereas a single appointment of an American to a judgeship was certain to provoke critical comments.

In view of the fact that stability of government was the most important element in preparing the Filipinos for nationality, it behooved the government to proceed in this matter of Filipinization with due caution. The logical policy of advancing men from the lower positions, and testing them well before their permanent promotion was determined, conformed to the American plan of giving the Filipinos sound training in self-government and was believed by thoughtful American and Filipino observers to be the one under which the advance toward a really stable government by Filipinos would ultimately prove to be most rapid.

It would have been hard to find in any government or even in private business the equal of the American members of the Philippine service for loyalty, enthusiasm, diligence, and the spirit that wins. None of them worked merely for pay; their interest was in the service. None of them watched the clock; they knew not when their day's work ended. They all worked to the limit of their capacity to work — and that was great. One cannot speak in too high terms of these men who, in an alien country and a strange climate, with an ungrateful government at home giving them half-hearted support, which later failed most of them altogether, devoted themselves consistently and unselfishly to their hard and altruistic work for a people who at the time had little appreciation of the full measure of their service.

The measure of success achieved by the administration in the Islands was principally due to the admirable quality of men who had finally worked their way to the positions of responsibility in administering the bureaus and offices of the government. It is an axiom of business that a good manager can make almost any business succeed, and a poor manager can make almost any business fail. The bureaus of the Philippine government were fortunate in having almost uniformly superlatively good managers, men who have subsequently made their mark in various activities — and this holds true not only of the chiefs of the bureaus but also of many of their assistants and men holding lesser positions.

With all the misunderstandings, heartburnings, and mistakes on the part of Americans and Filipinos, still in the last analysis it could be fairly said that the old hostile spirit of the insurrection had been lived down and that the United States enjoyed the friendship of the Filipinos.

The government was particularly strict in the rectitude of its employees toward government money and property, and even the acceptance or use of free passes or any other franking privilege by government employees was prohibited by executive order.

Among the many lines of governmental activity, five, either by reason of their importance or their backwardness, were receiving especial attention from the administration: first, road and bridge construction and maintenance; second, the reduction of rinderpest (the disease had been confined to one extremely limited area); third, placing the titles of the occupied lands in the hands of the occupants, for which an organized campaign was under way; fourth, control of locusts; and fifth, irrigation.

In these fifteen years of devoted labor there had been substantial progress in the matter of public works. The record of achievement included the construction of nearly six hundred schoolhouses, besides a number of provincial and municipal buildings and public markets; more than five thousand permanent bridges and culverts; the boring of nearly a thousand artesian wells, and progress on a number of irrigation projects.

More than seven thousand miles of general coast line had been surveyed and charted, over a hundred additional lighthouses had been built, and the coasts were comparatively safe for navigation.

The great port of Manila had been deepened, protected, and made safe. Cebu, Iloilo, and minor ports had also been developed, and the result was an improvement in commerce shown by an increase in oversea tonnage cleared from little over 300,000 in 1899 to nearly 2,000,000 in 1913.

Telegraph receipts increased from about eighty thousand dollars in 1906 to more than two hundred and eighty thousand in 1913.

The postal revenue had nearly trebled in the ten years 1903-13 and the money orders had increased from less than three million dollars to more than eight million dollars. A postal savings bank had been established where Filipinos could deposit their savings. The bank had forty thousand depositors, of whom thirty-three thousand were Filipinos, and deposits amounting to a million and a quarter dollars.

The English language was rapidly becoming a language for the people. Instruction in all the government schools was conducted in it. The annual enrollment in the public schools had been about four hundred and thirty thousand. By 1913 there must have been passed through the schools well over a million Filipinos who had learned enough English to communicate with each other.

Progress in health had been no less striking and satisfactory. The death rate in Manila had been reduced from 44 per 1000 population in 1901 to 22.48 in 1913, and for the civilized population throughout the Islands from 26.59 in 1904 to 18.82 in 1913.

A pure food and drugs law had been enacted and enforced.

Justice was being regularly administered in the courts. Although there was still occasional delay in reaching decisions, justice was administered more rapidly than is often the case in the United States.

The weather service was the most scientific and modern of any in the Orient.

Weights and measures had been defined by law and penalties provided for fraudulent practices. The Islands were in advance of the United States in that the metric system was established.

The system of taxation had been modernized: a land tax established, the customs tariff revised to bear more heavily upon luxuries, and internal revenue taxes imposed upon alcoholic liquors and manufactured tobacco. The per capita rate of taxation was lower than in any other country receiving the benefits of free primary schools and other modern public services. The public debt of the Islands was almost nominal, amounting in all to $12,000,000, or $1.27 per capita.

Sometime in 1912 the Governor-General asked the Commanding General how long he could defend Manila against a powerful invading force. General Duvall replied "Two weeks." The Governor then asked the Insular Treasurer how long it would take to move the treasure to Corregidor. The answer was six weeks.

Immediate plans were then made for the early construction of vaults and by June, 1913, the transfer of the treasure was complete. Later events proved this to have been a fortunate arrangement.

Financially the government was entirely solvent, and had been living comfortably within its revenues, its current expenses being about two-thirds of its usual income. One-fourth of the balance was needed for fixed charges, leaving usually about $3,500,000 a year available for extraordinary expenses and public works out of revenue. In the four years 1910–13, there had been about $11,000,000 of revenues spent on public works for the insular government only.

There had been an extraordinary growth in the business of the Islands, the gross foreign and internal trade having increased seventy-eight per cent in four years to the sum of $446,000,000. Of the increase about three-quarters was increase in the trade within the limits of the Islands.

It is a noteworthy fact that the commercial business of the Islands, from the retail trade — generally carried on by small Chinese tradesmen — to the important export houses, was almost entirely in the hands of foreigners. The business conducted by the Filipino in the early days was largely the development of natural resources.

A serious obstacle to the development of the tourist trade was the fact that before 1912 Manila did not possess an adequate and modern hotel.

One of the earlier mistakes made by the Commission had been the purchase for use as an office building of the best hotel building in the city. This action was severely criticized by the merchants, but there was neither the capital nor the degree of coöperation between Americans in the Islands necessary to build a new hotel. It was not until June, 1912, that the new Manila Hotel was opened to the public, the government having assisted in the construction by purchasing a substantial bond issue.

Sentiment in the United States in regard to the Philippine Islands varied from apathy on the part of many to keen interest on the part of those for whom the American experiment in the Islands had a romantic appeal. Some felt that the Islands were an unnecessary expense, and asked wherein their interests were served by the expenditure of a considerable sum of money to maintain sovereignty over an alien people on the other side of the world. They did not realize the importance of the trade relationship nor the advantages of a depot at the gateway to China.

The Anti-Imperialist League of Boston continued its protest against all Americans activities in the Philippine Islands. Their efforts might perhaps have been more effective if they had not been so violent in their denunciations of American administration in the Philippine Islands.

In January and February, 1913, the Honorable William A. Jones, representative in the United States Congress from Virginia and chairman of the House Committee on Insular Affairs, took occasion to rise on the floor of the House and deliver an extremely bitter attack on the Philippine administration in general and Governor-General Forbes in particular. His charges, replete with misstatements, were based largely on information given him by persons recently separated from the service and hence desirous of making things disagreeable for those who had got them out.

Mr. Jones gave especial attention to the failure of the government to agree with the Filipinos in the matter of appropriations, but the information from which he derived his material was so utterly at variance with the facts that he failed to mention correctly a single reason for the disagreement. For example, he gave as one of the causes of disagreement the high salaries paid to American Commissioners and secretaries of departments, whereas in fact the bill passed by the Assembly contained no change in these salaries, nor had the question been raised. He charged the Governor-General with arbitrary misuse of the power given him by law to carry on the appropriations of the preceding year, but did not mention that the changes which the Governor-General made amounted to less than three-twentieths of one per cent of the amount of items found in the previous bill.

In regard to the expenditure of public money by the Philippine government, Congressman Jones was especially vitriolic, charging "that much of it . . . was needlessly and shamefully wasted, and that the benefits derived from its expenditure, even in those cases where the expenditure was proper, have rarely, if ever, been commensurate with the cost." And he proposed at some later date to reveal "to what extent the Government we have imposed upon the Filipinos has been extravagant and wasteful."

Governor-General Forbes did not feel that he could let such a virulent attack go unanswered, and he employed, for the purpose of preparing an answer, the services of a sympathetic and very competent friend and lawyer practicing in Manila, Mr. J. Hamilton Lawrence, who drew a masterly reply setting forth the facts in parallel columns to the charges, which he published and distributed widely under the caption "Reply to Jones."

Presidents Roosevelt, Taft, and Harding, the two former while President and the latter as Senator of the United States and chairman of the Senate Committee concerned with Philippine affairs, publicly supported the insular administration in no uncertain terms.

President Roosevelt said:

. . . I believe that I am speaking with historic accuracy and impartiality when I say that the American treatment of and attitude toward the Filipino people, in its combination of disinterested ethical purpose and sound common sense, marks a new and long stride forward, in advance of all steps that have hitherto been taken along the path of wise and proper treatment of weaker by stronger races.

President Taft expressed his opinion of American policy in the Islands even more emphatically when he said in 1913:

Some criticism has been made of the character of the government in the Philippines as being tyrannical, and as also having been wasteful. I speak with very considerable knowledge of the government for the first half of the last decade, because I was in the islands, and with a good deal of information about the government since that time because I have been more or less responsible for it, and I affirm that there has been no such instance of success in colonial government in the history of world's colonies as the administration of the Philippine Islands. There has been no colony in which the welfare of the people of the colony has been the sole guide in its management, and in which there has been such an ambitious program for the education of the people and the fitting of them for self-government.

President Taft, moreover, in an interview with the Governor-General in 1912, made the statement that he had had it come back to him from every direction, from Americans and from foreigners, that the American experiment in the Philippine Islands was a success and a greater success than similar efforts in foreign countries. He said that sometimes they might not believe in the theories of government which had been established but that they had to admit the success of the work.

Senator Harding spoke in the Senate of America's work as "the most magnificent contribution of a nation's unselfishness ever recorded in the history of the world."

These expressions of approval of the work of the American government in the Philippine Islands cannot, however, be regarded as wholly impartial, as they came from the lips of men who held a measure of responsibility for the conditions they described; and it is gratifying to find these views supported by persons qualified to judge who were politically independent and in no way connected with the government.

One of the most authoritative endorsements which the Philippine government received came from Governor-General Lamothe of Cochin China in 1905. He said:

I spent four months in the Philippines, studying the results of American control. I was struck with the enormous progress made in such a comparatively brief period. This has been greater during the last four years than during the 350 years preceding the American occupation. The natives are being educated, are receiving the benefits of municipal and provincial liberty and are rapidly acquiring the spirit of republican institutions. France can take a most beneficial lesson from the splendid results of the American colonial system.

Competent judges of the administration of dependencies found much to praise in what they saw in the Islands. A good many came disposed to criticize and left filled with enthusiasm. One patriotic American told the Governor-General as he left that he had never been so proud of being an American citizen as he was after he had seen the work that was being done in the Philippine Islands.

During fourteen and a half years of American occupation of the Philippine Islands under Republican administrators in Washington, the government of the Islands had been conducted upon a strictly non-partisan basis. That this was carried out in practice was well proved by the character of the appointees, not only to the position of Governor-General of the Islands, but throughout the service.

Up to 1901 the administration had been in military hands, the officers being chosen primarily for military purposes. From the inauguration of Civil Governor Taft to the resignation of Governor-General Forbes, a period of twelve years and almost two months, the office of Governor-General was occupied by Republicans for only three years and fourteen days of the time. The Democrats, Governors-General Wright and Smith, held office for five years, three months, and twenty days; and Governor-General Forbes, an independent in politics, held the position for three years, nine months, and twenty days.

Ex-President Roosevelt in a letter to ex-Governor-General Forbes wrote: "As you know I administered the Islands absolutely without regard to politics. Both Luke Wright and Smith were Democrats and you, when I appointed you, were, as I understood it, either a Democrat or a Mugwump."

All the Governors and members of the Commission, whether Republican or Democrat, left their partisan views behind them when they sailed from the United States, and served purely as Americans. There was no fundamental difference of opinion among them as to the policies desirable in the administration of the Philippine Islands.

Moreover, the bureau chiefs and other American officers of government were absolutely non-partisan and held themselves generally aloof from political matters at home or in the Philippine Islands. Naturally enough, most of them had belonged to one or another party and a few remained active workers. The Philippine Islands were recognized in the national conventions of the Republican and of the Democratic parties in the United States and were given the right to elect delegates from the Islands to vote in national conventions. These delegates were consulted when it came to writing the Philippine plank for their party.

In 1912, the Democrats in the Islands found themselves in a somewhat difficult predicament. They were generally in sympathy with the policy of the United States in the Islands and as loyal Americans desired to support it, and yet they could not very well support and strengthen the Republican Party. The result of this situation was a split in the Democratic ranks and preparation of two sets of resolutions. Judge Ross, the leader of the regular conservative faction, asked, among other things, for "such legislation as will fix a definite policy with reference to this archipelago, providing for the retention of the islands until such time as, in the opinion of Congress, the Filipino people may be prepared for self-government, thus removing them from the arena of contending party politics in National elections."

A dissenting group bolted and prepared a sharp resolution condemning the Republican Party and its leader, President Taft, by name, whom they charged with "foisting an autocratic bureaucracy upon the people of these islands," and recommended "that in the best interests of the Filipino people, and for the most complete fulfilment of the moral obligation of the United States towards these people, that they should be declared by the Congress of the United States to be an integral part and territory of the United States of America."

It will be seen that neither of these platforms supported independence.

In 1912 Governor Woodrow Wilson, of New Jersey, was elected President. President Taft himself in a speech before the Ohio Society on January 29, 1913, expressed the opinion that the Philippine issue was in no sense a determining factor in the campaign.

The election of Wilson was hailed with great demonstrations of joy by the Filipinos. With the announcement of his election in Manila, they immediately assumed that great political concessions were to be made and perhaps even independence be given.

Interest naturally centered upon the personal views of the newly elected President in regard to the future status of the Islands. In a lecture delivered in 1907 he had said:

. . . Self-government is not a mere form of institutions. . . . It is a form of character. It follows upon the long discipline which gives people self-possession, self-mastery, the habit of order and peace and common counsel, and a reverence for law which will not fail when they themselves become the makers of law: the steadiness and self-control of political maturity. And these things cannot be had without long discipline. . . .

. . . We can give the Filipinos constitutional government, a government which they may count upon to be just, a government based upon some clear and equitable understanding, intended for their good and not for our aggrandizement; but we must ourselves for the present supply that government. . . . But we cannot give them self-government. Self-government is not a thing that can be "given" to any people, because it is a form of character and not a form of constitution. No people can be "given" the self-control of maturity. Only a long apprenticeship of obedience can secure them the precious possession, a thing no more to be bought than given. . . .

We of all people in the world should know these fundamental things and should act upon them, if only to illustrate the mastery in politics which belongs to us of hereditary right. To ignore them would be not only to fail and fail miserably, but to fail ridiculously and belie ourselves. Having ourselves gained self-government by a definite process which can have no substitute, let us put the people dependent upon us in the right way to gain it also.

In 1912, in a speech as Democratic nominee for President, he is reported to have said:

In dealing with the Philippines, we should not allow ourselves to stand upon any mere point of pride, as if, in order to keep our countenance in the families of nations, it were necessary for us to make the same blunders of selfishness that other nations have made. We are not the owners of the Philippine Islands. We hold them in trust for the people who live in them. They are theirs, for the uses of their life. We are not even their partners. It is our duty, as trustees, to make whatever arrangement of government will be most serviceable to their freedom and development. Here, again, we are to set up the rule of justice and of right.

Acting upon a suggestion made by his friend Walter H. Page, later his Ambassador to Great Britain, he sent Professor Henry Jones Ford, of Princeton, out to make a secret investigation of conditions in the Islands. Professor Ford traveled extensively through them without revealing to any official of the government the object of his visit, until finally he came to Baguio and showed his credentials to the Governor-General, asking for explanation of many points upon which he had heard critical comment.

In his report, presented in September, 1913, he devoted a good deal of attention to the character of the people, which he rated as high, and naturally dwelt at length on education, a quarter of the report being devoted to that subject. He paid a high tribute to the degree of literacy found in the Islands, dwelling on the very large proportion of the people who could read and write their native dialect.

He paid high tribute to the achievements in sanitation and road construction, and devoted a good deal of attention to the Benguet Road and to Baguio, the permanence of which as a health resort he felt "to be assured."

He described the situation as being "inflamed throughout" and said: "Filipino resentment of American rule is apparently not mitigated by appreciation of the achievements of American administration."

He found that the form of government was such as to produce "chronic discord," and spoke of a "continual friction . . . mitigated by the habitual suavity of the Assembly leaders."

He concluded that the American administration had been attended by greater success "in organizing the Philippines and fitting the country

ENTRANCE TO UNDERGROUND RIVER, PALAWAN

BACUIT BAY, PALAWAN

TYPICAL SCHOOL BUILDING

for self-government" than he had supposed; that the "present temporary form of government has done its work and has quite filled out its term of usefulness."

Finally, as he felt the work of the Philippine Commission had been accomplished, he recommended its abolition and the election of delegates to a convention to frame a constitution "establishing a government autonomous in character and republican in form," to go into effect at such time as the President of the United States should designate.

A supplementary report went so far as to indicate that unless an early change were made an insurrection was likely to ensue.

Professor Ford must have lent credence to singularly incompetent witnesses, as practically everyone conversant with the situation, whether army officer or civilian, foreigner, American, or Filipino, knew that there was absolutely no danger of insurrection and that any such representation disregarded the fundamental strength of the situation.

Meanwhile, President-elect Wilson had taken occasion, while making an address at Staunton, Virginia, on the 28th of December, 1912, to say: "The Philippines are at present our frontier but I hope we presently are to deprive ourselves of that frontier."

The effect of these few words was disastrous to the Philippine Islands. They settled down like a wet, cold blanket over the merchants, manufacturers, and other men of business. Up to the date of that speech the imports had exceeded the official estimates so that the customs revenues of the Islands were one-half million dollars more than had been figured in the forecast of the preceding year. Acting on this unexpected prosperity, the Legislature had been quite liberal in its appropriations, confident that the increase would continue. Beginning with the first of January, 1913, the customs fell off at the alarming rate of about two hundred thousand dollars per month, until by July 1 the loss of revenues reached a total of more than a million dollars.

Fortunately appropriations for public works contained the precautionary clause that they were not to be expended until released by executive action of the Governor-General. Thus all orders for public works which had not gone so far as to entail great loss to the government were cancelled. Each one of the bureaus was ordered to reduce all expenditure and return the largest possible amount of unexpended appropriation, and the government was ransacked for items and unexpended balances that could be covered back into the treasury.

To meet this situation the Governor-General issued an order for every bureau, excepting those of Education and Constabulary, to make a horizontal cut of five per cent in their expenses and, further, the Governor-General appointed an "Efficiency Committee" to scrutinize the operations of the bureaus and to recommend further economies.

On March 4, President Wilson took the oath of office. President Wilson in his first annual message to Congress outlined what seemed to be a consistent theory upon which the Democrats in Washington and their representatives in Manila were to proceed. He said:

Step by step we should extend and perfect the system of self-government in the islands, making test of them and modifying them as experience discloses their successes and their failures; that we should more and more put under the control of the native citizens of the archipelago the essential instruments of their life, their local instrumentalities of government. . . .

He proceeded to inject party politics squarely into the government of the Islands.

In August, 1913, President Wilson appointed Congressman Francis Burton Harrison, of New York, a member of Tammany Hall, to be Governor-General, the first to be appointed without any previous experience in the Islands to equip him for the complicated duties he was to undertake.

Interest naturally centered upon Representative Harrison's views in regard to the Islands. Four years previously he had made a speech on the floor of Congress, when the Payne Tariff Bill was under consideration, in which he had expressed himself as being sympathetic with the Filipinos' aspiration for independence, and urged that his people honestly endeavor to prepare them.

In his initial address, October 6, 1913, to the citizens of the Philippine Islands, Governor-General Harrison said among other things:

Every step we take will be taken with a view to the ultimate independence of the islands and as a preparation for that independence. And we hope to move toward that end as rapidly as the safety and the permanent interests of the islands will permit. After each step taken experience will guide us to the next.

The administration will take one step at once and will give to the native citizens of the islands a majority in the appointive Commission and thus in the upper as well as in the lower house of the legislature a majority representation will be secured to them.

Within the scope of my office as Governor-General I shall do my utmost to aid in the fulfillment of our promises, confident that we shall thereby hasten the coming of the day of your independence. . . .

In promising you on behalf of the administration immediate control of both branches of your legislature I remind you however that for the present we are responsible to the world for your welfare and your progress. Until your independence is complete we shall demand of you unremitting recognition of our sovereignty.

Almost immediately after Governor-General Harrison's arrival in the Islands, he requested the resignation of Commissioner Branagan and all four Filipino Commissioners, and cabled Washington requesting the immediate acceptance of Vice-Governor Gilbert's resignation. There were vacancies in the portfolios of Commerce and Police and of Interior at the time. The Filipino members of the Commission, able, loyal, and high-minded gentlemen, who had faithfully served the American government, were the Honorable José Luzuriaga, one of the first three Filipinos appointed to the Commission; the Honorable Gregorio Araneta, holding the portfolio of Finance and Justice; the Honorable Juan Sumulong; and the Honorable Rafael Palma.

The Filipinos were thunderstruck. The removal of the Americans could be understood, though only as a partisan measure. But why strike at loyal and capable Filipinos for no fault except support of the policies of the American administration? These patriotic and able Filipinos felt themselves humiliated by the new power in Washington. It is hard to conceive what good end could have been gained by this unmerited rebuke to loyal friends of America in the Islands.

With the exception of that of Commissioner Palma, the one Nationalist member of the Commission, who held over under appointment of June 30, 1908, all these resignations were accepted.

There was, however, no effort on the part of Governor-General Harrison to bring out a swarm of "deserving Democrats" and he resisted any pressure to this end brought to bear by aspirants for office or by Democratic party leaders.

President Wilson appointed the Honorable Henderson S. Martin, of Kansas, a Democrat, Vice-Governor, with the portfolio of Public Instruction; General Clinton L. Riggs, of Baltimore, a Democrat, Secretary of Commerce and Police; and Winfred T. Denison of New York, a Progressive, Secretary of the Interior. The last appointment was undoubtedly intended to preserve the appearance of a nonpartisan Commission. The Republicans were not represented; nor had any American appointed any experience whatever in the Philippine Islands or in the administration of any other dependency; nor could any of them speak Spanish.

The Filipino vacancies upon the Commission were filled by the immediate appointment of four new Filipino members, the Honorable Victorino Mapa, transferred from the Supreme Court to be Secretary of Finance and Justice, the Honorable Vicente Singson Encarnacion, a leader of the Progressive Party, the Honorable Jaime C. de Veyra, and the Honorable Vicente Ilustre, one of the irreconcilable group, reported to be anti-American in his sentiments.

Governor-General Harrison on the day of his arrival called for the resignation of the Assistant Executive Secretary, and shortly afterward for the resignations of other high officials of the government, including the Collector of Customs, Director of Lands, Chief of Police of the City of Manila, and some of their assistants.

It is hard to conceive the panicky frame of mind with which these announcements were received by the men who had devoted their lives to the service with the earnestness of crusaders, to use the phrase of one of the keenest of local observers. They had thrown in their fortunes for better or worse to serve the American government in the Philippine Islands. None of them had saved much, if any, money. Many had lost opportunities for a safe establishment at home in lucrative and permanent employment and had gone to those far-flung islands to do what they felt to be God's work in helping the Filipinos. Many of them found their health greatly impaired — too much so to return to a cold climate, such as that from which they had come, and begin again. Moreover, many of them had leave allowances which could be granted or withheld in the discretion of the Governor-General.

This feeling became so intense that Governor-General Harrison authorized Executive Secretary Carpenter to call a meeting of the bureau chiefs and inform them that no further resignations would be requested. The reassuring effect of this, however, was in large measure nullified by a peremptory call for two additional resignations on the following day.

Following these abrupt removals, important more for the high position of the men removed than for the number of persons concerned, Governor-General Harrison supported an appropriation bill, which shortly was unanimously passed by the reorganized Legislature, and which provided a horizontal cut in the higher salaries in a way that reduced the emoluments of the more important Americans in the service, who thus bore the brunt of the reduction. This satisfied a very insistent

demand on the part of the Filipinos for a reduction of the salaries paid
to the Americans in the service.

This action was received by the Americans in the service as aimed
directly at them. Many offered their resignations and all were so disturbed that Governor-General Harrison felt it necessary to issue what
he intended to be a further reassuring statement as follows:

> . . . I know of no reason for apprehension on the part of government em-
> ployees as to the permanence of their offices excepting as they may be affected by
> the consolidation of bureaus under plans which are already known to the public
> and which are being discussed daily in the newspapers.
>
> I wish, therefore, to make it plain that this administration does not contem-
> plate a wholesale reduction in either American or Filipino employees. Those men
> and women now in the employ of the government whose services have been satis-
> factory and continue to be satisfactory have not the slightest cause to fear that their
> positions will be taken away from them.
>
> I hope this announcement will settle finally the unrest and uncertainty which
> I am told has followed certain changes deemed necessary soon after my arrival
> here, and put down the unfounded and dangerous rumors which I am now told
> are in circulation. I wish government employees to continue to enjoy that sense
> of security, which I promise shall surround them so long as they deserve such
> consideration.
>
> As I have pointed out, the financial condition of the government does not war-
> rant the fear that the policy of retrenchment which will be followed will affect in
> any great degree the personnel of the government.

In spite of these reassuring words, separations from the service continued. Among those leaving were to be noted several bureau chiefs and
many especially qualified men. On July 1, 1920, there were but 582
Americans left in the service, and an analysis of the roster for 1921 discloses the fact that of those left only 298 had been in the service at the
time of Governor-General Harrison's arrival in the Islands. Of the
more than 2600 American employees to whom he addressed his assurances in the fall of 1913, only eleven per cent were on the roster eight
years later, and of these nearly one-half were teachers.

In the earlier years of Governor-General Harrison's administration this
matter became the subject of extremely bitter comment and criticisms
which found their way into the public press. The Governor-General
himself devoted nearly a third of his first report to an analysis of the
changes and the causes leading up to them.

The uncertainty in regard to the political future of the Islands probably contributed more than anything else to the continued uneasiness

that prevailed among the American civil servants in the Islands, and this reached such a pitch that the bureau chiefs gave their unanimous approval to a so-called retirement act supported by Governor-General Harrison. The bill provided a retirement allowance for those who had six years' service graded upward to a maximum of a year's full pay to those who had ten years' service, but with the extraordinary proviso that to avail themselves of the provision of the act officials of the government must tender their resignations in writing before the first of the ensuing July.

The practical effect of this law was to deprive every officer of the government who presented his resignation of the protection offered him by the civil service law. By merely accepting the resignation without giving any reason the Governor-General could terminate such officer's employment. A further provision reducing the salary attached to a position so vacated to two-thirds its former amount practically precluded the possibility of replacing Americans with other competent Americans.

In 1916 Governor-General Harrison reported: "With 50 exceptions, all the 1064 Americans who were eligible applied before the date on which applications ceased to be permissible. . . ."

The annual record of separations of Americans from the service from 1903 is shown in the table on the following page.

Professor Thomas Lindsey Blayney, a Democrat and friend of President Wilson, visited the Philippine Islands and other parts of the Orient and took occasion to study the Philippine situation, making every effort to inform himself by interviewing men in all walks of life. He did not hesitate in 1916 to speak of the policies of the administration of his party in the Islands as "demoralizing."

In his first message to the Legislature and in his later reports, Governor-General Harrison commented with some bitterness on the condition of the treasury which he found and severely criticized the financial conduct of the government by his predecessor. The points he made were: first, that the balance available for appropriation, or surplus, in the treasury was too low; second, that the scale of expenditures upon which the government was embarked was greater than the prospective revenues could support; and third, that the preceding administration had for the three years prior to 1913 paid out annually from one to one and a quarter million dollars, and in the calendar year 1913 alone more than three and a half millions, in excess of its ordinary income, thus reducing what he spoke of as the "available surplus."

There can be no question that Governor-General Harrison was mis-informed by the Auditor. The government had tried to carry a reserve of two million dollars for unforeseen contingencies. Such a contingency had arisen in the early months of 1913 in the loss of more than a million dollars of revenue from the collection of customs only, following Presi-dent-elect Wilson's Staunton speech, and in spite of every effort to re-

[Sources: Reports of the Bureau of Civil Service, 1918 and 1926.]

Fiscal year	Number of Americans in the service at middle of fiscal year	Number of separations of Americans			Per cent of separations of Americans		
		Voluntary	Involuntary	Total	Voluntary	Involuntary	Total
1903	2777	617	269	886	22	10	32
1904	3228	787	313	1100	24	10	34
1905	3307	614	195	809	18	6	24
1907	2616	536	90	626	20	4	24
1908	2479	407	77	484	17	3	20
1909	2659	376	62	438	14	2	16
1910	2633	508	92	600	19	4	23
1911	2633	481	71	552	18	3	21
1912 ,.............	2680	412	50	462	15	2	17
1913	2623	461	44	505	17	2	19
July–December, 1913 (half year)	2623	187	98	285	7	4	11
1914	2148	478	155	633	22	7	29
1915	1935	322	35	357	16	2	18
1916	1730	485	22	507	28	1	29
1917	1310	393	24	417	30	2	32
1918	948	359	28	387	38	3	41
1919	760	243	19	262	32	3	35
1920	582	223	36	259	38	6	44
1921	614	104	10	114	17	2	19
1922	604	117	22	139	19	4	23
1923	562	112	11	123	20	2	22
1924	526	109	13	122	21	2	23
1925	506	103	7	110	23	1	24
1926	462	98	10	108	21	2	23

duce expenses, at the time of closing the books at the end of the fiscal year, two months before the appointment of Governor-General Harri-son, the surplus available for appropriation amounted to but $826,490, or a little less than half the surplus it was hoped to carry.

In regard to Governor-General Harrison's second point, while it was true that the reduction of revenues called for a corresponding reduction of expenditures, it was also true that there was sufficient margin for such reduction within the optional expenditures lying at the discretion of the Governor-General; and furthermore it was a fact that the ordinary expenses of running the bureaus and offices, in spite of the sharp reduction of receipts, were several million dollars within the anticipated revenues of the government. For fourteen years the government had paid all its expenses from its revenues, and in addition to that, had met all its fixed charges, and since 1903 had expended annually on public works an average of nearly two million dollars out of revenue. In the four years 1910–13, the aggregate amount thus expended on public works for the insular government only had been nearly eleven million dollars. As expenditures for construction of public works were optional, it had been, as previously set forth, an entirely simple matter to proportion the expenditures to the receipts.

And in regard to Governor-General Harrison's third point, due undoubtedly to careless wording of the Auditor's reports, there is a curious confusion between moneys available for expenditure and those available for appropriation. The reductions he mentioned had occurred in moneys available for expenditure, which are not properly describable as "surplus." The money available for appropriation at the end of the fiscal year 1913 was a little more than a million dollars less than the balance or reserve at the close of 1910. Yet in spite of the heavy drain due to the unforeseen drop in revenues early in 1913, this surplus had been increased substantially over what it had been in 1911 and 1912.

There is no doubt of a serious falling off of business due in large measure to the uncertainty as to the policy of the Democratic administration in Manila and Washington. Congressman Austin, of Tennessee, who visited the Islands at that time, reported "depression in business" and "general dissatisfaction on the part of the business element."

The Governor-General did not allay this uncertainty when in his first message to the Legislature he made the unusual assertion that "business is intended to serve the Government, not the Government to serve business."

In spite of a denial by Congressman Jones that there was any serious disturbance of "financial, economic and industrial conditions," there is no doubt that Governor-General Harrison was confronted with a serious financial situation when he arrived in the Islands in October, 1913. The surplus available for appropriation, as has been seen, was low. The revenues both from customs and internal revenue were falling off, and the repeal of the export tax by the Underwood Tariff of 1913 was expected to reduce the revenues of the government by a further million dollars a year. To meet this situation Governor-General Harrison urged upon the Legislature the adoption of "a drastic program of economy," stating that without it the government was faced with a probable deficit of about two and a quarter million dollars.

Governor-General Harrison, at the time of the passage of his first annual appropriation bill, estimated that his expenditures would be fully three million dollars less than 1913, and he said optimistically in his message to the Legislature, October 16, 1914, that the reduction could be made "with an increase rather than impairment of the efficiency of the government, and without interruption of any important functions of administration or necessary construction." However, he felt it necessary to ask the Legislature for new taxation in a message in which he set forth the comparatively low rate of taxation paid by the Filipinos and expressed belief in their capacity to pay higher rates. The Legislature acted upon this recommendation the ensuing year, made substantial increases in several schedules of the internal revenue taxes, and imposed certain new ones. The most important item of the internal revenue — the percentage tax on business — was multiplied by three, and the revenues of the government from this source alone increased from a little over $1,000,000 in 1913 to something over $8,500,000 in 1920.

The law as originally enacted provided that these increases in taxation should be effective for one year only, and they were set forth in the report of the Governor-General as being necessary to meet the "emergency" which existed at the end of the year. Yet the increased percentage tax on business and many other items in the new schedule were extended for two years, and later made permanent.

In his message to the Legislature in October, 1913, Governor-General Harrison said:

These Islands have need of a simple and scientific form of government. Instead of that, we find a complicated and top-heavy system of bureaucracy. Much can be done toward simplifying this bureau form of government, and in this connection I invite your consideration to a possibility of a reduction in the number of the bureaus by consolidation or otherwise.

Further familiarity with the situation seems to have changed Governor-General Harrison's views in regard to this matter, as the total number of bureaus and offices of thirty-four which he criticized at the beginning of his régime, instead of being reduced during his incumbency, was increased to a total of forty-one, and the number of executive departments increased from five to seven. The reports of the Insular Auditor show an increase during the period 1913–20 of more than one hundred per cent in cost of operation, while the expenditures for salaries and wages, in spite of the number of Americans who, as has been seen, had left the service, showed an increase of fifty-six per cent. The increase in the cost of the legislative branch of the government amounted to more than one hundred and sixty-five per cent. A comparative analysis of the expenditures of the Executive Department brings out among other interesting facts that the discretionary expenditures in 1920 exceeded those of 1913 by one hundred and eighty per cent.

In his effort to give the Filipinos as far as possible their own way in the management of their affairs, Governor-General Harrison yielded to their desire to permit the provincial officers to manage the rinderpest campaign. The Legislature in December, 1913, passed an act transferring the control of the campaign to the provincial boards in order to get rid of the unpopular quarantine. In his first report, Governor-General Harrison, after paying tribute to the service rendered by the Scouts, told of the decision to withdraw them from the quarantine duty "inasmuch as after two years of operation it was felt no considerable improvement was noticeable." The result was not what he expected, as the number of deaths of cattle grew from 2787 in 1913 to 35,740 in 1921.

The government's careful plan for the registration of lands was radically affected by the immediate removal of the efficient American Director of Lands and the forced resignation of the assistant director. The abolition of the land court resulted in further delay. Though the new system was designed in the words of Governor-General Harrison "to expedite the registration of land titles," after it had been in force for only six months he reported "the results so far indicate the necessity, in several provinces, of greatly increased attention to cases of land registration by judges of first instance." In fact, the records show that instead of giving titles to the land at the rate of one hundred thousand parcels a year, as had been planned and was under way in 1913, the work slowed up, as set forth in an earlier chapter, to an extent that resulted in the issuance of less than that number of titles in the following seven-year period.

Governor-General Harrison wisely retained the highly efficient Director of Public Works, under whom important works were pushed to completion with great rapidity. Especial attention was paid to road building; construction of bridges, concrete schoolhouses, and provincial buildings; the boring of artesian wells; and the improvement of the ports. These measures were popular with the Filipinos and had attained an impetus of popular approval that made it easy to secure appropriations and hearty legislative support.

During this period there was no tendency on the part of the Governor-General or of the Philippine Legislature to slow up the work of the Department of Public Instruction. New schools were opened, money was appropriated and made available for the University, and the enthusiasm of the people in general and the legislators in particular for educational progress found expression in continued activity along the lines of practical and theoretical training.

Governor-General Forbes and General Pershing had already recommended to the War Department that the time had come for the appointment of a civilian governor for the Moro Province.

Governor-General Harrison fell in with this plan and recommended it to the Secretary of War, and with his approval appointed the Executive Secretary, Frank W. Carpenter, to succeed General Pershing upon the completion of his tour of duty in December, 1913.

Governor-General Harrison's administration, while bitterly denounced by Americans doing business in the Islands, and especially by those who had served in the government before the era of rapid Filipinization, was not without its cordial adherents, some of whom were men of high public standing, holding positions in which they had access to reliable sources of information.

In 1915, President Wilson cabled to Governor-General Harrison, then sojourning in Baguio: "Please accept my congratulations upon the success of your administration. . . ."

The *New York Times* reported Secretary of War Garrison as having said that "conditions governmentally considered were never better than they are today in the Philippine Islands," and that the government had "in the main been carried out in the most worthy way."

The later Secretary of War, the Honorable Newton D. Baker, cabled Governor-General Harrison on the occasion of his retirement:

On the eve of severing our official relations, I wish to extend my congratulations to you on your self-sacrificing work in the Philippines, and upon the many evidences of good will of the Filipino people toward you and America as a result, in a large part, of your labor.

From observers who cannot be charged with partiality because of direct association with the Democratic government, came further words of praise. Ex-Commissioner W. Morgan Shuster said:

The Philippine Islands are to-day better governed than ever before in their history. Governor General Francis Burton Harrison, in his two and a half years' stay, has done a great piece of administrative work. For the first time the United States has approximated successful colonial administration — so far at least as the Philippine Insular Government is concerned.

.   .   .   .

I am convinced that conditions to-day in the Islands reflect greater credit on the American people and the American flag than any which have ever existed since my acquaintance with things Philippine.

There can be no doubt of Governor-General Harrison's skill in dealing with the Legislature and in securing the passage of measures he wanted. Of this work a Manila paper said in 1915:

On the whole, the Governor General may well be proud of his record with the Legislature. He has displayed a parliamentary skill in handling the Assembly which no other American chief executive has equalled. One may pick flaws in the general appropriation bill; one may point out instances where the Assembly's approval was bought with political coin; but one may not deny that in the main purpose of legislation, the providing of funds on which the government may operate, Mr. Harrison has made a great record.

There is no doubt that for a while at least the Filipinos were greatly pleased with the concessions given to them, and there resulted an era of good feeling between Filipinos and Americans. Proof of this is found in the words of Eleanor Franklin Egan, who wrote in 1918:

For the first time Occupation Day has been celebrated by Filipinos and Americans alike, with joint ceremony and with mutual congratulation and compliment. It was on the whole a most significant day, marking as it did the beginning of the end of the old antagonism and ingratitude with which these people, whom we could not with honor set adrift, have met every effort we have made to benefit and assist them.

Commissioner Worcester, usually chary of praise, vigorously commended the Governor-General's support of Dr. Heiser, Director of Health, on the occasion of certain unjust attacks on the part of the Filipinos. Commissioner Worcester wrote:

Gov. Gen. Harrison has proved himself to be a stanch friend of sanitation in the Philippine Islands and has given effective support to the Bureau of Health during some very trying times, undeterred by the fact that this has made a serious drain on his popularity in certain quarters.

Thus comments upon the policy of Governor-General Harrison ranged from extreme praise by Democrats to bitter denunciation on the part of his critics.

President Wilson gave Governor-General Harrison a fairly free hand and, in general, support. He did not, however, take any steps toward giving the Philippine Islands their independence during the period when both houses of Congress had Democratic majorities. The World War and the subsequent peace negotiations were fully occupying his attention at this time.

The government of the Philippine Islands has compiled certain significant statistics indicative of civic advance. These include, among other data, figures of imports and exports, post and telegraph receipts, bank resources, tonnage of inter-island shipping cleared, postal savings bank deposits, and aggregate resources of commercial banks. All of these show a steady and healthy growth throughout the period of American administration and some of them show the remarkably stimulating effect upon Philippine activities when the markets of the United States were made free to Philippine products. Almost all these lines show steady progress under Governor-General Harrison and prove that, however much his course may be criticized, it had not resulted in preventing the progressive development of the people.

Congressman William A. Jones secured in 1916 the passage by Congress of a bill reorganizing the government of the Philippine Islands on a basis of greatly extended autonomy.

During the consideration of this measure, Senator Clarke, of Arkansas, very nearly threw the Islands unprotected upon the world by securing the passage by the Senate of an amendment to the Jones Bill, granting the Filipinos complete independence at the end of not less than two and not more than four years from the date of the approval of the act. The vote on the Clarke amendment was 41 to 41, and Vice-President Marshall cast the deciding vote in favor of its adoption. The Committee on Insular Affairs of the House of Representatives recommended to the House on April 7, 1916, the passage of the Jones Bill as passed by the Senate, including the Clarke amendment.

Senator Clarke frankly admitted his amendment was solely in the interests of America, and he even stated that he would be willing to have Japan ultimately take over control of the Islands.

Evidence of Filipino opposition to the Clarke amendment found expression in numerous telegrams and remonstrances to the authorities in Manila and Washington.

The *New York Evening Sun* said:

   The passage of an act of Congress committing the United States to the evacuation of the Philippines in two years or in four or at any specific time in the near future would be a criminal blunder.

And again a week later:

No more reckless or mistaken act was ever contemplated than the abandonment of the Philippines now or at any time in the next generation. It means a brief period of internal disorder and corruption, then seizure by one of the nations in need of colonial opportunity. There are no two opinions on the question among those who understand it.

The *Boston Transcript* said:

After America, Japan. That is what would inevitably be the disposition of the Philippines, if the present scheme for scuttling were fulfilled.

The *New York Times* quoted a special cable from Manila:

Popular unrest is growing on account of the increased immigration of Japanese. The people are alarmed, and anti-independence sentiment is found everywhere.

The leaders of all the native parties are privately opposed to the Clarke amendment.

The Honorable Lindley Garrison, Secretary of War, wrote to President Wilson:

I consider the principle embodied in the Clarke amendment an abandonment of the duty of this nation and a breach of trust toward the Filipinos; so believing, I cannot accept it or acquiesce in its acceptance

and resigned when the President failed to stand with him squarely on the issue.

The *New York Times* commented:

The bill should be laid aside. It is not to the interest of our wards in the Pacific, whom we have undertaken to develop in the arts of civilization, that it should become a law. . . . The sentiment of this country is strongly opposed to the Philippines bill.

The Clarke amendment was not destined to survive. It was defeated in the House of Representatives very largely through the attitude of that wing of the Democrats associated with the Roman Catholic Church.

On August 29, 1916, the so-called Jones Bill became law. It was entitled, "An Act to declare the purpose of the people of the United States as to the future political status of the people of the Philippine Islands, and to provide a more autonomous government for those Islands."

From an historical point of view the most important part of the bill was the declaration of purpose contained in the following preamble:

Whereas it was never the intention of the people of the United States in the incipiency of the war with Spain to make it a war of conquest or for territorial aggrandizement; and

Whereas it is, as it has always been, the purpose of the people of the United States to withdraw their sovereignty over the Philippine Islands and to recognize their independence as soon as a stable government can be established therein; and

Whereas for the speedy accomplishment of such purpose it is desirable to place in the hands of the people of the Philippines as large a control of their domestic affairs as can be given them without, in the meantime, impairing the exercise of the rights of sovereignty by the people of the United States, in order that, by the use and exercise of popular franchise and governmental powers, they may be the better prepared to fully assume the responsibilities and enjoy all the privileges of complete independence . . .

This act provided for an elective Philippine Senate as well as House of Representatives; it did away wholly with any difference in legislative control over the territory inhabited by the civilized peoples and that inhabited by the Moros and tribal peoples, but provided that the Moros and tribal peoples should be represented in both houses of the Legislature by senators and representatives appointed by the Governor-General. The law contained a provision, similar to the one in the former organic act, that, in case of failure on the part of the Legislature to enact appropriations necessary for the support of government, the last preceding appropriations should be deemed to be reappropriated. The Governor-General was given a right to veto legislation or items in the appropriation bill. Measures passed over the veto by the Legislature were subject to veto or approval by the President of the United States. The Philippine Senate was given the power to confirm or decline to confirm all appointments made by the Governor-General, except of members of the Legislature to represent the Moros and tribal peoples.

The public domain was, in the following words, placed under the control of the Philippine government "to be administered or disposed of for the benefit of the inhabitants thereof, and the Philippine Legislature shall have power to legislate with respect to all such matters as it may deem advisable; but Acts of the Philippine Legislature with reference to land of the public domain, timber, and mining, hereafter enacted, shall not have the force of law until approved by the President of the United States. . . ."

Subject to approval by the President of the United States it gives the Philippine government the right to enact a tariff law, except as to trade between the Islands and the United States. The indebtedness of the Philippine government was limited to $15,000,000.

The law provided that "the supreme executive power shall be vested in an executive officer, whose official title shall be 'The Governor-General of the Philippine Islands.' . . . He shall have general supervision and control of all of the Departments and Bureaus of the Government in the Philippine Islands . . . and shall be commander in chief of all locally created armed forces and militia."

The law provided specifically for a Vice-Governor who should be the head of the Department of Public Instruction, which should include the Bureaus of Education and Health.

Throughout the Taft régime the line between the legislative, executive, and judicial functions had been carefully drawn, except in so far as the Governor-General and the members of the Commission who held portfolios had both legislative and executive duties, and provincial officials and the municipal presidents also had executive and limited legislative functions. In no case had these officers failed to defend their executive or legislative prerogatives against encroachments.

The Speaker of the Assembly had always had executive control of the legislative body over which he presided and its secretariat. His executive powers stopped there. Repeated efforts had been made by the Assembly to give its committees executive functions, above all to place the expenditure of the money appropriated for irrigation under control of a committee of its members.

In 1916 the Philippine legislators began a series of progressive encroachments upon the executive power, and, in spite of an injunction of the Secretary of War to permit no such encroachments, Governor-General Harrison failed to exercise the veto power in a single instance to prevent measures carrying invasion of the executive power from becoming law. These encroachments sometimes took the form of enactments of law requiring executive officers, including the Governor-General, to obtain the consent of the presidents of the two houses of the Legislature before performing certain functions.

The presiding officers of both houses were given the following functions which should properly belong solely to the executive. Their approval was required to enable the Philippine National Bank to guarantee bonds of certain corporations (Act No. 2747, Philippine Legislature, February 20, 1918); to the proclamation by the Governor-General reducing the weight and fineness of Philippine coins, and to the issue by the Governor-General of temporary certificates of indebtedness (Act No. 2776, May 6, 1918); to the suspension by the Governor-General, upon the initiative of the Secretary of Finance, of the construction on certain public works projects (Act No. 2786, December 21, 1918); to the transfer of unexpended portions of certain appropriations by the department secretary (Act No. 2980, February 21, 1921); to action by the Governor-General in connection with the issue by a province and sundry municipalities of bonds for permanent public improvements (Act No. 3222, September 16, 1925).

They even went so far as to require the Secretary of War to obtain the consent of the presidents of the two Philippine chambers in regard to the terms on which certain bonds could be offered for sale. A careful perusal of the restrictions sought to be placed upon the executive power by these legislative enactments reveals a determination on the part of the Philippine leaders to tie the hands of the Govenor-General and place in their own hands the ultimate power in dealing with many important executive matters.

The Legislature further enacted laws placing certain important powers, properly within the province of the Governor-General, in the hands of lesser officers, usually secretaries of departments. There is no doubt that these acts of the Legislature were contrary to the spirit and to the letter of the fundamental law under which they were operating, and were enacted with the deliberate intention of taking power away from American officers and placing it in the hands of the Filipinos. A conspicuous example of this is to be found in the dismemberment of the Bureau of Health, which was required by the provisions of the Jones Law to be under the Secretary of Public Instruction, who was also Vice-Governor and an appointee of the President. Many of his important functions regarding the health service were taken away and transferred to the secretary of another department.

They even went so far in 1919 as to enact legislation endeavoring to limit to "matters of general policy" the supervision and control which Congress had provided that the Governor-General should have over all departments and bureaus of the government.

The Filipinos wanted a parliamentary form of government, based upon the English model rather than upon the American where the lines are drawn sharply between the executive and legislative functions. They insisted that the secretaries of departments should be responsible to the Legislature, and in furtherance of this conception of the fundamental structure of government they required by law that the term of secretaries of departments should expire with the convening of each new Legislature and that these officers should then be reappointed or new secretaries appointed, their idea being by this device to enforce a party government and make it possible for the Senate, by exercising its right of disapproving appointments made by the Governor-General, to compel the appointment of men pertaining to the dominant party. It was not long before the Senate began making use of this power of confirmation to force the Filipinization of the service. With succeeding years the practice grew of declining to confirm the appointment of any but Filipinos to most positions in the government.

In October, 1918, a Council of State was organized by executive order of Governor-General Harrison "to advise him on matters of importance affecting the welfare of the country." This Council comprised the presiding officers of both houses of the Legislature and the secretaries of the executive departments. The Governor-General presided and Speaker Osmeña of the House of Representatives was vice-chairman of this body. Following the creation of the Council of State, the trend of legislation was to vest in the Council powers which previously had been in the hands of the presidents of the two houses of the Legislature.

A study of the laws of this period, 1918–21, reveals that, in addition to the functions that Governor-General Harrison later described as really legislative, the Council of State was given many functions really executive. This was especially notable during the period between the election and the inauguration of President Harding.

The Council of State having been created by executive order could, of course, be abolished in the same way at the discretion of the Governor-General. Having in view the prospective change in régime in 1921, the Legislature undertook to perpetuate this serious encroachment upon the powers of the executive.

The government, beginning in 1916, embarked upon various enterprises usually left, in American practice, to private initiative. The voting control of the stock of the corporations formed for these purposes, at first vested in the Governor-General, was soon placed in the hands of a committee of three, consisting of the Governor-General and the presidents of the two chambers of the Legislature, later known as the Board of Control. As the government entered more and more into business by successive purchases of existing corporations, such as the railroad and hotel, and the creation of new ones, such as the Philippine National

Bank, National Development Company, National Coal Company, National Cement Company, and others, the responsibilities of those exercising voting control of the stock increased and the presiding officers of the two houses obtained an intervention in executive matters out of keeping with the spirit of American institutions. The Board of Control appeared definitely by name in the revised charter of the National Bank, the original charter having vested the power of voting stock in the Governor-General. It is noteworthy that this revision is dated January 30, 1921, after the election in the United States had assured a Republican President and Republican majorities of both houses of Congress, but before President Harding had taken office.

In November, 1926, acting upon the advice of the Attorney-General of the United States, Governor-General Wood by executive order abolished the Board of Control on the ground that the law creating it was constitutionally void. His action was sustained by a powerfully worded decision of the Philippine Supreme Court in April, 1927. Since that time the management of these administrative matters has pertained to the administrative head of the government. In the course of this decision the principle is set forth: "The legislature cannot lawfully exercise powers which are in their nature essentially executive or judicial. The legislature cannot make a law and then take part in its execution or construction." The decision of the Philippine Supreme Court was confirmed by the United States Supreme Court early in 1928.

Not only did the government embark upon the practice of extensive ownership in public utilities and other enterprises, but also, early in 1921, it went on record, by means of a joint resolution of both houses of the Legislature, as proposing to obtain control of public utilities whenever they could be obtained under favorable conditions and funds were available.

Although legislation did not specifically provide for paid committees to sit when the Legislature was not in session, yet the appropriation bills were so drawn as to give great latitude to the presidents of both houses in the matter. It is common knowledge that such committees multiplied until they menaced the representative character of the government, for, by withholding appointments to paid committees, the president of either house could make things less easy for legislators who did not vote as desired.

The annual cost of the Philippine Assembly, starting at about $280,-000 in 1908, ran along at somewhere about $220,000 until 1914, the first year when both the Assembly and Commission had Filipino majorities, when the expenditures increased about twenty per cent. With the creation of the Senate under the Jones Law, the cost of the Legislature increased to $480,000 in 1917, and that again has more than doubled in the ensuing ten years, the appropriation for 1927 reaching nearly a million dollars.

The appropriation act for 1917 and those for following years gave the President of the Senate and the Speaker of the House extraordinary powers over their appropriations. They could use the funds appropriated for the Legislature for any purpose they saw fit, whether specifically mentioned in the appropriation bill or not, the only limitation put upon these public moneys being that they be used for objects which, in the discretion of these officers, promoted "the efficiency of the service."

It was hardly to be expected that the Filipinos would realize the importance of paying adequate salaries for the higher positions in the government. Their experience during Spanish days was one of low salaries eked out by perquisites of office the receipts from which never appeared in published accounts. The rates which Americans knew it was necessary to pay in order to get first-class executives continued to look very high to the Filipinos, nor did they realize the extent of the relief given the community by the abolition of fees and exactions.

The scale of salaries established by the Filipinos has been the pitifully inadequate maximum of $3600 for such officers as the Insular Collector of Customs and the Director of Public Works. The difficulty of securing the right men for some positions is met in some cases by contracts under which certain American officers have been retained at the old figure of $6000, and perhaps in a few instances at higher rates. In 1919 and 1920, to meet unusual cost of living, the Legislature provided a bonus of twenty-five per cent on the lower salaries and fifteen per cent on salaries above $1200 with certain exceptions. The legislators did not, however, vote themselves a bonus.

In 1916, the increased price of silver caused the Philippine government to sell to the government of British India and to Chinese interests fifteen million silver pesos from the silver certificate reserve fund, the price received giving a profit of nearly a million dollars to the Philippine government. By this operation there was substituted a gold equivalent for the silver withdrawn, with a corresponding reduction in the required amount of the gold standard fund, the purpose of which was to maintain the parity of the bullion and face values of the silver coinage. The gold thus substituted for the silver reserve was placed on interest-bearing deposit in banks in the United States.

The careful protection given to the gold standard fund by the law enacted by the American Commission, requiring that no more than twenty-five per cent of this fund should be deposited in any one bank in the United States, was changed by the Filipino Legislature by removing the restriction in favor of the Philippine National Bank, into which unsound institution these funds were gradually transferred with unfortunate results.

One effect of the operations of the National Bank was a breakdown in exchange during the heavy demand in 1919. The government had recourse to relief by issuing temporary certificates of indebtedness and selling public works bonds. The exchange difficulty continued during 1920, the rate being raised to eleven per cent for telegraphic transfers.

A period of deflation ensued; the banks raised their rates of interest and pressure was brought to bear for liquidation of accounts. Heavy importations resulted in an unfavorable trade balance, and in 1921 the rate of exchange rose to sixteen per cent.

On March 7, 1919, the Legislature adopted an income tax law, modeled more or less closely upon that in effect in the United States, including a tax on undivided profits.

One interesting development arising from Filipino fear that the advent of capital would defeat their ambition for independence is to be found in a clause first inserted in the advertisements for the sale of the government ice plant. In this clause the grantee was required to set forth that he had read President Wilson's message to the Philippine people of October 6, 1913, and the reply by the Philippine Assembly, and to bind himself not to aid by cash or otherwise any propaganda inimical to these policies and the aspirations of the Filipino people. This clause was later incorporated in practically every franchise granted by the Philippine Legislature, appearing in no less than forty-five between 1914 and 1926.

Although the Filipinos were given the majority of both houses of the Legislature in 1914, it was not until five years later that the Legislature voted to restore to the Philippine people the right to fly their own flag and use the insignia of the insurrection, rights which they had lost twelve years previously. Not only did the Legislature restore the right to use the flag but later required that it be used publicly as the official flag.

Evidence is not lacking that after the adjournment of the Legislature a good deal of tampering with the wording of laws, in some instances materially changing the meaning, was indulged in by officers charged with preparation in final form of the laws — this in spite of the penalties of imprisonment, fine, and permanent disqualification from office, imposed on any public officer guilty of falsification of a document.

The period of Filipinization is noteworthy for the number of boards created. A perusal of the laws enacted after the Filipinos came into control of the Legislature reveals a tendency toward the creation of a multiplicity of boards, not only important ones, such as the Boards of Control, of Public Utility Commissioners, and of Public Welfare, but numerous others, such as the Board of Dental Hygiene, the re-creation of the Board of Health as the Council of Hygiene, the Central Sugar Board, Coconut Products Board, and others.

The official standing of the English language was not dealt with in an adverse spirit. In March, 1917, an act of the Legislature provided that the English text was to govern in interpretation of a law officially promulgated in English and Spanish, but in case of ambiguity, omission, or mistake, the Spanish might be consulted to explain the English text. And the status quo in the courts was continued for a decade by an enactment in 1919 that, besides English, Spanish should also be an official language of the courts and their records until January 1, 1930.

In 1917 the Filipinos at last placed a divorce law upon the statute book. Other measures passed in this period were a law requiring that commercial account books be kept in English, Spanish, or a local dialect, the naturalization law, the granting of a life pension to General Aguinaldo, an appropriation for inter-island immigration, an act providing mutual insurance on work animals, and a law penalizing publication of libels against the government of the Philippine Islands or of the United States during the war.

Many praiseworthy activities were undertaken by the government. In 1921, the sum of $150,000 was appropriated for public charities and for treatment of leprosy. Protection was given to labor by a law passed in the same year providing that loans payable in agricultural produce are void unless the produce is appraised at the market price, and the rate of interest is not to exceed that fixed by law. In 1917, an appropriation of $125,000 was made for immunization of cattle and to prevent the spread of rinderpest, and in 1919 the sum of $500,000 was appropriated for loans to facilitate the purchase of cattle to be used in cultivating new

rice and corn lands. Another excellent measure, passed in 1919, authorized municipalities to regulate signs and billboards, and, in passing, it
may be said that the roads in the Philippine Islands are more sightly
and less defaced by ugly advertising than are those in the United States.

The importance of sports is not lost upon the Filipino. In 1916, a sum
was appropriated to send a team to the Olympic games at Tokyo and
in 1921 an appropriation was made to send representatives of the Philippine Islands to the Olympic games in Shanghai.

In the World War the attitude of the Filipinos toward the United
States was helpful. Many Filipinos enlisted; some fought in France, and
many served in various capacities in the navy. In 1917 the Philippine
Militia was created and a National Guard division was organized. The
complement of officers included many from the United States Army
and the Constabulary. About 28,000 enlisted men were enrolled. The
authorities at Washington authorized a total of only 14,000 mustered
into the federal service and for the period of one month. The total
expenditures are stated to have been $515,000 from the United States
treasury and $2,406,000 from the Philippine treasury. Moreover, the
Philippine government voted to build and pay for a destroyer and a
submarine and these boats were built and placed in commission. They
were not completed, however, until the war was over, and in view of
the then seriously depleted condition of the Philippine treasury, the
United States never collected the amount. But the generous loyalty
which prompted the building is as much to the credit of the Filipinos
as though the United States had seen fit to draw upon the Philippine
treasury for the cost.

Throughout the history of American administration in the Philippine
Islands there has never been a tendency on the part of the Philippine
legislators to reduce appropriations for public works. On the other hand,
in the period during which the Filipinos had virtually absolute control,
they showed a praiseworthy desire to encourage them. In 1918, a law
was passed authorizing the establishment of municipal irrigation systems and making an appropriation of $50,000 a year to assist in this
work. In December, 1918, an appropriation for $1,250,000 was made
for the construction of a new pier in the harbor of Manila, Pier No. 7,
which at the time of its completion was superior to any other pier in
the Orient. It is constructed throughout of steel and concrete, and has
landing facilities of the most modern types for four large steamers
simultaneously.

As was to be expected, the Legislature provided liberally for education. Several laws are noted granting the Secretary of Public Instruction supervisory powers in connection with private schools and colleges.

In 1925 a concurrent resolution was passed reciting the desire of the Filipino people to establish an independent and democratic self-governing state, which "to be stable and enduring requires an enlightened citizenry," education being recognized as the bulwark of modern democracy, and stating that it is the sense of the Philippine Legislature that the first duty of government is toward the education of the masses, insuring to every child of school age as soon as possible free elementary education, to which end the finances of government should be largely devoted.

An analysis of the work of this period reveals a recognition by the Filipinos of their responsibility toward the tribal peoples and the importance of caring for their welfare. Large appropriations were made to be expended among the tribal peoples, and also among the Mohammedans, for public works, public schools, hospitals, and public health.

The appropriation bills for current expenses carried under various headings substantial amounts each year to be used in promoting friendly relations with Mohammedans and tribal peoples.

Nevertheless the mistake was made of sending successively two unsuitable Filipino governors to replace the American who had done such good service in administering the Mountain Province in Luzon. Abuses crept in and great dissatisfaction ensued. When Governor Early was promoted to be governor of the Mountain Province by Governor-General Wood, he found that the records for several years had never been filed. He disposed of twelve clerks, after which the arrears were made up, and current work carried on, with a force not exceeding three.

In 1921 a member of the Wood-Forbes investigating party traveled over the road via Cervantes to Tagudin. He found the sections had been reduced from about nine to less than four miles each. Over each section a high-priced foreman was placed whose salary exhausted the funds, so that there was practically no money left for laborers and the trail was rapidly going to pieces. In 1925, however, under Governor-General Wood, this was all changed; the trail was improved and widened, and in the latter part of 1926 it became passable for automobiles all the way through to Bontoc.

CHAPTER XIII

A SURVEY AND THE WOOD ADMINISTRATION

WITH HIS ELECTION in 1920, President-elect Harding found himself confronted with the troublesome problem of deciding how to administer the Philippine Islands.

A man of very open mind, he had been chairman of the Committee on Territories and Insular Possessions of the United States Senate, so that he was peculiarly equipped to deal with Philippine matters. Information from various sources made him skeptical of the correctness of President Wilson's statement in his message to Congress of that year that the Filipinos had complied with all the conditions, and that it was now the duty of the United States to give them independence. President Wilson undoubtedly did not know when he wrote this message that the treasury was embarrassed, that trust funds had been dissipated, currency depreciated, that the coin and bullion value supposed to be deposited to secure the issue of paper currency had, to an important measure, been withdrawn and expended, and that financially the government was in a bad way. The only saving aspect in the financial situation was to be found in the fact that the debt of the Islands was small compared with their assets and revenues.

President Harding determined to send a mission out to the Islands to study and report upon their readiness for independence, and to render judgment whether "the Philippine government is now in a position to warrant its total separation from the United States Government. . . ."

Major-General Leonard Wood was named as chairman of the mission. He had been three years governor of the Moro Province, and had served as Commanding General of the United States land forces in the Philippine Islands. His varied personal experience especially equipped him for this undertaking. The other member was ex-Governor-General Forbes, who had been Secretary of Commerce and Police for five years, and Vice-Governor during one year of that period, and Governor-General of the Islands for four years. Both members of the mission spoke enough Spanish to need no interpreter either for the conduct of interviews or in making public addresses.

A group of competent younger men was obtained as associates to the mission. Colonel, later General, Frank R. McCoy was chief of staff — a man of consummate ability and tact, and of long experience in responsibility, including several years' service in Cuba and in the Philippine Islands. Mr. Ray Atherton, representing the Department of State; Lieutenant-Colonel Gordon Johnston, who had seen long service in the Philippine Islands; Major Edward Bowditch, Jr., who had spent seven years in the service of the Islands in various civil capacities; Lieutenant-Commander Stewart F. Bryant, representing the United States Navy; Professor H. Otley Beyer, of the University of the Philippines, an ethnologist of note who had devoted himself for many years to the study of Philippine conditions, were attached to the mission, in addition to which there were aides, secretaries, and orderlies.

President Harding gave the impression of being a man utterly unconscious of self, whole-heartedly desiring the good of the cause to which he was at the moment devoting his attention, and interested in a proper solution of it without thought of its political effect on himself or his party.

The Wood-Forbes Mission arrived at Manila in May, 1921. The reception which was prepared for them was brilliant and cordial.

Governor-General Harrison had handed in his resignation effective the last day of President Wilson's administration, March 4, 1921. He left the Islands on that day. His place was taken temporarily by Vice-Governor Charles E. Yeater, a conscientious and capable American who, representing an administration that had gone out of power, very properly did not feel free to initiate new policies, and merely carried on until such time as the representative of the new administration should assume charge. He so impressed the members of the mission with his earnestness and capacity that, before they left the Islands, a cablegram was sent to President Harding, signed by both General Wood and ex-Governor-General Forbes in the spirit of non-partisanship that had characterized the administration previous to 1913, urging his appointment as Governor-General, at least until the new appointee should arrive. By this time, however, it was becoming evident that President Harding hoped to get General Wood to remain as Governor-General, and he was not prepared to make any other appointment.

Arriving in the Islands, the mission immediately set to work to get all the information needed to render its report, and a thorough inspection was made of the Islands, province by province and municipality by municipality. When it is remembered that there were more than eight hundred of these latter, the magnitude of the task can be realized. Four months were spent by the mission in the Islands. In the course of that time the archipelago was traversed from end to end and from side to side. Every province but one was visited, besides many of the sub-provinces; four hundred and forty-nine municipalities were inspected, and in all of them public sessions were held. In the great majority of cases, visits were made by one of the two members of the mission in person; in the large capitals both members jointly held public sessions, and then received those who wished to be heard privately.

Two steamers were made available for the trips of the mission, whose members separated and took different routes. The work was arduous and the mission worked from early morning until late at night. At the public sessions everyone desiring to speak was given a hearing; private interviews, and inspection of private buildings, including jails, were conducted.

It was made clear wherever public sessions were held that the mission did not want to hear only from the men of wealth and position, but wanted especially the views of the laboring men. Word of this was passed ahead and some rather amusing episodes resulted. In more than one place gentlemen of leisure were dressed up to resemble field laborers, and, responding to the request, stood up and said their part. In Cebu one of these impersonators made his speech and a member of the mission stepped forward and shook him by the hand. Afterward, as the investigating party drove off in the car, a senator of the district asked the member of the mission why he had shaken hands with that particular orator. When he was told that it was to feel whether or not the orator's hand was calloused, the senator commented with a laugh, "You are not missing very many tricks, are you?"

The following speech with which the public session in Oroquieta, in the province of Misamis, was opened is fairly typical:

Our mission has come here at the request of the President of the United States. He wants us to get in touch with the Philippine people. He wants to know what you are thinking about. He wants to know how your government is functioning; whether justice is being administered impartially and promptly and without favor; whether you are getting your land titles promptly; whether your government costs more than it ought to; whether your officials are promoting agriculture, education, sanitation, and public works.

We have come in a most friendly spirit. We bring a message of good will from the American people to the Philippine people. We are not trying to find things to criticize; it gives us great pleasure to find things we can honestly praise. We are glad to say we have found many things which we can report to the President as having been done well. We wish we could tell him that everything has been done well. We are glad to see the great interest in the public schools. . . . We are glad to find that the condition of public order throughout the archipelago is admirable. And there seems to be a friendly feeling between the Americans and the Filipinos throughout the Islands. All this is most encouraging. Another thing we have been glad to see has been the activity shown by the women in civic matters; there has been a great development in women's clubs and the services which they render are admirable. It is hoped that women will enter more and more into your political affairs, because their influence is for good.

Now, my friends, we have come here hoping that if any of you have anything to say you will feel free to speak. We shall be glad to hear from anybody, man or woman, workman or *principal*; anybody is welcome. Our only request is that whoever speaks shall be brief, because our time is short and our work has been very hard.

A young schoolmaster of the province, speaking in excellent English, replied in the following words:

The people of this town request you to convey to President Harding our heartiest thanks for your altruistic motives. We are very glad to have you once more in our country. When your investigation is over and when you have left the Islands and when you stand face to face with President Harding, we will ask you to submit your report free from prejudice and make it as strong and emphatic as possible for independence. You may have noticed some changes in this town. We have had a temporary setback because of the crisis, but the heart of the people remains unchanged in its aspiration for independence. Right here on this plaza and behind that church lie the bodies of Filipinos who died for independence. Call them ignorant, what you will, but give them credit for their ideals and sacrifices. It was their own fault, you might say, but was it not the same spirit that caused America to send millions to France? Was it not the same fate that caused the allied nations to send millions to death? It was the same spirit and fate that caused many of our own boys to go to France and fight for the cause of freedom. The Filipino boys did their bit in the Great War for self-determination of small nations. Are the Philippine people going to be denied their request? You have heard this cry many times, the cry that means the love of our country.

The mission found the desire for independence to be so general as to be almost universal, but it was tempered among the more worldly-wise, particularly the property owners and the people who lived in the larger cities, such as Manila and Cebu, with the realizing sense that they were not nearly ready for it. Some who expressed the hope that the mission would be able to report that they were ready, intimated that they knew very well that this hope was probably vain. They fully appreciated their own unreadiness. It was inevitable that there should be a number of fire-eaters who wanted independence immediately at any cost.

Some of the sessions were quite dramatic. In a public session in the province of La Union, the municipal president began by making a very careful and thoughtful speech in English, pointing out in well-ordered phrases the excellent work done for the Filipinos by Americans, and gracefully expressing his people's gratitude. He then referred to the pledges made by Americans to the Filipinos and demanded their fulfillment and asked for independence. Asked whether or not he wanted a protectorate, he replied that his people would accept what was given them. If America cared to assume a protectorate, they would accept that. He was told that America was quite unlikely to give protection without retaining power, and was forthwith asked point-blank what he would prefer. To this he replied sturdily: "Absolute independence, without a protectorate." He was told that that was a very serious matter. The American people wanted to please the Philippine people and to give them what they wanted if it could be done without disaster to them. The supposititious case was presented to him of an offer of two documents, both giving the Filipinos what they called independence, one under the protection of the United States which undertook to use ships and troops to defend the Islands, and the other giving them absolute independence with all forces of the United States withdrawn, leaving the Filipinos to fight their own battles, defend their own soil, pay their own bills, without access to United States' markets and without any privileges or preferences. He was asked which he would accept if his were the final responsibility to accept and decide for his own people. He replied: "I would take absolute independence without protection."

At this a young woman jumped up and said, "I think the *presidente* must be crazy." Then turning and speaking directly to the president: "I think anybody who has any sense at all knows perfectly well that we are wholly unable to protect ourselves. We have not a place where we can make a gun in the Islands and no training necessary to defend ourselves. We would be just as helpless as a child in the hands of enemies. Even the common people know this. Only yesterday a laboring man came to my house and we got talking over the independence of the Islands, and I asked him whether he thought we wanted it. He said, 'Not yet; we are not ready.' I asked him whether he thought we could protect ourselves against foreign aggression with bolos?" She made a motion as of drawing a bolo from its sheath and raising it high over her head — a very dramatic movement and moment. She then turned and said she thought the president must be a little "nervous."

In a good many places the substance of the private interviews which were received did not conform to the substance of the speeches which were made in public. Often a man would ask for independence in public and in private declare that he wanted none of it, explaining his public request on the ground that he was a candidate for office and therefore it behooved him to establish his standing with his party. Things could be made extremely difficult for him if he failed to ask for independence. In fact, in more than one instance those who publicly opposed independence before the mission were subjected to disagreeable treatment, and even to violence, by their neighbors. Occasionally those who in private opposed the granting of independence begged that under no circumstances should this fact be revealed to their fellow townsmen, as it would expose them to most unpleasant consequences, but they thought it their duty to tell the members of the mission what they really felt.

A case in point was that of a young man speaking in an open session who gave about half a minute to independence, and talked about fifteen or twenty minutes about provincial matters. Afterward he came and asked for a private interview and gave a lot of written reasons why independence should not be given.

These interviews developed wide differences of opinion even among those wanting independence. The great majority made the reservation that it should be under the aegis of the United States.

In Jolo, in the Moro country, a petition was presented to the mission signed by almost all the leading men of the region except the Sultan of Sulu, requesting the United States to annex the territory occupied by the Moros and to give them a permanent government by Americans.

Although the Filipinos had made a great point, not only through their press, but in the speeches of their leaders, of early and rapid Filipinization of their own civil service, it was noticed that, once they were given control of the government over the Moros and the tribal peoples, they did not give the same consideration to the desires of the young Moros and tribal peoples that they claimed for themselves in their own government. In other words, there was no haste made in Moroizing the government of the Moros or utilizing the tribal peoples in their own government. It is true that the Moros were not educated in the art of government to a point where there was a very large choice of competent and dependable candidates, but there was some just cause for

complaint that such Moros as were available were not given consideration, which would have been very welcome to their people and would
have made the relations of the Filipinos with their neighbors, the Moros,
more harmonious. Another cause for just complaint was the tendency
to multiply offices, an unnecessary number of which were created and
filled by Filipinos themselves unfit. This fact also was recognized and
resented by the Moros.

When the investigating party reached Bontoc, the headquarters of the
tribal peoples in Luzon, the town was crowded with representatives
from all the neighboring provinces, who unanimously requested the
return of American governors, teachers, doctors, and police officers, and
a continuance of American rule. An old warrior, seamed, scarred, and
tattooed in a way that indicated he had taken many heads in his day,
said, "When the Americans came we were like wild horses that had
never been trained. They taught us the way to do things. They taught
us how to live. We were just beginning to learn; we were like horses
half-broken. Now we are going back to our wild state." Another warrior said, "We were like blind people who could not see, and the Americans came and opened our eyes and we began to see. Do not leave us,
because if you go back we shall lose all we have gotten and be blind
again."

General Wood, who had at first declined the offer by President Harding of the governor-generalship of the Islands, became so impressed by
the necessity of constructive action, that he reconsidered his determination and, when again urged by President Harding, gave up the important position he had been proffered as Provost of the University of
Pennsylvania, and decided to turn back to Manila to take over the work
of governing the Filipinos.

SUMMARY OF THE REPORT
OF THE
WOOD-FORBES MISSION

The mission specifically placed itself on record against any drastic
reversal of policy, but suggested that there be allowed "time for the Filipinos . . . to absorb and master what is already in their hands." It
pointed out the need to "build up an informed public opinion, a stronger
spirit of civic responsibility and a better appreciation of the obligations
of citizenship." The report mentioned the fact that the problem is not

one for the Islands only, but that other countries throughout the Orient are greatly influenced by the success or failure of self-government as demonstrated in the Philippine Islands.

In regard to independence, the report found that "the great bulk of the Christian Filipinos have a very natural desire for independence; most of them desire independence under the protection of the United States; a very small percentage desire immediate independence with separation from the United States; a very substantial element is opposed to independence, especially at this time." It found the Moros, tribal peoples, and Americans in the Islands almost universally desirous of the continuance of American control.

The mission found the administrative departments of the government, generally speaking, "top-heavy in personnel and enmeshed in red tape," and it made the further comment that "there is a lack of supervision and personal contact."

The mission found a "general opinion among Filipinos, Americans, and foreigners that the public services are now in many particulars relatively inefficient; that there has occurred a slowing down in the dispatch of business, and a distinct relapse toward the standards and administrative habits of former days. This is due in part to bad example, incompetent direction, to political infection of the services, and above all to lack of competent supervision and inspection. This has been brought about by surrendering, or failing to employ, the executive authority of the Governor-General, and has resulted in undue interference and tacit usurpation by the political leaders of the general supervision and control of departments and bureaus of the government vested by law in the Governor-General." The mission commented on a tendency on the part of the Legislature to demoralize the civil service and reported "numerous exemptions from the requirements of the civil service and many provisions for temporary employment," but it held forth hope that these errors would be corrected by the Philippine leaders themselves.

The Constabulary was reported to be "entitled to great credit for its morale, efficiency, and orderly and effective performance of duty," and the public order was found to be excellent.

As to justice, the mission paid high tribute to the Supreme Court, but found in the lower tribunals the administration of justice unsatisfactory and slow, and a fairly general feeling that influence had "undue weight in determining issues." The number of undetermined cases in the courts was pointed out as too high.

PHILIPPINE LABORING-WOMEN

YOUNG LADY IN TYPICAL PHILIPPINE DRESS

The mission found the situation in the matter of registration of land titles unfortunate, due to lack of experienced and trained personnel, to inefficient management, lack of funds, and to the abolition of the court of land registration. It recommended that the land court should be reëstablished.

In the matter of education, the mission found the progressive development of the school system phenomenal. Expansion had been so rapid that the number of well-trained teachers was inadequate and the shortage of English-speaking teachers was noted. The willingness of parents to make sacrifices to give their children education was favorably commented upon. The mission found the University of the Philippines "full of promise," but "not meeting the demands upon it in as satisfactory manner as could reasonably be expected," and urgently recommended the reëstablishment of the school of tropical medicine.

In regard to health, it found the appropriations insufficient, a steady increase in the number of deaths from preventable diseases, and a shortage of doctors, nurses, sanitary officers, and hospitals. The mission urged that effort be made to treat all lepers who might possibly be benefited with the new medicines that had already effected marked improvement in some, and practical cure in other, cases. It condemned the care of the insane as medieval and urged that steps be taken immediately to provide proper hospitals.

The mission reported many gratifying evidences of economic advance: increased deposits in the postal savings bank, a great development in business, also greatly augmented resources of commercial banks, an increase in money orders, in receipts from telegraph business, and railroad earnings.

It found the Islands "were suffering from the general world-wide depression," and continued: "It should be noted, however, that whatever mistakes have been made here, they have not been sufficient to arrest the steady rate of progress which these figures prove to have taken place." The mission pointed out the remarkable increase in trade, of which two-thirds was with the United States, and the serious effect that some Philippine industries would suffer were the markets of the United States closed to the Islands.

The mission devoted a good deal of space to the Philippine National Bank, which it criticized sharply.

In regard to public works, the mission found an undue increase in the cost and a deterioration in the quality of the work performed. It gave credit for "a great deal of excellent work done," and characterized the Director as a Filipino of "unusual capacity and foresight." Progress in irrigation was noted. While the miles of road rated as first-class had increased, the standard had been lowered. The system of road maintenance had not been kept up and the roads had noticeably deteriorated, due in part to the introduction of heavy motor trucks carrying loads greater than the road surfacing was designed to support.

The mission found the government had entered into "certain lines of business usually left to private initiative" and recommended that the government as far as possible should "get out of and keep out of such business."

The elections were found to have been conducted in an orderly manner and with a "quiet acceptance by the minority of the results of the popular vote," although the Executive Bureau was found to have been deluged with complaints, and the courts loaded with "fraudulent election cases."

The report contained twelve general conclusions, among them the statement "that the Government is not reasonably free from those underlying causes which result in the destruction of government." This was a direct answer to a question as to whether such was the case, put by the Secretary of War in his letter of instructions to the mission. It was concluded also that many Filipinos have shown marked capacity for government service, but that the people are not organized economically to maintain an independent government.

The report ended with the following words:

We feel that with all their many excellent qualities, the experience of the past eight years, during which they have had practical autonomy, has not been such as to justify the people of the United States relinquishing supervision of the Government of the Philippine Islands, withdrawing their army and navy, and leaving the islands a prey to any powerful nation coveting their rich soil and potential commercial advantages.

In conclusion we are convinced that it would be a betrayal of the Philippine people, a misfortune to the American people, a distinct step backward in the path of progress, and a discreditable neglect of our national duty were we to withdraw from the islands and terminate our relationship there without giving the Filipinos the best chance possible to have an orderly and permanently stable government.

Recommendations

1. We recommend that the present general status of the Philippine Islands continue until the people have had time to absorb and thoroughly master the powers already in their hands.

2. We recommend that the responsible representative of the United States, the Governor General, have authority commensurate with the responsibilities of his position. In case of failure to secure the necessary corrective action by the Philippine Legislature, we recommend that Congress declare null and void legislation which has been enacted diminishing, limiting, or dividing the authority granted the Governor General under . . . the Jones bill.

3. We recommend that in case of a deadlock between the Governor General and the Philippine Senate in the confirmation of appointments that the President of the United States be authorized to make and render the final decision.

4. We recommend that under no circumstances should the American Government permit to be established in the Philippine Islands a situation which would leave the United States in a position of responsibility without authority.

The report received a great deal of attention and much publicity. It was not well received by most of the Filipino leaders, although it abounded with pleasing allusions to their good qualities. The mission had not, however, minced words nor hesitated to point out weaknesses in the situation. One of the best-informed Americans, who had been in the Islands and knew the tenor of the confidential information upon which the mission based many of its findings, remarked that "it was the most restrained document he had ever seen." It was prepared with the utmost care, every statement in it being a careful understatement of fact, of which supporting evidence was on file in Washington as exhibits to the report.

General Leonard Wood had been runner-up to President Harding for the Republican nomination in 1920, and this, together with his brilliant and conspicuous success in many and varied capacities, gave him an enviable prestige, so that when he accepted the governorship of the Philippine Islands, one frequently heard the remark, "If Wood can't do it, nobody can."

The position of Governor-General was peculiarly difficult just then because the policy of the Democrats had been that of allowing the Filipinos so large a share in the direction of their affairs that many functions placed by law in the hands of the Govenor-General had come to be exercised by Filipinos. As has been seen, numerous laws had been passed aimed directly at reducing the executive power of the Governor-General. And among the Filipino leaders there were not lacking those who, even after the arrival of Governor-General Wood, expected the American Governor-General to be a mere figurehead, with Filipinos exercising the real control. These people were calculating without General Wood, who would never occupy any position as a mere figurehead. It was inevitable that before long there should be some clash between General Wood and those who expected that he would not undertake to exercise the powers conferred upon him by law, and would fail to uphold the dignity of his country. He surprised even his close friends and admirers by his patience and forbearance in dealing with Filipinos who had become accustomed to an easy-going acquiescence on the part of their previous American ruler.

The diminution of the number of Americans in the civil service had brought the Governor-General's staff almost to the vanishing point. General Wood was accustomed to having a staff of able American assistants about him, and his wisdom was nowhere better demonstrated than in his selection of these men, nor was his power in any way better illustrated than in the personal magnetism with which he attached these men to his service. The General had Colonel Frank R. McCoy, afterwards General, as executive officer, and Lieutenant-Colonel Gordon Johnston and Major Edward Bowditch, Jr., all men of marked ability, charm of manner, fine presence, and tact. They were fluent in Spanish, experienced in the affairs of the Islands, pleasant in dealing with the Filipinos, and sympathetic with their ideals.

General Wood did not disband the Council of State which had been created by Governor-General Harrison.

It is not out of place here to indicate briefly the powers of the Governor-General granted since the Democrats had come into power in 1913. In 1921, the Governor-General had the veto power and could disapprove items in the appropriation bill. The supervision of provincial and municipal governments was retained by the Chief of the Executive Bureau, as he was now called, under the control of the Secretary of the Interior. By the time General Wood arrived, this supervision had been largely discontinued, and the organization in the Executive Bureau for following up and disciplining provincial and municipal officers had been weakened.

In 1921 the Governor-General's contact with the Legislature was much less direct than before 1916, and for the legislative support of his administrative measures he had to deal wholly with the elective representatives of the people. It is true he had the power of appointment of two senators to the upper and nine representatives to the lower house to care for the interests of the tribal and Mohammedan peoples. Although nothing in the law required that these should be Filipinos, in every instance they had been such. In case of failure on the part of the

Legislature to agree upon an appropriation bill, the previous bill carried over, as had been the rule before, but with certain limitations and provisions as to detail which made the powers a little less flexible.

Appointments by the Governor-General before 1916 were subject to approval by the Philippine Commission, and after 1916 by the elected Philippine Senate. The Philippine Senate had its first clash with General Wood over appointments, and adopted the policy of declining to confirm the appointment of any American whom the Governor-General might name to succeed a Filipino, unless it were done as a trade for some other position, equally or perhaps more important, to which a Filipino was appointed.

The first major job that confronted Governor-General Wood was the rehabilitation of the government finances, which he found at a very low ebb. The depleted trust funds had to be restored; depreciated currency brought back to normal; the treasury put in a position to enable the provinces and municipalities to withdraw and use the deposits which they had been compelled to place in the Philippine National Bank and which then had been largely lost.

The most encouraging circumstance was the extremely low bonded indebtedness of the archipelago and it was clearly necessary for the Philippine government to borrow enough money, first, to put the Philippine National Bank in such a position that it could honor drafts of the provinces and municipalities; and, second, to put the insular government in the same position in regard to its own deposits, and, further, to restore the sinking funds and the currency reserve. For these purposes Governor-General Wood, under Congressional authorization, increased the bonded indebtedness by $35,250,000. With this he paid off certificates of indebtedness and restored the currency reserves and trust funds. By the end of 1923 the Philippine government was in good solvent condition. The financial achievements in Governor-General Wood's first two years were summarized in an official memorandum prepared in 1924 for the Secretary of War, which stated that he had, first, restored the currency of the Islands to parity with the gold standard; second, reduced budget expenditures of the government thirty-five per cent and brought them within current revenues; third, secured legislation protecting the sinking funds of the government, and operating within the terms of the law assured material profits to the government from the use of the funds; and fourth, "restrained the government in its previous policy of squandering its funds in politically controlled commercial and industrial enterprises," while protecting large investments. Throughout General Wood's incumbency this improvement continued.

In July, 1923, a serious clash occurred between Governor-General Wood and the Filipino leaders who expected him to relinquish the powers given him by law. It arose over an American named Conley, employed in the secret service branch of the Manila police department, who incurred the enmity of certain Filipinos and as a result became the victim of a conspiracy, or what is commonly called in these days a "frame-up," in which charges were preferred against him. The moment any officer of the government gets on the trail of a malefactor, the latter invents charges and moves to force an investigation into the officer's conduct and affairs. In this case charges had been made repeatedly against Conley, and, with the approval of the Governor-General, he had been suspended. However, in view of the apparently prejudiced attitude of Filipino officials, the Governor-General insisted that Conley be given a fair trial in the courts. This was not what the instigators of the charges wanted; they sought his removal. After a prolonged trial before a Filipino judge, the charges were dismissed. The Governor-General then ordered an administrative investigation, which resulted in a recommendation for reinstatement, in effect confirming the previous findings of the chief of police that the charges had been instigated by gamblers whose operations had become unprofitable due to Conley's activities as chief of the vice squad. Upon receipt of instructions from the Governor-General to reinstate Conley, the Secretary of the Interior and the Mayor of Manila, both Filipinos, resigned. Conley was then reinstated by the chief of police on the order of the Governor-General.

The Filipino leaders felt that this was an intrusion by the Governor-General into a purely domestic matter, which they had endeavored by various devices to take out of the hands of the Governor-General and place exclusively in the hands of the Filipino secretaries of departments. In protest, the presiding officers of both houses of the Legislature resigned from the Council of State and the Filipino secretaries of executive departments resigned their portfolios.

These resignations were tendered in a letter dated July 17, 1923, addressed to the Governor-General and signed by the presiding officers of the two houses and five secretaries of departments, in which they charged him with the "policy and desire . . . to intervene in and control even to the smallest details, the affairs of our government, both insular and local, in utter disregard of the authority and responsibility of the department heads and other officials concerned." The letter then mentioned the Conley case, and charged that the Governor-General's actions in that connection were a clear violation of the fundamental law, naming the provisions of the law, and a "curtailment of Filipino autonomy."

It is doubtful if the secretaries expected that their resignations would be accepted. But Governor-General Wood did accept them, writing that they caused him regret and surprise, and continuing: "I beg to state most definitely and emphatically that each and every declaration made in your statement which charges neglect of the prerogatives and rights of the secretaries or disregard for the organic law is without the slightest foundation in fact."

The work of the departments was carried on by the undersecretaries, and the secretaryships, with the exception of that of the Department of the Interior, remained vacant, as the men whom Governor-General Wood wished to appoint to these places could not receive the affirmative votes of the Senate, not on the ground of merit, but because the President of the Senate confused the confirming power with the selecting power, and took a position which virtually meant confirmation only of appointees of his own selection. Governor-General Wood was not a man to submit to any such invasion of his prerogatives. He let the bureaus and departments continue under the assistant chiefs.

During this trying period Governor-General Wood showed patience as well as determination. As was natural, the Filipinos were not too happy over the loss of their most important executive positions.

These incidents, however, confirmed many American observers in the feeling that it had been a mistake on the part of the framers of the Jones Law to grant the Philippine Senate final power of disapproval of the appointees of the American Governor-General. The very situation invited some such clash as occurred.

In July, 1923, the "Commission of Independence," consisting of the members of both houses of the Legislature, passed a resolution endorsing the position taken by the presidents of the two houses and the resigning secretaries, and a later resolution, among other things, requested the appointment of a Filipino as Governor-General. In October, the two houses of the Legislature in joint session passed a resolution making their own the two above resolutions.

The Governor-General at this juncture received fine support from Washington. The Secretary of War cabled him:

After personal conference with the President and recognizing the necessity of bringing about coöperation between the branches of the Philippine government, executive, legislative, and judicial, maintaining the clear line of demarcation between them which is essential to well-balanced government, it seems well to make the following authoritative statement of the views of the administration here.

The personal sacrifice involved in your acceptance of your present office is proof of your desire to serve the Filipino people as you have served the United States. You are entitled to the support of the administration, and you have it.

In January, 1924, a commission visiting the United States in the interest of independence, headed by Speaker Roxas of the Philippine House of Representatives and the two Resident Commissioners, presented a memorial to the United States Senate and House of Representatives. They claimed that the time had now come for independence. They traced the history of the recent trend of events, pointed to the recommendation of President Wilson that independence be granted, and the assurance of President Harding in 1922 that no "backward step" was contemplated, and then entered into a bitter rhetorical tirade against Governor-General Wood.

To this President Coolidge replied at length, one sentence of his letter dismissing the charges as follows: "The American Government has information which justifies it in the confidence that a very large proportion, at any rate, and possibly a majority of the substantial citizenry of the islands does not support the claim that there are grounds for serious grievance."

After dealing at some length with the question of Filipino readiness for independence, the President went on to say:

. . . There have been evidences of a certain inability or unwillingness to recognize that this type of governmental organization rests upon the theory of complete separation of the legislative, executive, and judicial functions. There have been many evidences of disposition to extend the functions of the legislature and thereby to curtail the proper authority of the executive. It has been charged that the present Governor General has in some matters exceeded his proper authority, but an examination of the facts seems rather to support the charge that the legislative branch of the insular government has been the real offender through seeking to extend its own authority into some areas of what should properly be the executive realm.

The Government of the United States has full confidence in the ability, good intentions, fairness, and sincerity of the present Governor General. It is convinced that he has intended to act and has acted within the scope of his proper and constitutional authority. Thus convinced, it is determined to sustain him and its purpose will be to encourage the broadest and most intelligent coöperation of the Filipino people in this policy.

The most searching analysis of Governor-General Wood's work will not reveal a single act which was not wholeheartedly and unselfishly designed for the welfare of the Filipino. He demanded efficiency in the government service but did not require the substitutions of Americans generally for Filipinos, although to some positions he appointed Americans and secured their confirmation.

Among other noteworthy achievements of Governor-General Wood it is appropriate to emphasize the care of lepers, of the insane, and other unfortunates, which always engaged his interest.

He also encouraged steps taken to relieve the very serious lack of hospital facilities prevailing throughout the Islands.

Another important measure was an act passed by the Legislature in 1922 providing for the medical inspection of children in all government elementary schools at least once a year.

The healthy interest in sports previously noted continued, and in 1925 the Philippine Legislature, in an act granting a charter to the Philippine Amateur Athletic Federation, created in the Department of Public Instruction the office of National Physical Director.

The administration of justice was another object of Governor-General Wood's special attention. In 1923 he secured legislation providing for eleven additional judges of first instance.

During this period additional taxes were levied, the most noteworthy of which was an increase of the percentage tax on business from one per cent to one and one-half per cent. This increase of the "sales" tax rate was made effective for a year at a time, so that it appeared to have been devised as a temporary measure. This rate is a serious burden on business and becomes prohibitive where property is bought and resold.

A tax, this time eminently opportune, was levied upon gasoline, the proceeds to be utilized for the maintenance of roads, a measure urgently needed because of the great wear on insular roads by motor trucks, which were finding their way into every part of the Islands.

Renewed interest in the construction of irrigation systems caused the Legislature in 1922 to appropriate for this purpose the proceeds of a bond issue of ten million dollars.

Noteworthy contributions by the Legislature during this period were the habitual criminal law; a law prohibiting the use of tickets or other substitute for legal tender currency in payment of labor; special appropriations for the "continuation of the treatment and diagnosis of leprosy"; a copyright law; laws requiring the correct labeling of commercial fertilizers, strengthening the pure food and drugs act, making appropriations for the extermination of agricultural pests, for extension of public health service among the Mohammedans and tribal peoples, providing pensions for public school teachers, making further provisions for Constabulary pensions, and for the pension and retirement of officers of the public health service.

The tendency of the Legislature to insert in their enactments provisions giving the presiding officers, or committees, of both houses and the secretaries of departments powers properly belonging to the Governor-General persisted during the administration of Governor-General Wood, but with decreasing frequency.

The investigating mission of 1921 had found that the expenses of government had increased while the efficiency had decreased, due in part to the inevitable tendency to multiply government positions, and in part to the unduly rapid Filipinization, which placed many untrained Filipinos in responsible posts. The cost of collecting customs per dollar of customs revenue may be taken as an example of the increased expense of government. In 1903–13 the cost ran about five and seven-tenths cents per dollar collected. In 1914 it jumped to eight and nine-tenths cents, and throughout the incumbency of Governor-General Harrison it averaged slightly over eight cents, in spite of the greatly increased collections which should have materially reduced the cost per dollar collected. By 1925 the cost had been cut nearly in half, the figure being four and six-tenths cents.

In dealing with the Legislature, Governor-General Wood was greatly embarrassed by the fact that most laws were passed in the last few hours of the legislative session, and under the provisions of the Jones Law, he had but thirty days after adjournment in which to decide whether to approve or disapprove them. Clerks of the Legislature took nearly the whole month to prepare the laws for his consideration, and thus many came up to him within a few days of the expiration of the time allotted him to study the various measures and determine whether to approve or veto them. This placed a very unfair onus upon the Governor-General. If these laws could have been sent him while the Legislature was still in session, they could have been returned for changes in accordance with his views and then enacted with great advantage to the public interest. This was impossible when the Legislature was not in session and it meant that these bills had to be reintroduced and go through the whole legislative procedure again in the ensuing year, very likely not be reached until the last days, and again to come up only to be vetoed for some preventable defect.

Governor-General Wood was above all things an inveterate worker and no task was too difficult for him to undertake. When the avalanche of enactments by the Legislature finally reached him, he was to be found surrounded by his secretaries of departments and bureau chiefs, and legal and financial advisers. He always exercised extraordinary endurance and patience in giving consideration to every measure and assent to all that he felt could become law without injury to the Islands.

Governor-General Wood however used his veto power freely and was greatly criticized for it by the Filipinos, who in an appeal by the Legislature to the President took the untenable position that there was an implied limitation to the classes of legislation upon which the Governor-General could exercise the veto and that purely domestic matters were excluded.

The President upheld the Governor-General and stated: "By the organic law it is made the duty of the Governor General either to approve or disapprove every bill which is passed by the Philippine Legislature."

Even a cursory study of the statistics of business and finance during General Wood's régime reveals marked evidence of advance, and, if the excellence of a government is measured by the increased prosperity of the people, then the Philippine government was good.

The most salient points are the growth of the gross business of the Islands upon which the percentage tax is paid. This is found to have increased from less than $200,000,000 before the era of free trade with the United States to nearly $650,000,000 in 1925. Coastwise tonnage cleared shows an increase from less than five hundred thousand in 1900 to two and one-quarter million tons in 1925, while the foreign tonnage cleared shows an even greater increase. Records of the postal savings bank also reveal healthy growth both in numbers of depositors and in amounts deposited. The receipts of the Bureau of Posts in twenty years multiplied by over eight, from less than $125,000 to more than $1,000,-000. The telegraph receipts in the same period showed an increase of nearly nine times, from about $80,000 a year to $700,000; while money orders sold rose in twenty years from about $3,500,000 to $23,500,000. The mileage of improved roads steadily increased, in 1925 reaching 3500 miles of first-class roads, and more than 3000 of second and third class. The total number of permanent bridges and culverts reached 7779, artesian wells 1751, and lighthouses in operation 194 as compared with 48 in 1902. The business done by the street railway and lighting company in Manila increased from $380,000 to more than $2,400,000.

In 1927 Governor-General Wood, after six years of toil, returned to the United States for a well-earned leave of absence. The effects of an early injury to his head, which had resulted in the necessity for two operations before 1912, had increased to an alarming extent, and only an indomitable will enabled him to work on. He gradually lost more and more of his muscular control, and at last, in May, he left for the United States, announcing that it was his intention to return after but a short leave of absence.

Early in August, while undergoing a brain operation, he died, a martyr to his devotion in public service.

Vice-Governor Eugene A. Gilmore served as Acting Governor-General until the arrival in the Islands on March 1, 1928, of the Honorable Henry L. Stimson, of New York, who had been appointed Governor-General. He had held the position of Secretary of War in the cabinet of President Taft, and had other notable qualifications for the post of Governor-General.

CHAPTER XIV

THE INDEPENDENCE MOVEMENT

THE PLATFORM of the Katipunan, or of any of the political parties prior to American occupation, made no mention of independence. At the beginning of the insurrection against Spain in 1896, there was "merely a crude idea in the minds of the masses that they were somehow going to shake off their masters, get rid of the whites, and divide up the big estates not only of the friars but of Filipino land-holders as well."

The Schurman Commission reported:

> . . . it would be a misrepresentation of facts not to report that ultimate independence — independence after an undefined period of American training — is the aspiration and goal of the intelligent Filipinos who to-day so strenuously oppose the suggestion of independence at the present time.

After considering all the evidence concerning the insurrection of 1896 against Spain, the Commission found that "the rebellion (in which the United States has merely succeeded to Spain's place) arose out of definite grievances and sought redress for definite wrongs." And further: ". . . This movement was in no sense an attempt to win independence, but was merely an effort to obtain relief from abuses which were rapidly growing intolerable."

In the course of the report of the Schurman Commission, of which he was one of the five members, Admiral Dewey denied having made any promise "directly or indirectly" of independence to the Filipinos. In the early days of American activity in the Islands, many misunderstandings of this sort occurred, and were largely due to faulty interpretation, sometimes intentional and sometimes by reason of imperfect knowledge of one or the other language by the interpreters themselves.

It is not fair to the many admirable Filipinos who espoused the cause of national independence and fought for it, and who gave up their homes, lives, sons, brothers, and husbands to the cause, to question the purity of their motives or the genuineness of their desire for an ideal with which no American proud of his history can fail to sympathize. Not only were the Filipinos filled with a proper pride of race, but they had reason to distrust and dislike the Americans. Taught by their leaders to believe that the representatives of the United States had given assurance that they would be given independence, they were honest in the belief that the United States had not lived up to its promises. It was a series of disastrous misunderstandings.

It has been told how the insurrection was put down by force of American arms, and, while fighting was still in process, the United States testified its good will in the form of early establishment of educational facilities and the appointment of a civil commission, composed of Americans very sympathetic to the Filipino point of view and aspirations, who entered upon their duties in the years 1900 and 1901, and began immediately giving autonomous governments to the lesser units in the Islands. These enlightened measures did much to allay growing hostility against the United States and to make the Filipinos feel that a new day had dawned, and that the new régime would not permit the intolerable abuses of the Spanish régime.

The United States authorities, both military and civil, encouraged in the schools a study of the history of the United States and of the American struggle for independence. It was the practice to read aloud the Declaration of Independence at public gatherings on the Fourth of July throughout the Islands, and this was done both by the military and by civilian Americans, and nothing was done to discourage the study or the thought of independence.

While the display of the Katipunan flag for a while was prohibited, there was nothing in the law that prohibited oratorical pleas for its repeal and for the right to fly their own flag, and these appeals became favorite themes for Filipino orators with political aspirations.

The platform of the first Philippine political party organized during the American régime, the Federalist, favored annexation and declared against cession to any foreign power.

Nothing that Governor-General Wright ever said or did was calculated to discourage the desire or aspiration for independence. He merely pointed out the necessity of an adequate period of preparation.

That the Filipinos have ample justification for feeling that the United States has not intended permanently to withhold independence if the Filipinos ultimately desire it, is abundantly proved by official statements of successive Presidents of the United States from Theodore Roosevelt to Coolidge inclusive, and supported from time to time by the Secretaries of War.

President McKinley said: "The Philippines are ours, not to exploit but to develop, to civilize, to educate, to train in the science of self-government."

President Roosevelt's attitude was cordial and impulsive, although in the early years of his presidency he didn't mention independence. In 1908, he did, and spoke of giving the Filipinos an opportunity to develop the capacity for managing their own affairs. In his message to Congress in December of that year, he said: "I hope and believe that these mark the beginning of a course which will continue till the Filipinos become fit to decide for themselves whether they desire to be an independent nation." Further on in the same message he expressed the hope that within a generation the Filipinos would be ready to decide for themselves, and he intimated very strongly that he thought intelligent self-interest would lead them to desire an association with the United States.

In 1905, Mr. Taft as Secretary of War spoke of the time when the Filipino people "have reached the condition in which they shall be competent to determine what form of government is best for them. Whether they shall become an independent nation, or whether they shall prefer by reason of mutual benefit to maintain the bond between the two peoples, as is done between the United States and Cuba or between England and Canada, England and Australia, or what the form autonomy may take, may well be left to the future, and to the circumstances and to the individuals who shall be in control of the two nations at that time."

Colonel Roosevelt, in a letter dated January 4, 1915, wrote: ". . . I administered the Islands absolutely without regard to politics. . . . I . . . peremptorily refused to promise independence, save in the very careful language I used on the one or two occasions when I spoke of the subject, because to promise independence without the sharpest qualification is inevitably taken as meaning Independence in the near future."

Although Colonel Roosevelt, writing in the *New York Times* in 1914, took the position that the United States should grant independence to the Philippine Islands because he felt that they considered that a promise had been made to them, he later, in a letter dated May, 1916, which is undoubtedly his last word on the subject, wrote:

. . . I would unquestionably advocate the retention of the Islands *upon the condition* that first, no promise of independence is authoritatively given, and second and even more important, that our policy of armament should be made to conform with the requirements of the situation. In other words, this means that the government of the people must in emphatic manner take the proper attitude toward our position as a world power, and therefore toward the establishment and maintenance of a great naval and military programme, which alone would be adequate to maintain such a position.

In his successive capacities as President of the Philippine Commission, Civil Governor, Secretary of War, and President of the United States, Judge Taft's expressions on the subject of independence were numerous and authoritative. As Civil Governor, on December 17, 1903, he spoke of the frequent recurrence in authoritative expressions of the Executive of the motto

that "the Philippines are for the Filipino and that the Government of the United States is here for the purpose of preserving the Philippines for the Filipinos," for their benefit, for their elevation, for their civilization. . . .

And further said

Whether an autonomy or independence or quasi independence shall ultimately follow in these islands ought to depend solely on the question: Is it best for the Filipino people and their welfare?

In his speech at the opening of the Philippine Assembly on October 16, 1907, Secretary Taft said in part:

. . . As this policy of extending control continues, it must logically reduce and finally end the sovereignty of the United States in the islands, unless it shall seem wise to the American and the Filipino peoples, on account of mutually beneficial trade relations and possible advantage to the islands in their foreign relations, that the bond shall not be completely severed.

Addressing the Military Order of the Carabao in Washington, in January, 1911, President Taft gave further expression to his views. He said:

My judgment is that we are likely to retain the Philippines for a considerable time. I am willing, when we can honorably, to part with them. But we cannot honorably part with them until they are able to have a government in which due process of law will be observed, and which shall be responsible and able to meet responsibility toward all the nations of the world. That means some time. I do not like to say that we shall never part with the Philippines, because I hope that the time will come when we shall be willing to let them go.

President Taft took occasion to reiterate in many speeches his belief that the time necessary for the Filipinos to assure all of the elements of stability in their government was a long one.

When a bill offered by Congressman Jones in 1912 was under consideration in Congress, similar in many respects to that which finally

THE HONORABLE LEONARD WOOD, GOVERNOR-GENERAL

GENERAL DOUGLAS MacARTHUR

passed, but granting complete independence at the end of eight years, President Taft said in a message to Congress:

. . . Such a proposal can only be founded on the assumption that we have now discharged our trusteeship to the Filipino people and our responsibility for them to the world, and that they are now prepared for self-government as well as national sovereignty. A thorough and unbiased knowledge of the facts clearly shows that these assumptions are absolutely without justification. As to this, I believe that there is no substantial difference of opinion among any of those who have had the responsibility of facing Philippine problems in the administration of the islands. . . .

. . . we are endeavoring to evolve a homogeneous people fit to determine, when the time arrives, their own destiny. We are seeking to arouse a national spirit and not, as under the older colonial theory, to suppress such a spirit. . . .

.   .   .   .

Popular self-government ultimately must rest upon common habits of thought and upon a reasonably developed public opinion. No such foundations for self-government, let alone independence, are now present in the Philippine Islands . . . it is sufficient to point out that under liberal franchise privileges only about 3 per cent of the Filipinos vote and only 5 per cent of the people are said to read the public press. To confer independence upon the Filipinos now is, therefore, to subject the great mass of their people to the dominance of an oligarchical and, probably, exploiting minority. Such a course will be as cruel to those people as it would be shameful to us.

. . . A present declaration even of future independence would retard progress by the dissension and disorder it would arouse. . . . It would be a disguised policy of scuttle. It would make the helpless Filipino the football of oriental politics, under the protection of a guaranty of their independence, which we would be powerless to enforce.

This message to Congress and President Taft's speeches about this time opposing the Jones Bill had a very strong general influence throughout the United States.

A month before relinquishing his high office, President Taft took occasion in 1913 to make a masterly review of the Philippine situation. His advice to his successor is contained in the following words:

Is it possible that a great party like the Democratic Party, now become responsible for the administration of this country, is going to reverse a policy that has vindicated itself so completely in ten years, for mere purposes of conformity to cobwebbed planks in forgotten platforms? . . .

Secretary Dickinson made his most important speech in the Islands on the subject of independence at the town of Lucena in the province of Tayabas. He said:

After the position taken by President McKinley, President Roosevelt and President Taft — and those are the only declarations in regard to the future of the Philippines that have been authoritatively made, — certainly the American people cannot raise any objection toward the Philippine people cherishing aspirations for independence.

A realization of such a fact cannot precede the desire, and the doctrine that was declared, "The Philippines for the Filipinos," certainly presupposes that spirit of independence in those who are to be fitted for independent government.

The most authoritative statement by Secretary Stimson, who succeeded Secretary Dickinson in President Taft's Cabinet, is to be found in his annual report for 1912, in which he said that the American policy toward the Philippine Islands should be carried to completion. He continued:

Until that time all proposals for independence are pleas for national recreancy on our part and for the repudiation of the heavy and difficult burden which thus far we have been bravely and consistently sustaining. Even more is it unjust to the great masses of Filipino people in whose behalf the high-sounding slogans of "liberty" and "independence" are shouted. After having been for centuries sunk in ignorance and held in economic subjection, they are now being aroused to self-supporting manhood and being welded into national solidarity. Along this line, and this line alone, lies the true course toward liberty and independence.

Governor-General Smith, always sympathetic with the Filipinos and with their aspirations and loyal in his support of the policies of the Taft régime in regard to independence, did not discourage the Filipino desire for it, but was thoroughly convinced of their then unreadiness.

Governor-General Forbes made it a point never by word or action to discourage the aspiration for independence, and wrote in his journal:

. . . I rather like, and applaud inwardly, the almost universal desire for independence, and am trying to steer this desire into a motive force for progress and material development. I don't write or speak in favor of independence, as I don't believe in it for them. I believe in the desire for it, and I never discourage that.

In a letter to one of the Resident Commissioners about that time he said:

If I were to be asked when the Filipinos will be capable of nationality I should reply: when there is an accumulation of wealth known to exist in the country of a per capita amount many times that in existence today; when the daily rate of wage for unskilled labor, the index of earning power, is three pesos [$1.50] per capita; when the imports and exports are five hundred million pesos [$250,000,000] a year; when the population has reached thirty millions; when the receipts of the government available for expenditure are twenty pesos [$10] per capita; when there are schools for all children of school age in the Islands; and when eighty per cent of the people are literate.

But in his journal, following some such series of qualifications, is found this added commentary:

. . . the Islands will then for the first time be strong enough to maintain a separate government. But whether the individuals will be strong enough to maintain order and dispense justice is another question. Each advance should be made tentatively under such circumstances that the step could be withdrawn if the ice seemed to be too thin.

Again in September, 1910, in a speech made in the Islands, Governor-General Forbes said that the rate of interest that business people had to pay could be taken as a fair gauge of their civilization; that the Filipinos could make no better study than that of lowering the rate of interest on loans, and the nearer that rate approximated three per cent, the nearer they would be to independence.

As to their readiness he wrote in 1907 that "one of the most cogent reasons why the Islands cannot run themselves, if not the very most cogent . . . is lack of an intelligent and trained body of people with the power of the ballot who have had the benefits of good local government long enough to demand and insist on it. This can only be obtained by giving them good government and letting them have it long enough to appreciate it."

The platform of the Democratic Party upon which President Wilson was elected in 1912 contained the following Philippine plank:

We reaffirm the position thrice announced by the Democracy in national convention assembled against a policy of imperialism and colonial exploitation in the Philippines or elsewhere. We condemn the experiment in imperialism as an inexcusable blunder which has involved us in enormous expense, brought us weakness instead of strength and laid our nation open to the charge of abandonment of the fundamental doctrine of self-government. We favor an immediate declaration of the nation's purpose to recognize the independence of the Philippine Islands as soon as a stable government can be established, such independence to be guaranteed by us until the neutralization of the islands can be secured by treaty with other Powers. In recognizing the independence of the Philippines our Government should retain such land as may be necessary for coaling stations and naval bases.

There is nothing in this plank, however, which required any change of policy in regard to the Philippine Islands. If the President and his advisers and Congress felt that the government they would leave in the Islands did not conform to their ideas of stability, there was ample reason for continuing American control for an indefinite period. Stability cannot be measured by any rules laid down for the guidance of those having to judge. A Republican President might feel that a government was sufficiently stable and the time had come to withdraw, whereas his Democratic successor, scrupulously observing the terms of his party's platform, might feel that that time was still a generation away.

It was not only in the Philippine Islands that President-elect Wilson's Staunton speech [1] created a stir. The Hearst papers, usually Democratic in their leanings, loudly denounced President-elect Wilson's advocacy of withdrawing the frontiers. The *New York American* said:

> The American sincerely hopes that President-elect Wilson will not commit himself in advance to the contraction of American territory, nor permit Mr. Bryan to persuade him now or hereafter to do so.
>
> Mr. Bryan has always been wrong in advocating this un-American and un-Democratic policy. Mr. Bryan fought the campaign of 1900 on this issue of contracting our territory by relinquishing the Philippines. The people of the United States repudiated his plan by nearly a million votes.
>
> It would be an inauspicious beginning of President Wilson's administration to revive an advocacy which wrecked the Democratic Party twelve years ago.

And the thoughtful *Chicago Inter-Ocean* took occasion to say: "Let us hope that President-elect Wilson spoke without real thought, that he will speedily inform himself as to the facts and cease to give the sanction of his great station to a policy both cowardly and war-breeding."

That Secretary of War Garrison was not entirely in sympathy with an early withdrawal from the Philippine Islands was indicated by his statement before a Senate committee in January, 1915. He was quoted as saying:

> . . . The United States has assumed responsibilities with respect to the Philippines, which, in the highest spirit of self-respect, it must discharge rightfully, at whatever cost. It has pledged itself in certain ways to the Filipino people, and those pledges must be kept in the utmost honor. We have no right to lay down the burden and shirk our duty because we find it difficult or costly or dangerous.

The passage of the Jones Bill in 1916, with its preamble, served to suspend further agitation for independence for a time. The world's attention was turned to the events in Europe and the World War, into which the United States was rapidly being drawn, and which finally occupied the public mind everywhere.

[1] In this speech, in December, 1912, President-elect Wilson said: "The Philippines are at present our frontier but I hope we presently are to deprive ourselves of that frontier."

After the election of Republican majorities in both houses of Congress and the emphatic defeat of his own party in the election of 1920, President Wilson sent a message to Congress in which he said:

Allow me to call your attention to the fact that the people of the Philippine Islands have succeeded in maintaining a stable government since the last action of the Congress in their behalf, and have thus fulfilled the condition set by the Congress as precedent to a consideration of granting independence to the Islands. I respectfully submit that this condition precedent having been fulfilled, it is now our liberty and our duty to keep our promise to the people of those Islands by granting them the independence which they so honorably covet.

The cynical will observe that this message was sent toward the end of eight years of administration, and at a time when the President was no longer able either to influence legislation or to put his recommendation into effect.

There is no doubt that Governor-General Harrison went to the Islands imbued with the idea that it was America's duty and to her interest to withdraw from the Islands at an early date, and he is said, upon relinquishing his position as Governor-General after nearly eight years, to have felt aggrieved that this policy had not been supported by the administration.

In his first four reports, or until 1918, Governor-General Harrison made no recommendation that independence be granted to the Philippine Islands. He spoke of the Jones Bill and alluded to the aspirations of the Filipinos; and in his report for 1917 he said that "the world conflict renders discussion of the immediate independence of the islands inopportune," but expressed the hope that after the war the United States would "present the claims of the Philippines to an independent existence to the congress of nations."

In his reports for 1918, 1919, and 1920, he placed himself definitely on record as believing that the Filipinos had established the stable government set forth in the Jones Law, and that, having fulfilled this requirement, they were entitled to their independence.

For the Filipinos the case was complete. Both houses of Congress had declared the intention of the United States to grant independence as soon as a stable government should be established; the two highest authorities, the President of the United States and the Governor-General of the Islands, had publicly announced the condition to have been fulfilled, the stable government to have been established. And the Filipinos asked for the fulfillment of the pledge.

The election of President Harding directed attention to his position in regard to the Philippine Islands. He had been chairman of the Senate Committee on Territories and Insular Possessions, and as such was known to be well informed in regard to Philippine matters. In a speech made in the Senate in 1916 Senator Harding had said: "I think it impossible for us to honorably withdraw. I think it is impossible, first, because of our obligations to the Filipino people themselves."

President Harding as has been seen met the condition thrust upon him by sending out a mission, to investigate and report. Although no public announcement was made to that effect, it was generally felt that the report expressed the policy of the administration.

President Harding told the members of a Philippine independence mission in 1922 that the time had not come to grant them independence. He spoke of looking forward to a continued progress which would make it easy to sever the bonds between the two countries or rivet them more firmly, in accordance with their desires, and then made this very important declaration of purpose: "No backward step is contemplated. No diminution of your domestic control is to be sought."

The Honorable John W. Weeks, Secretary of War, was very definite. In May, 1922, a New York newspaper, reporting an interview, quoted him as saying: "I am not in favor of granting immediate independence to the Philippines, and the President is not."

President Coolidge's messages to the people of the Philippine Islands have been direct, incisive, and unequivocal. They mark an epoch in American relations with the Islands. Replying in 1924 to a visiting Philippine independence mission, the President wrote:

It is . . . a matter of congratulation, which I herewith extend, that you have chosen to carry on this discussion within the bounds of lawful claims and means. That you have thus declared the purpose to restrict your modes of appeal and methods of enforcing it is gratifying evidence of the progress which the Filipino people, under American auspices, have made toward a demonstrated capacity for self-government.

.   .   .   .

. . . Their [the Filipinos'] position in the world is such that without American protection there would be the unrestricted temptation to maintain an extensive and costly diplomatic service and an ineffective but costly military and naval service. It is to be doubted whether with the utmost exertion, the most complete solidarity among themselves, the most unqualified and devoted patriotism, it would be possible for the people of the Islands to maintain an independent place in the world for an indefinite future.

As to sentiment in the United States, the President indicated that Philippine independence was favored largely by those who did not feel it would benefit the Filipinos, but thought it would benefit the United States, and in that connection he said:

. . . Feeling as I do, and as I am convinced the great majority of Americans do regarding our obligations to the Filipino people, I have to say that I regard such arguments as unworthy. The American people will not evade or repudiate the responsibility they have assumed in this matter. The American Government is convinced that it has the overwhelming support of the American Nation in its conviction that present independence would be a misfortune and might easily become a disaster to the Filipino people. Upon that conviction the policy of this Government is based.

. . . In education, in cultural advancement, in political conceptions, and institutional development, the Filipino people have demonstrated a capacity which can not but justify high hopes for their future. But it would be idle and insincere to suggest that they have yet proved their possession of the completely developed political capacity which is necessary to a minor nation assuming the full responsibility of maintaining itself in the family of nations. I am frankly convinced that the very mission upon which you have addressed me is itself an evidence that something is yet lacking in development of political consciousness and capability.

After commenting upon the failure of the Filipinos to preserve the checks and balances between legislative and executive functions, he continued:

. . . the American Nation could not entertain the purpose of holding any other people in a position of vassalage. . . .

. . . It is not conceivable that they would desire merely because they possessed the power, to continue exercising any measure of authority over a people who could better govern themselves on a basis of complete independence. If the time comes when it is apparent that independence would be better for the people of the Philippines from the point of view of both their domestic concerns and their status in the world, and if when that time comes the Filipino people desire complete independence, it is not possible to doubt that the American Government and people will gladly accord it.

Frankly, it is not felt that that time has come.

In a message to Congress, December, 1926, the President said: "The economic development of the Philippine Islands is very important. They ought not to be turned back to the people until they are both politically fitted for self-government and economically independent." And then came these epoch-making words: "No one contemplates any time in the future either under the present or a more independent form of government when we should not assume some responsibility for their defense."

If this declaration of the President is accepted as the permanent policy of the United States, it establishes a doctrine similar in effect to the Monroe Doctrine but applicable to those islands that fringe the coast of Asia and are comprised in the Philippine group.

In response to comments published in the United States to the effect that the Philippine people did not desire independence, the Philippine Legislature passed a law providing for a plebiscite so that the people could have an opportunity by vote to demonstrate their desire for independence. Governor-General Wood vetoed this measure and it came up to President Coolidge on appeal.

On April 6, 1927, President Coolidge in a masterly document supported the veto of the Governor-General, giving his reasons in full. He criticized the requirement of the law that the voters must vote categorically "Yes" or "No" as to whether or not they desired "immediate, absolute and complete independence" on the ground that it gave to those who might wish to qualify their vote no chance to do so. He pointed out that no adequate provision was made to obtain the expression of the desires of the tribal and Mohammedan population.

The position which the United States would probably take were the Philippine Islands to sever completely their political relationship was vigorously dealt with. Apropos of the material assistance given to the Philippine Islands by the United States, the President said:

This phase of the question has not received careful consideration in the Islands because of the misapprehension which seems to be quite general there that America, even though she granted full independence to the Islands, would still assume the heavy responsibility of guaranteeing the security, sovereignty and independence of the Islands. In my opinion, this is wholly erroneous. Responsibility without authority would be unthinkable. American defense is a correlate of American sovereignty, not of foreign sovereignty. Where there is no sovereignty there is no obligation of protection. The best security to the Philippine Islands is the protection of and by the United States.

Governor-General Leonard Wood's attitude toward Philippine independence was set forth in a cable to the Secretary of War, March 14, 1924, in which he said:

. . . I sympathize deeply with the desire of the Filipino people for independence, but know they are not yet prepared to assume its responsibility, either from the standpoint of instructed public opinion, preparedness for defense, common language, or economic resources.

In years of presidential elections, the platforms of both political parties in the United States have usually touched upon the Philippine Islands. In 1900 and 1904 the platforms of the Republican Party justified, and those of the Democratic Party condemned, the Philippine policy of the Republican administration.

In 1908, the Republican platform spoke of "leading the inhabitants step by step to an ever-increasing measure of home rule." The Democratic Party in that year condemned "the experiment of imperialism as an inexcusable blunder" and favored "an immediate declaration of the nation's purpose to recognize the independence of the Philippine Islands as soon as a stable government can be established," the independence to be guaranteed by the United States "until the neutralization of the islands can be secured by treaty with other powers." The Democrats, however, favored the retention of land for coaling stations and naval purposes.

In 1912, the Republican platform set forth in one sentence that the Philippine policy of their party "has been and is inspired by the belief that our duty toward the Filipino people is a national obligation which should remain entirely free from partisan politics." The Democrats repeated almost verbatim the plank of four years earlier.

In 1916, the Republicans expressed adherence to the Philippine policy of their former leaders, asserting that it had already resulted in greatly improved conditions, and "if persisted in" would "bring still greater benefits in the future." They continued: "We accepted the responsibility of the islands as a duty to civilization and the Filipino people. To leave with our task half done would break our pledges, injure our prestige among nations and imperil what has already been accomplished." They ended by condemning the Democratic administration for "its attempt to abandon the Philippines," which the platform claimed was prevented by the Republican opposition in Congress. The Democrats in that year endorsed the provisions of the so-called Jones Bill, and reiterated their endorsement of the purpose of ultimate independence expressed in the preamble of that measure.

In 1920, the Republican platform was silent on the subject, but the Democratic platform came out squarely and very definitely for independence in these words, "We favor the granting of independence without unnecessary delay. . . ."

In 1924, the Republican platform declared in favor of a continuation of the existing policy in the Philippine Islands, while the Democratic platform contained almost the exact words of President Wilson in his message to Congress in December, 1920, recommending the immediate grant of independence.

The Republican platform in 1928 made no mention of the Philippine Islands, and the Democratic platform repeated its Philippine plank of 1924.

The fact that up to 1920 there was no essential difference between the Republican and Democratic Philippine planks, so far as immediate administrative action was concerned, did not escape close observers of the situation.

The matter of giving independence to the Philippine Islands has come repeatedly before Congress. From the first appearance of the Resident Commissioners in Washington in 1908, the first commissioner representing the Nationalist Party — Señor Ocampo — and later all the commissioners, have not failed at least once in each session to present the desire of the Filipinos for independence to the House of Representatives, to which they were accredited, making from time to time appeals not lacking in eloquence.

It is pertinent to mention a few significant instances indicative of the attitude of Congress on the subject of Philippine independence.

In 1907, the United States Senate voted 39 to 18 against a proposed measure providing that independence should be granted to the Islands upon the establishment of a stable government.

Congressman William A. Jones, of Virginia, in 1911, became chairman of the House Committee on Insular Affairs. In 1912 the committee reported favorably on his Philippine bill, providing for full and complete independence in 1921, but the bill was not voted upon by the House.

In 1916 the Clarke amendment to the Jones Bill passed the Senate, providing for complete independence of the Philippine Islands in not less than two years and not more than four years.

The amendment was defeated in the House by a vote of 213 to 165, and the bill enacted as we have seen with its preamble declaring that "as soon as a stable government can be established therein" independence was to be granted.

Senator O'Gorman, the Democratic leader in the Senate, came out squarely against the Jones Bill. In 1913, Cardinal Gibbons, the most distinguished and powerful representative of his church in the United States at the time, had expressed himself as follows: "I am convinced that, for the present, at least, the welfare of the islands will be better safeguarded under the care and direction of the United States. There is a great difference between independence and liberty. There are countries which have independence but no liberty or freedom, whereas the Philippine Islands, although for the present not enjoying independence, have freedom and liberty."

The attitude of Congress toward the Philippine Islands has undergone some very marked changes. In 1924 the Secretary of War found the House and Senate committees concerned with Philippine affairs strongly inclined to recommend cutting the Islands altogether adrift, and he was led to believe that a measure carrying with it complete Philippine independence, with no obligation of the United States to care for the Islands, might be passed. As a result, the Fairfield Bill was introduced in Congress providing for the creation of a supervised republic — to be known as the "Commonwealth of the Philippines" — the supervision to be exercised by a United States commissioner, who was to have certain emergency powers subject to decision by the President in Washington, in whom the power of intervention would reside.

This bill was reported favorably by the House Committee on Insular Affairs, and the Secretary of War let it be understood that it would have the sanction of the administration provided it were acceptable to the Filipinos. Although, with the sanction of the administration behind it, the bill stood an excellent chance of being enacted into law, it was not acceptable to the Filipinos because of the provision that they were not to have their independence for a long period (30 years).

The support of the administration was given because a complete separation — threatened by the attitude of Congress at that time — would have been so disastrous to the Philippine Islands, and incidentally to the relations of the United States with the Orient, that the administration felt that, of the compromises most likely to prevail, the Fairfield Bill was the least harmful. The Congress to which the bill was presented went out of existence, however, without taking definite action.

Had this measure become law, the machinery for exercise of power by the United States would have been diminished to such a degree that the United States would have been virtually in a position of responsibility without adequate means of intervention. The most glaring defect was the lack of power given to the American commissioner. The bill carrying the proposed limitations would not have given him the prestige necessary to his position, especially in an Oriental country.

Congress later seemed to have changed its attitude toward the Filipinos. There was less independence sentiment and both Senators and Representatives seemed much more inclined to watch the course of events and judge of the capacity of the Filipinos by the use they might make of the concessions already granted to them.

In the Islands the elective Legislature has consistently advocated independence. Whether or not the legislators in their hearts wanted independence — and some of them certainly did not — it soon developed that none of them could actively oppose independence and retain his seat, and the result has been a fairly uniform attitude on the part of the Filipino legislators in asking for independence.

At the close of the first session of the First Legislature, Speaker Osmeña made an address in which he spoke of the desire of the Philippine people for independence; and the first legislative notice taken of independenec was a vote by the Assembly supporting the position of the Speaker. The leader of the Progressive Party in the Assembly, in concurring in this resolution, did so with a reservation excepting that clause which claimed the country "to be now ready for independence."

Again, at the close of the session in 1909, the Speaker delivered a stirring address to the Assembly which was followed by a resolution requesting Resident Commissioner Quezon to urge upon Congress the granting of independence. The Speaker thereafter closed each session of the Assembly with a similar discourse.

In its advocacy of independence the Philippine Legislature did not at first use the word "complete." The word "immediate" was frequently used, but in the early days, when the people who asked for independence were pinned down, it was usually found they wanted it under an American protectorate and within the tariff wall of the United States.

As time went on the words "complete and absolute" came to be more and more frequently inserted in their demands. This has been more noticeable since the publication of the Wood-Forbes report, in which among the general conclusions were to be found the words: "We find a general failure to appreciate the fact that independence under the protection of another nation is not true independence."

With the emphasis placed in that report also upon the unwillingness of the United States to assume responsibility without authority, there has developed a tendency to become very emphatic in the demand for "immediate, absolute, and complete independence."

When, in 1926, both houses of the Philippine Legislature passed an independence resolution, a notable feature was that the representatives of the Mountain and Moro provinces joined in the vote.

The overwhelming Republican victory in the national elections of 1920 in the United States having given President-elect Harding a satisfactory majority of Republicans in both houses of Congress, and shown that the end of the régime of the Democratic Party was near, the Philippine Legislature made a continuing annual appropriation of five hundred thousand dollars for promoting independence. An independence commission was created and authorized to use the independence fund for its expenses and for publicity. Offices were opened in the Islands and in the United States. A press bureau was established and an agent maintained in Washington. A number of American newspapers were supplied with material, and a further mass of propaganda was sent out for publication by different periodicals throughout the United States.

When the Insular Auditor in 1924 ruled that the appropriation for the promotion of independence was illegal, an effort was made to secure an independence fund by popular subscription. In addition, the Legislature thereafter provided in the appropriation acts fifty thousand dollars annually for the expenses of committees to present petitions to Congress, although the nature of the petitions was not specified in the laws.

In the years 1919, 1922, 1923, 1924, and 1925, independence missions from the Philippine Islands were sent to the United States. Some of the members of these missions were very earnest and competent patriots, and some of them had no hesitation in admitting privately that they came because their political fortunes demanded activity in favor of independence, whatever their convictions might be.

Members of the 1919 mission, on reaching San Francisco, began speaking most conservatively, mentioning increased trade relations and improved means of communication. Later they changed their policy and made guarded appeals for independence in all their speeches, indicating that the cabled reports of their earlier speeches had not been satisfactory in Manila, and that it had been intimated to them that they were expected to make direct appeals for independence. The 1919 mission reached Washington while President Wilson was in Europe.

Speaker Roxas, of the Philippine House of Representatives, who headed the independence mission which arrived in Washington late in 1923, addressed to Congress a vigorous memorial.

In 1924 an independence mission consisting of Senate-President Quezon, Senator Osmeña, and Representative Recto, joined Speaker Roxas, who had headed a mission the preceding year.

In 1925 Senator Osmeña was designated by the Legislature to visit Washington on a political mission, and with great dignity and tact he endeavored to secure from Congress some further concessions for his people. He and Resident Commissioner Guevara presented to Congress a formal petition for independence.

As early as 1910 some of the Filipino leaders began agitating to secure from the Congress of the United States authority to adopt their own constitution. A proposed joint resolution to that effect was passed by the Philippine Legislature December 5, 1910, and the concurrence of the Commission requested. The resolution asked Congress to recognize the "inherent, inalienable" right of every civilized people to prepare and adopt its own constitution. The Commission did not concur.

In 1925 Senator Osmeña asked Congress to authorize the Philippine people to prepare a constitution for submission to Congress for approval. This does not appear to have been considered by Congress.

The attitude of Americans residing in the Islands toward independence varied between two extremes. A few, usually a small group of Democrats, espoused the cause of Philippine independence — and it is fair to them to assume that they believed in it. A larger group of Democrats, who organized and sent delegates to the Democratic national convention, but whose platform was not in conformity with that of the national party, urged some permanent political relationship. The rank and file of Americans resident in the Islands — including army officers, civilians, missionaries, public and private employees, soldiers and ex-soldiers, some of them expecting to pass the rest of their lives in the Islands, many of them married to Filipino women and settling down to the soil, and visitors, either on business or pleasure, but with a desire to know facts at first hand and form reliable opinions — almost to a man believed in a continuance of American rule over the Islands for an indefinite period of years. They felt that it would be madness to change from the slow but sure process of evolution, of gradually placing more and more in the hands of Filipinos the management of their affairs under the strong and guiding hand of the United States, to the uncertain degree of stability in which the Philippine Islands would be left without United States credit and administration. They knew that financial disaster would inevitably follow were the markets of the United

States suddenly closed to Philippine products, a disaster that might bring in its train a social upheaval.

There have been many Americans in the Islands, including some of the leading businessmen, who have advocated the permanent retention of the Islands. The American Chamber of Commerce of the Philippine Islands on August 14, 1920, at a meeting at which more than two hundred and fifty members were present, adopted a resolution expressing a desire for "a territorial government under the sovereignty of the United States." While all but six of the members present voted in favor of this resolution, there was no agreement as to the form of government.

Americans who oppose independence have been well represented by Judge Daniel R. Williams, who has contributed to magazines and newspapers in the United States many articles opposing the grant of greater political powers to the Filipinos, and in his book, "The United States and the Philippines," has argued against Philippine independence. Judge Williams contends that Congress is without power to withdraw the sovereignty of the United States.

President-Emeritus Charles W. Eliot of Harvard wrote:

The puzzle about the bringing-up of a backward race under the control of superior is, that there is no natural time-limit to the control exercised by the abler race; and the backward race will remain dependent so long as they are subject to the active control of the superior. Childhood in a family has a natural limit; and in the process of growth, physical and mental, the control of the parents gradually and naturally diminishes until it ceases completely, — often before the real maturity of the child. When the child becomes free, he or she is seldom as wise or as prudent as his parents. Nevertheless, liberty is essential to the development of a robust character. In the bringing-up of a backward race by one more advanced, there seems to be no natural, gradual transition from a condition of thralldom to one of liberty; and yet the experience of liberty is necessary to the development of any vigorous national character.

The Right Reverend Charles H. Brent, Episcopal Bishop of the Philippine Islands, a man of unusual breadth of character and vision, said:

It appears to me that it would be a measure of quixotry beyond the most altruistic administration to stand sponsor for the order of an experimental government of more than doubtful stability 10,000 miles from our coast. When the Philippines achieve independence they must swallow the bitter with the sweet and accept the perils as well as the joys of walking alone. There are national risks involved, even in a limited protectorate, to which I trust America will never expose herself.

. . . .

The people of the Philippines require our rule. We are not in the Philippines for our pleasure or profit. If we were it would be the most natural thing in the

world to say that the game is not worth the candle as soon as intense difficulties
and dangers arise, and leave the Philippines to go to perdition in their own way.
But we cannot do that.

Throughout the first years of American administration in the Philippine Islands, the Filipinos were being constantly incited to further
efforts on behalf of their own independence by the actions of the Anti-
Imperialist League, with headquarters in Boston. Emissaries from this
league made their appearance from time to time in the Islands, and invariably sought out things to criticize, and sent them in. It seemed the
Anti-Imperialists felt that the best way to prove that the Filipinos were
ready to govern themselves was to demonstrate that the Americans
were incapable of governing them, this being the spirit shown by their
agents.

It is a common trait among the Filipinos to make extravagant claims
and their orators of the period repeated asseverations of a "unanimous"
desire on the part of the people for independence, ignoring the existence
of that large body of careful and thoughtful Filipinos who knew that
their people were not ready to go alone, ardently as some of them wished
that they were. The word "unanimous" was on occasion written into
the text of resolutions which were passed with dissenting votes made of
record.

The natural desire for independence, however, was so strong that few
felt it expedient openly to oppose it. Officeholders or aspirants for office
not espousing independence were likely to lose the next election. Some
prominent Filipinos actually did transfer their property out of the
Islands when the Jones bill of 1912, providing for independence in 1921,
was pending, and numbers of them privately said they proposed to move
where they could still be under the American flag. Others indicated
the desire to go to France or Spain. These, however, formed a very
small minority. The great majority of wealthy Filipinos stayed in their
country, threw in their lot with their own people, and took their chances.

With the passage of time, the Filipinos seemed to acquire greater confidence in the capacity of their own people to govern, perhaps because
they had seen power being put in the hands of their fellows in increasing measure as the years went by and noted that the country still progressed. Thus the demand for independence became more insistent and
the votes for it more whole-hearted, while the voices raised against it became smaller. Notwithstanding, when the Wood-Forbes Mission visited
the Islands in 1921, in the private interviews which were given after the

public sessions were held, a surprising number of persons vehemently opposed independence. And it was surprising that these opponents of independence were found in no one class or stratum of society, but were quite generally distributed; some were schoolboys and girls, some were students returned from the United States, some laborers, people from the fields, factory hands, others were businessmen, professional men, and persons of social standing, society leaders in Manila, men of importance and standing in the provinces, their sons, wives, and daughters. On the other hand, those who favored independence were also drawn quite generally from all those classes. In other words, it seemed to be a matter of individual judgment and in no sense a question of social groupings, although the proportion of those who favored continued American retention of the Islands was greater among the educated and property-holding classes than it was among the illiterate.

The people closest in touch with the Filipinos were Americans living in the provinces, schoolteachers, Constabulary officers, and engineers. One of the provincial engineers, after living for some years among the people, writing in 1913 of the political situation, said: "If the worthy gentlemen who waste so much time and paper discussing independence would devote a year's time to the study of the matter — not as official visitors received with brass bands and banquets, but as unofficial workers among the rank and file of the Filipino people — they would soon discover that there is no independence question. . . . For the rank and file of the Filipinos do not want independence."

After his visit to the Islands in 1915, General McIntyre, Chief of the Bureau of Insular Affairs, reported to the Secretary of War: "I am convinced that no serious part of the Filipino people desires separation from the United States at this time."

Professor Thomas L. Blayney, a Democrat and friend of President Wilson, after visiting the Islands in 1915, wrote:

Certainly one of the most surprising things to the visitor, if he is fortunate enough to have heart-to-heart talks with representative Filipinos who are not themselves political aspirants, will be to learn that independence is not desired at this time by men of this type. *Every one of them gave it as his opinion that revolution would certainly follow the lowering of the Flag.*

In 1932 a Philippine Independence Mission composed of a few leading Filipinos, Señores Quezon and Osmeña, a senator representing the opposition party, Señor Roxas, Speaker of the House, and two floor leaders representing the Nationalist and opposition parties, was formed, to come to Washington and negotiate with American leaders the terms of independence. Senator Quezon, however, did not accompany the party to Washington and remained throughout the course of the negotiations in Manila.

They found Senator Hawes of Missouri desirous of sponsoring such a measure, and the result was the so-called Hawes-Cutting bill.

Senator Vandenberg and Secretary of War Hurley both had taken occasion to visit the Islands in an effort to reach some agreement to the terms of some measure that would meet the aspirations of the Filipinos and at the same time protect them from exploitation either political or economic.

On his return from service as Ambassador to Japan, ex-Governor-General Forbes conferred with the senate leaders and suggested some changes in the bill, which commended themselves to Senator Hawes and were adopted by the Senate. It was unfortunate that the Senator in presenting his bill to Congress should have mentioned these amendments and their source, as this was used to support the opposition to the bill in Manila.

All the steps leading up to the presentation of the bill in its final form had been taken with the cognizance and assent of the Philippine Independence Mission then sitting in Washington and the terms of the bill met their approval. It finally passed Congress in 1932, was vetoed by President Hoover, and early in 1933 was passed over the President's veto, and became law. It was, however, not to become effective until accepted by the Philippine Legislature.

The principal items in the law were the granting of absolute and complete independence at the expiration of ten years, and in the meantime there was to be established a supervised commonwealth under the sovereignty of the United States, but with an elected Philippine President and under a constitution to be adopted.

At this period the supporters of Señores Quezon and Osmeña were striving each for the mastery of their leader; Senator Quezon from his vantage point in Manila, it appeared, was marshaling his forces to oppose whatever bill his rivals supported, and in October 1933 under his leadership the Philippine Legislature voted not to accept the law.

After this Senator Quezon came to Washington, and while he was there the so-called Tydings-McDuffie bill was drafted and received his approval. It differed from the previous bill in certain particulars, the principal difference lying in the fact that no military bases were agreed upon to be retained by the United States; and the matter of naval bases was left for later determination by negotiation. The influence of Senator Quezon was such that the bill was unanimously approved by the Philippine Legislature and was ratified by the Philippine people at a plebiscite on May 14, 1935. The most important item of this bill was the grant of complete independence to become effective on the 4th of July, 1946.

The Filipinos soon became conscious of the fact that they had achieved too much. The absolute closing of United States markets to their products at the time independence came in 1946 would have been economically extremely disastrous. So Señor Osmeña made another trip to Washington and secured the passage of an additional bill, the principal provisions of which were providing quotas on a 5 per cent annually diminishing basis which would give a total of twenty years for closing the markets of the United States to the principal products of the Philippines, namely, sugar, coconut oil, tobacco, embroideries, and cordage. This, it was hoped, would give time for the Filipinos to develop new markets so that their principal industries should not be ruined.

The constitution of the Philippine Islands was adopted by the Filipinos at a constitutional convention in Manila on the 8th of February, 1935, approved by the President of the United States shortly afterward, and ratified by the Philippine people at a plebiscite on the 4th of May, 1935. This constitution provided for a unicameral legislative body, called the National Assembly. It also fixes the territory as that which was ceded to the United States by Spain in the Treaty of Paris, and further specifies that it includes "all territory over which the present Government of the Philippine Islands exercises jurisdiction." It specifies that the Philippines is a republican state in which the sovereignty resides in the people and that all government authority emanates from them. War is renounced as an instrument of national policy. The usual bill of rights, adequately expressed, is clearly set forth. While not providing for woman suffrage, it provides that the National Assembly should extend the right of woman suffrage if adopted by a plebiscite.

The President of the Philippines has the veto power but this may be overridden by a two-thirds vote of the Legislature; he may veto separate items in the appropriation and revenue bills, with certain limitations. Property "used exclusively for religious, charitable or educational purposes" is exempt from taxation. The President and Vice-President were elected for terms of six years and the President was not eligible for re-election. A later amendment to the constitution in 1940 by referendum shortened the term from six to four years with one re-election permitted. Later in the year 1935 certain amendments to the constitution were adopted and approved; these had to do purely with trade relations with the United States. In April, 1940, a further change in the constitution was made which provided for a two-chamber legislature. Elections for the senate and the house of representatives were held in November, 1941, less than a month before the war with Japan began.

The sovereignty of the United States was represented in the Philippine Islands by an official to whom the title of High Commissioner was given. The first High Commissioner was the Honorable Frank Murphy, who relinquished his title of Governor-General to take the new position under the Philippine Commonwealth. He was succeeded by the Honorable Paul V. McNutt in 1937, who in turn was succeeded by the Honorable Francis B. Sayre in 1939, who held the position in Manila until compelled by the exigencies of the invasion to move to Corregidor.

There was a wide difference of opinion, even among military men, as to whether the American occupation of the Philippines was a source of military strength or weakness.

It was not only the desire for the acquisition of the Philippines, rich as they are, that would induce any people to attack them. It is obvious that any such attack would be merely part of a greater plan and the possession of the Philippines would be merely a steppingstone towards its consummation, namely: world domination. Viewed in this light the war in the Pacific, of which the capture of the Philippine Islands would be an incident, would bring America face to face with a choice between two unpleasant alternatives:

1. The defeatist attitude of the isolationist, abandoning any claim to be a world power, giving up our freedom to traverse the oceans, and send our ships, our commodities, and our travelers over the world.

2. To fight and put an end once for all to tyranny and the hostile control of the avenues of trade.

The question lay in the final analysis between progressive or retrogressive world civilization. Looked at in this light the control of the Philippines was a military asset; and the question of how practical this asset was to prove itself lay in the degree of friendliness we were able to build up by years of association between Americans and Filipinos. If this degree of friendship was such that the Filipinos stood squarely on the side of progress, civilization, morality, and decency, then they were a very definite source of strength. And such they have proved to be.

CHAPTER XV

CONCLUSION

PRESIDENT MCKINLEY's instruction enjoined the Taft Commission to treat the Philippine people "with the same courtesy and respect for their personal dignity which the people of the United States are accustomed to require from each other." Thus was the golden rule applied to the administration of a dependency.

This injunction is the key to the spirit in which America approached her great task in the Philippine Islands, and, it is believed, sounds a high note of practical morality which must be observed, not only by the American people, but by all peoples if they are to achieve success in the administration of dependencies and end the growing resentment of foreign domination and European control which manifests itself in an increasing degree, especially among Asiatic peoples. One cannot help speculating as to whether the general application of this rule would not serve to prevent future changes of sovereignty in colonies now under European administration.

It is appropriate to look back to the early days of colonial administration. The records of early Spanish, Portuguese, British, Dutch, and other conquests, show that they were designed wholly for the expansion of trade, or for the extension of religious beliefs; and even where religion was the moving force, it is noteworthy that economic advantages were not neglected and that exclusive trade privileges were claimed as an accompanying prerogative. For centuries the Dutch in Java did not permit their colonists to have any European trade except with their own people. Similarly, the Spaniards for more than two hundred years excluded all other Europeans from trade relations with the Philippine Islands.

During these early centuries the controlling motive in colonial enterprises was the profit to the colonizing country, with comparatively little consideration for the welfare of the peoples colonized, although some of the early administrators were able and kindly men whose natural goodness made them interest themselves in the welfare of those they governed. Many of the governments as a matter of practice did greatly benefit the governed races, but this benefit was supplemental to the development of trade. The history of the Dutch administration of their East Indian colonies reveals the interesting fact that a very large sum was annually drawn from those impoverished peoples to defray expenses of the Netherlands government at home.

One should approach the study of colonial problems today with full realization of the fact that, except in the case of the over-sea possessions of the United States, practically all colonies have the historical background of acquisition for the purposes of trade advantage, and colonial administrators have for centuries measured their success by the profits they have provided to their merchants at home.

Little by little the idea gained ground that it was good business and good policy to win the good will of the governed people, and that kind treatment resulted in better trade relations and less draft on the home treasury than putting down rebellions. Even the Dutch had to spend large sums in quelling insurrection.

It is many years since the colonists of any of these countries have been restricted to trading exclusively with the sovereign country. But preference is given by differential freight rates, customs dues, and such natural advantages as those that flow from a common language and currency and from ease of communication. And the citizens of the sovereign country usually control the banks and through them the credits.

In the instructions of President McKinley, and in those of all the Presidents of the United States to their administrators in the Philippine Islands, a high note of altruism is maintained. They are enjoined to remember that the government is designed solely for the welfare of the Philippine people. Nowhere in their instructions, nor in any official instructions to the American administrators in the Philippines, nor in other dependencies of the United States, is found any clause requiring consideration of the welfare of the American people.

It is true that, in establishing free trade with the Philippine Islands, the United States has created a preferential trade advantage which has greatly benefited the merchants of our own country. But that advantage is reciprocal; the benefit is also extended to the merchants of the Islands and through them to the Philippine people, and no one can study the economic growth of the Islands in the past three decades without reaching the conclusion that the advantages from the trade relations accruing to the Philippine people have exceeded those accruing to the people of the United States.

Colonizing countries whose dependencies have been and still are to a large extent administered in the interest of trade have acted on what appears to an American eye a fallacy. They have failed to grasp one of the essential economic factors in the situation. In the effort to promote trade, they have almost uniformly conducted their colonies on the theory that by obtaining their labor cheap they were promoting the welfare of their merchants, manufacturers, and agricultural proprietors. Instead of devoting their best energies toward raising the standard of living among the laboring men, certain colonial powers have deliberately held the standard low and in some extreme cases resorted to artificial devices to accomplish this result. The British in Jamaica, for example, went so far as to import natives of India under ten-year contracts to work for twenty-five cents a day when the going rate of wages in the West Indies exceeded one dollar a day. The inevitable result of this act of social injustice and economic fallacy was to drive the competent Jamaican negroes out of the island: they emigrated in thousands to Panama, Cuba, and other Central American countries where they did not have to meet this kind of competition.

Americans in the Philippine Islands have done exactly the opposite, and the policy they have adopted has been proved economically sound. Americans have believed that the best measure of their success in the administration of the Islands can be found in an increase in the rate of wages for unskilled labor. They have gone on the principle that the world in the long run receives about what it pays for; if it pays a man twenty-five cents a day for his work, it will get twenty-five cents' worth of work out of him; if it pays him two dollars a day, it will get two dollars' worth of work out of him. It cannot pay more than the laborer is worth, because the money in which this labor is paid is derived from the work of his hands and the sale of the products he makes; and it is, therefore, an economic impossibility to pay too much for labor for any protracted period of time. Social injustice carries its own nemesis in a deterioration of the quality of the work performed. Education, emulation, and opportunity are the great factors in stimulating men to intelligent effort. Education arouses ambition and enables the laborer to learn and to apply scientific methods to make his work more efficient. Emulation is aroused as soon as there is opportunity to secure better living conditions by putting forth better efforts.

It is, therefore, in the treatment of labor that the greatest fundamental divergence of American practice from that of other colonizing countries is to be found. When the Americans arrived in the Philippine Islands many Filipinos were working for five and ten cents a day. The prevailing rate of wages for common labor was about twenty cents, except in the seaports and the largest centers of population, where it ran somewhat higher. Under the inspiration of education and opportunity all this has changed. Throughout the Islands the laborer looks for better things. Wages gradually increased; in the cities the laborer as early as 1930 was earning as high as one dollar a day, three or four times what he could earn before. Agricultural enterprises paid from about thirty to sixty-five cents a day for unskilled labor, and for skilled labor up to two dollars.

There has been, and persists to this day, a prejudice among colonial administrators against the education of the masses in countries of vast populations living necessarily a more or less primitive life and subsisting on very little, such as India, Java, and certain regions in Africa. In the early centuries there was no general system of primary education in Europe, and the colonizing countries themselves could not have been expected to provide for their dependencies privileges of which they did not see the use for their own people. Belief in universal education has been of slow and comparatively recent growth, and, as applied to colonies, has followed the example set by the United States.

The detail, mentioned earlier, by the American army of soldiers to open schools before fighting had ceased is a convincing proof of the American attitude toward the value of education, and this is later shown by the comparatively large proportion of Insular revenue appropriated for the schools.

On the other hand the Dutch, after two hundred and fifty years of control of their East Indian possessions, in 1870, out of revenues exceeding 34 millions, allocated but $120,000 for education. Thirty years later, with revenues one-third more, they spent $563,000 for the education of the natives; and at that time about $1,000,000 to educate Europeans residing in these colonies. This was later largely increased, but in 1924 their expenditures came to 24 cents per capita, while in that year Philippine expenditure for education reached $1.10 per capita.

The British Indian government year book for 1921–1922 has the following revealing paragraph:

. . . without education, India will be confronted in no long time with that supreme peril of modern states, an uninformed democracy. Indeed from almost every point of view, education remains the prime question in India to-day.

ON THE WAY TO IWAHIG

THE PABELLONES

CLIFF AND ROCK

A prevalent but less excusable failure on the part of old colonizing sovereignties is the scanty attention paid to public health. In the early centuries knowledge of prevention and cure of disease was so small that it is not surprising that little should have been done about it, but statistics prove conclusively that Dutch and British colonial sanitation has not kept abreast of modern advances in preventive medicine, hygiene, and hospital facilities.

The Dutch colonies in 1870, for example, spent but $200,800 a year for medical service. Even as late as 1924 they spent on health but six and a half millions of dollars, or about three per cent of the total expenditures for all purposes of government. This amounted to twelve and one-half cents per capita. This may be compared with the Philippine expenditure of twenty-seven cents per capita in 1924.

British and Dutch administrations present many admirable features and to an important degree compare favorably with the best governments in the world. Justice, finance, and the protection of the native in the ownership of his land are among the admirable features to be found in their systems, that of the Dutch in the last respect being especially worthy of note.

Another good feature of British and Dutch colonial administration lies in its continuity and the choice of really high-class men who devote their lives to a service in which their government assures them a career. The history of India is replete with stirring stories of brilliant individual service and sacrifice from the days of John Lawrence, who came to the front in the days of the Mutiny, through to the present day. British administrators especially are chosen from among the best in their country. They are gentlemen by birth, by instinct, and by training. They deal justly as between man and man among the natives of the countries they rule. They pass from colony to colony using the experience gained in one to assist them in the work done in another, and above all they are clean-lived, truth-speaking, and scrupulous in the application of public funds. The recent Dutch administrators have a similar background.

It is largely due to this continuity of service that Great Britain has reached her eminence as a colonial power.

It is too much to expect that there could be any such continuity of service in a democracy, where every few years a change of administration is possible and once in a while inevitable.

In the United States such supervision as is exercised over dependencies and protectorates until recently was divided rather illogically among the Departments of State, Interior, War, and Navy. Were all this work done by one department, there would be highly attractive careers offered to a desirable class of young men with a genius for administration and a desire for over-sea and venturesome service, who could move from place to place as vacancies occurred and ultimately reach positions of responsibility and importance commensurate with their experience and ability, just as is done in the diplomatic service. The problems confronting these various dependencies are cognate, and a man trained in one will find himself admirably fitted to meet and solve the problems that will confront him in the next.

The United States consumes annually two billion dollars' worth of tropical products, much of which comes from the tropical portions of South America, Central America, and the West Indies, including Cuba. Cuba enjoys reciprocal trade relations and Porto Rico free trade with the United States.

The increase in both the external and internal trade of the Islands predicated a corresponding growth in the productive activity of the Philippine people and in their accumulation of wealth.

All in all, there is abundant cause to feel that the great American statesmen concerned with Philippine development were wise and their policies fundamentally sound. As Mr. Taft phrased it:

> We were not the guardians of the small portions of the educated and the wealthy in the Philippines. We were guardians especially of the poor, the ignorant, and the weak, and we could not discharge our duty as such guardians unless we remained there long enough to give to the poor, the weak, and the humble a consciousness of their rights, and a certainty that they would be preserved under any government to which we might transfer sovereign power.

No fair-minded person can study the course of events in the Philippine Islands without realizing that in the main the United States has notably improved the condition of the Filipinos and prepared them for nationality.

INDEX

INDEX

Abaca, 8, 30

Administration, Manila, 40–42; sentiment toward, in United States, 45; insurgent government not recognized, 48–49; nonrecognition leads to warfare, 50–51; Filipinos resist, 51–57; guerrilla warfare continues, 57–59; end of hostilities, 59–60, 68–69; opposition to Philippine policy, 60–62; civil government established, 62, 65; Schurman Commission, 63–66; Taft Commission, 66–68; military government terminated, 69; Philippine Commission assumes executive control, 70–73, 79; Payne Bill, 80, 120, 121, 123, 307; municipal governments organized, 81–85; Provincial Government Code enacted, 85–88; Americans in service, 90–93; Wright reorganizes, 93–97; Jones Bill, 97–99, 130, 158, 307–308, 368–369, 372, 373; revenue and expenditure, 118, 119, 327–330; separation of Church and State, 296–297; struggle for confidence and friendship, 297–302, 332; weaknesses of early, 298–299, 300; 1898–1913 summarized, 310–319; non-partisan character of early, 317–319; Wilson injects party politics into, 322; growth under American, 333; under Taft régime, 336; Wood-Forbes Mission on, 352; and American political platforms, 371–372, 377–378; Fairfield Bill, 379; Hawes-Cutting Bill, 386; spirit of American, 389–394

Aglipay, Gregorio, organizes schism, 297

Agricultural Bank of the Philippine Government, 138

Agriculture, resources, 8–9; growth of, 30, 148; veterinary service, 167; education in, 182–183; Constabulary coöperates with Bureau of, 208; Bureau of, 249–252; loans payable in produce protected, 342; pest extermination, 362

Aguinaldo, Emilio, insurgent leader, 34–35, 43, 44; confers with Pratt at Singapore, 47–48; Dewey's relations with, 48–49; proclaims independent government,

49, 50–51; capture of, 54–55, 56–57; on guerrillas, 60; capture of, 68; takes oath of allegiance, 78; on outlaws, 113–114; visits Baguio, 218; visits Iwahig, 231; on Americans in Philippines, 298; pensioned, 342

Alcalde, mayor of Manila, 84

Alexander VI, Pope, fixes demarcation line, 20

Algué, José, Chief of Weather Bureau, 161, 253–254, 255

Ali, Datu, Moro outlaw, 283

Allen, Henry T., organizes Constabulary, 92, 105–106

Amburayans, tribal people on Luzon, 265

American Board Mission, 272

American Chamber of Commerce of the Philippine Islands, votes for retention, 383

American Circulating Library Association of Manila, 194

American Trading Company of Borneo, 28

Americans, population in Islands, 10 *n.*

Anda, Simón de, resists British in Philippines, 26

Anderson, Thomas M., arrives in Philippines, 41; and Aguinaldo, 49

Animals, 15–16; domestic, 249–251; mutual insurance on work, 342

Anito stick, 265

Annexation, of Islands recommended, 319

Anthrax, 250

Anti-Imperialist League, opposes acquisition of Islands, 61, 78, 80, 315; abets beet sugar interests, 151; incites to independence, 384

Ants, 16

Apayaos, tribal people in Luzon, 260, 266–267

Apo, Mount, 5

Appropriations, law and operation of, 306; Jones attacks administration on, 315–316; under Jones Bill, 335; legislative power over, 340; encouraged for public works, 343